Drug Testing in the Workplace

Research Advances in Alcohol and Drug Problems

Volume 11

RESEARCH ADVANCES IN ALCOHOL AND DRUG PROBLEMS

Drug Testing in the Workplace

Research Advances in Alcohol and Drug Problems

Volume 11

Edited by

Scott Macdonald
Addiction Research Foundation
London, Ontario, Canada

and

Paul Roman
University of Georgia
Athens, Georgia

SPRINGER SCIENCE+BUSINESS MEDIA, LLC

The Library of Congress cataloged the first volume of this title as follows:

Research advances in alcohol & drug problems. v. 1–

New York [etc.] J. Wiley, 1974–
v. 24 cm. annual.
"A Wiley biomedical health publication."
ISSN 0093-9714

1. Alcoholism—Periodicals. 2. Narcotic habit—Periodicals.
RC565.R37 616.8′6′005 73-18088

ISBN 978-0-306-44557-6 ISBN 978-1-4615-2399-4
DOI 10.1007/978-1-4615-2399-4

Originally published by Plenum Press, New York in 1994

Contributors

SHAHID ALVI, Conference Board of Canada, Ottawa, Ontario, Canada
JUDITH C. BLACKWELL, Department of Sociology, Brock University, St. Catharines, Ontario, Canada
TERRY C. BLUM, School of Management, Georgia Institute of Technology, Atlanta, Georgia
BARBARA BUTLER, Barbara Butler & Associates Inc., Toronto, Ontario, Canada
ROBERT B. COAMBS, Treatment Research and Development Department, Addiction Research Foundation, Toronto, Ontario, Canada
R. V. DENENBERG, Denenberg Associates, Red Hook, New York
TIA SCHNEIDER DENENBERG, Denenberg Associates, Red Hook, New York
JOHN DINARDO, Department of Economics, University of California, Irvine, California
DAIL L. FIELDS, School of Management, Georgia Institute of Technology, Atlanta, Georgia
BHUSHAN KAPUR, Clinical Laboratories, Addiction Research Foundation, Toronto, Ontario, Canada
JOAN M. KRAFT, Institute for Behavioral Research and Department of Sociology, University of Georgia, Athens, Georgia
RISA L. LIEBERWITZ, New York State School of Industrial and Labor Relations, Cornell University, Ithaca, New York
SCOTT MACDONALD, Social Evaluation and Research, Addiction Research Foundation, London, Ontario, Canada
JOAN A. MARSHMAN, Addiction Research Foundation, Toronto, Ontario, Canada
JACK K. MARTIN, Institute for Behavioral Research, University of Georgia, Athens, Georgia
MARY PAT McANDREWS, Treatment Research and Development Department, Addiction Research Foundation, Toronto, Ontario, Canada
STUART H. MILNE, School of Management, Georgia Institute of Technology, Atlanta, Georgia

MICHAEL D. NEWCOMB, Division of Counseling and Educational Psychology, University of Southern California, Los Angeles, California
MONIQUE PINSONNEAULT, Attorney, Auckland, New Zealand
PAUL M. ROMAN, Institute for Behavioral Research, University of Georgia, Athens Georgia
DAVID TRANTER, Barbara Butler & Associates Inc., Toronto, Ontario, Canada
MARTIN SHAIN, Workplace Program, Addiction Research Foundation, Toronto, Ontario, Canada
CHESTER S. SPELL, School of Management, Georgia Institute of Technology, Atlanta, Georgia
SAMANTHA WELLS, Social Evaluation and Research, Addiction Research Foundation, London, Ontario, Canada

Preface

Drug testing is one of the most controversial and complex issues facing the workplace in North America today. Ethical, legal, and social issues arise in just about any discussion of such testing. Limitations in research approaches and applications of scientific methods further obfuscate these issues.

This book examines the broad contours of drug testing in terms of research findings and perspectives. The reader is faced with several poignant questions:

- What are the costs of alcohol and drug use in the workplace?
- What can drug testing reveal about an employee?
- Are drug tests accurate and reliable?
- How effective are drug screening programs?
- What are the consequences of testing?
- How can one evaluate the effectiveness and/or cost-effectiveness of testing?
- What are the legal implications of testing?
- What alternative approaches can be used in the workplace?
- What are the perspectives and attitudes of unions toward the numerous issues surrounding drug testing?
- What are the sociological implications of drug testing?

These questions and more are addressed in fifteen chapters, which are grouped into two parts: research findings (Part I) and perspectives on drug testing (Part II). This book presents a wide range of findings, ideas, and perspectives related to drug testing. These may help the reader understand the complex and multitiered nature of drug-testing issues. It is hoped that researchers, program planners, policymakers, and employees will find this material useful for developing, evaluating, and refining workplace programs and policies. Likewise, these materials can guide research to address the many questions that remain unanswered.

Contents

PART I. RESEARCH FINDINGS

Drugs in the Workplace

I

RESEARCH FINDINGS

1

Extent and Impact of Alcohol and Drug Use Problems in the Workplace

A Review of the Empirical Evidence

JACK K. MARTIN, JOAN M. KRAFT, and PAUL M. ROMAN

To suggest that there is a contemporary concern in North America for understanding the prevalence and consequences of the use of drugs, both licit and illicit, is to state the obvious. Accounts of the social costs of drug use and the problems experienced by drug users appear routinely in the popular media. Scientific and professional treatments of drug-related issues are now commonplace in scholarly literature. Despite this attention, however, there have been few systematic attempts to document these behaviors empirically among employed persons (Backer, 1987; Roman, 1990).

This is a curious omission in light of the popular view that drug use by employees exacts significant social and economic costs (for both employees and employers) in the form of lowered productivity, increased health care costs, and impaired job performance (Gerstein & Grossman, 1989; Martin, Blum, and Roman, 1992). In this chapter we bring together a range of fragmentary evidence on the patterns and consequences of drug and alcohol use among employed persons. As a practical matter, much of the discussion centers on patterns of

---

JACK K. MARTIN, JOAN M. KRAFT, and PAUL M. ROMAN • Institute for Behavioral Research and Department of Sociology, University of Georgia, Athens, Georgia 30602. Joan M. Kraft acknowledges support from Training Grant No. T32-AA-07473, awarded to the University of Georgia by the National Institute on Alcohol and Alcoholism (NIAAA). Paul M. Roman acknowledges partial support from Research Grants Nos. R01-AA-07218 (awarded to the University of Georgia) and R01-DA-07417 (awarded to the Georgia Institute of Technology) from the NIAAA. The authors also thank Lori Holyfield for her research assistance, and Linda White for preparing the manuscript.

Research Advances in Alcohol and Drug Problems, Volume 11: Drug Testing in the Workplace, edited by Scott Macdonald and Paul M. Roman. Plenum Press, New York, 1994.

alcohol use and abuse, because the vast majority of the published research focuses on employees' abuse of alcohol (Hollinger, 1988).

This is less problematic than it may seem. The distinction between alcohol and drug use is somewhat artificial, in that the data indicate that most drug users do not limit consumption to a single substance (Clayton & Ritter, 1985; Stein, Newcomb, & Bentler, 1988): most notably, the use of illicit drugs tends to be associated with the use of alcohol (Newcomb & Bentler, 1986). Studies of the extent of employees' use of drugs other than alcohol, however, constitute an emerging body of research. Although this research is less common, several recent studies and national data bases examining this phenomena are described in this review.

Throughout this chapter, our focus is on contemporary empirical evidence. First we discuss a number of studies that focus on four commonly identified work-related consequences of employee substance abuse: absenteeism, accidents, lowered job performance, and turnover. We then turn our attention to the extent of employee use of alcohol and other drugs, reviewing published reports of U.S. workers and a scattering of Canadian studies that examine substance use patterns across and within occupations. Finally, in a third section we examine recent evidence of the prevalence of workers' use of alcohol and other drugs in the U.S. labor force by bringing together secondary data from several U.S. national surveys.

1. WORK-RELATED OUTCOMES OF EMPLOYEES' SUBSTANCE USE/ABUSE PATTERNS

There has been much speculation as to the socioeconomic costs of employees' alcohol and drug use (see Chapter 3 for a review of these costs). The research literature addressing the economic outcomes of workers' substance abuse has focused on the costs to employers in the form of alcohol and drug users' presumed higher levels of absenteeism, increased risk for accidents and fatalities at work, reduced levels of job performance, higher medical insurance costs, and increased turnover rates (Webb, Redman, Hennrikus, Rostas, & Sanson-Fischer, 1990). In this section we review several empirical studies that examine these hypothesized outcomes.

Absenteeism

Perhaps the best documented work-related outcome of employees' alcohol and drug use is higher rates of absenteeism. In one of the earliest studies, Maxwell (1960, 1972) found that 53% of recovered alcoholics (n = 406) recalled moderate to severe levels of half- or full-day work absences during their problem drinking period. In addition, these respondents reported high rates of moderate to severe on-the-job absenteeism, including leaving work posts temporarily (44.2%), leaving work early (39.3%), taking longer lunch periods (39.8%), and arriving late (32.6%). Trice (1962), using a similar methodology in two samples of Alcoholics Anonymous members (n = 84 and n = 552), found that 70% of respondents indicated that absenteeism increased as their drinking problem developed. Moreover, Trice suggests that the absenteeism rates among the 552 alcoholics surveyed in the second study were four to five times higher than typical (p. 502). In a case control study by Pell and D'Alonzo (1970), identified and suspected alcoholics were found to have approximately twice the rate of sickness absences of the control group ($p < .001$).

Absenteeism seems to be a marked characteristic of employed problem drinkers. Rates of two to three times that of non-problem-drinking workers are commonly cited (see Observer & Maxwell, 1959; Thorpe & Perry, 1959), and rates as high as eight times normal have been reported (Bross, Pace, & Cronin, 1992). The data are also clear in indicating that this relationship generalizes cross-nationally. High absenteeism among problem drinkers has been documented in studies of workers in France (Godeau & Quaetel, 1958; Cavalie, 1956, cited in Trice and Roman, 1978), Sweden (Lingren, 1957, cited in Trice and Roman, 1978), Australia (Schlossler and McBride, 1984), and Great Britain (Beaumont and Hyman, 1987; Lucas, 1987).

Although less numerous, recent studies provide evidence of an association between absenteeism rates and the use of drugs other than alcohol. For example, in a national sample of 300 registered nurses recovering from alcohol and/or drug dependency (Sullivan, Bissell, & Leffler, 1990), self-reported attendance problems were the second most frequently mentioned on-the-job effect of their drug dependence, mentioned by 35% of respondents. Similarly, a 5-year study of chemically dependent workers at a single manufacturing site (Bross et al., 1992) found these workers to average 5.71 periods of multiday absence (totaling 181 days), compared to 0.86 periods of absence (totaling 25 days) among workers in a non–chemically dependent control group.

Accidents and Fatalities

An additional body of research has sought to demonstrate the association of employee substance abuse patterns to the frequency of accidents and injuries both on and off the job. These studies, however, have appeared less frequently. For example, in a review article, Weingard and Room (1977) were able to identify only three studies of U.S. workers that examined accidents of workers with drinking problems. Moreover, a subsequent review by Roizen (1982) found no additional treatments of this hypothesized relationship. (See Webb, 1992, and Shain, 1982, for additional reviews of this literature.)

With few exceptions (see Beaumont & Hyman, 1987; Trice, 1962, 1965), studies of problem-drinking and drug-using employees support the hypothesis that accident rates are higher for these workers. Observer and Maxwell (1959) found that problem drinkers experienced an average of 3.6 more accidents than workers in the control group. Webb et al. (1992) found that 67% of problem drinkers were in work accidents, compared to 43% of non–problem drinkers. This relationship became even stronger when minor accidents (those requiring no leave from work) were partialed out: About 26% of problem drinkers had work absences attributable to injuries, as compared to only 10% of non–problem drinkers. Maxwell (1960, 1972) indicates that 10% of the recovered alcoholics he studied retrospectively reported moderate to serious occurrences of on-the-job accidents, and 18% reported moderate to serious occurrences of accidents off the job. Maxwell's study is less useful for assessing prevalence, given the lack of a nonalcoholic control group.

Though many studies of the impact of impairment on industrial accidents have failed to use control groups (see, e.g., Baker, Samkoff, Fisher, and Van Buren, 1982; Copeland, 1985; Papoz et al., 1986), Wechsler, Kasey, Thum, and Demone (1969) utilized controls in a study of 969 emergency room patients who sustained injuries on the job. In this case, subjects injured on the job were 1.7 times more likely to have measurable blood alcohol levels (BALs) than were members of the control group. A similar study of Zambian copper miners (Buchanan, 1988), although not providing control data, reported that across the 6-month study interval 30% of the 309 workers who experienced an on-the-job accident had measurable blood alcohol levels. Blood alcohol levels were also examined in studies of occupational fatalities in Texas (Lewis & Cooper, 1989) and Alberta (Alleyne, Stuart, and Copes, 1991). According to these data, 13.3% of 173 autopsies in Texas found measurable blood alcohol levels, and in Alberta 10.7% of 373 fatalities tested for the presence of alcohol produced measurable blood alcohol levels. Similarly, Lederman and Metz (1960) estimated that workers with high BALs were 10 to 11 times more likely to be involved in work accidents. Finally, Metz and Marcoux (1960) discovered that in 7.4% of work accidents workers with high BALs were victims, and that 15% of all serious work accidents resulting in time off involved alcohol.

Three recent studies have also sought to examine the relationship of the use of drugs other than alcohol to occupational accidents or fatalities. In the Texas study of occupational fatalities mentioned above, 7.0% of the autopsies were positive for the presence of drugs that could have altered the worker's reaction time or coordination (Lewis & Cooper, 1989, p. 25), although in only one case was an illicit drug (marijuana) present. In the Canadian study 8.5% of urine tests were positive for marijuana, 8.5% were positive for prescription drugs, and an additional 6.7% were positive for the presence of nonprescription drugs (Alleyne et al., 1991).

Drug use and accidents have also been examined with survey data. In a telephone survey of a random sample of 2,565 residents of New England (Hingson, Lederman, & Walsh, 1985), 26% of employees who reported weekly drug use also had experienced an accident in the previous year, compared to 17% of their non-drug-using counterparts. It is important to note that this study also found evidence that workers who averaged five or more drinks daily were significantly more likely than drug users or those who did not drink to have had an accident that required medical attention, to be hospitalized as a result of an accident, and to have had an accident at work (Hingson et al., 1985, p. 301). Further, 40% of respondents who reported weekly on-the-job drinking had experienced injury-producing accidents in the previous year, and 8% had required hospitalization.

Additional evidence of the association of drug use and accidents is provided in the Bross et al. (1992) study of chemically dependent workers in a manufacturing setting. Compared to controls, chemically dependent workers in this study had significantly higher rates of strains and sprains, fractures and dislocations, and lacerations and contusions. Finally, using self-reported data on drug use, Crouch, Webb, Peterson, Buller, and Rollins (1989) found that those reporting drug use were five times more likely to have had a reportable vehicle accident than a non-drug-using sample matched by age, sex, occupation, years of service, and geographic location.

Job Performance

It has been suggested that perhaps the most direct effect of workers' substance use and abuse is a decline in performance at work, particularly with respect to alcohol abuse (Trice & Roman, 1978). Indeed, the few studies that have sought to examine this issue provide support for the assertion. Maxwell (1960, 1972) reports that between 57.8% and 72.3% of problem-drinking respondents retrospectively indicate reductions in performance at work. Specific behaviors included putting things off (72.3%), spasmodic performance (69.2%), neglecting details (65.8%), lowered quantity (59.6%), mistakes or errors in judgment (58.3%), and lowered quality (57.8%); in each case, respondents indicated moderate to severe occurrence of these behaviors. Trice (1962) presents similar findings in studies of alcoholic workers, where virtually all respondents retrospectively reported substantial work-role impairment associated with their abuse of alcohol. Additional evidence of reduced job performance among employees with a drinking problem is provided by Warkov, Bacon, and Hawkins (1965). Supervisory ratings of those with drinking problems were significantly lower than ratings for a random sample of employees. For example, supervisors rated 34% of the problem-drinking group as performing at levels below average, compared to only 6% of their non-problem-drinking counterparts (Warkov et al., 1965).

In perhaps the most systematic study of job performance among problem-drinking and non-problem-drinking workers, Blum, Roman, and Martin (1992) provide clear evidence of lowered performance levels associated with heavier levels of drinking. For 136 employed respondents, presumably objective collateral assessments of four dimensions of performance at work were collected. These included technical performance, ability to exercise self-direction at work, conflict avoidance, and functioning in interpersonal relationships. Collateral assessments of the focal respondent's job performance in each of the four domains were significantly lower for those workers who were in the upper quartile (i.e., 52 or more drinks per month) on monthly alcohol consumption.

Cursory evidence also ties the use of drugs other than alcohol to lowered job performance, although some studies have been unable to document this connection (see Haas & Hendlin, 1987; Kagel, Battalio, & Miles, 1980; McDaniel, 1989; Zinberg & Weil, 1969). For example, in a study of 224 employed alcohol and drug abusers who were new clients of an employee assistance program at a 10,000-employee industrial plant (Walsh et al., 1991), net of controls, cocaine use was found to be associated with job warnings from supervisors. In a study of nonmedical drug use among armed forces personnel (Burt, 1981), 10% of enlisted personnel who used drugs in the previous year reported lowered job performance associated with that use. Additionally, 3% of respondents reported receiving lowered efficiency or performance ratings as a function of their drug use. In a longitudinal study of 310 U.S. "baby boomers" (White, Aidala, & Zablocki, 1988), 21.2% of current marijuana users reported being less productive at work in the previous year as a result of their marijuana use, nearly three times the proportion of current drinkers reporting similar impairment as a result of their use of alcohol. Finally, in their study of drug-dependent nurses, Sullivan et al. (1990) indicated that 12% of these respondents reported poor performance at work associated with their drug use.

Turnover

The final job-related outcome of employee substance abuse considered in this review is turnover. As in the case of job performance, evidence for a relationship of substance abuse to turnover rates is unclear. According to Trice (1962), Trice and Roman (1978), Straus and Bacon (1951), and Strayer (1957), the majority of problem drinkers continue to be employed in a single job as their alcohol dependency progresses. In a study of 161 employed male alcoholics (Schollaert, 1977), 36% experienced turnover during the 5 years prior to their entry into treatment; further, variables describing drinking behavior were central to the turnover process. Unfortunately, Schollaert provides no data to suggest that the turnover rates experienced by respondents in his sample were different from turnover rates in the general population of employed persons.

The relationship between turnover rates and the use of drugs other than alcohol appears to be better established in the literature. For example, in the White et al. (1988) study described previously, 2.6% of the respondents who were current marijuana users indicated that they had lost a job as a result of their drug use. Among the 300 recovering registered nurses surveyed by Sullivan and her colleagues (1990), 16.7% reported changing work sites to find easier access to drugs. Finally, several recent studies of young persons in the United States (Kandel & Davies, 1990; Kandel, Davies, Kraus, & Yamaguchi, 1986; Kandel & Yamaguchi, 1987) suggest that the turnover rate is higher for workers who use drugs than for those who do not. Kandel and Davies (1990) report that drug use, especially cocaine use, is positively related to the likelihood of job separation.

It would appear that there is ample empirical evidence documenting the four hypothesized negative outcomes of employees' use of alcohol and other drugs. Knowing that large numbers of employees are afflicted with problems related to substance abuse may be an important realization; however, it provides only a gross appreciation of the extent of the problem. In an attempt to develop a finer-grained analysis of the consequences of workers' use of alcohol and other drugs, in the next section we turn our attention to the extent of such substance use. In this regard we review existing data on the occupational influences on workers' use of alcohol and other drugs.

2. OCCUPATIONAL INFLUENCES ON EMPLOYEES' SUBSTANCE USE/ABUSE PATTERNS

Evidence suggests that the vast majority of workers who experience or develop alcohol- and drug-related problems are nonetheless able to maintain relatively stable employment (Chodorkoff, Krystal, Nunn, & Wittenberg, 1961; Scanlon, 1991). This is true particularly during the early and middle developmental stages of increasing abuse (Archer, 1977). Moreover, although estimates of the extent of employee involvement with drugs vary depending on the particular substance of concern (e.g., marijuana, cocaine, or alcohol), estimates by the National Institute on Alcohol Abuse and Alcoholism (NIAAA) and the National Institute on Drug Abuse (NIDA) place the proportion of the active U.S. work force who experience late-stage substance abuse (e.g., alcoholism or drug addiction) at 10% (Wrich, 1988). Other estimates place the proportion of the work force who will be substance abusers at some time during their careers at between 12% and 15% (Delaney, 1987). In other words, perhaps as many as 13 million to 20 million workers in the United States alone will experience moderate to serious problems related to their use of drugs and alcohol at some time during their working life.

In perhaps the most comprehensive review of the literature available on the epidemiology of alcohol abuse among employees, Fillmore and Caetano (1982) emphasize the extraordinary difficulty involved in arriving at reliable estimates of the prevalence of alcohol problems in the labor force. Indeed, these authors liken the task of reviewing the research literature to that of a "ragpicker" (p. 34) who is able to glean only fragments of a larger picture. Unfortunately, little has changed in the past decade to bring that image into sharper focus. Reliable data documenting substance use and abuse patterns for the U.S. population and the use of survey techniques and probability samples to detail these patterns go back to the 1950s for alcohol (W. B. Clark, 1991) and to the 1970s for drugs. These large surveys, however, include minimal information about employment. Variability in patterns of substance abuse are extensively evident in detailed reports of these epidemiological surveys, yet these variations are typically limited to sociodemographic attributes other than employment status or occupation (age, race, gender, region of residence, etc.; Martin, Roman, and Blum, 1992).

In the absence of employment-related data obtained from representative samples of the labor force, the research literature continues to utilize a wide variety of operations and populations to assess levels of workers' maladaptive uses of alcohol and drugs (Hollinger, 1988). This is problematic because estimates of the prevalence of employee substance abuse vary significantly depending on the population studied and the measures utilized. For example, in a recent review of 12 studies of the prevalence of alcohol problems among a variety of different kinds of workers and types of employing organizations (Webb et al., 1990), prevalence estimates ranged from a low of 1.2% (in a population of more than 76,000 employees of a single company when alcohol problems were diagnosed clinically by physicians; Pell & D'Alonzo, 1973) to a high of 20.9% (when alcohol problems were assessed by Short Michigan Alcoholism Screening Test [SMAST] scores in a survey of 2,820 employees of federal agencies and manufacturing plants; Cahill & Volicer, 1981).

Given the range of available prevalence estimates, it is unlikely that a consensual estimate of alcohol or drug abuse rates can be obtained from the research literature. Examination of industry- and occupation-specific data on the prevalence of alcohol problems and, to a lesser extent, drug problems, however, does suggest three broad generalizations that have been supported in earlier reviews:

1. Employee substance abuse has been found to be inversely related to occupational status (Martin, 1990).
2. Within broad occupational and industry categories, workers in specific occupations (e.g., food and beverage servers, transportation workers, sailors and seamen) appear to be at greater risk for the development of problems related to the heavier use of alcohol and drugs (Hitz, 1973).

3. Regardless of occupational membership, the highest rates of substance use and abuse are found among younger and male workers (Fillmore & Caetano, 1982; Hollinger, 1988).

We now provide an overview of the evidence underlying each of these generalizations.

Inverse Association of Occupational Status Level

A large number of studies demonstrate that as occupational status increases, substance use/abuse decreases. Members of lower-status occupations in the United States have been found to consume alcohol at higher levels (Cahalan & Cisin, 1968; Cahalan & Room, 1972; Hitz, 1973), to be more prone to experience alcohol problems related to heavier drinking (Cahill & Volicer, 1981; Hitz, 1973; Parker & Brody, 1982; Parker, Kaelber, Harford, & Brody, 1983; Warkov et al., 1965), to be more likely to be diagnosed as active alcoholics according to DIS/DSM-III criteria (Helzer, Burnam, & McEvoy, 1991), and are more likely to be represented in treated or institutionalized populations (Archer, 1977; R. Clark, 1949; Ethridge & Ralston, 1967; Falkey & Schneyer, 1957; Malzberg, 1960; Schuckit & Gunderson, 1974; Scott, 1954; Taylor, 1957; Ullman, Demone, Stearns, & Washburne, 1957). These patterns are not limited to the United States; similar occupational patterns exist in Canada (Smart, 1979), Sweden (Ojesjo, 1980), Australia (Webb et al., 1990), and Great Britain (Plant, 1977).

The inverse relationship of occupational status to alcohol use and abuse also appears to generalize to the use of other drugs, particularly marijuana. For example, among employed persons in the United States, self-reports of current use of marijuana (Cook, 1989; Mensch and Kandel, 1988; Voss, 1989) and cocaine (Voss, 1989) have been found to be higher among blue-collar workers. Similarly, among availability samples of regular Canadian users of marijuana and cocaine abusers in treatment, semiskilled and unskilled workers were the largest occupational category represented (Erickson, 1989; Smart & Adlaf, 1992). Finally, in a 1985 U.S. study of 172 individuals treated for cocaine dependence (Schnoll, Karrigan, Kitchen, Daghestani, & Hansen, 1985), more than 58% of subjects reported membership in blue-collar and lower-status white-collar occupations (e.g., clerical and sales).

Employees' Substance Use/Abuse Patterns within Specific Occupations

Studies of substance abuse, primarily alcohol abuse, among workers in specific occupations have examined a number of occupations that presumably place workers at greater risk for the development of problems. Occupations commonly examined and found to have higher than expected levels of abusive patterns of drinking behavior include food and beverage servers (Fillmore, 1990; Hitz, 1973), sales workers (Hitz, 1973), brewery workers (Plant, 1978, 1979), members of the armed forces (Polich & Orvis, 1979; Schuckit & Gunderson, 1974) sailors and seamen (Brun-Gulbrandsen & Irgens-Jensen, 1967; Casswell & Gordon, 1984; Heath, 1945; Powdermaker, 1945), protective service workers (Fillmore, 1990; Hitz, 1973; Violanti, Marshall, & Howe, 1983), workers in domestic services (Straus & Winterbottom, 1949), transport operatives (Fillmore, 1990; Guinn, 1983; Manello & Seaman, 1979), journalists and workers in the newspaper trades (Caswell & Gordon, 1984; Hitz, 1973), extractive workers (Buchanan, 1988), and workers in construction trades (Casswell & Gordon, 1984; Sonnenstuhl & Trice, 1987). It is also important to note that this literature has found that cross-nationally, many of these occupations have uniformly high rates of abusive behavior (see Brun-Gulbrandsen & Irgens-Jensen, 1967; Casswell & Gordon, 1984; Olkinuora, 1984; Plant, 1978).

Unfortunately, like the research on the broader influences of occupational status, studies of workers in specific occupations have not utilized standard measures of alcohol and drug use. As such, studies of this sort are only marginally useful in assessing overall differential prevalence rates (Fillmore & Caetano, 1982, p. 71). From a methodological point of view, however, it is encouraging to note that studies examining more or less standard measures of alcohol abuse (i.e., standardized mortality ratios and DIS/DSM-III diagnostic criteria) have found many of the specific occupational groups discussed above to be at significantly higher risk for alcohol problems or alcohol-related deaths (Fillmore & Caetano, 1982; Guralnick, 1963; Mandell, Eaton, Anthony, & Garrison, 1992; Plant, 1979).

Influences of Age and Gender on Employees' Patterns of Substance Use/Abuse

Although short on evidence comparing drug use among male and female employees, empirical work clearly indicates that male workers are more likely to drink and to develop drinking-related problems than female workers (Cahill & Volicer, 1981; Fillmore & Caetano, 1982; Loughlin & Kayson, 1990). In a study of 2,820 employees of federal agencies and manufacturing plants, Volicer, Cahill, and Smith (1981) indicate that 11.7% of men, but only 4% of women, drink at least 3 or 4 drinks on two or more occasions a week. Further, in this study 17.3% of male employees, but only 8.7% of female employees, were classified as possibly alcoholic or alcoholic according to scores on the SMAST.

Data on employed respondents from national samples of the United States also establish men and women's differential use of alcohol. In a sample of households, Lennon (1987) found that net of the influences of job characteristics, marital status, and race, employed men consume a higher number of drinks per day than employed women. Similarly, data from another survey of the United States (Johnson, 1982) indicate that employed men are also more likely than women to experience problems related to their drinking. In this study 25% of employed men, but only 16% of employed women, were found to have drinking-related problems (Johnson, 1982). Finally, gender differences in workers' drinking behavior have been noted in Canada (Smart, 1979), Australia (Webb, 1990), and Great Britain (Harvey, Butler, Thomas, & Jenkins, 1992).

As noted, the association of gender with employees' use of drugs other than alcohol is not as well established as the drinking-gender connection. There is, however, cursory evidence of this relationship. For example, in their previously described study of 224 EAP clients, Walsh et al. (1991) indicated that their subjects were overwhelmingly male (p. 19). Utilizing data obtained from a subset of 1,716 employed respondents in a nationally representative sample of U.S. households (n = 3,000), Cook (1989) also found gender to be significantly related to current use (i.e., use in the last month) of marijuana and cocaine. In this study, among employed men, 14% reported current marijuana use, and 3% reported current use of cocaine. Among employed women, in contrast, current marijuana use was reported by 8%, and current cocaine use was reported by only 1%. Moreover, Cook (1989) found that these gender differences persisted in the face of controls for age. There is also limited evidence suggesting gender differences in the use of drugs on the job. For example, Hollinger (1988) reported that regardless of levels of job satisfaction, men are nearly three times more likely than women to go to work under the influence of alcohol and/or drugs.

At the level of the total population, the association between age and alcohol abuse is well established (see Cahalan, 1970; W. B. Clark & Hilton, 1991). Among employed persons, however, the data are less clear. For example, Seeman and Anderson (1983) reported that although age was negatively associated with the number of drinking occasions per month reported by the employed men in their sample, it did not significantly influence the most frequent quantity of alcohol consumed per occasion. These authors did report that age was related to two drinking-related problems, although the effects were mixed. Younger workers are more likely to miss work, but older ones are more likely to report drinking on the job (Seeman & Anderson, 1983).

As in the case of studies of gender and drug use among employees, research examining age effects on workers' use of drugs other than alcohol appears infrequently. The studies of Cook (1989), Walsh et al. (1991), and Hollinger (1988), however, do provide some evidence of this connection. Walsh et al. (1991) indicated that 117 (52.2%) of the 224 EAP clients they studied were less than 30 years of age, and more important, the 90 subjects reporting cocaine use in the previous 6 months were significantly younger than their counterparts who did not use cocaine. A similar pattern is reported by Cook (1989); age was the most significant predictor of marijuana and cocaine use among the employed respondents in his sample (p. 20). In this study 20% of young workers (ages 18–34) reported current marijuana use, compared to 6% of their counterparts between 35 and 44 years old, and only 2% of workers 45 and older. Similarly, cocaine use in the past year was reported by 12% of workers in the youngest age group, compared to 2% of older workers (p. 22). Hollinger (1988) also presents evidence that younger workers (i.e., younger than 30) are approximately four times more likely as their older peers to report to work under the influence of drugs or alcohol.

Although not meant to be exhaustive, the above literature review clearly indicates that the maladaptive use of alcohol and other drugs varies systematically as a function of occupational status, is disproportionately high for specific occupations within these broader categories, and is significantly higher for younger and male workers. As noted, however, these patterns provide little information regarding differential prevalence rates. In an attempt to address this important issue we turn to an analysis of the alcohol and drug use data that are available in recent national samples of the U.S. population.

3. ESTIMATES OF WORKERS' SUBSTANCE USE/ABUSE PATTERNS AVAILABLE IN NATIONAL SURVEY DATA

In this section we report estimates of employed respondents' annual and current use of drugs and alcohol, reports of job-related alcohol problems, and on-the-job use of these substances. The data discussed are drawn from our analyses of three primary sources:

1. The 1984 National Alcohol Survey (NAS), conducted by the NIAAA-sponsored National Alcohol Research Center, which includes detailed measures of alcohol use patterns and problems, as well as less detailed indicators of drug use in the past year
2. Published reports based on the NIDA 1985, 1988, and 1990 National Household Surveys of Drug Abuse (NHSDA), which report annual and current use of alcohol and other drugs
3. The 1984 National Longitudinal Survey of Labor Market Experience–Youth Cohort (NLSY), which includes information on whether respondents used or felt high from particular drugs or alcohol while on the job

The data presented from the NAS and NLSY studies, which have not been published elsewhere, are the result of our analyses of the primary data. Data reported from the NHSDA data sets have been synthesized from existing NIDA publications.

In discussing each data set, we focus only on the responses of individuals who were employed at the time of the survey. In most instances we provide estimates of whether respondents used alcohol or a particular drug during a particular year or month, but not of how frequently during that time the substances were consumed. Analyses include employees' self-reports of the use of heroin/LSD (or hallucinogens), cocaine, marijuana, alcohol, and psychotherapeutic drugs (prescription-type stimulants, sedatives, and analgesics). It should be pointed out that in most analyses the use of psychotherapeutic drugs is limited to illicit use (i.e., without prescription, or a larger than prescribed dose of a drug). In analyses utilizing the NAS data the use of psychotherapeutic drugs includes both licit and illicit use, but excludes analgesics from this category.

We present more detailed estimates of alcohol consumption, examining whether workers consumed 5 or more drinks on at least five different occasions in the past month, consumed 8 or more drinks on at least one occasion in the past month, and consumed enough alcohol to feel drunk at least once in the past month. We examine these patterns first for full-time and part-time workers, and then across occupational categories. When possible, the influences of the workers' age and gender are controlled.

Prevalence Rates and Employment Status

Using 1985, 1988, and 1990 NHSDA data, Tables 1 and 2 report the distributions of drug and alcohol use by employment status. Table 1 provides estimates for annual use of these substances, whereas Table 2 reports current use (i.e., use in the past month). Examination of these data reveals several interesting patterns. To begin, the data indicate a general decline in employees' use of both alcohol and illicit drugs since 1985. Moreover, these declines are observed regardless of workers' employment status or age. The proportion of workers reporting current use of any illicit drug (Table 2), in any age–employment status group, dropped by approximately 50% across this interval. For example, in 1985, 7.6% of full-time workers in the 18–25 age category reported cocaine use in the previous month; in 1990, however, the proportion of workers in the same age category reporting similar use dropped to 2.5%.

Changes in the proportion of workers who drink were not as dramatic. In 1985, nearly 70% of full-time workers over the age of 35 were current drinkers (Table 2); by 1988, the proportion had dropped to roughly 60%. The proportion of current drinkers remained essentially unchanged between 1988 and 1990 at 58.1% of full-time workers. Similarly, there were only nominal changes in the proportion of workers classified as current heavy drinkers across this same interval (Table 2).

For the most part, the data in Tables 1 and 2 reveal few differences in the substance use patterns of full-time and part-time workers. The largest difference observed is in the use of cocaine reported in 1990: Part-time workers were about half as likely as full-time workers (2.4% vs. 4.0%, respectively) to report annual

Table 1
Percentage of Employees Reporting Drug and Alcohol Use In the Past Year by Employment Status, 1985, 1988 and 1990 NHSDA

	1985	1988	1990
Hallucinogens			
Full-time	1.8	1.7	1.1
Part-time	1.9	2.4	1.1
Cocaine			
Full-time	8.5	5.6	4.0
Part-time	5.3	4.5	2.4
Marijuana			
Full-time	18.6	12.5	12.5
Part-time	16.6	12.6	10.6
Psychotherapeutic[a]			
Full-time	N/A	N/A	4.1
Part-time	N/A	N/A	5.3
Alcohol			
Full-time	84.2	79.4	77.8
Part-time	74.4	77.3	76.2

[a]Illicit use of prescription-type stimulants, sedatives, tranquilizers, and/or analgesics.
Note: "N/A" means data are not available.

use (Table 1). Controlling for age and examining current use patterns (Table 2), however, does suggest differences in the use of marijuana and alcohol among younger workers. Specifically, 12.8% of part-time workers in the 26–34 age category report current use of marijuana in 1990, compared to only 7.4% of their full-time counterparts. It is interesting to note that this trend is reversed for workers in the 18–25 and 35-and-over categories, where more full-time workers report current use. The 1990 data also indicate that regardless of age, full-time workers are somewhat more likely to drink, and to report the heavy use of alcohol.

The tendency for full-time workers to report higher levels of alcohol consumption is further illustrated in Tables 3 and 4. In these tables data are reported from the 1984 NAS to present more detailed estimates of the proportions of workers who drink heavily and who report various problems associated with drinking. The data in Table 3 reflect two potentially maladaptive use patterns: having consumed 8 or more drinks on at least one occasion in the past month, and having consumed enough alcohol at some time in the past month to have felt drunk. According to these data, when compared to their part-time counterparts, full-time workers are nearly twice as likely to have consumed 8 or more drinks

Table 2
Percentage of Employees Self-Reporting Use of Substances in the Last 30 Days by Age and Employment Status, 1985, 1988, and 1990 NHSDA

	1985			1988			1990		
	18–25	26–34	35+	18–25	26–34	35+	18–25	26–34	35+
Cocaine									
Full-time	7.6	6.8	1.0	5.0	2.5	—	2.5	1.9	—
Part-time	3.9	6.9	—	3.6	—	—	—	—	—
Marijuana									
Full-time	23.5	17.7	3.7	16.9	11.2	1.3	12.6	7.4	2.9
Part-time	15.2	19.5	2.4	14.2	9.8	2.7	12.0	12.8	—
Psychotherapeutic[a]									
Full-time	6.1	4.9	2.2	4.0	2.3	0.8	2.0	1.3	1.2
Part-time	5.2	4.4	—	2.7	—	—	3.3	—	—
Alcohol									
Full-time	76.3	74.2	69.9	73.1	69.2	59.9	71.2	68.0	58.1
Part-time	66.0	71.3	60.6	65.4	54.6	62.7	58.9	54.6	57.9
Heavy alcohol[b]									
Full-time	N/A	N/A	N/A	11.2	8.1	3.9	13.9	8.4	4.0
Part-time	N/A	N/A	N/A	12.0	4.4	—	9.2	5.2	3.1

[a]Illicit use of prescription-type stimulants, sedatives, tranquilizers, and/or analgesics.
[b]Drinking 5 or more drinks per occasion on 5 or more of the past 30 days.
Note: "—" means less than 0.05%. "N/A" means that data are not available.

recently (8.9% vs. 4.8%, respectively) and are somewhat more likely to have been drunk during the past month (8.4% vs. 6.2%, respectively). To a large extent, however, these differences can be attributed to gender differences in these patterns; specifically, women are more likely to be employed part-time and are less likely to consume alcohol at heavier levels (Roman, 1988). Indeed, the data in Table 3 indicate that employment status is associated with men's, but not women's, consumption patterns, although the pattern is not consistent. Men employed full-time are more likely to have consumed 8 or more drinks on one occasion in the past month (12.9%) than are men who are part-time workers (8.3%), but are less likely than male part-time workers to report having felt drunk during that period (11.5% vs. 13.9%, respectively).

In Table 4, NAS estimates are provided of the proportion of workers who have experienced job-related problems as a result of their drinking behaviors. Workers reported whether during the past year (a) drinking had a harmful effect on their employment opportunities; (b) they experienced a drinking-related illness that kept them away from regular job activities for a week or more; (c) they lost a job, or nearly lost one, because of their drinking; (d) people at work had

Table 3
Percentage of Employees Reporting Monthly Heavy Drinking by Employment Status and Gender, 1984 NAS

	Had 8+ Drinks			Felt Drunk		
	Total Sample	Men	Women	Total Sample	Men	Women
Full-time	8.9	12.9	3.1	8.4	11.5	3.3
Part-time	4.8	8.3	2.6	6.2	13.9	2.6

Table 4
Proportion of Employees Reporting Drinking-Related Problems by Employment Status and Gender, 1984 NAS

	Employment Status		Gender		Men		Women	
	Part-time	Full-time	Male	Female	Part-time	Full-time	Part-time	Full-time
Drinking had a harmful effect on employment opportunities	2.2	2.2	2.9	1.1	2.8	3.8	1.1	1.2
Illness connected with drinking kept you from working on regular activities for a week or more	0.2	0.0	.01	0.3	.01	0.0	0.3	0.0
You have lost a job or nearly lost one due to drinking	0.5	0.6	0.7	0.3	0.6	1.7	0.4	.01
People at work have indicated that you should cut down	0.9	0.6	1.0	0.6	1.0	1.6	0.8	.01
Drinking may have hurt your chance for promotion, or raises, or better jobs	0.4	0.7	0.6	0.3	0.4	1.8	0.4	0.0
Average number of problems	0.042	0.041	0.058	0.023	0.049	0.091	0.030	0.01[illegible]
Experienced only 1 problem	2.5	2.4	2.8	1.4	2.8	4.5	1.9	1.2
Experienced 2 or more problems	0.8	0.7	1.2	0.5	1.1	1.7	0.5	0.1

indicated that they should cut down on their drinking; and (e) drinking may have hurt their chances for promotions, raises, or better job assignments. According to the estimates in the table, the most commonly reported job-related alcohol problem is a negative effect on employment opportunities from drinking, reported by 2.2% of full-time and part-time workers. The remaining job-related problems are reported by less than 1% of workers, although nearly 1% of all workers do report the presence of two or more of these outcomes.

Although there are only nominal differences between full-time and part-time workers among the five job-related problems, controlling for the workers' gender does suggest certain contrasts between these groups. Although the differences are small, with the exception of experiencing an illness that kept them away from work, part-time male workers are somewhat more likely than their full-time counterparts to report problem outcomes associated with their drinking. These patterns are reversed for women, where full-time workers are more likely to have experienced similar problems. The patterns are also evident in differences in the average number of problems reported. On average, men who work part-time experience more problems (mean = .091) than men who work full-time (mean = .049); however, women who work full-time have a higher average number of problems (mean = .030) than women who work part-time (mean = .013).

The 1984 NAS data provide little direct evidence of the extent of alcohol or other drug use in the workplace. The 1984 NLSY data, though, permit estimates of on-the-job consumption patterns. According to the data in Table 5, marijuana

Table 5
Percentage of 19 to 26-Year-Old Workers Who Use Drugs or Alcohol While on the Job by Employment Status and Sex, 1984 NLSY

	Total	Men	Women
Cocaine			
Full-time	1.2	1.6	0.7
Part-time	1.0	1.2	0.8
Marijuana			
Full-time	5.3	7.5	2.5
Part-time	4.9	8.6	2.1
Psychotherapeutic drugs			
Full-time	2.4	2.3	2.3
Part-time	2.5	3.1	2.1
Alcohol			
Full-time	3.3	4.8	1.3
Part-time	2.6	3.6	1.9

is used most frequently at work, and cocaine is used least frequently. Among workers aged between 19 and 26 in 1984, approximately 5% of workers (5.3% of full-time and 4.9% of part-time) used marijuana and approximately 3% (3.3% of full-time and 2.6% of part-time) consumed alcohol at work during the previous year. As before, gender differences in these behaviors are evident, with men being more likely to report on-the-job consumption. Indeed, the highest proportion of on-the-job users of marijuana are male part-time workers (8.6%), and the highest users of alcohol at work are full-time men (4.8%).

Prevalence Rates and Occupational Status

As noted, the variable having perhaps the most frequently documented association with workers' substance use patterns has been occupational status. In Tables 6 through 9 we extend the previous analyses by explicitly considering the evidence of differential prevalence rates across five occupational categories.

Table 6 presents 1984 NAS estimates of the proportion of workers who reported drug use during the past year. Consistent with previous research, these data indicate a relatively clear inverse relationship of drug use to occupational status. With the exception of LSD/heroin use (reported by few respondents), employees in the highest-status occupations are less likely to use drugs. In general terms, marijuana, cocaine, and psychotherapeutic drug use is highest among blue-collar workers. In this regard, semiskilled blue collar workers emerge as the occupational group most likely to use illicit substances; more than 16% of these workers reported marijuana use and nearly 10% reported cocaine use in the previous year. A high proportion of skilled blue-collar workers also reported marijuana (13.5%) and psychotherapeutic drug (13.2%) use.

Table 6
Percentage of Employees Reporting Drug Use in Past Year by Occupation, 1984 NAS

	LSD/Heroin	Cocaine	Marijuana	Psychotherapeutics[a]
Professional/ managerial	0.5	4.1	11.2	1.5
Technical/ administrative	1.0	6.0	11.2	14.0
Service workers	1.4	7.9	11.2	8.5
Skilled workers	0.9	5.5	13.5	13.2
Semiskilled workers	1.0	9.7	16.6	11.2

[a]Excludes analgesics; includes licit and illicit use.

Because public attention focuses on marijuana and cocaine use, and because few workers report the use of other drugs during the past year, we examine information on the current use of these substances by occupation and age. NHSDA data on current use of marijuana and cocaine (reported in Voss, 1989, pp. 36, 40) are summarized in Table 7. Again, skilled and semiskilled blue collar workers report the highest current use of marijuana (approximately 16%) and cocaine (approximately 5%). The overall distributions of use by occupation, however, mask considerable variation in these patterns related to workers' age. In particular, there appear to be larger differences in current use of marijuana by occupation among the youngest workers than for those in the two older age categories. Among workers aged 18 to 25, skilled workers are the most likely (34.9%) to report current marijuana use, followed by their semiskilled counterparts (28.2%). As might be expected, prevalence rates for marijuana and cocaine use in the youngest cohort are higher regardless of occupational status.

The NHSDA estimates in Table 7 reveal an unanticipated pattern among older (age 35 and over) workers. Specifically, in this group the relationship of occupational status and current marijuana use is positive; professionals and managers report the highest (4.8%) and semiskilled workers the lowest (2.0%) current use of this substance. This pattern is not evidenced with respect to current use of cocaine, as there are essentially no differences in use across occupational categories of older workers.

The inverse relationship of occupation and patterns of substance use is clearly shown with respect to alcohol consumption. These data are summarized in Table 8, which presents 1984 NAS estimates of the proportion of workers who report having consumed 8 or more drinks, or having felt drunk, on at least one

Table 7
Percentage Self-Reporting Use of Marijuana and Cocaine in the Last 30 Days by Age and Occupation, 1985 NHSDA

	Marijuana				Cocaine			
	Total	18–25	26–34	35+	Total	18–25	26–34	35+
Professional/ managerial	9.7	22.0	16.5	4.8	1.9	5.1	2.8	1.1
Technical/ administrative	9.4	15.7	15.7	3.1	4.3	5.5	9.5	1.0
Service workers	12.2	18.1	22.8	4.2	3.2	3.8	8.8	0.5
Skilled workers	15.8	34.9	21.8	2.7	4.6	10.3	7.5	—
Semiskilled workers	15.8	28.2	21.2	2.0	5.5	11.2	8.0	1.0

Source: Reported in Voss (1989, pp. 36, 40)

Table 8
Percentage of Employees Reporting Monthly Heavy Drinking by Occupation and Gender, 1984 NAS

	Had 8+ Drinks			Felt Drunk		
	Total Sample	Men	Women	Total Sample	Men	Women
Professional/managerial	3.2	5.5	0.0	4.0	7.1	0.0
Technical/administrative	5.4	9.8	3.0	4.9	7.0	3.6
Service workers	9.8	15.4	6.0	11.4	17.8	7.0
Skilled workers	14.1	15.1	5.3	14.0	14.7	7.3
Semiskilled workers	16.3	22.8	2.9	13.0	17.9	2.7

occasion in the past month. According to these data, blue-collar workers are much more likely to report these behaviors. In skilled blue-collar occupations, 14.1% of workers reported having consumed 8 or more drinks on at least one episode in the previous month, and 14.0% reported having been drunk at least once during the same period. For semiskilled workers, 16.3% had consumed 8 or more drinks and 13% indicated having been drunk sometime in the past month. Professionals and managers, and technical and administrative workers, were least likely to engage in these consumption patterns.

Controlling for gender reveals that the inverse association of occupation to the potentially problematic drinking behaviors examined in Table 8 applies primarily to men. Again semiskilled blue collar workers appear to be at greatest risk, with 22.8% and 17.9%, respectively, indicating extensive consumption (8 or more drinks) and having been drunk at least once in the past month. For women, the relationship of occupation to these patterns is not consistent, with the highest prevalence of extensive consumption and having been drunk found for service workers (6.0% and 7.0%, respectively) and skilled blue-collar workers (5.3% and 7.3%, respectively). Substantially lower rates are observed, however, for women in semiskilled, technical or administrative, and professional occupations.

The final set of relationships examined in this section consider the differential prevalence rates of on-the-job use of marijuana, cocaine, and alcohol across occupational categories. These data are drawn from the 1984 NLSY and are summarized in Table 9. According to these estimates, with few exceptions young workers in service, skilled blue-collar, and semiskilled blue-collar occupations emerge as being most likely to report on-the-job use during the previous year. Briefly, cocaine use at work is reported infrequently, regardless of occupation or gender, although 1.8% of all service workers (and 3.0% of men in service occupations) do report on-the-job use of cocaine. Marijuana use at work is most

Table 9
Proportion of 19 to 26-Year-Old Workers Who Use Drugs or Alcohol on the Job by Occupation and Sex, 1984 NLSY

	Cocaine			Marijuana			Alcohol		
	Total	Men	Women	Total	Men	Women	Total	Men	Women
Professional/managerial	0.5	0.6	0.4	2.1	3.4	1.1	2.3	3.9	1.0
Technical/administrative	1.0	1.3	0.9	3.7	6.5	2.2	3.0	5.7	1.4
Service workers	1.8	3.0	0.9	5.2	9.0	2.5	3.3	5.2	2.0
Skilled workers	1.0	1.1	0.0	8.9	9.1	7.4	3.5	4.0	0.3
Semiskilled workers	1.1	1.3	0.1	8.0	9.1	3.9	2.9	3.5	0.8

common among incumbents of lower-status service (reported by 5.3% of all service workers) and skilled (reported by 8.9%) and semiskilled (reported by 8.0%) blue-collar occupations. The data indicate, however, that marijuana use at work is primarily a male phenomenon, with approximately 9% of men in service and blue-collar occupations reporting this behavior. Women's self-reported substance use at work rivals men in one category, skilled blue-collar occupations; 7.4% of women in these occupations reported on-the-job use of marijuana. Finally, alcohol use at work is only nominally related to occupational status, with the highest rates reported by men in technical administrative (5.7%) and service (5.2%) occupations.

Summary and Discussion

Several consumption patterns emerging from our analyses of the national survey data are worth noting before proceeding with a more detailed discussion of the materials presented in this review. To begin, as expected, more workers report consumption of alcohol than the use of illicit drugs. NHSDA estimates reported in Table 1 indicate that since 1985, more than 75% of all workers drink. It is interesting to note, however, that these same surveys (Table 2) indicate that in 1990 roughly as many workers drank heavily (between 3.1% and 13.9%) as reported having used marijuana in the past month (between 2.9% and 12.6%). Also, according to these data (Tables 1, 2, and 6), regardless of year, relatively few workers report annual or current use of either cocaine, psychotherapeutic drugs, or hallucinogens.

A second general pattern that is evident in both the national survey data and much previous research is that more men than women drink heavily, use drugs, and experience negative consequences associated with these behaviors. For example, Table 3 reports that in 1984 12.9% of men employed full-time, but only 3.1% of their female peers, had consumed 8 or more drinks on at least one occasion in the past month. Similarly, 7.5% of men employed full-time, compared to only 2.5% of their female counterparts, reported feeling high from or using marijuana at work (Table 5).

Another overall pattern that emerges from the analyses of the secondary survey data reported here points to the clear inverse relationship of age to substance use and abuse. This pattern is particularly evident in self-reported use of marijuana and heavy drinking (see Table 2). In 1990 12.6% of younger full-time workers (18–25 years of age) reported current use of marijuana, and 13.9% reported current heavy drinking. Among their full-time counterparts aged 26 to 34, 7.4% of respondents indicated current marijuana use and 8.4% current heavy drinking, and among full-time workers age 35 or older, only 2.9% disclosed current marijuana use and 4.0% current heavy drinking.

Analyses of the national survey data reveal few differences in substance use and abuse patterns related to full-time or part-time employment status. The largest differences between these two groups of employees are observed in the 1984 NAS data on heavier drinking (see Table 3). In particular, drinking 8 or more drinks on a single occasion in the past month is reported by 8.9% of full-time workers, compared to only 4.8% of part-time workers. For the most part, however, the data from the three national surveys examined suggest only nominal differences in the consumption of licit and/or illicit drugs related to workers' employment status.

Lastly, in each of the national data sets, differential use patterns for both alcohol and drugs were evident across occupational status levels. Regardless of age and (to a lesser extent) gender, workers in lower-status service and blue-collar occupations consistently reported the highest use of marijuana and cocaine (Tables 6 and 7), were more likely to drink heavily (Table 8), and were more likely to use marijuana on the job (Table 9).

4. CONCLUSIONS

Thus, a review of existing materials and new analyses has revealed some important new dimensions of workplace drug use patterns, especially the parity between rates of heavy drinking and marijuana use. There are, however, several other inferential conclusions that are suggested by these data, some of which may challenge conventional wisdom. We consider these in terms of "costly" behavior patterns, gender differences, and distinctive classes of employed substance users and abusers.

First, patterns of job behaviors associated with employee substance abuse need not all be viewed in the category of costs. Accidents and job performance decrements are definite costs to the workplace, typically affecting both management and fellow workers. But the same does not necessarily hold for absenteeism. Earlier studies (Trice, 1962) revealed that substance abusers' absenteeism reflected efforts to protect themselves from harm that might occur if they tried to work; obviously this protection can extend to coworkers and to the workplace itself. While seemingly absurd, the suggestion that absenteeism can serve positive functions stands in the face of very imperfect systems of detection of employed substance abusers or implementing effective means for their behavioral change.

Parallel reasoning applies to the supposed cost of turnover associated with employee substance use. Again it can be suggested that employee turnover can save rather than exact costs for employers and coworkers, assuming that the substance abuser is disruptive and inconsistently productive. The significant point here may be that the oft-stated economic costs of workplace substance abuse may reflect tendencies toward inflation of the "drug problem" in the workplace rather than objective assessments of impact. Viewing absenteeism and turnover only as costs may reflect such inflation.

Second, the data suggest that there are subtle but perhaps important gender differences in workplace-related substance use and abuse. The rates of such use remain dramatically higher for men, although some movement toward parity is hinted by the data. The intense focus on illegal drugs and alcohol, however, overstates the significantly greater extent to which women are prescribed and utilize psychotherapeutic drugs. One cannot simply assume that because these drugs are used as medications, they have little or no impact on job behaviors. Further, such usage can become abuse, sometimes without the knowledge of the individual users or their significant others.

Of particular significance is the strong pressure toward defining the epidemic proportions of depression in North America, coupled with the increased biological orientation in defining depression and hence its psychotropic rather than psychosocial treatment (National Institute of Mental Health, 1991). Of equal or greater importance is the recognition of psychoactive drug therapies as means of managing health care costs in the United States, in some instances essentially substituting a drug regimen for routine counseling or periodic evaluation by a competent specialist.

Thus, gender and employment are important considerations in assessing workplace drug problems, not only from the perspective of possible convergence between the sexes in patterns of use (Roman, 1988) but also with awareness of the less obvious growth in the use of legal psychoactive substances by employed persons, a situation where women's rates of use outrun those of men.

Third, viewed from the perspective of effective intervention, a very important distinction is not readily evident in any overview of the distribution of substance abuse within employment settings. Of understated significance is employees' use of substances before or while working versus the behaviors of employed substance abusers who rarely if ever would use their substance(s) of choice during working hours or before coming to work. In several respects, members of the former class of substance abusers are less problematic in that the cues of their substance abuse are more obvious, behavioral impairment is probably more evident, and technologies may be implemented to detect much of such substance use. Linked to these advantages are the relative simplicity and straightforwardness of workplace rules, procedures, and penalties that can be publicized and implemented when on-the-job substance use or intoxication is detected.

By contrast, the aftereffects of off-hours substance abuse, or hangover, offer much less obvious cues and vary considerably across individuals. A typical observation is that such individuals often do not display patterned absenteeism and attempt to carry out their work regardless of the physical and psychological handicaps that are experienced (Trice & Roman, 1978). Thus, their impact in the workplace may be considerably more subtle than that of the on-the-job drug users in terms of impaired functioning or decision-making faculty.

The suggested means for dealing with this class of employed substance abusers in a manner that maximizes objectivity and opportunities for due process is a policy and procedure based on decrements in job performance that can be documented and acted upon by workplace supervision. It may be obvious that such an approach is attractive in theory, but it assumes an ease of measuring job performance that does not always exist (Roman, 1990).

The distinctiveness of two classes of employed substance abusers offers some explanation as to why various actions in the workplace seem to detect far fewer substance abusers than are suggested by a range of epidemiological estimates. In the case of all employed substance abusers, it is also critical to recognize the numerous barriers to detection that are embedded in the social networks and power relations within workplaces.

To some extent the gap between actual substance abuse and detected substance abuse reflects a variety of pressures toward cover-up. But this gap also likely represents the overestimation of impairment created by employees' use and abuse of a variety of psychoactive substances. Indeed, it likely describes the integration of the supposed impacts of these on- and off-the-job behaviors into the flow of everyday work life (Cosper, 1979; Roman, 1990).

REFERENCES

Alleyne, B. C., Stuart, P., and Copes, R., 1991, Alcohol and other drug use in occupational fatalities, *Journal of Occupational Medicine* **33**:496–500.

Archer, J., 1977, Occupational alcoholism: A review of issues and a guide to the literature, in: *Alcoholism and Its Treatment in Industry* (C. Schramm, ed.), pp. 2–28, Johns Hopkins Press, Baltimore.

Backer, T. E., 1987, *Strategic Planning for Workplace Drug Abuse Programs* (DHHS Publication No. ADM-87-1538), National Institute on Drug Abuse, Rockville, MD.

Baker, S. P., Samkoff, J. S., Fisher, R. S., and Van Buren, C. B., 1982, Fatal occupational injuries, *Journal of the American Medical Association* **248**:692–697.

Beaumont, P. B., and Hyman, J., 1987, The work performance indicators of problem drinking: Some British evidence, *Journal of Occupational Behavior* **8**:54–62.

Blum, T. C., Roman, P. M., and Martin, J. K., 1992, Alcohol consumption and work performance, *Journal of Studies on Alcohol* **54**:61–70.

Bross, M. H., Pace, S. K., and Cronin, I. H., 1992, Chemical dependence: Analysis of work absenteeism and associated medical illnesses, *Journal of Occupational Medicine* **34**:16–19.

Brun-Gulbrandsen, S., and Irgens-Jensen, O., 1967, Abuse of alcohol among seamen, *British Journal of Addiction* **62**:19–27.

Buchanan, D. J., 1988, Studies on blood alcohol in the workers of a Zambian copper mine, *Alcohol and Alcoholism* **23**:239–242.

Burt, M. R., 1981, Prevalence and consequences of drug abuse among U.S. military personnel: 1980, *American Journal of Drug and Alcohol Abuse* **8**:419–439.

Cahalan, D., 1970, *Problem Drinkers: A National Survey,* Jossey-Bass, San Francisco.

Cahalan, D., and Cisin, I. H., 1968, American drinking practices: Summary of findings from a national probability sample, II: Measurement of massed versus spaced drinking, *Quarterly Journal of Studies on Alcohol* **29**:130–54.

Cahalan, D., and Room, R., 1972, Problem drinking among American men aged 21–59, *American Journal of Public Health* **62**:1473–1482.

Cahill, M. J., and Volicer, B. J., 1981, Male and female differences in severity of problems with alcohol at the workplace, *Drug and Alcohol Dependence* **8**:143–156.

Casswell, S., and Gordon, A., 1984, Drinking and occupational status in New Zealand men, *Journal of Studies on Alcohol* **45**:144–148.

Cavalie, B., 1956, Influence de l'ethylsime chronique sur la morbidité et les accidents du travail, *Archives des Maladies Professionelles de Médecine du Travail et de Sécurité* **17**:98.

Chodorkoff, B., Krystal, H., Nunn, J., and Wittenberg, R., 1961, Employment characteristics of hospitalized alcoholics, *Quarterly Journal of Studies on Alcohol* **22**:106–110.

Clark, R., 1949, The relationship of alcoholic psychoses commitment rates to occupational income and occupational prestige, *American Sociological Review* **14**:535–549.

Clark, W. B., 1991, Some comments on methods, in: *Alcohol in America: Drinking Practices and Problems* (W. B. Clark and M. Hilton, eds.), pp. 19–25, State University of New York Press, Albany, New York.

Clark, W. B., and Hilton, M., eds., 1991, *Alcohol in America: Drinking Practices and Problems,* State University of New York Press, Albany, New York.

Clayton, R. R., and Ritter, C., 1985, The epidemiology of alcohol and drug abuse among adolescents, *Advances in Alcohol and Substance Abuse* **4**:69–97.

Cook, R. F., 1989, Drug use among working adults: Prevalence rates and estimation methods, in: *Drugs in the Workplace: Research and Evaluation Data,* NIDA Research Monograph, No. 91, U.S. Government Printing Office, Washington, DC.

Copeland, A. R., 1985, Fatal occupational accidents—The five-year Metro Dade County experience, 1979–1983, *Journal of Forensic Sciences* **30**:494–503.

Cosper, R., 1979, Drinking as conformity: A critique of sociological literature on occupational differences in drinking, *Journal of Studies on Alcohol* **40**:868–891.

Crouch, D., Webb, D., Peterson, L., Buller, P., and Rollins, D., 1989, A critical evaluation of the Utah Power and Light Company's substance abuse management program: Absenteeism, accidents and costs, in: *Drugs in the Workplace: Research and Evaluation Data,* NIDA Research Monograph, No. 91, U.S. Government Printing Office, Washington, DC.

Delaney, T. J., 1987, The EAP part of the personnel function, *Public Personnel Management* **16**:359.

Erickson, P. G., 1989, Living with prohibition: Regular cannabis users, legal sanctions, and informal control, *International Journal of the Addictions* **24**:175–188.

Ethridge, D., and Ralston, J., 1967, Occupational backgrounds of institutionalized alcoholics: Comparative data and implications for rehabilitation, *Mental Hygiene* **51**:543–548.

Falkey, D., and Schneyer, S., 1957, Characteristics of male alcoholics admitted to the medical ward of a general hospital, *Quarterly Journal of Studies on Alcohol* **18**:67–97.

Fillmore, K., 1990, Occupational drinking subcultures: An exploratory epidemiological study, in: *Alcohol Problem Prevention in the Workplace: Employee Assistance Programs and Strategic Alternatives* (P. Roman, ed.), pp. 77–94, Quorum, New York.

Fillmore, K., and Caetano, R., 1982, Epidemiology of alcohol abuse and alcoholism in occupations, in: *Occupational Alcoholism: A Review of Research Issues,* NIAAA Research Monograph 8, pp. 21–88, U.S. Government Printing Office, Washington, DC.

Gerstein, D. R., and Grossman, E., 1989, Building a cumulative knowledge base about drugs in the workplace, in: *Drugs in the Workplace: Research and Evaluation Data,* NIDA Research Monograph, No. 91, pp. 319–333, U.S. Government Printing Office, Washington, DC.

Godeau, L., and Quaetel, R., 1958, L'alcoolisme dans les arnsenaux, *Revista de Medicina de la Universidad de Navarra* **13**:75–78.

Guinn, B., 1983, Job satisfaction, counter-productive behavior and circumstantial drug use among long-distance truckers, *Journal of Psychoactive Drugs* **15**:185–88.

Guralnick, L., 1963, Mortality by occupational level and cause of death among men 22 to 64 years of age: United States, 1950, *Vital Statistics Special Reports* **53**(5): 439–612.

Haas, A. P., and Hendlin, H., 1987, The meaning of chronic marihuana use among adults: A psychosocial perspective, *Journal of Drug Issues* **17**:333–348.

Harvey, S., Butler, T., Thomas, R. L., and Jenkins, R., 1992, Patterns of alcohol consumption in white-collar workers: A cross-sectional and longitudinal study, *British Journal of Addiction* **87**:91–102.

Heath, R. G., 1945, Group psychotherapy of alcohol addiction, *Quarterly Journal of Studies on Alcohol* **5**:555–562.

Helzer, J. E., Burnam, A., and McEvoy, L., 1991, Alcohol abuse and dependence, in: *Psychiatric Disorders in America: The Epidemiologic Catchment Area Study* (L. Robbins and D. Regier, eds.), pp. 81–115, Free Press, New York.

Hingson, R. W., Lederman, R. I., and Walsh, D. C., 1985, Employee drinking patterns and accidental injury: A study of four New England states, *Journal of Studies on Alcohol* **46**:298–303.

Hitz, D., 1973, Drunken sailors and others: Drinking problems in specific occupations, *Quarterly Journal of Studies on Alcohol* **34**:496–505.

Hollinger, R. C., 1988, Working under the influence (WUI): Correlates of employees' use of alcohol and other drugs, *Journal of Applied Behavioral Science* **24**:439–454.

Johnson, P. B., 1982, Sex differences in women's roles and alcohol use: Preliminary national data, *Journal of Social Issues* **38**:93–116.

Kagel, J. H., Battalio, R. C., and Miles, G. C., 1980, Marihuana and work performance: Results from an experiment, *Journal of Human Resources* **15**:372–395.

Kandel, D. B., and Davies, M., 1990, Labor force experiences of a national sample of young adult men: The role of drug involvement, *Youth and Society* **21**:411–415.

Kandel, D. B., and Yamaguchi, K., 1987, Job mobility and drug use: An event history analysis, *American Journal of Sociology* **92**:836–878.

Kandel, D. B., Davies, M., Kraus, D., and Yamaguchi, K., 1986, The consequences in young adulthood of adolescent drug involvement, *Archives of General Psychiatry* **43**:746–754.

Lederman, D., and Metz, B., 1960, Les accidents du travail et l'alcool, *Population* **15**:301–316.

Lennon, M. C., 1987, Sex differences in distress: The impact of gender and work roles, *Journal of Health and Social Behavior* **28**:290–305.

Lewis, R. J., and Cooper, S. P., 1989, Alcohol, other drugs, and fatal work-related injuries, *Journal of Occupational Medicine* **31**:23–28.

Lingren, G. M., 1957, Alkohol och arbete, *Svenska Lakartidn* **54**:3613–3620.

Loughlin, K. A., and Kayson, W. A., 1990, Alcohol consumption and self-reported drinking-related problem behaviors as related to sex, work environment, and level of education, *Psychological Reports* **67**:1323–1328.

Lucas, E. G., 1987, Alcohol in industry, *British Medical Journal* **294**:460–461.

Malzberg, B., 1960, *The Alcoholic Psychoses: Demographic Aspects at Midcentury in New York State,* Yale Center of Alcoholic Studies, New Haven, CT.

Mandell, W., Eaton, W. W., Anthony, J. C., and Garrison, R., 1992, Alcoholism and occupations: A review and analysis of 104 occupations, Unpublished manuscript.

Manello, T. A., and Seaman, F. J., 1979, Prevalence, costs and handling of drinking problems at seven railroads, Final Report, University Research Corporation, Washington, DC.

Martin, J. K., 1990, Jobs, occupations, and patterns of alcohol consumption: A review of literature, in: *Alcohol Problem Prevention in the Workplace: Employee Assistance Programs and Strategic Alternatives* (P. Roman, ed.), pp. 45–66, Quorum, New York.

Martin, J. K., Blum, T., and Roman, P., 1992, Drinking to cope and self-medication: Characteristics of jobs in relation to workers' drinking behavior, *Journal of Organizational Behavior* **13**:55–71.

Martin, J. K., Roman, P. M., and Blum, T. C., 1992, Employment and drinking: Results from a U.S.A. national survey, Unpublished manuscript.

Maxwell, M. A., 1960, Early identification of problem drinkers in industry, *Quarterly Journal of Studies on Alcohol* **21**:655–678.

Maxwell, M. A., 1972, Alcoholic employees: Behavior changes and occupational alcoholism, *Alcoholism* **8**:174–180.

McDaniel, M., 1989, Does pre-employment drug use predict on-the-job suitability? in: *Drugs in the Workplace: Research and Evaluation Data,* NIDA Research Monograph, No. 91, U.S. Government Printing Office, Washington, DC.

Mensch, B. S., and Kandel, D., 1988, Do job conditions influence the use of drugs? *Journal of Health and Social Behavior* **29**:169–84.

Metz, B., and Marcoux, F., 1960, Alcoolization et accidents du travail, *Arch. Mal. Prof.* **21**:750–752.

National Institute of Mental Health, 1991, *What to Do When an Employee is Depressed* (DHHS Publication No. ADM-91-1792), U.S. Government Printing Office, Washington, DC.

Newcomb, M. D., and Bentler, P. M., 1986, Cocaine use among adolescents: Longitudinal associations with social context, psychopathology, and use of other substances, *Addictive Behaviors* **11**:262–273.

Observer, and Maxwell, M. A., 1959, A study of absenteeism, accidents, and sickness payment in problem drinkers in one industry, *Quarterly Journal of Studies on Alcohol* **20**:302–312.

Ojesjo, L., 1980, The relationship to alcoholism of occupation, class, and employment, *Journal of Occupational Medicine* **22**:657–666.

Olkinuora, M., 1984, Alcoholism and occupation, *Scandinavian Journal of Work and Environmental Health* **10**:511–515.

Papoz, L., Weill, J., L'Hoste, J., Chich, Y., Got, C., and Goehrs, Y., 1986, Biological markers of alcohol intake among 4,796 subjects in accidents, *British Medical Journal* **292**:1234–1237.

Parker, D., and Brody, J., 1982, Risk factors for alcoholism and alcohol problems among employed men and women, in: *Occupational Alcoholism: A Review of Research Issues* (NIAAA Research Monograph 8), pp. 99–127, U.S. Government Printing Office, Washington, DC.

Parker, D., Kaelber, C., Harford, T., and Brody, J., 1983, Alcohol problems among employed men and women in metropolitan Detroit, *Journal of Studies on Alcohol* **44**:1026–1039.

Pell, S., and D'Alonzo, C. A., 1970, Sickness absenteeism of alcoholics, *Journal of Occupational Medicine* **12:**198–210.

Pell, S., and D'Alonzo, C. A., 1973, A five-year mortality study of alcoholics, *Journal of Occupational Medicine* **15:**120–25.

Plant, M., 1977, Alcoholism and occupation: A review, *British Journal of Addiction* **73:**309–316.

Plant, M., 1978, Occupation and alcoholism: Cause or effect? A controlled study of recruits to the drink trade, *International Journal of Addiction* **13:**424–435.

Plant, M., 1979, *Drinking Careers, Occupations, Drinking Habits and Drinking Problems,* Tavistock, London.

Polich, J. M., and Orvis, B. R., 1979, Alcohol problems: Patterns and prevalence in the U.S. Air Force, U.S. Air Force Project Report, No. R-2308AF, Rand Corporation, Santa Monica, CA.

Powdermaker, F., 1945, Review of cases at merchant marine rest centers, *American Journal of Psychiatry* **10:**650–654.

Roizen, J., 1982, Estimating alcohol involvement in serious events, in: *National Institute on Alcohol Abuse and Alcoholism, Alcohol Consumption and Related Events,* Alcohol and Health Monograph No. 1 (DHHS Publication No. ADM-82-1190), pp. 179–219, U.S. Government Printing Office, Washington, DC.

Roman, P. M., 1988, *Women and Alcohol Use: A Review of the Research Literature* (DHHS Publication No. ADM-88-1574), U.S. Department of Health and Human Services, Rockville, MD.

Roman, P. M., ed., 1990, *Alcohol Problem Prevention in the Workplace: Employee Assistance Programs and Strategic Alternatives,* Quorum, New York.

Scanlon, W. F., 1991, *Alcoholism and Drug Abuse in the Workplace: Managing Care and Cost Through Employee Assistance Programs,* 2d ed., Praeger, New York.

Schlosser, D., and McBride, J. W., 1984, *Estimating the Prevalence of Alcohol and Other Drug Related Problems in Industry,* New South Wales Drug and Alcohol Authority Research Grant Report Series No. B84/3, New South Wales Drug and Alcohol Authority, Sydney, Australia.

Schnoll, S. H., Karrigan, J., Kitchen, S. B., Daghestani, A., and Hansen, T., 1985, Characteristics of cocaine abusers presenting for treatment, in: *Cocaine Use in America: Epidemiologic and Clinical Perspectives,* NIDA Research Monograph No. 61, pp. 171–181, U.S. Government Printing Office, Washington, DC.

Schollaert, P., 1977, Job-based risks and labor turnover among alcoholic workers, in: *Alcoholism and Its Treatment in Industry,* (C. Schramm, ed.), pp. 177–185, Johns Hopkins Press, Baltimore.

Schuckit, M., and Gunderson, E., 1974, The associations between alcoholism and job type in the U.S. Navy, *Quarterly Journal of Studies on Alcohol* **35:**577–585.

Scott, W., 1954, Recorded inebriety in Wisconsin: An analysis of arrested inebriates in two Wisconsin counties, *Sociology and Social Research* **39:**104–111.

Seeman, M., and Anderson, C. S., 1983, Alienation and alcohol: The role of work, mastery, and community in drinking behavior, *American Sociological Review* **48:**60–77.

Shain, M., 1982, Alcohol, drugs and safety: An updated perspective on problems and their management in the workplace, *Accident Analysis and Prevention* **14:**239–246.

Smart, R. G., 1979, Drinking problems among employed, unemployed, and shift workers, *Journal of Occupational Medicine* **21:**731–736.

Smart, R. G., and Aldaf, E. M., 1992, Recent studies of cocaine use and abuse in Canada, *Canadian Journal of Criminology* **34:**1–13.

Sonnenstuhl, W. J., and Trice, H. M., 1987, The social construction of alcohol problems in a union's peer counseling program, *Journal of Drug Issues* **17:**255–271.

Stein, J. A., Newcomb, M. D., and Bentler, P. M., 1988, Structure of drug use behaviors and consequences among young adults: Multitrait-multimethod assessment of frequency, quantity, work site, and problem substance abuse, *Journal of Applied Psychology* **73:**595–605.

Straus, R., and Bacon, S. D., 1951, Alcoholism and social stability: A study of occupational integration of 2,023 male clinic patients, *Quarterly Journal of Studies on Alcohol* **12:**231–260.

Straus, R., and Winterbottom, M. T., 1949, Drinking patterns of an occupational group: Domestic servants, *Quarterly Journal of Studies on Alcohol* **10:**441–460.

Strayer, R., 1957, A study of employment adjustment of 80 male alcoholics, *Quarterly Journal of Studies on Alcohol* **18:**276–287.

Sullivan, E. J., Bissell, L., and Leffler, D., 1990, Drug use and disciplinary actions among 300 nurses, *International Journal of the Addictions* **25:**375–391.

Taylor, F., 1957, A study of white male alcoholic patients, admitted to Connecticut State hospitals during the fiscal year 1956, *Connecticut State Medical Journal* **21:**703–706.

Thorpe, J. J., and Perry, J. T., 1959, Problem drinking: A follow-up study, *Archives of Industrial Health* **19:**24–29.

Trice, H., 1962, The job behavior of problem drinkers, in: *Society, Culture and Drinking Patterns* (D. Pittman and C. R. Snyder, eds.), pp. 493–510, Wiley, New York.

Trice, H., 1965, Alcoholic employees: A comparison of psychotic, neurotic, and "normal" personnel, *Journal of Occupational Medicine* **7:**94–99.

Trice, H., and Roman, P., 1978, *Spirits and Demons at Work,* 2d ed., Cornell University, Ithaca, New York.

Ullman, A., Demone, H., Stearns, A., and Washburne, N., 1957, Some social characteristics of misdemeanants, *Journal of Criminal Law and Criminology* **48:**44–53.

Violanti, J., Marshall, J., and Howe, B., 1983, Police occupational demands, psychological distress and the coping function of alcohol, *Journal of Occupational Medicine* **25:**455–458.

Volicer, B. J., Cahill, M. H., and Smith, J. L., 1981, Sex differences in correlates of problem drinking among employed males and females, *Drug and Alcohol Dependence* **8:**175–87.

Voss, H. L., 1989, Patterns of drug use: Data from the 1985 Household Survey, in: *Drugs in the Workplace: Research and Evaluation Data,* NIDA Research Monograph, No. 91, U.S. Government Printing Office, Washington, DC.

Walsh, D. C., Hingson, R. W., Merrigan, D. M., Cupples, L. A., Levenson, S. M., and Coffman, G. A., 1991, Associations between alcohol and cocaine use in a sample of problem-drinking employees, *Journal of Studies on Alcohol* **52:**17–25.

Warkov, S., Bacon, S. D., and Hawkins, A. C., 1965, Social correlates of industrial problem drinking, *Quarterly Journal of Studies on Alcohol* **26:**58–71.

Webb, G., 1992, The relationship between alcohol and work injuries: A review of the evidence, Presented to the Fifth Winter School in the Sun, Brisbane, Australia.

Webb, G. R., Redman, S., Hennrikus, D., Rostas, J. A. P., Sanson-Fisher, R. W., 1990, The prevalence and sociodemographic correlates of high-risk and problem drinking at an industrial worksite, *British Journal of Addiction* **85:**497–507.

Webb, G. R., Redman, S., Hennrikus, D. J., Kelman, G. R., Gibberd, R. W., and Sanson-Fisher, R. W., 1992, The relationships between high-risk and problem drinking and the occurrence of work injuries and related absences, Unpublished manuscript.

Wechsler, H., Kasey, I. H., Thum, D., and Demone, H. W., 1969, Alcohol level and home accidents: A study of emergency service patients, *Public Health Reports* **84:**1034–1050.

Weingard, D., and Room, R., 1977, Alcohol and home, industrial, and recreational accidents, in: *Alcohol, Casualties, and Crime* (M. Aaren, T. Cameron, J. Roizen, R. Room, and D. Weingard, eds.), pp. 39–119, Social Research Group, Berkeley.

White, H. R., Aidala, A., and Zablocki, B., 1988, A longitudinal investigation of drug use and work patterns among middle-class, white adults, *Journal of Applied Behavioral Science* **24:**455–469.

Wrich, J. T., 1988, Beyond testing: Coping with drugs at work, *Harvard Business Review* **66:**120–130.

Zinberg, N. E., and Weil, A. T., 1969, The effects of marihuana on human beings, *Addictions* **16:**26–43.

2

Predictors of Drug Use and Implications for the Workplace

MICHAEL D. NEWCOMB

1. INTRODUCTION

Drug use and abuse have been parts of civilization since before recorded history (e.g., see Siegal, 1989; Westermeyer, 1988). It is certainly not a new problem, but one that receives recurring attention. In the recent centuries, we have faced the gin epidemic in England, the opium wars in the Orient, and the woefully forgotten cocaine patent-medicine tragedies at the turn of the 20th century. More recently, we have witnessed the heroic attempt and dramatic failure at Prohibition, "reefer madness" in the 1940s, the drug cultures of the 1960s, and the heroin epidemic of the 1970s. In the United States, cocaine is perceived as a major threat, in particular in its newest and more virulent forms of crack and rock cocaine. Unfortunately the current "war on drugs" conspicuously overlooks the abuse of alcohol and nicotine, which are currently among the largest killers of the U.S. population (Newcomb, 1992a). Tobacco is responsible for nearly 400,000 deaths in the United States per year, and alcohol accounts for nearly 100,000 more fatalities (Julien, 1992).

By many accounts, the United States has a culture oriented toward and dedicated to the use, and perhaps even abuse, of drugs. Drugs are used daily by

---

MICHAEL D. NEWCOMB • Division of Counseling and Educational Psychology, University of Southern California, Los Angeles, California 90089-0031. Writing of this chapter was supported by Grant DA 01070 from the National Institute on Drug Abuse. Variants of portions of this chapter were contributed to the National Institute of Medicine Committee on Drug Use in the Workplace. Appreciation for manuscript and table preparation is warmly extended to Sherilee Aragon.

Research Advances in Alcohol and Drug Problems, Volume 11: Drug Testing in the Workplace, edited by Scott Macdonald and Paul M. Roman. Plenum Press, New York, 1994.

millions of people to wake up in the morning (with coffee or tea), to get through the stresses of the day (with cigarettes), and to lull away worries in the evening (with alcohol). U.S. culture and society have made role models of the Marlboro man, the Virginia Slims woman, and the Coors Silver Bullet (Newcomb & Bentler, 1989). Drugs are pushed by Madison Avenue, pharmaceutical companies, congressmen such as Jesse Helms, and the local crack dealer. Drugs are peddled as remedies to cure all of life's ills, from stress to headaches, depression, and physical illness.

Therefore, for many people—young and old alike—drug use provides an immediate, but short-lived respite from dealing directly with the complex problems and stresses faced in life. A virtual pharmacopoeia of legal and illegal substances are available to relieve our discomfort, to improve our mood, and to help us forget our problems, at least temporarily. This may be only one facet or symptom of a much bigger problem: the commonly held attitude and approach to life that emphasizes the "quick fix" of a problem rather than a more effective and lasting, but more demanding solution (Newcomb, 1992a). Through various means we are taught that an immediate short-term solution to complex problems is adequate and acceptable. At the same time, little instruction, opportunity, or encouragement are provided for the creativity, persistence, and endurance necessary to provide more complete and satisfying solutions.

A thorough review of the historical patterns and movements regarding drug use and abuse is beyond the scope of this chapter and has been published elsewhere (e.g., Buchanan, 1992; Siegal, 1989; Westermeyer, 1988). Nevertheless, it is critical to point out that actual prevalence of drug use and abuse and societal perceptions of these problems are affected largely by political motives and social agendas. To a substantial extent, drug abuse is a social, political, and economic construction, too often with tragic consequences (e.g., Mosher & Yamagisako, 1991).

There is, however, an interesting history of drug use at work that has been reviewed recently by Fillmore (1984). She concludes that many of the changes in regard to the acceptability of drug use on the job have arisen as a result of the Industrial Revolution and the temperance movement. In fact, she points out that "prior to the industrial revolution, work and drinking appear to have been inseparable in the U.S. Although the drunken worker was disapproved, especially among the Puritans, drinking in the workplace was considered normal behavior. Drink was long associated with hard work" (p. 41). Thus, the condemnation of drug use in the workplace is a relatively recent reaction. Even more recent is a growing awareness of the diverse costs related to alcohol and drug abuse on the job. This may be exacerbated with more detailed and demanding jobs (e.g., oil tanker captain), more employees placed in charge of public welfare (e.g., school bus drivers and nuclear-power workers), or higher value on work products (e.g., film producers).

2. ETIOLOGY OF DRUG USE

An overview of the various theoretical and empirical causes of drug use provides a background to appreciate the complexity of evaluating the consequences associated with drug use on the job. The influences that cause drug use and abuse are varied and far from clearly understood. Although most drug use initiation occurs during adolescence with friends or peers who are also using drugs, the stage for this event has been set much earlier by family, community, and society.

Hundreds of variables have been studied for their ability to predict the onset of drug use. Many individual and social influences have been investigated and can be conceptualized as reflecting (a) cultural/societal environment, (b) immediate community, (c) interpersonal forces (e.g., school, peers, and family), and (d) individual factors (genetics, personality, attitudes, etc.). An individual can be considered "at risk" because of factors or forces within each of these areas. A great deal of attention has been devoted to each of these possible influences and can be reviewed from both theoretical and empirical perspectives in several sources (e.g., Glantz & Pickens, 1992; Galizio & Maisto, 1985; Lettieri, 1985; Lettieri, Sayers, & Pearson, 1980).

Hawkins, Catalano, and Miller (1992) reviewed the possible risk factors for youthful drug use and identified 17 potential causes, reflecting the four general areas listed above (see Table 1). Cultural/societal factors include laws and norms favorable toward drug use, availability of drugs, extreme economic deprivation, and neighborhood disorganization. Interpersonal forces include family alcohol and drug behaviors/attitudes, poor and inconsistent family management practices, family conflict, peer rejection in elementary grades, and association with drug-using peers. Psychobehavioral influences include early and persistent problem behaviors, academic failure, low degree of commitment to school, alienation and rebelliousness, attitudes favorable to drug use, and early onset of drug use. Finally, biogenetic factors include potential heritability of drug abuse and psychophysiological susceptibility to the effects of drugs.

Although not mentioned by Hawkins et al. (1992), certainly the best predictor of future behavior is past behavior. This is no less true for drug use and abuse than for other behaviors; therefore, the strongest predictor of current drug use is past drug use. All other potential predictors must exhibit a unique influence on altering drug use or abuse beyond that accounted for by prior involvement with drugs.

Another obvious factor related to drug use initiation is the age of the individual. The risk for initiating drug use increases for most drugs to a peak during middle to late adolescence and decreases thereafter (Kandel & Logan, 1984). Tobacco has the youngest age of peak vulnerability at about 16 years; increased likelihoods for beginning use of alcohol, marijuana, and psychedelics occur

Table 1
Summary of Risk Factors for Drug Use

Domain	Risk Factor
Culture and society	• Laws favorable to drug use
	• Social norms favorable to drug use
	• Availability of drugs
	• Extreme economic deprivations
	• Neighborhood disorganization
Interpersonal	• Parent and family drug use
	• Positive family attitudes toward drug use
	• Poor/inconsistent family management practices
	• Family conflict and disruption
	• Peer rejection
	• Association with drug-using peers
Psychobehavioral	• Early/persistent problem behavior
	• Academic failure
	• Low commitment to school
	• Alienation
	• Rebelliousness
	• Favorable attitudes toward drug use
	• Early onset of drug use
Biogenetics	• Inherited susceptibility to drug abuse
	• Psychophysiological vulnerability to drug effects

during the next two years of life. Interestingly, the most hazardous age for trying cocaine typically occurs in young adulthood (about the mid-twenties). The pattern for cocaine may be changing, however, because of the insurgence of crack, an inexpensive and smokable form of cocaine that may be more alluring to teenagers.

Starting at a basic level, some types of alcohol and drug abuse appear to have a genetic component, although environmental, social, and psychological factors have received primary attention regarding the initiation of drug use and progression to drug abuse (e.g., Sadava, 1987; Zucker & Gomberg, 1986). Although biogenetic influences certainly affect the potential emergence of drug use disorders, these forces are clearly shaped and modified by other personal attributes and environmental conditions (e.g., Marlatt, Baer, Donovan & Kirlahan, 1988). For instance, some types of alcohol abuse appear to have a genetic component (Vaillant, 1983), although the magnitude and mechanism of such a factor have not been clearly established. There is also a growing body of literature, in both animal and human studies, that has shown biogenetic factors to play an important role in use and abuse of drugs other than alcohol (Cadoret, 1992; Merikangas, Rounsaville, & Prusoff, 1992).

Genetic influences clearly play an important—but not exclusive (Zucker & Gomberg, 1986)—role in the etiology of alcoholism (Crabbe, McSwigan, & Belknap, 1985). Among the most famous studies in this area is the work of Goodwin (1976, 1985). For instance, using adoptees from alcoholic and non-alcoholic fathers in Denmark, he determined that sons of alcoholics were at four times greater risk for developing alcoholism than their peers with a nonalcoholic father. Twin and animal studies have also demonstrated a genetic factor for alcoholism. Nevertheless, even monozygotic twins have far from 100% concordance for alcoholism (Crabbe et al., 1985), establishing that alcoholism is not totally genetic and that other personal, environmental, and societal factors play important roles (Newcomb, in press).

One of the classic studies of heritability of alcoholism described two patterns of genetic transmission (Bohman, Sigvardsson, & Cloninger, 1981; Cloninger, Bohman, & Sigvardsson, 1981). Type I is called *milieu limited* and involves both genetic and environmental factors, affects both men and women, is associated with late onset, and is associated with few or no alcohol or criminal problems in the parents. Type II is called *male limited* and is affected little by environment, is restricted to male transmission, has an early onset and association with criminal behavior, and is related to fathers with severe alcoholism, extensive treatment, and extensive criminality. Although these heritability patterns are interesting and informative, they have received substantial criticism on methodological bases (e.g., Searles, 1988) and must be considered with caution.

An important question concerns what precisely is inherited if there is a genetic influence for alcoholism or other drug abuse. Research evidence, primarily but not exclusively based on animal models, suggests at least two mechanisms (e.g., Bardo & Risner, 1985). Those at genetic risk for drug abuse may inherit a biological vulnerability to the hedonic affects of the drug, so that for them the drug effect is more attractive than for others. It is also possible that those at genetic risk for drug abuse may not experience the withdrawal effects as severely as those not at risk (e.g., less likelihood of hangover). These proposed mechanisms and perhaps others (e.g., inherited behavioral traits; Tarter, 1988), however, must be evaluated more conclusively in further research (Schuckit, 1987).

Establishing correlates of substance use has been the primary basis for inferring etiological variables, although this approach is seriously flawed for inferring causal effects (Newcomb, 1987, 1990). Despite the compelling idea that the causes of drug abuse may be different from the causes of use (Long & Scherl, 1984), little systematic research exists that verifies such a hypothesis, although data and results are accumulating to support the notion (Glantz & Pickens, 1992). Newcomb (1988) has suggested and given support to the notion that any type of drug used (perhaps with the exception of tobacco or over-the-counter and prescribed medications) in the workplace in fact reflects drug abuse. The reasons people begin using drugs seems different from those factors that contribute to continued or escalated drug use; for instance, several researchers have found that most people start using drugs as a result of social influences, whereas abuse of drugs is often more strongly tied to psychological factors (see Carman, 1979; Kandel, Kessler, & Margulies, 1978; Newcomb & Bentler, 1990; Paton, Kessler, & Kandel, 1977).

Some have suggested that involvement with drugs progresses in a fixed sequence from licit drugs to illicit substances (e.g., Kandel, 1975; Kandel & Faust, 1975). Thus, a typical (but not universal) progression in an individual may start with beer, wine, or cigarettes, then move to hard liquor, later to marijuana, and subsequently to other illicit drugs such as amphetamines, cocaine, or heroin. Of course, these shifts from a lower stage to a higher stage are probabilistic, but not guaranteed (O'Donnell & Clayton, 1982). Involvement at one stage does not necessarily lead to involvement at the next stage, but involvement at the next stage is unlikely without prior involvement in the previous stage. This notion has been tested in various cross-sectional and longitudinal studies (e.g., Hays, Widaman, DiMatteo, & Stacy, 1987; Mills & Noyes, 1984; Newcomb & Bentler, 1986c). Results have generally confirmed the stage hypothesis, with some variations. For instance, Donovan and Jessor (1983) found that problem drinking occurred higher in the progression than general alcohol use. In contrast, Newcomb and Bentler (1986c) found that several mini-sequences accounted for drug involvement from early adolescence to young adulthood when the role of cigarettes and nonprescription medications were included.

This progression is certainly dependent upon the drugs available to a particular individual and the allure or abuse liability of the drug. It is possible that highly addictive drugs, such as crack cocaine, may alter this sequence of drug progression. Because of its severe addictive potential and wide and inexpensive availability, use of crack may occur much earlier in the sequence than other illicit drugs or even licit drugs. Although this seems likely, there are few data currently available to test this notion. The mechanism that drives such staging (e.g., availability, anxiety reduction, peer group norms, or physiological vulnerability perhaps associated with learning to appreciate the positive effects of a drug) is not known, although there are some hints that these factors may not be the same at all stages; for example, psychopathology has been implicated primarily at later stages or higher levels of drug involvement and not at initiation.

A wide range of correlates and influences on initial involvement in substance use have been identified. Because of the inevitable correlation of other problem behaviors with drug use (see discussion below on problem behaviors), many predictors of drug involvement are similar to predictors of general problem behavior or deviance. The main mechanism for clearly establishing unique predictors of drug use has been longitudinal studies controlled for other deviant behaviors and attitudes, with statistical controls substituted for the more desirable experimental control, and analyzed using structural equation modeling methods (e.g., Bentler, 1980; Newcomb, 1990).

Nevertheless, peer influences (e.g., modeling use, provision of substances, encouraging use) are the most consistent and strongest of all factors. In addition to the roles of prior behavioral experience with drugs and peer influences, other factors associated with initial involvement with drugs include such social structural variables as socioeconomic status (with generally heavier use among more disadvantaged groups), family role and socialization variables (with greater use in families adult drug use models and lack of family structure and responsiveness), educational variables (with poor school attachment and performance associated with greater drug use), psychological variables (e.g., low traditionalism and high need for stimulation), attitudinal variables such as tolerance for deviance (with nontraditionalism associated with greater drug use), behavioral variables such as deviant behaviors or low law abidance (implying greater substance use), emotional variables (e.g., anxiety or need for excitement), psychopathology (with greater depression and antisocial personality related to higher drug use), and temperament, as well as exposure to stressful life events (see Hawkins et al., 1992; Newcomb & Bentler, 1989).

Many of these varied influences have been related to involvement with drug use or abuse, but none have ever been found to be the primary factor involved. Because the range of variables leading to initial involvement in drug use is so large, recent views of this phenomenon have emphasized the risk-factor notion that is often used in medical epidemiology (Bry, McKeon, & Pandina, 1982; Newcomb, Maddahian, & Bentler, 1986; Newcomb, Maddahian, Skager, & Bentler, 1987; Scheier & Newcomb, 1991a, b). At this time, it seems highly unlikely that any one factor (or even a few) will ever be found to account fully and totally for all variations of drug involvement. As might be expected, based on the list of correlates and antecedents noted above, the risk factors include environmental, behavioral, psychological, and social attributes.

Therefore, drug involvement must be considered as multiply determined and as generated by many factors. This approach suggests that the more risk factors someone is exposed to that encourage drug use, the more likely it is that he or she will use or abuse drugs. Exposure to greater numbers of risk factors not only is a reliable correlate of drug use but influences the increase in drug use over time, implying a true etiological role for these variables (Newcomb et al., 1986; Scheier & Newcomb, 1991b). This approach indicates that drug use is one possible attempt at coping with these stressful risk conditions, with the likelihood of use increasing as the individual is exposed to more and more conditions. The particular factors are not as important as the simple accumulation of more vulnerability factors in the person's life.

The flip side of risk factors for drug use are protective factors that reduce the likelihood and level of drug use and abuse. Protective factors are those psychosocial influences that have a direct effect on limiting or reducing drug involvement (Newcomb, 1992b). Very recently, this risk-factor approach to drug use and abuse has been expanded to test for multiple protective factors as well (Newcomb, 1992b; Newcomb & Felix-Ortiz, 1992).

Protective factors also may operate in a different manner than simply through a direct effect on reducing drug involvement. They may, in fact, buffer or moderate the association between risk factors and drug use and abuse (Brook, Cohen, Whiteman, & Gordon, 1992; Newcomb & Felix-Ortiz, 1992; Stacy, Newcomb, & Bentler, 1992). Protective factors that moderate the relationship between risk for drug use or abuse can involve aspects of the environment (e.g., maternal affection; Brook, Nomura, & Cohen, 1989) or the individual (e.g., introversion or self-acceptance; Stacy et al., 1992). For instance, Stacy et al. (1992) found a significantly stronger relationship between peer use of hard drugs and self-use of hard drugs for those low in self-acceptance compared to those with high self-acceptance (for whom there was little association between hard drug use by peers and self). Newcomb and Felix-Ortiz (1992) have also tested the buffering effects of multiple protective factors on the relationship between multiple risk factors and drug use and abuse. Several significant effects were noted, primarily for illicit drugs.

3. PREVALENCE OF DRUG USE ON THE JOB

One serious ambiguity that affects all issues discussed in this chapter and elsewhere in this book is variations in what is meant by "drug use on the job." In a strict sense, this means the ingestion of drugs at the work site during explicit periods of employment. Based on this definition, a three-martini lunch or two-joint break would not be considered drug use on the job. On the other extreme, many drugs have long half-lives and may affect work performance hours, if not days, subsequent to ingestion. Should this be considered drug use on the job? This ambiguity is reflected and compounded by the variants of self-report measures of workplace drug use. The most typical assessment asks whether the respondent has used a particular drug on the job; it is unclear, though, whether the employee would interpret this question to include drugs used just before work, during breaks, or at lunch. These latter three instances may not be construed as strictly using drugs on the job, but they reflect temporal periods of drug ingestion that quite likely may account for being intoxicated at work. Being drunk, high, or stoned at work may be the more appropriate question to ask, but this is rarely assessed (with the exception of Newcomb, 1988). Other variations in types of questions asked and interpretations of these by the respondent may account for the disparity in conclusions sometimes noted in studies discussed in this chapter.

Few studies describe the actual extent of drug use on the job. It remains an arguable assumption that those who drink or use drugs away from work will also do so on the job or in other inappropriate settings. This may be the case, but it is certainly not firmly established. As such, these types of studies of general drug use (as reported above) provide some background for investigating drug use on the job, but they cannot truly inform us about this behavior.

Although some estimates exist, debate continues regarding the extent of drug use on the job. Most employers have been confronted with an employee who is using drugs at work. This does not indicate that "everyone is doing it," however, as some articles in the popular press have indicated. For instance, some personnel experts believe that the furor about drugs on the job may have been distorted or exaggerated by the media and other sources (e.g., Crew & Hartman, 1992; Gordon, 1987).

When some estimates of the prevalence of drug use at work appear, though, they are of a magnitude that cannot be taken lightly. For instance, according to Backer (1987), "Experts estimate that between 10 and 23 percent of all U.S. workers use dangerous drugs on the job." These estimates are based on best guesses, however, and not on any reliable assessment of use of drugs on the job. These estimates are typically based on two types of data: prevalence rates of addicted individuals seeking treatment who admitted using drugs on the job, and estimates of the prevalence of alcohol or drug problems of individuals in various occupations (not stipulating that the problematic use of drugs occurred on the job). Although important and indirectly related to problems of drug use on the job, these data fail to establish the actual extent of involvement with drugs in the workplace and can be misleading (Alden, 1986).

For example, Washton and Gold (1987) found that 75% of the callers to the national cocaine hotline (800-COCAINE) had used drugs on the job. Not surprisingly, cocaine was the most prevalent drug used by these callers in the workplace, and 92% had performed their job while under the influence of some drug. These estimates are certainly biased in at least two ways. First, cocaine abusers (as opposed to the general population or abusers of other drugs) are most likely to call a cocaine hotline. Second, those having problems with drugs are most likely in general to call the hotline. These selection factors restrict the generalizability of these figures to only those who admit having a problem with cocaine and are willing to call a hotline. Similarly, Levy (1973) found that all but two of a group of 95 former addicts had used drugs on the job. This approach is the reverse in some ways of finding the percentage of people using drugs on the job, and it reflects the inherent biases of studying only those who are in treatment, somehow identified as drug abusers, or personally acknowledge severe difficulty with drug use. Therefore, these results only tell us what a small group of severe abusers or addicts seeking treatment have done on the job. There is no adequate way to generalize these conclusions to all employees or a random community sample.

4. CONTEXT AND DRUG USE ON THE JOB

Particular occupations have long been associated with heavy drinking, as have certain countries. Differences in drug usage certainly exist between different types of jobs and across different countries, although the reasons behind these differences are not so clear. Most of studies of these differences have focused on alcohol consumption and not on other drugs.

As determined by per capita consumption levels of alcohol, France, Italy, and Spain have the highest rates of alcohol use. The United States is sixteenth on this list, with all but France evidencing an increase over time (Helzer, 1987). In contrast, the United States ranks sixth in prevalence of mortality resulting from cirrhosis, a much clearer indicator of alcohol abuse than use (Helzer, 1987). These differences may reflect differing national climates or attitudes toward drug use, or competing causes of mortality. It is not clear how such standards affect the likelihood of using drugs in the workplace beyond providing a sociocultural context that may be conducive to or constraining upon such behavior.

The social dynamics of particular jobs or occupations are more easily identified than specific national characteristics that foster drinking and may help account for the differential levels of drug use across occupations. Olkinuora (1984) and Plant (1981) identified several risk factors that were related to the connection between occupation and alcoholism. These included the availability of alcohol at work, social pressure to drink on the job, separation from normal social relationships, freedom from supervision, very high or very low income, collusion by colleagues, stresses or hazards, and preselection of high-risk people.

A variety of methods have been used to establish links between alcoholism and occupation. These have included studying alcohol treatment populations, agency surveys, population surveys of drinking habits, and mortality studies, particularly of deaths attributable to cirrhosis (e.g., Olkinuora, 1984; Plant, 1977). Results from these studies have identified occupations at high and low risk for alcohol problems. Jobs in the high-risk category involve entertainment, the liquor trade, caterers, seamen, executives, the military, service workers, laborers, doctors, lawyers, and medical students (Olkinuora, 1984; Plant, 1977, 1981; Slattery, Alderson, & Bryant, 1986). Jobs at low risk for alcohol treatment and mortality as a result of cirrhosis include engineering foremen, jewelers, farmers, chemists, public drivers, construction employees, gardeners, and shopkeepers (Slattery et al., 1986). These low-risk occupations were characterized by threat of job loss for "drunkenness (e.g., drivers) and skilled craftsmen who underwent a lengthy period of apprenticeship or those who still work with their hands as well as their brains" (p. 933).

Several recent studies have identified industries that are at high and low risk for employees using drugs specifically on the job. Lehman, Farabee, Holcom, and Simpson (1991) found the highest rates of drug use in the workplace for skilled, technical, paraprofessional, and service occupations (ranging from 3% to 4%), and the lowest rates for professional and cleric positions (from 0% to 1%). Mensch and Kandel (1988) also identified specific occupations that were differentially associated with using drugs on the job. The pattern of their findings is more complicated and differs by type of drug and gender. Among men, entertainment and recreation jobs were associated with the highest rates of alcohol, marijuana, and cocaine use on the job, followed by construction for being high on marijuana at work. Among women, alcohol use at work was most related to agriculture, forestry, and fisheries; marijuana use on the job most often occurred in construction jobs; and cocaine was most prevalent on the job in the transportation sector. Gleason et al. (1991) found that the highest prevalence rates of drug use on the job were in the construction and entertainment/recreation industries, whereas the lowest rates were found within the professional services and public administration industries.

The High School Senior Survey follow-up has also examined prevalence and trends in use of drugs at work by occupational status (O'Malley, 1992). Respondents indicated in which of 14 occupations they were most recently employed. These 14 types of jobs were grouped into seven categories that were roughly ordinal in degree of "prestige," ranging from semiskilled to professional. Military and protective services reported very low rates of drug use at work, with little variation among the other categories. Alcohol use at work was highest for males in the top three categories (professional, skilled, and managerial) and the lowest grouping (semiskilled). Females' rates were only slightly lower and slightly higher for the clerical category; there were substantial gender differences for use of marijuana at work. Skilled and semiskilled male workers had much higher rates than other categories in use of marijuana and cocaine at work.

One question that naturally arises when perusing this literature is whether a person who is predisposed to alcohol or drug problems is attracted to specific professions or whether certain professions contribute to the alcohol or drug problems. In other words, individuals may choose a particular job for reasons that allow or are associated with their involvement with drugs. Thus, an association between drug or alcohol use and certain jobs may be accounted for by a confounding factor located within the individual and not the work setting. On the other hand, certain jobs or work conditions may socialize or promote drug use among its employees (Ames & Janes, 1987).

Plant (1978, 1979) attempted to tease apart these different hypotheses by studying new recruits to the liquor or brewery trade (a very high-risk occupation) to those applying for jobs at low risk for alcohol problems. He found that those who applied to the liquor jobs had poorer employment records and were heavier drinkers prior to their employment than were applicants to lower-risk occupations. This supports the preselection hypothesis. Interestingly, however, Plant also found that those in the liquor industry increased their drinking behavior (including use on the job) in conformity to perceived social norms. Thus, for at least this occupation there is a self-selection process *and* an environmental-pressure process occurring that account for the higher rates of alcoholism. Similarly, Newcomb (1988) found that drug use on the job was associated more with personal characteristics than with any of the job characteristics he considered (e.g., turnover, satisfaction). Such findings, although rather convincing, may be accounted for by other factors, such as available employment opportunities.

Cosper (1979) and Cosper and Hughes (1982) challenged the notion that occupations associated with heavy drinking actually reflect alcohol abuse or alcoholism. They suggested that the frequency, but not the quantity, of drinking is higher in certain occupations and may not reflect problem levels. They propose that conformity to unique norms of an occupation may generate these differences, and thus may not indicate deviance or low social conformity. Although this may be true in certain jobs (they studied naval officers and journalists), it does not account for either the differential treatment rates or the mortality differences observed in other studies.

5. POLYDRUG USE

Much previous research has revealed that use of drugs is not typically limited to one specific substance, but often involves use of various drugs. This is particularly true for teenagers and those who use illicit drugs (e.g., marijuana, cocaine), but it has been documented among young adults (Newcomb & Bentler, 1988) and adults (Newcomb, 1992b) as well.

Clayton and Ritter (1985) reviewed many studies of drug use and found that "more often than not, the persons who are using drugs frequently, are multiple drug users" (p. 83). For instance, cocaine users reported significantly higher prevalence rates for all other types of drugs—including cigarettes, alcohol, cannabis (marijuana), over-the-counter medications, hypnotics, stimulants, psychedelics, inhalants, narcotics, and PCP—compared to those who had not used cocaine (Newcomb & Bentler, 1986a). These large differences were found for both men and women, and they were prevalent during adolescence as well as young adulthood (e.g., Newcomb & Bentler, 1986b). The association between various types of drug use is so high that latent constructs of general polydrug use (Newcomb & Bentler, 1988) and polydrug use in the workplace (Newcomb,

1988; Stein, Newcomb, & Bentler, 1988) have been identified distinctly and reliably.

In a series of analyses regarding drug use in the workplace, one of the overriding conclusions reached by Newcomb (1988) was that substance use in the workplace was not typically restricted to using a single substance but was highly related to using substances from the same class of drugs, as well as different classes of substances, at work. In other words, it is highly likely that someone caught using marijuana at work has also used hashish or alcohol or hard drugs on the job. In fact, the multivariate analyses in this study suggest that substance use in the workplace is best characterized as polydrug use at work. Detailed information on conditional hazard rates for use of specific substances at work confirmed these correlational analyses; the use of one substance at work increased by several times the likelihood of using other drugs in this context.

6. STAGE THEORY OF DRUG USE

Another way to understand drug involvement has been with the progression or stage theory of Kandel (Kandel, 1975; Kandel & Faust, 1975), described earlier in this chapter. Newcomb (1988) found preliminary support to extend this stage-theory hypothesis to drug use in the workplace. Using Guttman scaling analyses, he found that drug use at work occurred after both alcohol and cannabis use for men and subsequent to cocaine use for women. Thus, using drugs at work implies a degree of drug involvement somewhere between cannabis and cocaine use (on the one hand) and other hard drug use (on the other). The different scaling results for men and women suggest that using drugs at work occurs sooner in the sequence of drug involvement for men than for women. This may help explain the gender differences obtained in studies of prevalence of substance use in the workplace.

These conceptualizations of drug involvement as both staged and involving multiple drugs are not mutually exclusive, but may reflect different levels of abstraction (e.g., Newcomb & Bentler, 1986c). For instance, even though there may be a sequence or progression of involvement with drugs, those who have tried drugs high in the sequence may also be characterized by a general involvement with many drugs.

7. RELATIONSHIP BETWEEN DRUG USE ON AND OFF THE JOB

It is expected that general drug use away from work and drug use on the job might be related and reflect a life-style of drug involvement. Substance use away from work is substantially more prevalent than substance use at work; many people may use drugs regularly, but not at work or school. Others may use drugs both at work and away from the job. In addition, it is likely that some people limit their substance use to the workplace, although this group is probably relatively small.

There is little literature that addresses this issue. Researchers have only begun to confront the degree of correspondence between a general proclivity to use drugs and actual drug use on the job. Unfortunately, there is an unspoken assumption that the association is quite high, if not perfect. For instance, virtually all discussions of drug use on the job cite statistics of general drug use for various populations to argue that workplace use must be rampant (e.g., Backer, 1987). This may not be a reasonable conclusion, however, since even heavy users of drugs may either obey internal prohibitions and social sanctions against using drugs on the job or restrict their use or even abuse to circumstances and situations that would not interfere with their work duties and responsibilities. A more reasonable assumption is that at least some general drug use must precede use of drugs on the job for most people.

Newcomb (1988) directly tested these issues and arrived at several conclusions. First, drug use at work and general drug use were highly, but not perfectly, related (i.e., high general use of drugs did not guarantee use of drugs in the workplace). In most cases, knowing the extent of general drug use predicted less than 50% of the variance of using drugs on the job. Thus, those researchers who rely upon prevalence rates of general drug use to characterize the extent of disruptive drug use may be quite misleading, since there is far from a one-to-one relationship.

8. PREDICTORS OF DRUG USE ON THE JOB

Although hundreds of studies have examined correlates of general drug use, only a few could be found that specifically examined factors associated with drug use on the job. With the exclusion of Newcomb (1988, 1989), who examined multiple substances with prospective data, most of these were cross-sectional and limited to use of any drug on the job.

Many believe that job conditions are important risk or protective factors associated with using drugs on the job. This is a logical assumption based upon the occupational differences in drug use behaviors and the clear evidence regarding the social-environmental influences on drug use. Theoretical contributions have emphasized various characteristics of the work environment as influences on drug use of employees, including organizational frustration and job stress (Milbourn, 1984), distancing forces, attractions, and constraints (Gupta & Jenkins, 1984), norms regarding drug use of coworkers and the occupation (Shore, 1986), and the drug use-enabling aspects of the work environment (Ames, 1990; Roman, Blum, & Martin, 1992).

In quantitative or qualitative tests of these expectations, the primary focus has been on correlates with general drug use rather than drug use on the job. For instance, Markowitz (1984) found that indicators of general alcohol misuse were significantly correlated with less responsibility and autonomy in the workplace. Martin, Blum, and Roman (1992) found that self-medicating use of alcohol was significantly associated with more pressure and fewer extrinsic rewards on the job, although demographic factors (being divorced and living in an urban area) were far more important than these job characteristics.

A few studies have directly examined job characteristics as they relate to actual drug use on the job. For instance, Lehman and Simpson (1992) found that substance use at work was significantly correlated with 13 variables: (a) younger age, (b) being male, (c) lower education, (d) low self-esteem, (e) more depression, (f) not working in the office, (g) little faith in management, (h) low job involvement, (i) job dissatisfaction, (j) high job tension, (k) low organizational commitment, (l) more accidents, and (m) more absences. In a more specific analysis of this data set, Lehman et al. (1991) found seven unique predictors of substance use at work in a multiple regression analysis: (a) not being married, (b) having been arrested, (c) low self-esteem, (d) high peer drug use, (e) working alone or in a small group, (f) a high-risk job, and (g) low job involvement.

Mensch and Kandel (1988) examined various job dimensions as possible correlates of on-the-job marijuana use for men and women. They found eight small, but significant correlates of using marijuana at work among the men: (a) low skill discretion, (b) low decision authority, (c) high job insecurity, (d) low supervisor support, (e) high physical demands, (f) high hazardous exposure, (g) low substantive complexity, and (h) high motor skills. Among the women, marijuana use on the job was significantly correlated with five job characteristics: (a) low skill discretion, (b) low decision authority, (c) high coworker support, (d) low substantive complexity, and (e) high physical demands.

Mangione and Quinn (1975) examined relationships between drug use on the job and job satisfaction for men and women in two age groups (younger and older than 30 years). There were no significant correlations between drug use in the workplace and job satisfaction for either group of women. Among older men, a small but significant correlation was found between more drug use on the job and less job satisfaction ($r = -.12$).

In several ethnographic studies, Ames (1990) reported that certain aspects of the work environment, as well as ambiguous or conflicting responsibilities of supervisors, encouraged drinking on the job. They characterized these aspects of the working environment as enabling influences for on-the-job alcohol use.

Newcomb (1988) has presented a comprehensive set of both cross-sectional and prospective findings on the correlates and predictors of drug use in the workplace. He examined many personal, social, and work-related factors in terms of their associations with using drugs on the job. In regard to background and demographic information, he found that those most likely to engage in drug use in the workplace were male, either black (for use of marijuana) or white (for use of other drugs), had few educational plans, had cohabited sometime in their life, had no children, and were not currently married. Higher income was related to greater use of cocaine and hard drugs on the job.

A wide range of personality, emotional functioning, social support, and life-problems variables were examined as possible correlates of drug use in the workplace. In general, several small but significant effects were found. Using drugs at work was only slightly related to relationship and family problems and emotional distress. Drug use at work was most highly related to having drug and alcohol problems, lacking law abidance, being liberal, feeling powerless, and lacking injury hysteria (i.e., low fearfulness). In other words, drug use in the workplace was not typically a result of life problems or general unhappiness (although a few small associations with these variables were found); it was most related to being nonconforming and having some trouble with an intimate relationship, as well as the factors noted above.

In terms of job conditions, drug use at work was not highly related to many work-related variables, including income, collecting public assistance, amount of work, and support for work problems. Drug use on the job was most related to job instability (frequently being fired), committing vandalism at work, and (to a lesser extent) job dissatisfaction. It was only slightly related to problems and unhappiness in the workplace.

To summarize, these studies reveal that drug use in the workplace appears to be more a function of the individual and his or her personal qualities rather than his or her environment, regardless of whether the environment is defined as at work or home. Such use is strongly related to individual characteristics suggesting a rebellious, nonconforming, deviant, and perhaps acting-out personality that was also evident earlier in life (as noted in the prospective studies). Based on these limited studies, it appears that drug use on the job is not largely or generally determined situationally, but rather is a manifestation of a general syndrome of problem behaviors both related to and separate from drug use.

These issues have been examined in several reviews of the literature, all of which have arrived at similar conclusions. For instance, Harris and Heft (1992) summarized that "though statistically significant in some cases, the relationship between work conditions and drug/alcohol consumption appears to be quite small" (p. 241). More than a decade earlier, Herold and Conlon (1981) reached the same conclusion regarding the association between work factors and alcohol abuse, noting that "unequivocal evidence of such linkages is scarce" (p. 337).

There are problems with this general conclusion, which is based on existing literature, theory, and empirical studies. These problems emphasize the necessity of not ruling out the work environment as a contributing or interactive factor for generating drug use among workers or protecting them from it. One limitation is that all of the studies contrasting various predictors of drug use on the job have been biased because of an imbalance of available measures of the individual versus directly assessed measures of job conditions and attitudes. For instance, some studies have included very few assessments of on-the-job conditions compared to personal characteristics and may have overemphasized the role of individual factors, since the personal qualities measured were of greater abundance in these studies.

The primary problem with these studies is that *none* of them were designed to examine the predictors of drug use in the workplace and instead were adapted to such a goal. In contrast, several studies have numerous and careful assessments of job characteristics, but fail to consider an adequate range of individual qualities. Even in these studies, however, the weak individual measures predominate over those for work conditions (e.g., Martin et al., 1992). Therefore, no existing study has been designed to test directly and explicitly whether drug use on the job is associated more or less with personal qualities (e.g., traits) or job characteristics (e.g., role ambiguity, stress, dissatisfaction) where appropriate and thorough measures of both domains have been gathered.

Finally, most studies of job conditions assume a direct or main effect of work environment on drug use either on or off the job. Such a conceptual model may be too narrow and limited. Several reviewers and researchers have noted that such a simplistic depiction is unrealistic and that the associations are far more complex (e.g., Martin et al., 1992) and may involve intervening variables (e.g., Violanti, Marshall, & Howe, 1983), generalization processes (e.g., Martin et al., 1992), or individual differences (Conway, Vickers, Word & Rahe, 1981), as well as the critical importance of interactions or moderated relationships between personal characteristics and job conditions (e.g., Brief & Folger, 1992). Therefore, we must not prematurely dismiss the potential impact of the work environment on drug use by the worker, both on and off the job, without comprehensive analyses and tests of these more realistic theories and processes.

9. GENERAL DEVIANCE AND DRUG USE ON THE JOB

One typically overlooked concern is whether drug use on the job is associated with various other deviant attitudes and behaviors that may also affect job performance and may be more important than drug use on disrupting performance on the job. In other words, is using drugs in the workplace a relatively independent form of inappropriate behavior, or is it linked to other problems or part of a general deviant life-style of irresponsible attitudes and behavior? This is an important distinction that has important implications for how to handle and treat drug use at work. If drug use in the workplace is strongly associated with other types of defiant attitudes and behavior, addressing only the inappropriate drug use may not correct a general life-style problem of deviance.

Drug use and abuse do not occur as isolated events, nor as distinct aspects of an individual's behavior. They are typically only components of a cluster of behaviors and attitudes that form a syndrome or life-style of problem behaviors or general deviance (McGee & Newcomb, 1992; Newcomb & McGee, 1991). Problem behavior theory was developed by Jessor and Jessor (1977, 1978) and provides a useful conceptualization to understand how teenage drug use is only one aspect of a deviance-prone life-style. Adolescent substance use is considered only one facet of a constellation of attitudes and behavior that are considered problems, unconventional, or nontraditional. These problem behaviors have been defined as "behavior that is socially defined as a problem, a source of concern, or as undesirable by the norms of conventional society . . . and its occurrence usually elicits some kind of social control response" (Jessor & Jessor, 1977, p. 33). For adolescents, these deviant behaviors include alcohol abuse, illicit drug use, precocious sexual involvement, academic problems, frequency of various sexual activities, deviant attitudes, and delinquent behavior.

This theory has been tested in several confirmatory factor analysis studies (Donovan & Jessor, 1985; Gillmore et al., 1991; McGee & Newcomb, 1992; Newcomb & McGee, 1991). These studies have identified a syndrome of problem behaviors among adolescents and young adults and revealed that either one common latent factor accounted for the correlations among the several indicators of problem behavior or that all of these constructs were highly correlated. For instance, Newcomb and Bentler (1988) found that teenage polydrug use was correlated highly with low social conformity (r = .69), criminal activities (r = .42), a deviant friendship network (r = .46), early sexual involvement (r = .52), and low academic potential (r = −.34).

Unfortunately, most of these studies have examined teenagers for whom many of these behaviors are age-status offenses (i.e., they would not be considered problematic at an older age). Nevertheless, some research has studied this cluster of problem behavior at older ages. Some have suggested that the syndrome may lose coherency and unidimensionality at later points in life (e.g., Newcomb & Bentler, 1988; Osgood, Johnson, O'Malley, & Bachman, 1988).

McGee and Newcomb (1992) used higher-order confirmatory factor analyses to examine the construct of general deviance at four ages from early adolescence to adulthood. They found that the construct was highly reliable at all ages, although in adulthood sexual involvement became somewhat detached from the cluster of deviant attitudes and behaviors captured by drug use, low social conformity, and criminal behaviors. In young adulthood, however, Newcomb (1988) identified a construct of general deviance that also included polydrug use in the workplace. Other indicators of this construct included general polydrug use, low social conformity, criminal behaviors, sexual involvement, and dealing drugs.

More specifically, Newcomb (1988) found that in terms of magnitude of association, various use of most drugs in the workplace was most highly correlated with low law abidance and selling drugs, followed by thefts and confrontational acts, and then the sexual involvement variables. Alcohol use on the job was less tightly bound to other types of deviance than use of other drugs in the workplace. Although significant, the deviance variables accounted for only 6% of the variance of alcohol use on the job, whereas these deviance variables accounted for variance proportions ranging from 20% (for cocaine use at work) to 36% (for hard drug use on the job).

Newcomb (1988) also asked to what extent using drugs on the job implies that other problems with drugs exist for an employee. Analyses on this issue revealed that compared to those who did not use drugs on the job, those who did use them were (a) 3.1 times more likely to admit having trouble with alcohol during the past 4 years; (b) 3.9 times more likely to admit having trouble with drugs in the past 4 years; (c) 2.6 times more likely to have had an accident that was drug related in the past 6 months; (d) 2.2 times more likely to have been arrested for or convicted of driving while intoxicated during the past 4 years; (e) 4.4 times as likely to have been arrested for or convicted of selling or possessing drugs in the past 4 years; (f) 2.3 times as likely to have attended an alcohol treatment program in the past 4 years; (g) 12.8 times as likely to have sold any illegal drugs during the past 6 months; and (h) 3.8 times more likely to have had a bad reaction to marijuana during the past 6 months. Certain non-drug-related problems associated with drug users have been identified in the employment setting. For instance, *Newsweek* (1983) has noted that the employed drug user is "late three times more often, requests time off 2.2 times more often, has 2.5 times as many absences of eight days or more, uses three times the normal level of sick benefits, is five times more likely to file a workmen's compensation claim, and is involved in accidents 3.6 times more often than other employees" (p. 57). Gardner (1982) cites other such employment correlates of drug use as lunchtime lateness, many short-term absences (especially on Mondays and Fridays), and injuries (particularly on the afternoon shift). In light of the general deviance syndrome, however, it may be quite likely that these other problems are not caused by drug use as much as they all reflect a general tendency toward deviance and irresponsibility that includes drug use and job behaviors.

REFERENCES

Alden, W. F., 1986, The scope of the drug problem: A national strategy, *Vital Speeches of the Day,* 751–756.

Ames, G. M., 1990, The workplace as an enabling environment for alcohol problems, *Anthropology of Work Review* **11**:12–16.

Ames, G. M., and Janes, C. R., 1987, Heavy and problem drinking in an American blue-collar population: Implications for prevention, *Social Science and Medicine* **8**:949–960.

Backer, T. E., 1987, *Strategic Planning for Workplace Drug Abuse Problems,* National Institute on Drug Abuse, Rockville, MD.

Bardo, M. T., and Risner, M. E., 1985, Biochemical substrates of drug abuse, in: *Determinants of Substance Abuse: Biological, Psychological, and Environmental Factors* (M. Galizio and S. A. Maisto, eds.), pp. 65–99, Plenum Press, New York.

Bentler, P. M., 1980, Multivariate analysis with latent variables: Causal modeling, *Annual Review of Psychology* **31**:419–456.

Bentler, P. M., and Newcomb, M. D., 1986, Personality, sexual behavior, and drug use revealed through latent variable methods, *Clinical Psychology Review* **6**:363–385.

Bohman, M., Sigvardsson, S., and Cloninger, C. R., 1981, Maternal inheritance of alcohol abuse: Cross fostering analysis of adopted women, *Archives of General Psychiatry* **38**:965–969.

Brief, A. P., Folger, R. G., 1992, The workplace and problem drinking as seen by two novices, *Alcoholism: Clinical and Experimental Research* **16**:190–198.

Brook, J. S., Cohen, P., Whiteman, M., and Gordon, A. S., 1992, Psychosocial risk factors in the transition from moderate to heavy use or abuse of drugs, in: *Vulnerability to Drug Abuse* (M. D. Glanz and R. Pickens, eds.), pp. 359–388, American Psychological Association, Washington DC.

Brook, J. S., Nomura, C., and Cohen, P., 1989, Prenatal, perinatal, and early childhood risk factors and drug involvement in adolescence, *Genetic, Social, and General Psychology Monographs* **115**:223–241.

Bry, B. H., McKeon, P., and Pandina, R., 1982, Extent of drug use as a function of number of risk factors, *Journal of Abnormal Psychology* **91**:273–279.

Buchanan, D. R., 1992, A social history of American drug use, *The Journal of Drug Issues* **22**:31–52.

Cadoret, R. J., 1992, Genetic and environmental factors in initiation of drug use and the transition to abuse, in: *Vulnerability to Drug Abuse* (M. D. Glanz and R. Pickens, eds.), pp. 99–114, American Psychological Association, Washington, DC.

Carman, R. S., 1979, Motivations for drug use and problematic outcomes among rural junior high school students, *Addictive Behaviors* **4**:91–93.

Clayton, R. R., and Ritter, C., 1985, The epidemiology of alcohol and drug abuse among adolescents, *Advances in Alcohol and Substance Abuse* **4**:69–97.

Cloninger, C. R., Bohman, M., and Sigvardsson, S., 1981, Inheritance of alcohol abuse: Cross fostering analysis of adopted men, *Addictive Behaviors* **4**:91–93.

Conway, T. L., Vickers, R. R., Ward, H. W., and Rahe, R. H., 1981, Occupational stress and variation in cigarette, coffee, and alcohol consumption, *Journal of Health and Social Behavior* **22**:155–165.

Cosper, R., 1979, Drinking as conformity, *Journal of Studies on Alcohol* **40**:868–891.

Cosper, R., and Hughes, F., 1982, So-called heavy drinking occupations, *Journal of Studies on Alcohol* **43**:110–118.

Crabbe, J. C., McSwigan, J. D., and Belknap, J. K., 1985, The role of genetics in substance abuse, in: *Determinants of Substance Abuse: Biological, Psychological, and Environmental Factors* (M. Galizio and S. A. Maisto, eds.), pp. 13–64, Plenum Press, New York.

Crew, S. M., and Hartman, S. J., 1992, Drugs in the workplace: Overstating the problems and the cures, *Journal of Drug Issues* **22**:923–937.

Donovan, J. E., and Jessor, R., 1983, Problem drinking and the dimensions of involvement with drugs: A Guttman scalogram analysis of adolescent drug use, *American Journal of Public Health* **73**:543–552.

Donovan, J. E., and Jessor, R., 1985, Structure of problem behavior in adolescence and young adulthood, *Journal of Consulting and Clinical Psychology* **53**:890–904.

Fillmore, K. M., 1984, Research as a handmaiden of policy: An appraisal of estimates of alcoholism and its cost in the workplace, *Journal of Public Health Policy* March:40–64.

Galizio, M., and Maisto, S. A., eds., 1985, *Determinants of Substance Abuse: Biological, Psychological, and Environmental Factors*, Plenum Press, New York.

Gardner, A. W., 1982, Identifying and helping problem drinkers at work, *Journal of Social and Occupational Medicine* **32:**171–179.

Gillmore, M. R., Hawkins, J. D., Catalano, R. F., Jr., Day, L. E., Moore, M., and Abbott, R., 1991, Structure of problem behaviors in preadolescence, *Journal of Consulting and Clinical Psychology* **59:**499–506.

Glantz, M. D., and Pickens, R. W., 1992, Vulnerability to drug abuse: Introduction and overview, in: *Vulnerability to Drug Abuse* (M. Glanz and R. Pickens, eds.), pp. 1–14, American Psychological Association, Washington, DC.

Gleason, P. M., Veu, J. R., and Pergamit, M. R., 1991, Drug and alcohol use at work: A survey of young workers, *Monthly Labor Review,* August, pp. 3–7.

Goodwin, D. W., 1976, *Is alcoholism hereditary?* Oxford University Press, New York.

Goodwin, D. W., 1985, Alcoholism and genetics: The sins of the fathers, *Archives of General Psychiatry* **42:**171–174.

Gordon, J., Drug testing as a productivity booster? *Training,* **24:**22–34.

Gupta, N., and Jenkins, G. D., 1984, Substance use as an employee response to work environment, *Journal of Vocational Behavior* **24:**84–93.

Harris, M. M., and Heft, L. L., 1992, Alcohol and drug use in the workplace: issues, controversies, and directions for future research, *Journal of Management* **18:**239–266.

Hawkins, J. D., Catalano, R. F., and Miller, J. Y., 1992, Risk and protective factors for alcohol and other drug problems in adolescence and early adulthood: Implications for substance abuse problems, *Psychological Bulletin* **112:**64–105.

Hays, R. D., Widaman, K. F., DiMatteo, M. R., and Stacy, A. W., 1987, Structural equation models of current drug use: Are appropriate models so simple(x)? *Journal of Personality and Social Psychology* **52:**134–144.

Helzer, J. E., 1987, Epidemiology of alcoholism, *Journal of Consulting and Clinical Psychology* **55:**284–292.

Herold, D. M., and Conlon, E. J., 1981, Work factors as potential causal agents of alcohol abuse, *Journal of Drug Issues* **11**(3)**:** 337–356.

Jessor, R., and Jessor, S. L., 1977, *Problem Behavior and Psychosocial Development,* Academic Press, New York.

Jessor, R., and Jessor, S. L., 1978, Theory testing in longitudinal research on marijuana use, in: *Longitudinal Research on Drug Use: Empirical Findings and Methodological Issues* (D. B. Kandel, ed.), pp. 41–71, Hemisphere, Washington, DC.

Julien, R. M., 1992, *A Primer of Drug Action,* 6th ed., Freeman and Co., New York.

Kandel, D. B., 1975, Stages in adolescent involvement in drug use, *Science* **190:**912–914.

Kandel, D. B., and Faust, R., 1975, Sequence and stages in patterns of adolescent drug use, *Archives of General Psychiatry* **32:**923–932.

Kandel, D. B., Kessler, R. C., and Margulies, R. Z., 1978, Antecedents of adolescent initiation into stages of drug use: A developmental analysis, in: *Longitudinal Research on Drug Use: Empirical Findings and Methodological Issues* (D. B. Kandel, ed.), Hemisphere, Washington DC.

Kandel, D. B., and Logan, J. A., 1984, Patterns of drug use from adolescence to young adulthood, I: Periods of risk for initiation, continued use, and discontinuation, *American Journal of Public Health* **74:**660–666.

Lehman, W.E.K., Farabee, D. J., Holcom, M. L., and Simpson, D. D., 1991, Prediction of substance use in the workplace: Unique contributions of demographic and work environment variables, Unpublished manuscript.

Lehman, W.E.K., and Simpson, D. D., 1992, Employee substance use and on-the-job behaviors, *Journal of Applied Psychology* **77:**309–321.

Lettieri, D. J., 1985, Drug abuse: A review of explanations and models of explanations, *Advances in Alcohol and Substance Abuse* **4:**9–40.

Lettieri, D. J., Sayers, M., and Pearson, H. W., eds., 1980, *Theories on Drug Abuse: Selected Contemporary Perspectives,* National Institute on Drug Abuse, Rockville, MD.

Levy, S. I., 1973, A case study of drug-related criminal behavior in business and industry, in: *Drug Abuse in Industry* (J. M. Sher, ed.), Thomas, Springfield, IL.

Long, J. V. F., and Scherl, D. J., 1984, Developmental antecedents of compulsive drug use: A report on the literature, *Journal of Psychoactive Drugs* **16:**169–182.

Mangione, T. W., and Quinn, R. P., 1975, Job satisfaction, counterproductive behavior, and drug use at work, *Journal of Applied Psychology* **60:**114–115.

Markowitz, M., 1984, Alcohol misuse as a response to perceived powerlessness in the organization, *Journal of Studies on Alcohol* **45:**225–227.

Marlatt, G. A., Baer, J. S., Donovan, D. M., and Kivlahan, D. R., 1988, Addictive behaviors: Etiology and treatment, *Annual Review of Psychology* **3:**223–252.

Martin, J. K., Blum, T. C., and Roman, P. M., 1992, Drinking to cope and self-medication: Characteristics of jobs in relation to workers' drinking behavior. *Journal of Organizational Behavior* **13:**55–71.

McGee, L., and Newcomb, M. D., 1993, General deviance syndrome: Expanded hierarchical evaluations at four ages from early adolescence to adulthood, *Journal of Consulting and Clinical Psychology* **60:**766–776.

Mensch, B. S., and Kandel, D. B., 1988, Do job conditions influence the use of drugs? *Journal of Health and Social Behavior* **29:**169–184.

Merikangas, K. R., Rounsaville, B. J., and Prusoff, B. A., 1992, Familial factors in vulnerability to substance abuse, in: *Vulnerability to Drug Abuse* (M. Glanz and R. Pickens, eds.), pp. 75–98, American Psychological Association, Washington, DC.

Milbourn, G., 1984, Alcoholism, drug abuse, job stress: What small business can do, *American Journal of Small Business* **8:**36–48.

Mills, C. J., and Noyes, H. L., 1984, Patterns and correlates of initial and subsequent drug use among adolescents, *Journal of Consulting and Clinical Psychology* **52:**231–243.

Mosher, J. F., and Yanagisako, K. L., 1991, Public health, not social warfare: A public health approach to illegal drug policy, *Journal of Public Health Policy* **12:**278–323.

Newcomb, M. D., 1987, Consequences of teenage drug use: The transition from adolescence to young adulthood, *Drugs and Society* **1:**25–60.

Newcomb, M. D., 1988, *Drug Use in the Workplace: Risk Factors for Disruptive Substance Use Among Young Adults,* Auburn House, Dover, MA.

Newcomb, M. D., 1989, Drug use and sensation seeking: Latent-variable comparisons among adolescents, Paper presented at the Western Psychological Association Meeting, Reno, NV.

Newcomb, M. D., 1990, Losing the war on drugs: Are we too addicted to the quick fix to seek the ultimate fix?, Paper presented to United States Congress sponsored by the Federation of Behavioral, Psychological and Cognitive Sciences, Washington DC.

Newcomb, M. D., 1992a, Substance abuse and control in the United States: Ethical and legal issues, *Social Science and Medicine* **35:**471–479.

Newcomb, M. D., 1992b, Understanding the multidimensional nature of drug use and abuse: The role of consumption, risk factors, and protective factors, in: *Vulnerability to Drug Abuse* (M. D. Glantz and R. Pickens, eds.), pp. 255–297, American Psychological Association, Washington DC.

Newcomb, M. D., in press, Families, peers, and adolescent alcohol abuse: A paradigm to study multiple causes, mechanisms, and outcomes, in: *Development of Alcohol Problems: Exploring the Biopsychosocial Matrix of Risk* (R. Zucker, G. Boyd, and J. Howard, eds.), National Institute of Alcoholism and Alcohol Abuse, Rockville, MD.

Newcomb, M. D., and Bentler, P. M., 1986a, Cocaine use among adolescents: Longitudinal associations with social context, psychopathology, and use of other substances, *Addictive Behaviors* **11**:263–273.

Newcomb, M. D., and Bentler, P. M., 1986b, Cocaine use among young adults, *Advances in Alcohol and Substance Abuse* **6**:73–96.

Newcomb, M. D., and Bentler, P. M., 1986c, Frequency and sequence of drug use: A longitudinal study from early adolescence to young adulthood, *Journal of Drug Education* **16**:101–120.

Newcomb, M. D., and Bentler, P. M., 1988, *Consequences of Adolescent Drug Use: Impact on the Lives of Young Adults*, Sage, Newbury Park, CA.

Newcomb, M. D., and Bentler, P. M., 1989, Substance use and abuse among children and teenagers, *American Psychologist* **44**:242–248.

Newcomb, M. D., and Bentler, P. M., 1990, Antecedents and consequences of cocaine use: An eight-year study from early adolescence to young adulthood, in: *Straight and Devious Pathways from Childhood to Adulthood* (L. Robins, ed.), pp. 158–181, Cambridge University Press, New York.

Newcomb, M. D., and Felix-Ortiz, M., 1992, Multiple protective and risk factors for drug use and abuse: Cross-sectional and prospective findings, *Journal of Personality and Social Psychology*, **63**:280–296.

Newcomb, M. D., and McGee, L., 1991, The influence of sensation seeking on general deviance and specific problem behaviors from adolescence to young adulthood, *Journal of Personality and Social Psychology* **61**:614–628.

Newcomb, M. D., Maddahian, E., and Bentler, P. M., 1986, Risk factors for drug use among adolescents: Concurrent and longitudinal analyses, *American Journal of Public Health* **76**:525–531.

Newcomb, M. D., Maddahian, E., Skager, R., and Bentler, P. M., 1987, Substance abuse and psychosocial risk factors among teenagers: Associations with sex, age, ethnicity, and type of school, *American Journal of Drug and Alcohol Abuse* **13**:413–433.

Newsweek, 1983, Taking drugs on the job. August 22, **102**:52–60.

O'Donnell, J. A., and Clayton, R. R., 1982, The stepping-stone hypothesis: Marijuana, heroin, and causality, *Chemical Dependencies: Behavioral and Biomedical Issues* **4**:229–241.

Olkinuora, M., 1984, Alcoholism and occupation, *Scandinavian Journal of Work and Environmental Health* **10**:511–515.

O'Malley, P. M., 1992, Report to the National Institute on Medicine Committee on Drug Use in the Workplace, IOM, Washington, DC.

Osgood, D. W., Johnston, L. D., O'Malley, P. M., and Bachman, J. G., 1988, The generality of deviance in late adolescence and early adulthood, *American Sociological Review* **53**:81–93.

Paton, S., Kessler, R. C., and Kandel, D. B., 1977, Depressive mood and illegal drug use: A longitudinal analysis, *Journal of Genetic Psychology* **131**:267–289.

Plant, M. A., 1977, Alcoholism and occupation: A review, *British Journal of Addiction* **72**:309–316.

Plant, M. A., 1978, Occupation and alcoholism: Cause or effect? A controlled study of recruits to the drink trade, *International Journal of the Addictions* **13**:605–626.

Plant, M. A., 1979, Occupations, drinking patterns and alcohol-related problems: Conclusions from a follow-up study, *British Journal of Addiction* **74**:267–273.

Plant, M. A., 1981, Risk factors in employment, in: *Alcohol Problems in Employment* (B. D. Hore and M. A. Plant, eds.), Croom Helm, London.

Roman, P. M., Blum, T. C., and Martin, J. K., 1992, Enabling of male problem drinkers in work groups, *British Journal of Addiction*, **87**:275–298.

Sadava, S. W., 1987, Interactional theories, in: *Psychological Theories of Drinking and Alcoholism* (H. T. Blane and K. E. Leonard, eds.), Guilford, New York.

Scheier, L. M., and Newcomb, M. D., 1991a, Differentiation of early adolescent predictors of drug use versus abuse: A developmental risk factor model, *Journal of Substance Abuse* **3**:277–299.

Scheier, L. M., and Newcomb, M. D., 1991b, Psychosocial predictors of drug use initiation and escalation: An expansion of the multiple risk factors hypothesis using longitudinal data, *Contemporary Drug Problems* **18:**31–73.

Schuckit, M. A., 1987, Biological vulnerability to alcoholism, *Journal of Consulting and Clinical Psychology* **3:**301–309.

Searles, J. S., 1988, The role of genetics in the pathogenesis of alcoholism, *Journal of Abnormal Psychology* **97:**153–167.

Siegel, R. K., 1989, *Intoxication: Life in Pursuit of Artificial Paradise,* Dutton, New York.

Slattery, M., Alderson, M. R., and Bryant, J. S., 1986, The occupational risks of alcoholism, *International Journal of the Addictions* **21:**929–936.

Stacy, A. W., Newcomb, M. D., and Bentler, P. M., 1992, Interactive and higher-order effects of social influences on drug use, *Journal of Consulting and Clinical Psychology* **56:**189–196.

Stein, J. A., Newcomb, M. D., and Bentler, P. M., 1988, Structure of drug use behaviors and consequences among young adults: Multitrait–multimethod assessment of frequency, quantity, work site, and problem substance use, *Journal of Applied Psychology* **73:**595–605.

Tarter, R. E., 1988, Are there inherited behavioral traits that predispose to substance abuse? *Journal of Consulting and Clinical Psychology* **56:**189–196.

Vaillant, G. E., 1983, *The Natural History of Alcoholism: Causes, Patterns, and Paths to Recovery,* Harvard University Press, Cambridge, MA.

Vaillant, G. E., and Milofsky, E. S., 1982, The etiology of alcoholism: A prospective viewpoint, *American Psychologist,* **37:**494–503.

Violanti, J., Marshall, J., and Howe, B., 1983, Police occupational demands, psychological distress and the coping function of alcohol, *Journal of Occupational Medicine* **25:**455–458.

Washton, A. M., and Gold, M. S., 1987, Recent trends in cocaine abuse as seen from the 800-COCAINE hotline, in: *Cocaine: A Clinician's Handbook* (A. M. Washton and M. S. Gold, eds.), pp. 10–22, Guilford Press: New York.

Westermeyer, J., 1988, The pursuit of intoxication: Our 100 century-old romance with psychoactive substances, *American Journal of Drug and Alcohol Abuse* **1:**175–187.

White, H. R., Aidala, A., and Zablocki, B., 1988, A longitudinal investigation of drug use and work patterns among middle-class, white adults, *The Journal of Applied Behavioral Science* **4:**466–469.

Zucker, R. A., and Gomberg, E. S. L., 1986, Etiology of alcoholism reconsidered: The case for a biopsychosocial approach, *American Psychologist* **41:**783–793.

3

A Critical Review of the Estimates of the Costs of Alcohol and Drug Use

JOHN DiNARDO

1. INTRODUCTION

Estimates of the "costs" of alcohol and drug use play a major role in public policy. They are sometimes used to justify expansions in drug treatment programs and widespread implementation of drug screening programs. A series of studies have attempted to calculate these costs for the United States (Berry & Boland, 1977; Cruze, Harwood, Kristiansen, Collins, & Jones, 1981; Harwood, Napolitano, Kristiansen, & Collins, 1984; Rice, Kelman, Miller, & Dunmeyer, 1990); they are widely cited by authorities on drug testing (Coombs & West, 1990; Decresce, Lifshitz, Mazura, & Tilson, 1989), by journalists (Kelley, 1989), and by the government. When considering these estimates, a number of questions need to be addressed: Are they useful? Are they accurate? What do they attempt to measure? What do we *really* know about the costs of alcohol and drug abuse? These and other questions will be answered in this chapter. I will also discuss the empirical basis of cost estimates, as well as the often-neglected role that substitution among drugs plays in assessing appropriate drug control policies.

JOHN DINARDO • Department of Economics, University of California, Irvine, California 92717.
I would like to thank Harry Leder and Peter Reuter for their criticisms of an earlier draft. Funding for research related to this work was provided by RAND's Drug Policy Research Center, which is supported by the Ford and Weingart Foundations and the National Institute on Alcoholism and Alcohol Abuse. None of the persons mentioned above should bear any responsibility for the analysis herein.

Research Advances in Alcohol and Drug Problems, Volume 11: Drug Testing in the Workplace, edited by Scott Macdonald and Paul M. Roman. Plenum Press, New York, 1994.

Three key ideas are stressed in this chapter. First, an analysis of what the "costs" are, and to whom they apply, will be presented. The two accounting schemes that help policymakers and concerned citizens calculate these costs are the economic or benefit-cost (BC) analysis framework and the human capital–cost of illness (HC–COI) framework, the latter of which is used in the works cited above. The choice of framework is not a mere academic issue. The HC–COI framework addresses the wrong questions. In particular, in thinking about the costs of alcohol, drug use, and mental (ADM) disorders, the following question should be posed: Compared to what? Surely we will never completely eradicate all ADM disorders. In the language of most relevant studies, there is no single policy or group of policies that will reduce these costs to zero. As a consequence, we need to think about real policies, not a single magical policy that will completely eliminate ADM disorders.

Second, the fundamental empirical motivation for studying the costs of alcohol and drug use is suspect. Stated simply, the argument is that people who use drugs are less productive than those who do not. In fact, much of the current literature points in the opposite direction, although there are grave problems with this research. Furthermore, the literature has not resolved the empirical problem that drug users may differ from nonusers in ways other than their drug intake. As a consequence, we know very little about the effects of drug use on productivity. Similarly, we know very little about the effects of drug use on crime or health care costs.

Finally, we have no reason to believe that current estimates of the cost of alcohol and drug use are too high, too low, or about right. Both conceptually and empirically, the enterprise rests on very shaky foundations. This does not mean that progress is impossible or unlikely; alternative strategies and ways of thinking about the problem are presented in this chapter. It should be noted that the foregoing is a limited critique—that is, I criticize HC-COI studies on their *own* terms. It is obvious that the complex of problems we call "alcohol and drug abuse" will not be solved by simple scientific calculus. Many of the problems are beyond the scope of a few well-designed government policies. A limited critique is useful, however, if we do not lose sight of the larger picture. In particular, no simple calculus can objectively determine how much such values as democracy, civil liberties, freedom, or the quality of life are worth. Although these issues are ultimately more important, they will not be discussed here.

The paper is organized as follows. The first section discusses the standard economic approach to these types of problems (i.e., BC analysis). Next, the HC–COI approach is considered in detail. The scientific basis for the various components of these estimates are discussed. I then return to the question: Why do we care about the costs of ADM disorders? Finally, the *benefits* of alcohol and drug use are presented, followed by a discussion and conclusion.

2. BENEFIT-COST ANALYSIS

I begin by outlining how a typical economist might set up the problem of estimating the cost of drug and alcohol use. Of necessity this discussion will be somewhat superficial, because some important methodological questions will be omitted; however, some discussion of standard approaches to BC analysis is helpful to understanding the limitations of estimates of the cost of drug and alcohol use currently used by policymakers. First, an economist would not start with a question like "What are the costs of alcohol consumption, drug use, and mental disorders?" Economists usually deal with BC analysis, in which a more typical question would be "Will social welfare be enhanced by instituting drug or alcohol policy X?"

More generally, "Benefit-cost analysis is considered a good tool to use when considering the impact of a policy measure on the allocation of resources" (Gramlich, 1991). A good example is an excise tax on cigarettes or alcohol (Manning, Keeler, Newhouse, Slouss, & Wasserman, 1989); taxing cigarettes is likely to reduce smoking and thus reduce the amount of money spent on collectively financed health insurance, pensions, group life insurance, disability insurance, and so forth. Once an appropriate policy is chosen, "winners and losers" have to be identified. In the cigarette-tax case, society wins, because fewer people die of cancer and less has to be spent on hospital care. Conversely, smokers contribute to social security, but do not live long enough to collect the payments; as a consequence, when a high proportion of people stop smoking, nonsmokers "lose" subsidized pensions.

Next, the various gains and costs have to be valued. Costs of a specific program can be easily estimated using budget costs. Gains, however, are usually harder to estimate. Often these are gleaned from the market. For instance, if a policy saves lives by making jobs safer, then we can look at the wages workers are willing to accept for employment with a low probability of dying on the job, compared to wages for jobs with a higher probability of death (Dillingham, 1985; Fisher, Chestnut, & Violette, 1989; Moore & Viscusi, 1988), recognizing that such a calculation is not independent of the distribution income or a host of other aspects of the economy, including how well-informed individuals are of job risks.

Another aspect of the valuation problem is dealing with time and uncertainty. Benefits gained three years into the future are worth less than benefits gained today; if a person is risk averse, a certain gain is worth more to him or her than an uncertain gain. Because information in this area is often scarce or impossible to get, analysts often choose to do "sensitivity analysis," which is nothing more than recalculating the benefits and costs under different assumptions. Such an analysis is often useful because if the lowest estimated value of a specific program still yields a substantial net benefit, the project can be recommended even if there is some uncertainty about the exact magnitude of the benefits.

Finally, the analyst considers various distributional issues. Many (though certainly not all) would agree that a dollar given to a poor person is worth more than that same dollar given to a rich person; in this case, benefits accrued by the poor are given more weight than those accrued by the rich. Once all of this is done, the researcher is ready to compare the costs to the benefits. If the latter are extremely large and the former very small, then it may be reasonable to conclude that the specific policy is a good idea.

In sum, the hallmarks of the BC approach are as follows:

1. It specifies a particular policy to evaluate. Raising the minimum drinking age, raising the excise tax on cigarettes, and imposing mandatory drug testing are examples of policies that, in principle, could be evaluated by the BC approach. It also evaluates the effect of the policy on incentives; for instance, in evaluating the effects of building a subway, it is necessary to consider the subway's impact on consumer demand for buses or other transportation systems.
2. It determines both the costs and benefits of a policy, and it identifies who gains and loses. In the previous example on smoking, both the contribution of smokers to social insurance programs and the drain they put on health insurance programs are identified.
3. Whenever possible, it seeks to evaluate the value *individuals* place on specific changes wrought by the policy. Often this means looking to the market. If people reveal that they are willing to pay more for a reduction of one type of health risk than to reduce another, then the former yields more benefits.

3. THE HUMAN CAPITAL–COST OF ILLNESS APPROACH

So-called human capital estimates take a fundamentally different approach. In the economics literature, this is more commonly known as the discounted future earnings (DFE) approach; it is often used in legal contexts. In the United States there has been a proliferation of studies using such estimates (Berry & Boland, 1977; Cruze et al., 1981; Harwood et al., 1984; Rice et al., 1990), whose method has been described as follows:

> An individual's value to society is his or her production potential. If markets are functioning well, individuals will be paid a wage equal to the value of the output they produce. Thus the value of a person to society can be measured by his or her earnings and the value of life would be the future earnings stream. This stream of earnings is discounted using a discount rate that reflects the trade-off between the values of a dollar today and a dollar tomorrow. (Rice, Kelman, Miller, and Donmeyer, 1990)

The core of this approach which we will discuss at great length later in the chapter, rests on the appropriateness of calculating the "lost" output resulting from various disorders. For example, according to this theory, people who consume illegal drugs or alcohol lower their productivity—that is, they do not work as long or as well. This productivity is "valued" by society in terms of the wage the person receives. If a person receives $5 an hour and works 1 less hour because of alcohol or drug consumption, then society loses $5 of production value. Likewise, if a business executive earning $200,000 a year dies 5 years earlier than he or she would have had he or she not consumed alcohol, society "loses" $1 million.

The distinguishing characteristic of this approach is that the cost of illness is estimated *without* consideration of an explicit policy alternative. HC–COI analysis does not evaluate a specific policy; it does not look at the impact of such a policy on incentives; it does not identify both gains and losses; and in general, it does not consider individuals' evaluation of risks.

Table 1 presents a summary of the calculations in one recent estimate of the costs of ADM disorders for the United States (Rice et al., 1990). This study is typical of such estimates; because it is so well documented, it will be used as a prototype on which to center the discussion, which will necessarily be brief and incomplete. The table also lists the major categories to which costs are ascribed; each category will not be discussed, but the reader will be given some idea of what is being calculated.

Table 1
Estimated Costs of ADM by Type of Cost, 1988 (Millions of Current Dollars)

Type of Cost	Total	Alcohol Abuse	Drug Abuse	Mental Illness
Total	273,333	85,790	58,279	129,264
Core costs	206,506	70,184	12,896	123,426
Total direct costs	66,744	8,729	2,656	55,389
Treatment	61,956	8,126	2,407	51,423
Support	4,818	603	249	3,966
Total indirect costs	139,732	61,455	10,240	68,037
Morbidity	91,173	32,953	7,194	57,026
Mortality*	42,559	28,502	3,046	11,011
Other related costs	61,809	13,769	42,202	5,838
Direct costs	28,479	9,589	16,782	2,108
Indirect costs	33,330	4,180	25,420	3,730
Special disease groups	5,018	1,837	3,181	—
AIDS	3,181	—	3,181	—
Fetal alcohol syndrome	1,837	1,837	—	—

*6 percent discount rate.
Source: Rice et al., 1990.

Cost of illness studies are often divided into two major categories; core costs, and other related costs. "*Core costs*" are those "resulting directly from the illness," and "*other related costs*" are the costs of "secondary, nonhealth effects of illness." These categories in turn have two components: "*direct costs*" costs for which "payments are actually made, and "*indirect costs,*" costs for which "resources are lost" (Rice, Kelman, and Miller, 1991, p. 281). "Core costs include all costs directly related to the treatment and support of persons with [the various disorders] as well as the indirect costs associated with these disorders. Indirect costs are the value of lost output resulting from reduced productivity, lost work, and housekeeping days, and losses due to premature death" (Rice, Kelman, Miller, and Dunmeyer, 1990, p. 9). Other related costs include the direct costs of crime, motor vehicle deaths, social welfare program administrative costs, and the indirect costs of productivity losses for victims of crime, incarceration, crime careers, and time spent to care for afflicted family members.

4. DOES ALCOHOL AND DRUG USE LOWER PRODUCTIVITY?

For alcohol and drug abuse, direct costs (i.e., income that doctors and others receive) do not make up the largest share of all costs. For drug use, these direct core costs ($2.6 billion) constitute less than 5% of the total costs ($58 billion).

In HC–COI studies, the negative relationship between income and alcohol or drug use is labeled a "cost" and multiplied by the number of users. Estimates of these costs are large; from Table 1, it can be seen that these indirect costs make up most of the costs of alcohol and account for 17% of drug-related costs ($10 billion). In this section the scientific basis for the view that ADM disorders *cause* this large amount of income loss is examined.

Drug Use and Income

Model (1991b) used data from the 1984 National Household Survey (NHS) to study the relationship between drug or alcohol use and income. In the NHS, because respondents were asked only total household income, occupational groupings were used to calculate predicted wages; also included was information on whether the respondent was a main earner or not. The full sample is large (4,716 observations), and the main-earner subset has 3,083 observations. Model used a fairly extensive list of covariates: Drug use was first broken into heavy or moderate use for several drugs, including cocaine, alcohol, depressants, codeine, marijuana, hallucinogens, and heroin.

Of the 56 coefficients reported, 20 were significant at conventional levels; of these, 12 were positive. In particular, Model found significant positive estimates for heavy and moderate alcohol and cocaine use. (Her estimates for the effect of marijuana were positive in the full sample, and negative in the main-earner subsample.) In all four of the specifications, she found that moderate alcohol use is *positively* related to income. In three of the four specifications, she found that moderate drug use was positively related to income; only for heavy drug or alcohol use did she find negative estimates. Model was reluctant, however, to conclude that moderate drug use by the main earner *causes* a rise in household income of 20%, or that alcohol use by the main earner in the household raises wages 50%.

Are Model's results likely an artifact of her income measure or her sample? Consider the recent studies by Kaestner (1991) and Rippey (1989), who used the National Longitudinal Study of Youth (NLSY). There is less useful detail in the NLSY about drug use, but more detail on income measures. Rippey (1989), whose approach most closely resembles Model's, found that only the use of marijuana, tranquilizers, and other narcotic drugs has significant detrimental effects on income. Kaestner (1991) attempted to deal with the obvious problem that causality may run in the other direction (i.e., higher wages could lead to greater drug use), but he also reported results using specifications that parallel the ones presented by Model and Rippey for cocaine and marijuana. For both sexes, he found a positive effect of lifetime cocaine prevalence; he found a positive effect of 30-day marijuana prevalence for women, and a negative estimated effect for men.

Gill and Michaels (1992) and Register and Williams (1992), also using NLSY data, attempted to confront a different set of statistical shortcomings. They also looked at the effect of drug use on labor supply. Gill and Michaels (1992) found that drug users received higher wages than nonusers. Register and Williams (1992) found positive productivity effects of marijuana and no statistically significant association between cocaine use and productivity. Labor supply effects in both studies were unclear.

DSM-III Criterion and Income

Perhaps mere *use* is an inappropriate measure. Many would argue that the presence or absence of alcoholism, or a comparable disorder, is more important than the level of consumption. Studies using some form of the DSM-III (American Psychiatric Association, 1980) criterion, however, find a similar lack of robustness or presence of "anomalous" results, even though the DSM-III criterion is perhaps closer to the appropriate disorder concept. Typically studies do not include measures of occupation, industry, or schooling, arguing instead that ADM disorders affect these variables. In general, these studies find negative effects for alcoholism and drug abuse, although (with the exception of alcohol use for men) most of the results are imprecise and not different from zero at conventional levels of significance; they find positive estimates for drug use for women, although these, too, are quite imprecise. Some of the additional disorders, however, are negative and significantly different from zero; for example, they find that affective disorders have large and quite precisely estimated effects on log income.

"Anomalies" of this sort are present in the earlier, less comprehensive studies of the costs of alcohol and drug use. Commenting on Harwood et al. (1984), Gill and Michaels (1992) wrote that "their measure of drug abuse seems quite arbitrary, as does their choice of results to present." It is also worth noting that because of data limitations, Harwood et. al. (1984) used a very limited set of regressors. In their regressions they included two measures of current marijuana use, and one measure of whether the person used marijuana in his or her lifetime. Although their estimates of the impact of having used marijuana once in a lifetime were large and negative, three of the six estimates of current use that they chose to report were positive. Further, they found "insignificant" impacts of hard drug use on income, despite the fact that the use of hard drugs should presumably have a greater negative impact than the use of marijuana. Similarly, it is hard to understand why, if marijuana negatively affects productivity, a current user of marijuana should have higher wages than someone who is not currently using marijuana but has done so in the past.

In their more exhaustive study of the effect of alcoholism on income, with ECA data, Mullahy and Sindelar (1991) generally found negative effects, although they did find positive estimates for the effect of alcoholism on income among those with college education. They also presented some evidence suggesting that the effect of alcohol use varies for different age groups. Benham and Benham (1982), using a criterion similar to the DSM-III found no significant impact of alcoholism on either weekly earnings or the probability of being in the labor force.

Some more recent studies have tried to deal with the problem that drug users are not identical to nonusers in all respects but drug use (see Berger & Leigh, 1988; Gill and Michaels, 1992). Unfortunately, most of these studies have not been entirely persuasive. These exercises generally point to the implication that whatever the negative impact of drug or alcohol use on wages is, it is overstated (too negative) for the obvious reason that drug users differ from nonusers in other (perhaps unobservable) ways besides drug or alcohol use.

Putting the Evidence Together: Implications for Measures of Indirect Costs

What is one to make of this evidence? Opinions are sure to vary, but one does not come away convinced that we have a lot of understanding of the causal link between ADM disorders and losses in productivity, or about the magnitude of these effects. One obvious problem is that these are merely observational studies, and attributing causality to the results is difficult. In one of the few controlled experiments of the effect of drugs or ADM disorders on "labor market productivity," however, the authors find that use of marijuana is positively related to productivity (Kagel & Miles, 1980). They are quite clear that they do not intend their results to apply to the general population, but they argue that the a priori case for a negative effect of marijuana on work performance is weakened.

Quite understandably, researchers attempting to estimate the effects of ADM disorders on income are more likely to accept imprecise negative results than they are to accept positive estimates. This tendency to ignore the imprecision of negative estimates or the occasional "anomalous" positive estimates, however, fundamentally undermines the claim usually made by authors that the estimates represent "lower bounds." A great many of the estimates in Rice's and similar studies are not significantly different from zero at conventional levels of significance. If their estimates were really lower bounds, why not estimate the productivity losses attributable to drug use at zero? Furthermore, as is typically the case, use of an extremely parsimonious set of explanatory variables in income regressions is further reason that the estimates of the effect of ADM disorders on income cannot reasonably be thought of as lower bounds. The Rice study, for instance, did not include variables such as occupation on the grounds that including occupation would *miss* the direct effects of ADM disorders on occupational choice. If occupation exerts an independent effect on income (apart from its correlation with drug use), however, then to the extent that drug users are more likely to be in lower-paying occupations, the estimated losses will be too large. These criticisms apply *mutatis mutandis* to all of the previous HC–COI studies (Berry & Boland, 1977; Cruze et al., 1981; Harwood et al., 1984; Rice, 1966; Rice et al., 1990).

Alcohol and common drugs of abuse can cause psychomotor impairment as well as other sorts of physical and mental dysfunctions that might adversely impact a variety of occupational tasks (see Chapter 4). Work activity, however, is more complex than a sequence of tasks. People vary as to how they integrate drug use into their daily routines. One of the interesting sidebars to the work of Kagel, Battalio, and Miles (1980) is that a majority of subjects avoided doing work immediately after their consumption of marijuana. Perhaps they were aware of the resultant impairment of psychomotor activity and sought to mitigate these effects by their timing of work and drug use activity. Furthermore, is it not possible that some drug use increases productivity? Unfortunately, not much research has been done in this area, but there is plenty of anecdotal evidence that people use cocaine or similar products to enhance productivity (R. K. Siegel, 1989) or, for example, that drugs can be used to mitigate some of the effects of sleep loss in pilots on long flights (Klein, 1972).

In summary, there is no persuasive evidence from the research reviewed here that mere exposure to psychoactive substances or the existence of a mental disorder *causes* decreased productivity in the workplace. What drugs do to users is likely a function of what the users do with the drugs. Most studies of the cost of ADM disorders, however, have little reluctance in attributing most of the measured correlation between income and alcohol or drug use to the use of these substances. When "anomalies" turn up, they are typically ignored. For instance, consider the response by Rice et al. (1990) to the positive correlation in their study between drug use meeting the severity criterion and income: "For women, the regression results for drug abuse presented the same problem as those for affective disorders *and were therefore unusable*. Imputations were made. . . . This resulted in an additional loss due to drug abuse of 2.4 billion" (Rice, Kelman, Miller, and Donmeyer, 1990, p. 260, emphasis added).

Ignoring the important question of whether estimates calculated this way are really lower bounds on the cost of drug use, one might attempt to determine whether there is anything meaningful in these "lost productivity" estimates. Not only is the scientific evidence for a primary causal role of ADM in reducing productivity not well established, there is little valid conceptual basis for attempting this type of calculation, a point to which I will return.

5. OTHER RELATED COSTS

The preceding section demonstrates that the empirical basis for productivity effects of alcohol and drug use is quite suspect. The focus of this section is the "other related direct costs" examined in the Rice study. This is the most recent, comprehensive, and well-documented study of its kind, and it supplies a nice comparison with previous studies.

> Other related direct costs of ADM include public and private expenditures for crime, motor vehicle crashes, social welfare program administrative costs, and costs associated with the destruction of property by fire. Indirect costs include the value of productivity losses due to the following: (1) victimization by crime; (2) incarceration for a criminal offense; (3) time spent by heroin and cocaine addicts in criminal activities (crime careers) rather than legal employment; and (4) time spent to care for family members. (Rice et al., 1990, p. 145).

Again, the empirical basis for estimates of the total amount of crime or crime costs caused by ADM disorders is weak. For example, no research convincingly establishes that mere exposure to drugs or alcohol causes criminal careers (except, of course, the crime of possession). Does alcohol and drug consumption cause crime, or do persons with criminal temperaments merely prefer to consume alcohol or drugs? Short of a controlled or natural experiment, tasks associated with disentangling cause and effect are likely to be very difficult or simply impossible.

In an interesting paper on labor supply in the underground economy (i.e., any income not reported to the tax authorities) in Quebec City, Canada, Fortin, Lemieux, and Frechette (1990) constructed and tested a simple economic model of the trade-off between work in the underground economy and work in the formal sector. Among other things, they found evidence that a simple neoclassical labor supply model can rationalize underground work. Participation in the underground economy is *simultaneously* a function of the wages of the regular sector, average income per hour in the irregular sector, and the marginal tax rate. In general, participation of the irregular sector is more likely given a higher marginal tax rate, higher returns in the underground economy, and lower wages in the regular sector.

Using an HC–COI approach, one could do a "cost of low wages" study in which one calculates the amount of crime *caused* by low wages, or a "cost of higher taxes" study in which one attributes the dollar value of underground work to higher taxation and the existence of high marginal tax rates for social insurance programs, or finally, a "cost of being good at underground work" study in which one attributes the dollar value of underground work to the "cost" of people being good at such labor. But even if one shared the costs across all three activities, it is not clear that we would learn anything useful from these exercises. The effect of high marginal tax rates will be different depending on the level of wages in the regular sector; if wages are extremely high, a high marginal tax rate will cause less underground labor than if wages are not so high.

One study of drugs and crime reports that most drug dealers have regular jobs (Reuter, MacCoun, & Murphy, 1990). The data are not of the sort in the aforementioned studies, so we cannot be sure if the same model applies; still, one is strongly tempted to think that the amount of drug dealing will vary with the tax rate on regular jobs or average wages. Surely it is not unreasonable to conjecture that the amount of drug crime might fall if average wages for those at risk for drug crime were to double, and if taxes on legal income were substantially reduced. If such is the case, why not attribute the crime costs to high taxation instead of drug abuse? There is no simple or convincing way to allocate costs across a variety of different "causes." In sum, even the simplest notions of causality pose great conceptual difficulties for HC–COI studies.

By employing the benefit-cost (BC) framework, however, these difficult issues can be avoided. This involves the analysis of policies by way of experiments or natural experiments. Cook (1990) summarized a number of fascinating natural experiments, including a workers' strike against the government-owned Norwegian wine and spirits monopoly that lasted for 9 weeks; in the first 4 weeks, the strike led to a cessation of the sale of wine and spirits by the monopoly's retail outlets. Cook notes that although beer consumption, moonshining, and trips across the border to Sweden increased, alcohol consumption declined between 20% and 30%. Comparing this period to the similar period the year before revealed that there was a 22% reduction in domestic disturbances and a 15% reduction in acts of violence.

The BC approach can be explained by the following example. If the decrease in alcohol consumption were 5% and the decrease in domestic violence were also 5%, then we could say that the elasticity of domestic violence with respect to alcohol is 1 (i.e., a 1% decrease in alcohol consumption "causes" a 1% decrease in domestic violence). This most closely resembles a controlled experiment.* The key is that if we look at a specific change that affects ADM behaviors (but is not influenced by the level of such disorders that prevails), we can look at the effect of that change on all the phenomena we want to measure (domestic violence, emergency room visits, etc.). This provides clean measures of the "costs" of drugs; however, unlike the HC–COI approach, it is generally tied to some potentially implementable policy.

Note that one would *not* want to calculate the crime costs of alcohol consumption by assuming that we could reduce alcohol consumption by 100%. Apart from the fact that 100% is well beyond the range where the estimated elasticity would be valid, it is highly unlikely that we could ever abolish all consumption. Instead, the BC approach would lead to the more valuable exercise of deciding whether it would be desirable to increase alcohol taxation (i.e., whether the current tax on alcohol is high enough to maximize social welfare).

6. WHY WE SHOULD NOT CARE ABOUT THE COSTS OF DRUG ABUSE

In BC analysis, we know why we care about the costs of policy X—we need to know whether these are less than or greater than the benefits. Conversely, why do we need to know the cost of drug abuse?

A frequent user for these cost estimates is the determination of appropriate spending priorities across various disorders. Heien and Pittman (1989) refer to this as claims-making activity. It is generally assumed that these estimates give policymakers a sense of the magnitude of the problem; if it can be shown that one problem is more costly than another, it should receive more government financing to eradicate. However attractive this view may be, it is not based on an internally consistent logic, economic or otherwise. The only economically meaningful statements about spending priorities depend on which policies the money is spent. Conceptually, there is no difficulty extending this analysis to the case where the outcomes of policies are uncertain. The most frequently used analysis (expected utility theory) generally has the implication that those policies that *on average* have the highest social benefits have the highest priority. The magnitude

*This way of thinking has several names. In the social sciences this is often called quasi experimentation, or a natural experiment.

of the costs is irrelevant here. One should not spend money where the costs are highest, but on acts that yield the highest net benefit.

There is yet another distinction between the two accounting frameworks: Whose productivity is being lost? Presumably, how much or how hard one works will affect how well off he or she becomes. If an individual decides to spend less time at work and more time with his or her family, would he or she want to estimate the "cost" of spending time with the family? If an employer pays for the value of an employee's marginal product, the employer does not lose. If an employee's mere absence for an additional several hours of work every week does not reduce everyone else's productivity, society does not lose. In having decided to spend more time at home, the employee is better off. The HC–COI approach, though, would say that costs had risen, even if everyone is better off!

Ultimately, the relevant question is social welfare. Furthermore, social welfare is ultimately a question of how well off individuals are. The problem with the HC–COI approach is that it ignores the fact that people make decisions (at least in part) based on their own self-interest. We might question individual judgments (do people always act in accordance with their self-interest?) or recognize that individual decisions to act in a certain way may be made without incorporating the externalities for others that their acts generate, but surely individuals' assessments should not be completely ignored.

On a related note, are the costs borne by the user on par with the costs he or she imposes on others? Suppose that in full knowledge of the likely outcome, I choose to drink heavily and decrease the length of my life. Is the cost of the person-years lost the same as those lost in the death of another as the result of someone's drunk driving? Most persons would argue that although one might like to spend money reducing both types of deaths, the costs to society from the latter are larger. The HC–COI theory implicitly puts both deaths on an equal footing. This is a problem if we think individual judgments should play a role in deciding what maximizes social welfare.

7. THE *BENEFITS* OF ALCOHOL AND DRUG USE AND THE ROLE OF SUBSTITUTION

One of the useful by-products of HC–COI estimates of the cost of ADM disorders is that they have brought attention to the fact that alcohol and drug use affects social welfare through many channels. As the BC approach makes clear, this fact is important in thinking about appropriate policies. One unfortunate consequence, however, is that it draws attention away from two other aspects of the problem. First, it fails to recognize that alcohol and drug use provide benefits, if the judgments of individuals are any guide. Second, the approach is ill equipped to deal with what I call *substitution*—the propensity of users to switch to lower-priced or more accessible drugs when the drug they are currently consuming becomes more costly or harder to get.

In BC analysis, the benefits are valued by observing people's choices. Little research, however, is done on the benefits of drug use; in particular, we know very little about the benefits of the use of illegal drugs. Presumably not all drug and alcohol consumption is the result of self-destructive choices made by individuals, but the lack of research in this area probably reflects the social consensus that *any* use of illegal drugs is abuse. On the second issue, though, there is more information. Substitution has implications for both policy-making and the empirical validity of estimates of the total costs of ADM disorders.

Evidence of Substitution

Alcohol or drug activity is rarely foisted upon an individual without some decision on the part of that individual. If a person is using cocaine, he or she has chosen one illegal substance from an array of psychoactive substances, some of which are legal. If use of one drug leads to a decline in alcohol use, one of the benefits of drug use would arguably be the reduction in alcohol use. An appropriate judgment would then necessarily involve an assessment of the costs of both behaviors.

In a recent paper, Model (1993) investigated the effect of marijuana decriminalization on hospital emergency room drug episodes. She used quarterly data from the Drug Abuse Warning Network (DAWN) between the years 1975 and 1978 and compared changes before and after various decriminalization laws were implemented in 8 of 21 standard metropolitan statistical areas (SMSAs). She found that marijuana use rose substantially; use of other drugs, however, declined much more than that for marijuana rose. Model interpreted this as evidence of substitution of other (more dangerous) drugs for marijuana.

Studies using data from the "Monitoring the Future" project (Bachman & Johnston, 1978) found similar evidence for high school seniors during the years 1980–1989 (DiNardo, 1991; DiNardo & Lemieux, 1992). In December 1983, a presidential commission on drunken driving recommended that the minimum age for purchase and public possession of any alcoholic beverage be increased from 18 to 21. Subsequently highway trust funds were tied to compliance with this recommendation, and by 1988 all states had a 21-year age minimum. Changes in the legal minimum drinking age during this period were associated with an increase in the 30-day prevalence of marijuana consumption (DiNardo & Lemieux, 1992). Researchers conducted a study of marijuana users to see what if any impact Operation Intercept, reportedly the largest "peacetime search and seizure operation by civil authorities" (*Belair,* 1969), had on the consumption of marijuana and other drugs (McGlothlin, Jamison, Rosenblatt, 1970). They, too, found evidence of substitution, with users turning to hashish and alcohol as marijuana became more scarce.

There is also historical evidence of substitution. Several authors have argued that the Eighteenth Amendment and the Volstead Act of 1920 (the beginning of the so-called Prohibition era) led to the first signs of "large scale marketing of marijuana for recreational use" (Brecher, 1972; R. K. Siegel, 1989). The evidence comes from reports of the sudden appearance of marijuana "tea pads" in New York City in 1920. These tea pads were tolerated as much as alcohol speakeasies were tolerated, although prices of marijuana were reported to be very low (Brecher, 1972).

Perhaps the leading case for the possibility of substitution between psychoactive substances is evidence on the use of alcohol by opioid addicts. S. Siegel (1986) noted that in the nineteenth century opiates were sometimes prescribed to alcoholics, the idea being that opium, though not perfectly safe, was safer than alcohol. The reverse was also noted to those treating opium addicts: "Unless care be taken, a drunkard results. The shore of post-poppy land is strewn with wrecks of those who, after escape from the narcotic peril, have taken to rum" (Mattison, 1902, p. 29). Increased use of alcohol in recovering heroin addicts has long been noted, although there is much debate on whether this reflects substitution and on the magnitude of the effect (Kolb, 1962; O'Donnell, 1969).

More recently, some have argued that cocaine and alcohol are substitutes. In the latter half of 1989 in the United States, 40% of emergency calls from persons under 35 years of age were for crack, and 38% were for alcohol. By the first third of 1991 the situation was reversed and the percentages were 33% and 44%, respectively (Taylor, 1991).

The evidence for substitutability with other drugs is more mixed, although there appears to be very little research in this area. At the request of the U.S. *Journal of Drug and Alcohol Dependence* the NIAAA searched 70,000 research papers for evidence on substitution, but it found none (Taylor, 1991).

The Implications of Substitution for Studies on the Cost of ADM Disorders

An examination of substitution causes severe difficulties in interpreting estimates of the costs of ADM disorders from the HC–COI approach. Suppose that instead of considering ADM disorders as a whole, one compares the relative costs of alcohol versus illegal drug use. Again, the important issue centers on feasible policies. It is, in general, not valid to look at any one drug in isolation, estimate the cost of its use or abuse to be X dollars, and conclude that it is a good idea to spend X dollars on the problem; ultimately we are concerned about the entire array of drug use. Presumably we would not welcome the total eradication of alcohol use if doing so meant that use of crack cocaine were to rise to meet the drop in alcohol consumption. As a consequence, if there were a policy that could eliminate all alcohol consumption for less money than the estimated costs of drinking, it might not be a good idea to implement it if it merely shifts the costs from one category to another. For cost estimates to be meaningful, specific policies must be evaluated, and their impact on *all* behavior (not just the intended behavior) must be investigated.

The results reported above on the link between ADM disorders and income were extremely muddled. Without exception, the authors of these studies recognized the difficulties in inferring causality. Part of the difficulty in estimating the effect of alcohol or drug use on income stems from the fact that alcohol and drug use represent individual choices. Substitution changes the proportion of people consuming a specific drug, and hence the correlation between income and drug use. In the HC–COI framework, because the estimates of productivity loss are based on observational studies, this would mean that the extent of the bias in measuring this productivity loss would vary as policies (implicit or explicit) vary. For example, if a program discouraged cocaine use at the expense of creating a greater number of marijuana users, there is little doubt that this would change our estimates of the impact of both marijuana and cocaine use on income. In this example, the program would almost necessarily change the proportion of high and low productivity people in both the class of cocaine users and marijuana users. After implementing such a policy only the more hard-core cocaine users would be left, and presumably they might be lower-productivity persons. Observational studies would point to an increased negative effect of cocaine use on income during these policy regimes. Likewise, if we accept the conventional wisdom that most people tried marijuana during the late 1960s, it is not unreasonable to conjecture that the analyst running regressions of income versus marijuana use would find less of an effect on income during this period than in a time where marijuana use was less common.

8. CONCLUSIONS

Studies of the costs of ADM disorders have certainly increased public awareness that alcohol and drug use affects social welfare through many channels. These studies can be very beneficial. The accounting framework used by these studies, however, has been criticized in this chapter. These estimates do not rest on a firm conceptual basis and cannot, in general, be used as a guide to making priorities on spending. They are not helpful in determining either the magnitude of the problem or changes in the magnitude over time (even if all the methodological difficulties in computing the estimates were solved) and so are not always useful in combination with other sorts of information. In sum, it is not clear whether the biases are positive or negative. Making a judgment about the size of the bias presupposes the existence of an unbiased estimate; without a conceptual foundation, there can be no "unbiased" estimate.

Furthermore, this lack of conceptual foundation is more than a mere academic debate about the right way to compute the estimates. Benefit-cost analysis is not without its difficulties; there are severe problems with measuring the value of life or evaluating net social gain. BC analysis comes much closer to the type of problem presumably faced by decision makers, however, than do unstructured estimates of the costs of ADM disorders.

The focus on actual policies that accompanies the BC accounting framework is also important empirically. The analysis of natural experiments is advocated to estimate the effectiveness of specific policies, such as (though not limited to) increased alcohol taxes and higher drinking ages, as in a series of studies (Cook, 1981; Cook & Tauchen, 1982, 1984; O'Malley & Wagenaar, 1991; Saffer & Grossman, 1987a, b). This type of empirical inquiry allows the analyst to generate reliable estimates without a complete description of the many and subtle links between ADM disorders and wages or other socially relevant outcome measures. The advantages of such analysis are well known (see Campbell and Cook, 1979, for a discussion).

> The United States and other modern nations should be ready for an experimental approach to social reform, an approach in which we try out new programs designed to cure specific social programs, in which we learn whether or not these programs are effective, and in which we retain, imitate, modify, or discard them on the basis of apparent effectiveness on the multiple imperfect criteria available. . . . Many feel we are already at this stage, that we are already continuing or discontinuing programs on the basis of assessed effectiveness. . . . It is not at all so. . . . Most ameliorative programs end up with no interpretable evaluation. (Campbell, 1969, p. 409)

Ultimately the issue in policy debate is what is to be done, *not* how much it costs us to do nothing.

Why do these HC–COI studies proliferate? Studies continue to be produced because there exists a demand for them. Perhaps this demand is a consequence of a sincere desire to understand the problems that accompany drug use, but a simultaneous reluctance to confront actual policies over which there might be intense political disagreement. Simple recourse to these estimates will do little to improve our understanding of the alcohol and drug problem, nor will it point us in the right direction. A careful evaluation of real policies is needed, along with a willingness to abandon policies if the best available evidence shows them to be ineffective. No amount of research can substitute for a willingness to confront real options.

REFERENCES

American Psychiatric Association, 1980, *Diagnostic and Statistical Manual*, 3rd ed., American Psychiatric Association, Washington, DC.

Bachman, J. G., and Johnston, L., 1978, The Monitoring the Future project: Design and procedures, Monitoring the Future Occasional Paper No. 1., Institute for Social Research, Ann Arbor, MI.

Belair, F., Jr., 1969, Mexico is asked to help combat drug smuggling, *The New York Times,* September 9, pp. A-1, A-32.

Benham, L., and Benham, A., 1982, Employment, earnings, and psychiatric diagnosis, in: *The Economic Consequences of Health* (V. Fuchs, ed.), pp. 203-220, National Bureau of Economic Research, University of Chicago, Chicago.

Berger, M. C., and Leigh, J. P., 1988, The effect of alcohol use on wages, *Applied Economics* **20:**1343–1351.

Berry, R. E., and Boland, J. P., 1977, *The Economic Cost of Alcohol Abuse,* Free Press, New York.

Brecher, E. M., and the Editors of *Consumer Reports,* 1972, *Licit and Illicit Drugs; The Consumers Union Report on Narcotics, Stimulants, Depressants, Inhalants, Hallucinogens, and Marijuana—Including Caffeine, Nicotine, and Alcohol,* Little, Brown, Boston.

Campbell, D. T., 1969, Reforms as experiments, *American Psychologist* **24:**402–429.

Campbell, D. T., and Cook, T. D., 1979, *Quasi-Experimentation: Design and Analysis for Field Setting,* 1st ed., Rand McNally College Publishing Company, Chicago.

Cook, P. J., 1981, The effect of liquor taxes on drinking, cirrhosis, and auto fatalities, in: *Alcohol and Public Policy: Beyond the Shadow of Prohibition* (M. H. Moore and D. Gerstein, eds.), pp. 255-285, National Academy Press, Washington, DC.

Cook, P. J., 1990, The social costs of alcohol use, in: *Expert Meeting on the Negative Social Consequences of Alcohol Use,* Paper No. 2, pp. 49–81, Norwegian Ministry of Health and Social Affairs, Oslo, Norway.

Cook, P., and Tauchen, G., 1982, The effect of liquor taxes on heavy drinking, *Bell Journal of Economics* **13:**379–390.

Cook, P., and Tauchen, G., 1984, The effects of minimum drinking age legislation on youthful auto fatalities, 1970–77, *Journal of Legal Studies* **13:**169–190.

Coombs, R. H., and West, L. H., eds., 1990, *Drug Testing: Issues and Options,* Oxford University Press, New York.

Cruze, A. M., Harwood, H. J., Kristiansen, P. L., Collins, J. J., and Jones, D. C., 1981, Economic cost to society of alcohol and drug abuse and mental illness—1977, Technical Report No. ADM 82-1179, Prepared for the Alcohol, Drug Use, and Mental Health Administration, Rockville, MD.

Decresce, R., Lifshitz, M. S., Mazura, A., and Tilson, J., 1989, *Drug Testing in the Workplace,* American Society of Clinical Pathologists Press, Chicago.

Dillingham, A., 1985, The influence of risk variable definition on value of life estimates, *Economic Inquiry* **24:**227–294.

DiNardo, J., 1991, Are marijuana and alcohol substitutes? The effect of state drinking age laws on the consumption of marijuana by high school seniors, Manuscript No. 22, RAND Drug Policy Research Center, Santa Monica, CA.

DiNardo, J., and Lemieux, T., 1992, Alcohol, marijuana, and American youth: The unintended consequences of government regulation, Working Paper No. 4212, National Bureau of Economic Research, Cambridge, MA.

Fisher, A., Chestnut, L. G., and Violette, D., 1989, The value of reducing risk of death: A note on new evidence, *Journal of Policy Analysis and Management.*

Fortin, B., Lemieux, T., and Frechette, P., 1990, An empirical model of labor supply in the underground economy, Working Paper No. 3392, National Bureau of Economic Research, Cambridge, MA.

Gill, A. M., and Michaels, R. J., 1992, Does drug use lower wages? *Industrial and Labor Relations Review* **45:**419–434.

Gramlich, E. M., 1991, *A Guide to Benefit-Cost Analysis,* 2nd ed., Prentice Hall, Englewood Cliffs, NJ.

Harwood, H. J., Napolitano, D., Kristiansen, P., and Collins, J., 1984, Economic costs to society of alcohol and drug abuse and mental illness: 1980, No. RTI/2734/00-01FR, Prepared for the Alcohol, Drug Abuse and Mental Health Administration, Research Triangle Institute, Research Triangle Park, NC.

Heien, D. M., and Pittman, D. J., 1989, The economic costs of alcohol abuse: An assessment of current methods and estimates, *Journal of Studies on Alcohol* **50:**89.

Kagel, J. H., Battalio, R. C., and Miles, C. G., 1980, Marihuana and work performance, *Journal of Human Resources* **15:**373–393.

Kaestner, R., 1991, The effect of illicit drug use on the wages of young adults, *Journal of Labor Economics* **8:**318–412.

Kelley, J., 1989, Poll: On-the-job drug use is "significant", *USA Today,* December 13, p. A-1.

Klein, K., 1972, Prediction of flight safety hazards from drug induced performance decrements with alcohol as a reference substance, *Aerospace Medicine,* **43:**1207–1213.

Kolb, L., 1962, *Drug Addiction: A Medical Problem,* Charles C. Thomas, Springfield, IL.

Lemieux, T., Fortin, B., and Frechette, P., 1991, Labor supply in the underground economy: An empirical analysis based on survey data, Unpublished manuscript, Massachusetts Institute of Technology, Cambridge, MA.

Manning, W. G., Keeler, E. B., Newhouse, J. P., Slouss, E. M., and Wasserman, J., 1989, The taxes of sin: Do smokers and drinkers pay their way? *Journal of the American Medical Association* **261:**1604–1609.

Mattison, J., 1902, *The Mattison Method in Morphinism,* E. B. Treat, New York.

McGlothlin, W., Jamison, K., and Rosenblatt, S., 1970, Marijuana and the use of other drugs, *Nature* **228:**1227–1229.

Model, K. E., 1991, The relationship between drug and alcohol use and income: An econometric model, Unpublished manuscript, Harvard University, Cambridge, MA.

Model, K. E., 1993, The effect of marijuana decriminalization on hospital emergency drug episodes: 1975–1978, Unpublished manuscript, Harvard University, Cambridge, MA.

Moore, M. J., and Viscusi, W. K., 1988, Doubling the estimated value of life: Results from using new occupational data, *Journal of Policy Analysis and Management* **7**(3)**:**476–490.

Mullahy, J., and Sindelar, J. L., 1993, Alcoholism, work, and income, Unpublished manuscript.

O'Donnell, J. A., 1969, Narcotics addicts in Kentucky, U.S. Public Health Service Publication No. 1881, National Institute of Mental Health, Chevy Chase, MD.

O'Malley, P. J., and Wagenaar, A. C., 1991, The effects of minimum drinking age laws on alcohol use, related behaviors and traffic crash involvement among American youth, 1976–1987, *Journal of Studies on Alcohol* **52:**478–491.

Register, C. A., and Williams, D. R., 1992, Labor market effects of marijuana and cocaine use among young men, *Industrial and Labor Relations Review* **45:**435–448.

Reuter, P., MacCoun, R., and Murphy, P., 1990, Money from crime: A study of the economics of drug dealing in Washington, D.C., RAND Report R3894-RF, RAND Corporation, Santa Monica, CA.

Rice, D. P., 1966, Estimating the cost of illness, Health Economic Series No. 66, Publication Number (PHS)947-6, Department of Health, Education, and Welfare, Rockville, MD.

Rice, D., Kelman, S., and Miller, L. S., 1991, Estimates of economic costs of alcohol and drug abuse and mental illness, 1985 and 1988, *Public Health Reports* **196:**280–291.

Rice, D. P., Kelman, S., Miller, L. S., and Dunmeyer, S., 1990, The economic costs of alcohol and drug abuse and mental illness: 1985, Report submitted to the Office of Financing and Coverage Policy of the Alcohol, Drug Abuse, and Mental Health Administration, U.S. Department of Health and Human Services, Institute for Health and Aging, University of California, San Francisco.

Rippey, E., 1991, Just say no? The effects of alcohol and drug use on the performance of individuals in the American labor market, Unpublished manuscript, National Bureau of Economic Research, Cambridge, MA.

Saffer, H., and Grossman, M., 1987a, Beer taxes, the legal drinking age and youth motor vehicle fatalities, *Journal of Legal Studies* **16:**351–374.

Saffer, H., and Grossman, M., 1987b, Drinking age laws and highway mortality rates: Cause and effect, *Economic Inquiry* **25:**403–417.

Siegel, R. K., 1989, *Intoxication: Life in Pursuit of Artificial Paradise,* 1st ed., Dutton, New York.

Siegel, S., 1986, Alcohol and opiate dependence: Re-evaluation of the Victorian perspective, in: *Research Advances in Alcohol and Drug Problems* (H. D. Cappell, F. B. Glaser, Y. Israel, H. Kalant, W. Schmidt, E. M. Sellers, and R. C. Smart, eds.), pp. 279–315, Plenum Press, New York.

Taylor, J., 1991, Cocaine users turn to alcohol, *Journal of Drug and Alcohol Dependence* **15:**1, 12.

4

The Effects of Psychoactive Substances on Workplace Performance

ROBERT B. COAMBS and MARY PAT McANDREWS

1. INTRODUCTION

Drug use in the workplace is often viewed as pleasure seeking by imprudent employees. This is sometimes true; however, drug use goes well beyond pleasure seeking, and many drugs are used because they are perceived to help the user deal more effectively with life and work demands (Alexander & Hadaway, 1982; Ashton & Stepney, 1982; Khantzian, Mack, & Schatzberg, 1974; Peele, 1985; Shiffman & Wills, 1985). For example, the truck driver who uses cannabis (marijuana) for pleasure, amphetamines and caffeine to remain awake, and opioids to alleviate back pain is using drugs to achieve certain ends, including adapting to the demands of his or her job. Many psychoactive substances affect human thought and behavior, and their use is often an attempt to control one's own thought processes and mental capacity. Thus, the effects of drugs on performance are likely to influence critically how they are used, and we should expect to find drugs in the workplace just as we would in any situation in which they have adaptive value.

A fundamental assumption of drug screening is that drug use impairs workplace performance and is associated with increased risks and hazards. For exam-

ROBERT B. COAMBS and MARY PAT McANDREWS • Treatment Research and Development Department, Addiction Research Foundation, 33 Russell Street, Toronto, Ontario, M5S 2S1, Canada. The views expressed here are those of the authors and do not necessarily represent those of the Addiction Research Foundation.

Research Advances in Alcohol and Drug Problems, Volume 11: Drug Testing in the Workplace, edited by Scott Macdonald and Paul M. Roman. Plenum Press, New York, 1994.

ple, an employer who discovers that he or she has an employee who is an ex-heroin addict, now maintained on methadone, is usually most interested in the possible effects of methadone on the employee's current productivity and safety.

It is relatively easy to see how acute drug intoxication could impair performance in virtually any type of workplace activity where speed and accuracy of thought and behavior are critical. More subtle impairments associated with chronic drug use and withdrawal, however, can also be relevant to workplace performance in many circumstances. Two complimentary methods have been used to investigate these two types of impairment: the information processing and neuropsychological approaches. They are two approaches in cognitive psychology, a discipline devoted to the study of higher mental processes, including perception, memory, reasoning, and judgment.

Approaches to Studying Cognitive Effects of Drugs

The information processing approach, which has become the central model in cognitive psychology, provides a means of analyzing the events that occur between the presentation of a stimulus and the output of a response in the performance of a task (Ashcraft, 1989). A defining assumption of this approach is that thought processes can be broken down into discrete processing elements, or stages, during which unique operations are performed on incoming information. For example, in a typical information processing task, the subject perceives a stimulus, uses formerly acquired knowledge to transform the stimulus in some way, decides whether the transformed stimulus conforms to a particular category, and responds based on the decision. Perception, memory, decision processing, and psychomotor functions are all involved in the execution of the task.

Information processing models have been a rich source of hypotheses regarding fundamental cognitive operations. The approach has also helped investigate changes in cognitive operations associated with alcohol (Marusarz & Koh, 1980; Sternberg, 1975), benzodiazepines (Coambs et al., 1986), cannabis (Tinklenberg & Taylor, 1984), and barbiturates (Williams, Rundell, & Landgrave, 1981).

Neuropsychology provides another important methodological approach to studying drug-induced cognitive impairments. Essentially, this is the study of the relationship between various cognitive domains (e.g., language, memory, and reasoning) and brain structure and function. Modern neuropsychological theory, which has been greatly influenced by the ideas of Jackson (1932) and Luria (1973), holds that basic processing activities are localized in discrete brain areas (e.g., rudimentary visual analysis in the occipital cortex). Superimposed on these processing elements is a hierarchical organization, with successive centers elaborating on and integrating the processing carried out in earlier regions. Most cognitive activities involve a combination of basic skills, and therefore they depend on many centers of processing. For example, writing includes fine motor coordination, visual perception, spatial localization, and feedback from muscles and joints in addition to verbal skills. Each of these may be localized processing activities, but the behavior requires integrated control and production.

Cognitive dysfunction is assessed using neuropsychological tests that evaluate different systems and capacities. Performance on such tests permits inferences about the integrity of brain structures and pathways (Lezak, 1983). This approach is widely used because such tests are convenient and flexible, objective and reliable, sensitive enough to detect early pathology, and grounded in clinical and normative data bases. Assessment batteries, constructed from existing tests whose diagnostic utility and validity are well established, are used to provide a comprehensive evaluation of cognitive functions.

The study of the neuropsychological effects of drugs makes our understanding of drug effects more comprehensive. Drug-induced changes in cognitive functions can be either short-lived and reversible, or permanent. The degree of impairment and eventual recovery undoubtedly depend on a number of factors, such as the level of consumption and duration of drug use, age and gender of the user, and concomitant use of other drugs. Other variables that are often associated with a drug-abusing lifestyle, such as head injury, poor diet, and damage to organs (e.g., the liver), may confound the search for direct consequences of drug use by altering drug-related deficits. Lack of knowledge about levels of functioning that preceded the drug use also increases the difficulty of determining whether impairment exists. Moreover, drugs appear to differ in the degree to which tolerance to cognitive impairment associated with acute administration develops over extended use.

The information processing and neuropsychological approaches have often been used separately in research on cognition and drugs. In general, information processing research has examined the acute effects of drug administration, whereas the neuropsychological approach has been used most often to assess long-term effects. These approaches are beginning to blend together, however, in experimental and clinical neuroscience. They are complementary in that both decompose complex mental functions—one via experimental manipulation of processing stages, the other by neurobehavioral analysis.

This chapter reviews the known effects of drugs of abuse on cognitive functioning. Most of the available information is based on laboratory or clinical research on psychomotor and cognitive functioning; however, we relate these findings to issues of workplace performance wherever possible. Data on central nervous system depressants, cannabis, stimulants, and solvents are reviewed with respect to their acute (i.e., short-term) and chronic (i.e., long-term) effects, as well as changes seen in withdrawal.

2. DRUGS OF CONCERN IN THE WORKPLACE

Alcohol

Acute Effects. One well-known acute effect of alcohol is its capacity to impair the operation of complex machinery (e.g., driving or flying; Modell & Mountz, 1990). Psychomotor skills, divided attention (Moskowitz & DePry, 1968), and high-speed decision making are all impaired (Tharp, Rundell, Lester, & Williams, 1974). Steele and Josephs (1990) suggest that an impairment in processing complex stimuli causes the main negative and positive behavioral effects of alcohol. The intoxicated individual is able to focus only on the most obvious stimuli; less obvious stimuli are not processed. This appears to contribute to aggressive behavior because knowledge of the consequences of aggression constrains sober individuals, whereas the intoxicated individual is less aware of these consequences. This phenomenon can impair the capacity to perceive the dangers or costs of any particular behavior (Modell & Mountz, 1990). An important benefit, however, is that it can help a drinker to avoid stressful thoughts. If the drinker focuses on a pleasant distraction before drinking, alcohol will help worries to recede into the background. Thus, the impairments in abstraction and reasoning may be critically related to the safety aspects of the drug, and to the causes of alcohol use itself.

Alcohol also disrupts memory functions. This is dramatically seen in periods of waking memory lapse, called blackouts (Sweeney, 1990). In the extreme form of blackout, total memory loss occurs for events that take place during the period of intoxication (Goodwin, Hill, Hopper, & Viesselman, 1975). While the person is in the blackout period, he or she has intact remote memory for events preceding intoxication and can utilize short-term memory to the extent that conversation and action are appropriate to the situation. The memory loss is caused by alcohol-induced deficits in storage processes, and similar, smaller impairments are observed when alcohol is ingested in smaller doses (Birnbaum & Parker, 1977; Petros, Kerbel, Beckwith, Sacks, & Sarafolean, 1985). Ironically, alcohol has been shown to *enhance* memory performance when it is administered after material has been learned but several hours before the recall test, perhaps because of a reduction in interference (Lamberty, Beckwith, Petros, & Ross, 1990; Parker and Weingartner, 1984).

Alcohol also causes "hangover": the cluster of physiological and psychological effects that occurs in some drinkers 4 to 12 hours after the peak blood alcohol level has been reached (C. M. Smith & Barnes, 1983). Hangover is not well understood, but preliminary evidence suggest that it causes marked deficits in performance in a wide range of daily human activities, including driving and the operation of complex machinery (Karvinen, Miettinen, & Ahlman, 1962; Kelly, Myrsten, Neri, & Rydberg, 1970; Seppälä, Leino, Linnoila, Huttunen, &

Ylikahri, 1976). These impairments appear serious enough to cause traffic mortality (Franck, 1983); however, little research exists to draw accurate conclusions regarding risk levels.

Chronic Effects. Alcohol has direct toxic effects on neurons (Harper, Kril, & Holloway, 1985; Walker, Hunter, Barnes, & Riley, 1980), and in association with other medical consequences of alcohol abuse (e.g., liver damage and inadequate nutrition) can result in significant and lasting cognitive deficits. Although there are no precise data on the incidence of neurological or cognitive impairment in alcohol abusers, 50% to 70% of individuals seeking treatment may present with some form of cognitive impairment. This is similar to estimates of liver dysfunction associated with chronic alcohol abuse.

The most well-known disorder associated with alcohol abuse is the Wernicke-Korsakoff syndrome. Victor, Adams, and Collins (1989) provide a comprehensive review of this disorder, with a description of more than 200 cases. The acute phase is associated with three main symptoms: abnormalities of eye movements; unbalanced walk; and a confusional state that includes poor responsivity, disorientation, and deficits in attention and memory. These symptoms usually improve substantially with appropriate treatment (thiamin). The chronic phase is marked by a profound memory deficit that includes an inability both to recall information from the remote past and to learn and retain new information. Although there may be other difficulties in other cognitive capacities, the level of general intellectual functioning, verbal abilities, and many other specific skills remain intact in these patients. Though partial or complete recovery from the amnesia is seen in some individuals, the majority show minimal or no recovery (Victor et al., 1989).

Less dramatic deficits that are far more common than Korsakoff syndrome have been described by many investigators over the last two decades. Again, general intellectual functioning is not affected, but selective impairments are seen in several cognitive domains when sensitive neuropsychological tests are used. Extensive reviews of these effects are available in Parsons, Butters, and Nathan (1987). The most prominent deficits are in complex visual-motor functions, particularly when speed of response is important. Thus, visual search, manual tracking, symbol copying, and other psychomotor functions are marked by imprecision and slowness. Problem-solving abilities (e.g., abstraction, hypothesis generation, and mental flexibility) are also deficient. Mild deficits are also apparent in new learning and memory, with pictorial material yielding more impairments than verbal material. The memory difficulties are increased when the task requires the patient to use strategies for organizing and retrieving the information.

Recovery of both brain and cognitive deficiencies has been reported. Carlen, Wortzman, Holgate, Wilkinson, and Rankin (1978) were the first to report reversibility in brain shrinkage after several months of abstinence, and this has since been replicated by others (Ron, Acker, Shaw, & Lishman, 1982; Zipursky, Lim, & Pfefferbaum, 1989). Various investigators have also shown recovery in the cognitive indices for 35% to 90% of patients. This improvement in functioning, however, depends critically on abstinence (Carlen & Wilkinson, 1987). In general, the more novel, complex, and rapid the information processing requirements of the task, the longer the time for recovery to normal levels of function.

In summary, there are at least two profiles of impairment associated with chronic alcohol abuse: the severe memory problems of Korsakoff syndrome, and the more moderate pattern of deficits seen in individuals without obvious neurological dysfunction. In addition, researchers have described a more profound, global decline in intellectual and cognitive abilities (called alcoholic dementia), but the criteria for this condition remain unclear (Cutting, 1978; Lishman, 1986). Even moderate forms of impairment that may remain undetected in gross behavior, however, can have significant impact on functioning within and outside the workplace. With prolonged abstinence, partial or complete recovery of function is possible. Finally, the extent to which these deficits may be evident in heavy or problem drinkers (i.e., those who would not meet DSM-III-R criteria for abuse or dependence) is still an open question. Further studies of specific risk factors related to consumption or to the individual should lead to better early identification of alcohol-related cognitive impairments.

Benzodiazepines

The benzodiazepines (e.g., diazepam) are among the most prescribed class of drugs in Western industrialized countries (Baldessarini, 1990, p. 424). These drugs are used as muscle relaxants, as sedatives, as anticonvulsants, as preanesthetics, and to reduce anxiety. In the last 15 years, however, it has become evident that there are serious side effects with benzodiazepines (Lister, 1985). These are chiefly toxic effects on behavior, rather than irreversible effects on tissue. The form and severity of the performance impairments vary across the benzodiazepines (Scharf, Fletcher, & Graham, 1988); the impairments are most marked in the elderly (Nikaido, Ellinwood, Heatherly, & Gupta, 1990).

Acute Effects. The main concern with benzodiazepines is with their acute effects on behavior. The acute impairments appear to be more severe, with more measurable impact on behavior than chronic impairments.

Memory. One of the most important toxic behavioral effects of benzodiazepines is their impairment of human memory (Ghoneim, Mewaldt, Berie, & Hinrichs, 1981). Shortly after the introduction of these drugs as a preanesthetic, it became evident that they cause memory loss (e.g., Clarke, Eccersley, Frisby, & Thornton, 1970). A critical focus of research in this area has been to identify the systems of memory in which the impairment is localized. These drugs produce little impairment of short-term storage, whereas numerous studies have shown that benzodiazepines produce significant effects on permanent storage (Coambs, Poulos, & Cappell, 1986; Ghoneim, Mewaldt, & Hinrichs, 1984; Lister, 1985). The form of permanent storage that appears most affected is memory for specific events (i.e., episodic memory; Lister, 1985; Tulving, 1983). The impairment, called anterograde amnesia, is where subjects have difficulty recalling material learned after the drug has been absorbed, but have normal recall for material learned prior to drug onset. Another form of memory, semantic memory (knowledge of the world), does not appear to be affected by these drugs (Brown, Brown, & Bowes, 1983; Ghoneim et al., 1984). Knowledge related to skill acquisition also appears to be unimpaired (Lister & File, 1984).

Other Performance Effects. Benzodiazepines produce deficits in a wide variety of psychomotor tasks (Kleinknecht & Donaldson, 1975; Wittenborn, 1979). It is difficult to determine the causes of the psychomotor effects, because of different results between studies (Wittenborn, 1979). Two psychomotor effects that show reliable impairment are driving performance and speech.

Benzodiazepines are commonly found in the bodies of fatally injured motor vehicle accident victims (Cimbura, Warren, Bennett, Lucas, & Simpson, 1980; Ellinwood & Heatherly, 1985; Skegg, Richards, & Doll, 1979), and the driving deficit arises from both motor and cognitive impairments (Moskowitz & Smiley, 1982). The blood levels found in these victims represent typical clinical doses of the drug. Diazepam also impairs performance in the operation of driving simulators (Linnoila & Hakkinen, 1974; Moskowitz & Smiley, 1982). The drug affects several driving skills, including (a) divided attention (Moskowitz & Smiley, 1982; Tinklenberg & Taylor, 1984); (b) eye-hand coordination, such as staying in a lane (Moskowitz & Smiley, 1982); and (c) high-speed decision making, such as selecting one of two accident-avoidance responses when one of two types of road obstacle appears (Coambs, 1987; Moskowitz & Smiley, 1982). These impairments closely resemble those produced by alcohol; both drugs impair divided-attention performance (Moskowitz & DePry, 1968; Tinklenberg & Taylor, 1984) and response selection processes (Huntley, 1974). It is particularly important that, when taken together, the two drugs have additive effects on both motor and cognitive measures of driving performance (Moskowitz & Smiley, 1982). Thus, diazepam may cause impairment in the operation of any complex machine, including industrial equipment and aircraft.

Several benzodiazepines disrupt speech: Sentence structure is more likely to be incomplete, and the message incoherent (Gottschalk, 1977). Gottschalk (1977) found that this effect persisted after 15 mg diazepam was administered daily for 2 weeks. Speech was more disorganized and repetitious than normal.

Chronic Effects. Chronic use of benzodiazepines does not appear to cause measurable physiological damage. If these drugs are used for long periods, however, they can begin to produce a phenomenon resembling reversible brain dysfunction. Individuals who use benzodiazepines for long periods do not develop tolerance to the memory impairments and certain other effects, and hence they behave as if they were suffering from a mild form of brain damage. The impairments cease if the individual stops using the drug, but months or years of life experience can be blurred or lost because of the memory impairments the drugs produced.

Memory. Of all the possible chronic effects of benzodiazepines, memory effects have been the most researched. Individuals do not develop complete tolerance to the impairment in permanent memory. In one study, 14 mg diazepam was administered orally to normal subjects in a 21-day laboratory study, and a significant reduction in delayed free recall at the end of the study period was found (Ghoneim et al., 1981). Clinical populations also do not become completely tolerant to the free-recall deficit. Lucki, Rickels, and Geller (1985) found that patients chronically maintained on typical clinical doses of benzodiazepines exhibited memory impairment 1 hour after receiving their prescribed drug. A similar result was obtained by Hendler, Cimini, Ma, and Long (1980), who found that patients chronically maintained on benzodiazepines showed more impairment on various neuropsychological tests than patients maintained on narcotics.

The full extent of the diazepam-induced impairment on memory and response selection processes is not likely to be immediately obvious to the casual observer, to the clinical interviewer, or even to the drug user. In one study that examined this, Hinrichs, Mewaldt, Ghoneim, and Berie (1982) measured the cognitive performance of subjects who received both diazepam and a placebo at different times. Although these subjects were given feedback about their own performance and were aware of the sedative action of the drug, their self-rating of mental ability in the diazepam condition was no different from that in the placebo condition.

In conclusion, one of the most unique aspects of the cognitive impairments caused by benzodiazepines is the specificity of impairments they produce. Even though they may not be obvious in gross behavior, they have significant implications for thought processes in workplace settings. Any task requiring long-term storage of memories for specific events (such as what occurred in yesterday's committee meeting), fast and accurate choices, or complex psychomotor performance appears to be impaired by benzodiazepines.

Barbiturates

Current clinical use of barbiturates is limited to certain neurological (e.g., status epilepticus) or psychiatric (e.g., severe emotional distress, diagnostic interviews) conditions where rapid and deep relaxation is required. Barbiturates are contained in combination drugs, such as certain preparations for migraine. Until the mid-1970s they were commonly used as hypnotics to treat insomnia and as major tranquilizers for anxiety disorders. The benzodiazepines have become the preferred drugs for insomnia and anxiety, however, given their milder side effects, lower likelihood of dependence, milder withdrawal syndrome, and greater safety with respect to overdose.

Acute and Chronic Effects. Barbiturates act as central nervous system depressants, and thus their acute and chronic effects on cognition are similar to those of alcohol and other depressants. There have been very few controlled studies, however, of these effects. Certain acute effects on visual perception and eye movement control that appear to be specific to barbiturates have been reported; these include disruption of pursuit eye movements (Schalen, Pyykko, Korttila, Magnusson, & Enbom, 1988) and slowed processing of stimuli (Tharp, Rundell, Lester, & Williams, 1975). Judd and Grant's study (1975) of polydrug users suggested that long-standing heavy barbiturate use may produce a pattern of cognitive dysfunction similar to that seen in chronic alcoholics. The authors showed that response speed, visual-motor coordination, learning, and conceptualization abilities were all impaired.

Cannabis

There has been a great deal of research over the past three decades on acute effects of cannabis on cognitive functioning, and less on effects of chronic use. Although there are clearly demonstrated acute effects, there are insufficient data on the effects of long-term use. Studies in this area are hampered by the lack of proper controls, concurrent use of other drugs in cannabis users, differing forms of the drug, and the fact that the potency of street cannabis is variable and has also increased nearly 200% since the early studies (Deahl, 1991). Therefore, it is somewhat difficult to compare across early and recent studies and to know whether earlier results are relevant to current use patterns.

Acute Effects. Cannabis intoxication leads to widespread changes in cognitive functioning. In his comprehensive review of the effects of cannabis on memory functioning, Ferraro (1980) noted that the drug disrupts learning, attention, mental efficiency, and concept formation. The most consistent impairments have been noted in learning and memory tasks. There is generally no impairment in retrieving information that was learned in a nondrug state, but performance is poor for new material presented during intoxication, even when tested in drug-free conditions. Recall and recognition are characterized in particular by an increase in false "recollection" of material that had not been presented (Darley & Tinklenberg, 1974; Dornbush, 1974; Hooker & Jones, 1987).

Cannabis intoxication also has important effects on complex perceptual-motor and decision-making processes. Murray (1986) reviews a number of studies showing disruption in time and distance estimates and slowed reaction time on a variety of psychomotor tasks following cannabis ingestion. As well, performance decrements have been observed on simulations of driving (Kvalseth, 1977) and airplane flight (Janowsky, Meachem, Blaine, Schoor, & Bozzetti, 1976; Yesavage, Leirer, Denari, & Hollister, 1985). The majority of studies indicate that cannabis in social doses can disrupt the complex psychomotor skills involved in operating machinery at home, at work, and on the road (Relman, 1982). The literature is mixed as to whether tolerance develops to the subjective effects and performance decrements associated with cannabis use (e.g., Cappell & Pliner, 1974; Relman, 1982). Virtually all of the studies where positive effects have been obtained, however, were conducted with non-naive users.

The potential for cannabis-related decrements to be seen in the workplace is heightened by the fact that it is the most commonly used illicit substance in Canada and the U.S. (U.S. Department of Health and Human Services, 1993). In a recent Canadian survey, use within the past year was reported by 24% of males aged 20 to 24 and 15% of males aged 25 to 34 (Eliany, Giesbrecht, Nelson, Wellman, & Wortley, 1990), with one quarter of male current users reporting that they used cannabis one or more times per week; the corresponding rates for females were approximately half those for males. Although we lack statistics on the situations and settings in which cannabis use is highest, the performance impairments and lack of complete tolerance observed in formal studies have disturbing implications for speeded analysis and decision-making in the workplace and elsewhere.

Chronic Effects. Numerous reports from the 1970s indicated few, if any, cognitive disturbances in chronic cannabis users (e.g., Bowman & Pihl, 1973; Grant, Rochford, Fleming, & Stunkard, 1973; Weckowicz & Janssen, 1973). Ray, Prabhu, Mohan, Nath, and Neki (1978), for example, found no deficits on tests of attention and concentration, visual-motor coordination, or memory functions, and Schaeffer, Andrysiak, and Ungerleider (1981) found no evidence of impairment across a wide range of tests despite the fact that many subjects were not abstinent during the period of testing. In fact, the 1980 National Institute on Drug Abuse report on marijuana to the U.S. Congress (U.S. Secretary of Health, Education and Welfare, 1980), indicated that there was little direct evidence of enduring cognitive impairment associated with the use of this drug. The lack of positive findings regarding cannabis use and mental deficits has helped fuel arguments favoring decriminalization.

Only recently have there been well-controlled studies of the cognitive effects of long-term cannabis use in abstinent individuals. Varma, Malhotra, Dang, Das, and Nehra (1988) tested long-term cannabis users after a minimum of 12 hours of abstinence; they found selective impairments in short-term memory and in perceptual-motor speed. Users were similar to controls, however, on many other measures of cognitive functioning, including attention, concentration, remote memory, delayed recall, and recognition. Schwartz, Gruenewald, Klitzner, and Fedio (1989) reported similar memory impairment, for both verbal and visuographic material, in a small sample of cannabis-abusing adolescents who had been abstinent for 6 weeks. This study also demonstrated a reduction in observed deficits over a 6-week test period, suggesting recovery similar to that seen in alcohol-related dysfunction. Mendhiratta et al. (1988) conducted a longitudinal study of users of cannabis (and matched controls) who had been evaluated initially 10 years previously. Because all prior users had continued their cannabis use, they were tested after a 12-hour abstinence. Significant impairments relative to controls were observed on tests of concentration (digit span backwards), memory (Bender VisuoMotor Gestalt) and psychomotor speed (tapping and verbal response time); these differences were apparent at both the initial and follow-up test occasions. Clearly, more research is needed to establish whether there is a reliable pattern of performance deficits associated with long-term cannabis use.

Opioids

Opioids are the class of natural and synthetic chemicals related to morphine and codeine. The legal opioid that is most commonly used in Canada is codeine, whereas in the U.S. it is propoxyphene (Darvon). Other commonly used drugs in both countries include demerol (pethidine), and morphine (International Narcotics Control Board, 1991). The users of these drugs include outpatients under treatment for pain, illegal users of heroin and diverted prescription drugs, and former opioid addicts maintained on methadone, a synthetic opioid.

Acute Effects. The acute effects of opioids include extremely pleasant or unpleasant feelings, drowsiness, apathy, lethargy, reduced physical activity, reduced visual acuity, inability to concentrate, and generalized depression of cognition, sometimes referred to as "mental clouding" (Chesher, 1989). The performance impairments produced by weaker opioids such as propoxyphene and codeine are less than those resulting from use of heroin, morphine, or Demerol, but the former substances are more likely to be used in the workplace because they are more available. Acute therapeutic doses of heroin and morphine produce impairment in functions related to perception, learning, memory, and reasoning (G. M. Smith, Semke, & Beecher, 1962). Acute therapeutic doses of codeine and propoxyphene produce slight impairment in driving-related functions (Bradley and Nicholson, 1986; C. Edwards, Gard, Handley, Hunter, & Whittington, 1982; Sokol, & Rodda, 1974; Linnoila & Hakkinen, 1974). With all opioids, the extent of the impairment is not always obvious to the observer, because even in high doses they do not produce excessive talkativeness, slurred speech, or obvious signs of incoordination (Chesher, 1989). Habitual opioid users develop extensive tolerance to the performance effects of these drugs, and even drug-free ex-addicts respond less strongly to an acute dose of opioid than naive users (Chesher, 1989).

Chronic Effects. Generally, after repeated administration of an opioid, tolerance develops to signs of depression (Chesher, 1989). Using various psychometric instruments, Hendler et al. (1980) examined the cognitive functioning of patients who were maintained on benzodiazepines and opioids. The benzodiazepines produced measurable impairment in overall test scores, but the opioids did not. This appears to be partly because tolerance develops to the opioid-induced cognitive impairments, and because some opioids do not produce cognitive impairment after initial drug administration (Ghoneim, Mewaldt, & Thatcher, 1975). Chronic opioid use also does not appear to produce permanent cognitive deficits. Most studies indicate that, compared to controls, users of legal opioids do not show neuropsychological deficits (Fields & Fullerton, 1975; Guerra, Solé, Camí, & Tobeña, 1987; Rounsaville, Jones, Novelly, & Kleber, 1982). Strang and Gurling (1989) found some neuropsychological changes in long-term, high-dose heroin addicts, but these may be attributable to alcohol use and/or head injury. In patients who are maintained on a stabilized dose of methadone, there appears to be little or no performance impairment produced by the drug (Chesher, 1989; Robinson & Moskowitz, 1985).

Thus, acute first-time doses of opioids appear to produce slight cognitive impairments in a range of human performance tasks. This effect could be expected to be particularly pronounced where other drugs are taken at the same time (Chesher, 1989). Tolerance appears to develop to these effects, however, and opioids do not appear to produce lasting neuropsychological deficits.

Amphetamines and Cocaine

Amphetamines and cocaine act as stimulants in that they increase excitatory neural transmission. In the 1980s there was a major escalation of cocaine abuse, particularly with the availability of inexpensive and smokable crack cocaine. The neurological consequences of stimulant abuse include hemorrhages in the brain, seizures, and strokes in a small proportion of users (Kramer, Locke, Ogunyemi, & Nelson, 1990; Mody, Miller, McIntyre, Cobb, & Goldberg, 1988; Pascual-Leone, Dhuna, Altafullah, & Anderson, 1990). Little research, though, has been published on cognitive changes associated with acute or chronic use of cocaine. Because of the similar excitatory and arousing effects of amphetamines and cocaine, they will be discussed together here.

Amphetamines, and to a lesser extent cocaine, are more likely to be used by some occupational groups than others to enhance their work. For example, students studying for exams and long-distance truck drivers are more likely to use amphetamines to reduce fatigue.

Acute Effects. As might be expected, stimulants can improve performance on many tasks, particularly when consistent attention or speed of response is important (Mackworth, 1950). Similarly, acute administration can reverse the effects of fatigue on performance (Newhouse et al., 1989; Resnick & Resnick, 1984). Studies of the effects of cocaine on cognitive event-related EEG responses indicate an increase in amplitude of such responses. This suggests that attentional resources may be improved by the drug (Herning, Hooker, & Jones, 1987). Performance impairments, however, have also been documented. These include an increase in errors of intrusion (i.e., false recollections) on memory tests, hyperactivity, and an increase in repetitive motor responses (Frith & Done, 1983). These findings suggest a somewhat paradoxical effect: increased orientation and preparation as a result of arousal, coupled with dysfunction in higher-order control processes.

Chronic Effects. There have been very few carefully controlled studies examining the effects of chronic stimulant abuse. One important obstacle to such research is that a withdrawal syndrome characterized by depression, fatigue, and concentration difficulties can persist several months after cessation of use (Gawin & Kleber, 1986). A second obstacle is that the majority of stimulant abusers also use other drugs (notably alcohol, tranquilizers, and marijuana) to reduce the dysphoria associated with the "crash." Therefore, it is difficult to determine the specific effects of stimulants.

Several early reports documented performance decrements in learning, memory, and attention in coca leaf chewers in South America (Negrete & Murphy, 1967; Zapata-Oritz, 1976). Manschreck et al. (1990) studied crack users after a 3-week period of abstinence. They reported a deficit in short-term auditory memory, although no impairments were observed in language, general intelligence, abstraction, or motor synchrony. A similar effect on learning and memory, for both verbal and pictorial material, has been reported by Uddo-Crane (1990). She also found greater impairment in subjects who used intravenous administration relative to those who chose smoking as the primary route of ingestion. O'Malley, Adamse, Heaton, and Gawin (1992) reported mild to moderate impairments in attention, memory, and abstraction abilities in recently abstinent cocaine abusers. Their findings also indicated significant recovery of function with prolonged (4-month) abstinence. In another study, moderate deficits were observed in short-term verbal memory and attention, and milder impairments were seen in nonverbal memory, naming, and abstraction (Ardila, Rosselli, & Strumwasser, 1991). Both sets of investigators found a correlation between consumption and impairment, suggesting a direct effect of cocaine on cognitive functioning. This pattern is consistent with the profile found in polydrug users who use stimulants (Adams, Rennick, Schoof, & Keegan, 1975; Carlin, 1986). Some studies have failed to demonstrate deficits in this population (Bruhn & Maage, 1975; Grant et al., 1978), but this may be because these users had not used enough stimulants for a long enough time to show measurable impairments.

Although the data are sparse, the findings indicate that attention and memory can be significantly reduced by chronic cocaine use. One way of interpreting minor or negative effects of stimulants on cognitive functioning is to assume a model that conceptualizes drug-induced cerebral dysfunction in terms of cumulative deterioration and compensation. According to this model, deficits will only become evident when drug-related deterioration has reached a particular threshold. The young age and relatively short abuse histories of many stimulant abusers might mean that few have reached this threshold.

Prolonged use of amphetamines or cocaine or acute use at toxic levels has been shown to induce paranoid-like psychosis. Symptoms include delusions of persecution and hallucinations, sometimes taking the form of the sensation of insects crawling under the skin (Fischman, 1984; Nicholi, 1984). Less dramatic symptoms such as paranoid ideation, depression, irritability, and anxiety are also commonly reported by users (Washton & Tatarsky, 1984). The presence of such symptoms has clear implications for disruption to functioning in the workplace, such as impaired relations with co-workers and clients.

Withdrawal Effects. Gawin and Kleber (1986) have described a withdrawal syndrome associated with cessation of a cocaine binge. The initial phase, which they labeled the "crash," lasts up to 4 days. In the early stages, agitation, depression, and cocaine craving are high, followed by fatigue and increased sleep. The second phase, withdrawal, is characterized by a protracted dysphoric syndrome. Sleep becomes normalized, but there is decreased activation, anxiety, and a sense of diminished normal pleasurable experiences. This phase induces a return of craving and possible resumption of use. The authors noted that if cocaine abusers can remain abstinent, this dysphoria lifts within 2 to 12 weeks. The third phase, extinction, is essentially a return to normal mood, although craving can reappear months or even years after cessation of cocaine use. There has been relatively little research on cognition in cocaine abusers in withdrawal, because the accompanying gross disturbances in mood and anxiety can independently disrupt performance on cognitive tasks.

Nicotine

It may at first seem surprising to find nicotine in a discussion of drug effects in the workplace. For smokers, however, nicotine has substantial effects on thought processes and psychomotor performance in many tasks related to work. Furthermore, there are cognitive and performance impairments that are caused by nicotine withdrawal (Hughes, Higgins, & Hatsukami, 1988). Most smokers indicate that they smoke, at least in part, to improve their cognitive performance. In a study of motives for smoking among university students, Wesnes and Warburton (1978) found that 83% agreed with the statement "Smoking helps me think and concentrate." Wesnes and Warburton (1984) also found that smoking was perceived by subjects as helping them with work, and that cigarettes helped them to think and concentrate. Smokers smoke a great deal at work; Meade and

Wald (1977) found that in the absence of smoking regulations, smokers working in offices smoked 56% of their cigarettes while at work and had their peak smoking hours during the working day. Nicotine's effects on cognition are short-term, occurring shortly after the use of the drug. Accordingly, only acute effects will be discussed.

Acute Effects. It is not precisely clear what the source is of smokers' belief that smoking helps them think and concentrate; nicotine does not appear to enhance cognitive performance in nonsmokers (Hindmarch, Kerr, & Sherwood, 1990). Although the withdrawal effects following abstention from tobacco are highly variable among smokers (Shiffman, 1979), nicotine withdrawal generally causes an impairment in cognitive functioning. For example, Wesnes and Warburton (1983) found a decrease in performance in a digit-sequence identification task in a nonsmoking control condition. In a sustained simulated driving task, Heimstra, Bancroft, and DeKock (1967) found significantly more tracking and vigilance errors in deprived smokers. Efficiency in sustained performance in a visual reaction time task also decreased when smokers were deprived of tobacco (Frankenhaeuser, Myrsten, Post, & Johansson, 1971). Hatsukami, Hughes, Pickens, and Suikis (1984) found significant increases in self-rated confusion, as well as an impairment in concentration, in smokers in withdrawal. In addition, Myrsten, Elgerot, and Endgren (1977) found that impaired concentration was a frequently reported symptom of withdrawal in the subjects they studied. Henningfield (1987) found that the concentration impairment lasts at least 10 days after quitting smoking.

Correspondingly, smokers who are deprived of nicotine for at least 12 hours improve their cognitive performance when nicotine is administered (Snyder & Henningfield, 1989). For example, J. A. Edwards, Wesner, Warburton, and Gale (1985) found that in smokers who abstained for at least 12 hours, target detection in a rapid digit-sequence identification task increased significantly in speed and accuracy in the first 10 minutes following smoking. Mangan (1982) has demonstrated improved performance in an auditory vigilance task following smoking. Research by Spilich (1987), however, suggests that although performance on simple cognitive tasks may be enhanced when smokers smoke, performance on more complex tasks (e.g., reading comprehension and simulated automobile driving) may be impaired.

Thus, nicotine withdrawal impairs cognitive performance, and nicotine administration reverses this effect; however, nicotine does not appear to enhance cognitive performance in nonsmokers. Therefore, the most likely explanation why smokers believe that smoking helps them "think and concentrate" is that smoking reverses the impairment caused by tobacco withdrawal. More research is needed to clarify this important issue.

It is generally accepted that nicotine withdrawal can strongly contribute to relapse to smoking (Shiffman, 1979). Nicotine gum can reduce withdrawal symptoms, including cognitive symptoms (Schneider, Jarvik, & Forsythe, 1984), as well as rates of recidivism relative to behavioral treatment alone (Musk & Shean, 1986). The concentration impairment caused by nicotine withdrawal also may lead to relapse in some smokers. Shiffman (1982) studied the environmental and cognitive experiences associated with relapse in smokers attempting to quit. He found that relapse "crises" in smokers attempting to quit were often associated with stressful experiences, usually related to interpersonal relationships or work.

The cognitive effects of nicotine and nicotine withdrawal can be expected to impair workplace performance primarily in the operation of complex machinery and the efficient performance of intellectual tasks. Several authors have observed a relationship between smoking and reduced driving performance. Heimstra et al. (1967) found that smokers in withdrawal performed worse in driving simulators compared to both nonsmokers and smokers who were permitted to smoke. Brison (1990) found that smokers were much more likely to cause motor vehicle crashes than nonsmokers; furthermore, those smokers who tended to smoke more while driving had a greater risk of accidents than those who tended not to do so. The cause of this effect could be distraction, behavioral differences, carbon monoxide toxicity, and/or the impairments in performance of complex tasks that some researchers have observed (Spilich, 1987).

The effects of nicotine on learning, memory, abstraction, and reasoning in work settings are more difficult to predict. Any occupation that requires either sustained attention or fast and efficient cognitive processing, however, may be affected by nicotine withdrawal (Snyder & Henningfield, 1989).

Solvents

An organic solvent is a chemical compound used to extract, dissolve, or suspend non-water-soluble materials (fats, oils, resins, lipids, etc.). Typical solvents are acetone, benzene, styrene, toluene, and xylene. There are a very large number of solvents in use, and they are particularly prevalent in industrial settings. The two main populations that are exposed to these compounds are solvent abusers and industrial workers. In a recent Addiction Research Foundation survey of Ontario students, approximately 2.7% had tried glue and/or solvents (Smart, Adlaf, & Walsh, 1991). Of all drugs of abuse, solvents are distinctive in their capacity to cause damage to the central nervous system after fairly limited exposure (Hartman, 1988).

Acute Effects. The early evidence that these drugs cause brain damage (Brecher, 1972) has focused most research attention on the neurology and neuropsychology of these substances. There has been relatively little study of the acute effects of intoxication in these drugs, because the evidence for brain damage is so strong that it would not be ethical to conduct controlled studies with volunteers.

Thus, information processing studies of the type conducted with alcohol or benzodiazepines in normal volunteers are not possible.

Clinical observations indicate that solvent intoxication progresses through stages (Hartman, 1988). First, the user experiences euphoria, excitation, dizziness, lightheadedness, "drunkenness," and hallucinations. Other symptoms include headache, dizziness, fatigue, muscle weakness, memory impairment, poor concentration, and poor problem-solving ability. This is followed by central nervous system depression, confusion, disorientation, dullness, loss of self-control, tinnitus, and blurred vision. The user then shows signs of sleepiness, incoordination, and diminished reflexes. Generally, the impairment resembles that of alcohol—which should not be surprising, because ethyl alcohol is itself a solvent with many similarities to other solvents.

Chronic Effects. The best available information on the neurotoxic effects of solvents is derived from industrial use, because a large number of workers are exposed to these chemicals, often for many years (Hartman, 1988). Such workers often have good premorbid functioning, with no history of substance abuse or of head injury or other neurological trauma. They are usually chronically exposed to only one chemical. Neuropsychological impairments occur in digit-symbol substitution, digit span, block design, visual memory, simple reaction time, paired associate learning, and sentence repetition tests (Hartman, 1988). These test impairments indicate that the patients have comprehensive deficits of short- and long-term memory. Chronic use of solvents produces symptoms of dementia, defined as "impairment in short- and long-term memory, associated with impairment in abstract thinking, impaired judgment, other disturbances of higher cortical function, or personality change. The disturbance is severe enough to interfere significantly with work or usual social activities or relationships with others." (American Psychiatric Association, 1987, p. 107). Cerebral blood flow is reduced, and sensitivity to pain, light touch, and vibration is diminished. Solvent abuse and chronic exposure can also produce brain damage, as shown by cortical shrinkage on computerized tomography (CT) scans (Fornazzari, Wilkinson, Kapur, & Carlen, 1983). These losses in tissue and function may or may not be partly recovered after solvent exposure ceases (Hartman, 1988).

The deliberate abuse of solvents can also occur in the workplace among young industrial workers, even if solvents are not readily available at the work site. Such individuals are more difficult to study than workers who suffer passive exposure, because the abusers are more heterogeneous. They are generally of lower intellectual functioning before the abuse begins, and they often have a history of other drug abuse, head injury, or hypoxia attributable to inhaling the substance from a restricted air source, each of which can have its own toxic effects on brain function.

Thus, exposure to solvents can be a serious problem for job performance and safety. Employees who exhibit intoxication of the type described in this section should be monitored closely for toxic exposure to solvents. Workplace exposure is often caused by inadequate or improper use of air filtration and ventilation equipment by the employee; usually the problem can be corrected before a dangerous situation arises by discussing the issue with the employee and altering the work environment as needed.

3. DISCUSSION

As this brief review shows, although much is known about the effects of drugs on performance, large gaps still exist. For example, even with such intensively studied drugs as alcohol, important questions remain regarding the durability of impairments, their relation to consumption indices, and the important risk factors determining individual susceptibility. In general, not enough is known regarding chronic versus acute effects of drugs, and the performance effects of barbiturates, amphetamines, and cocaine require more investigation. Given the substantial number of substance abusers who use several drugs, we also need more research on the effects of combinations of drugs on cognition.

One of the most important gaps is that few studies identify how performance deficits observed in the laboratory relate to the workplace. Most field studies have focused on impairments in functions that have obvious implications for workplace performance, such as perception, motor skills, attention, and decision making; however, such functions as judgment, abstraction, and reasoning, which are also essential for effective workplace performance, have not received much attention. It is possible, though, to draw many connections between laboratory studies and workplace performance. Toward this end, we have chosen four such categories of function: perceptual and motor skills, attention and high-speed decision making, learning and memory, and abstraction and reasoning. In Table 1, we summarize the effects of each drug on each category, with reference to the general effects on work performance.

Much of drug testing focuses on so-called safety-sensitive positions. Truck drivers and airline pilots are subject to testing, but aircraft engineers, physicians, judges, and politicians are not, even though serious consequences can result from drug-induced errors in these latter occupations. The effects of drugs on reasoning and abstraction are generally not well understood. With improved knowledge of the effects of drugs on higher cognitive functions, many occupations may come to be considered safety sensitive.

In conclusion, a large number of psychoactive substances influence cognitive function, and these cognitive effects are central to drug use: Some individuals specifically take drugs to control their own thought processes and mental capacity. Thus, we should expect to find drugs in any situation in which they are perceived to have cognitive utility, including the workplace. It is most desirable

Table 1
Workplace-Related Performance Impairments Induced by Certain Drugs

	Perceptual and Motor Skills	Attention and Decision Making	Learning and Memory	Abstraction and Reasoning
Alcohol	Impaired even at low doses and during hangover	Impaired even at low doses	Impaired at moderate doses	Impaired at moderate doses
Benzodiazepines	Impaired at moderate doses	Impaired at moderate doses	Impaired at moderate doses	Insufficient data
Barbiturates	Impaired at moderate doses	Insufficient data	Impaired at moderate doses	Insufficient data
Cannabis	Impaired at moderate doses	Impaired at moderate doses	Impaired at moderate doses	Insufficient data
Opioids	Some impairment at moderate doses	Some impairment at moderate doses	Drowsiness may cause impairment	Drowsiness may cause impairment
Amphetamines and cocaine	Not strongly affected	Can be impaired after chronic use	Can be impaired after chronic use	Insufficient data
Nicotine	Some impairment in nicotine withdrawal	Some impairment in nicotine withdrawal	Insufficient data	Insufficient data
Solvents	Impaired at moderate doses	Impaired at moderate doses	Impaired at moderate doses	Impaired at moderate doses

Note: Impairments noted refer to typical acute doses of the drug unless otherwise stated. This is a broad guideline only; refer to the text for the specific drug and process. Definitions of low, moderate, and high dosage levels are somewhat arbitrary and are based on typical doses for a particular drug.

for drug testing to emphasize the actual performance impairments produced by drugs. The large gaps that remain in our understanding of the effects of drugs on performance, however, need to be addressed. Without such knowledge, it is difficult or impossible to establish whether an employee is actually impaired by a particular drug. Future research on the effects of drugs on higher mental processes promises to enhance our understanding and use of the concept of safety-sensitive occupations.

REFERENCES

Adams, K. M., Rennick, P., Schoof, K., and Keegan, J., 1975, Neuropsychological measurement of drug effects: Polydrug research, *Journal of Psychedelic Drugs* **7:**151–160.

Alexander, B. K., and Hadaway, P. F., 1982, Opiate addiction: The case for an adaptive orientation, *Psychological Bulletin* **92:**367–381.

American Psychiatric Association, 1987, *Diagnostic and Statistical Manual,* 3rd ed.—revised, American Psychiatric Association, Washington, DC.

Ardila, A., Rosselli, M., and Strumwasser, S., 1991, Neuropsychological deficits in chronic cocaine abusers, *International Journal of Neuroscience* **57:**73–79.

Ashcraft, M. H., 1989, *Human Memory and Cognition,* Scott, Foresman & Company, Glenview, IL.

Ashton, A., and Stepney, R., 1982, *Smoking: Psychology and Pharmacology,* Tavistock, London.

Baldessarini, R. J., 1990, Drugs and the treatment of psychiatric disorders, in: *Goodman & Gilman's The Pharmacological Basis of Therapeutics,* 8th ed. (A. G. Gilman, T. W. Rall, A. S. Nies, and P. Taylor, eds.), pp. 383–435, Macmillan, New York.

Birnbaum, I. M., and Parker, E. S., 1977, Acute effects of alcohol on storage and retrieval, in: *Alcohol and Human Memory* (I. M. Birnbaum and E. S. Parker, eds.), pp. 99–108, Lawrence Erlbaum Associates, Hillsdale, NJ.

Bowman, M., and Pihl, R. O., 1973, Cannabis: Psychological effects of chronic heavy use: A controlled study of intellectual functioning of chronic heavy users of high potency cannabis, *Psychopharmacologia* **29:**159–170.

Bradley, C. M., and Nicholson, A. N., 1986, Effects of a mu-opioid receptor agonist (codeine phosphate) on visuo-motor coordination and dynamic visual acuity in man, *British Journal of Clinical Pharmacology* **22:**507–512.

Brecher, E. M., and the Editors of *Consumer Reports,* 1972, *Licit and Illicit Drugs,* Little, Brown and Company, Boston.

Brison, R. J., 1990, Risk of automobile accidents in cigarette smokers, *Canadian Journal of Public Health* **81:**102–106.

Brown, J., Brown, M., and Bowes, J. B., 1983, Effects of lorazepam on rate of forgetting, on retrieval from semantic memory and on manual dexterity, *Neuropsychologia* **21:**501–512.

Bruhn, P., and Maage, N., 1975, Intellectual and neuropsychological functions in young men with heavy and long-term patterns of drug abuse, *American Journal of Psychiatry* **132:**397–401.

Cappell, H. D., and Pliner, P., 1974, Regulation of the self-administration of marijuana by psychological and pharmacological variables, *Psychopharmacologia* **40:**65-76.

Carlen, P. L., and Wilkinson, D. A., 1987, Reversibility of alcohol-related brain damage: Clinical and experimental observations, *Acta Medica Scandinavica (Suppl.)* **717:**19–26.

Carlen, P. L., Wortzman, G., Holgate, R. C., Wilkinson, D. A., and Rankin, J. G., 1978, Reversible cerebral atrophy in recently abstinent chronic alcoholics measured by computed tomography scans, *Science* **200:**1076–1078.

Carlin, A. S., 1986, Neuropsychological consequences of drug abuse, in: *Neuropsychological Assessment of Neuropsychiatric Disorders* (I. Grant and K. M. Adams, eds.), pp. 478–497, Oxford University Press, New York.

Chesher, G. B., 1989, Understanding the opioid analgesics and their effects on skills performance, *Alcohol, Drugs and Driving* **5:**111–138.

Cimbura, G., Warren, R. A., Bennett, R. C., Lucas, D. M., and Simpson, H. M., 1980, *Drugs Detected in Fatally Injured Drivers and Pedestrians in the Province of Ontario,* Traffic Injury Research Foundation of Canada, Ottawa.

Clarke, P. R. F., Eccersley, P. S., Frisby, J. P., and Thornton, J. A., 1970, The amnesic effect of diazepam (Valium), *British Journal of Anaesthesiology* **42:**690–697.

Coambs, R. B., 1987, The effects of diazepam on decision processes and memory access, Doctoral dissertation, University of Toronto.

Coambs, R. B., Poulos, C. X., and Cappell, H. D., 1986, Diazepam impairs long-term memory storage and retrieval, but not short-term memory, in: *Proceedings of the 34th International Congress on Alcoholism and Drug Dependence,* pp. 160–162, International Council on Alcohol and Addictions, Lausanne, Switzerland.

Cutting, J., 1978, Relationship between Korsakoff's syndrome and alcoholic dementia, *British Journal of Psychiatry* **132:**240–251.

Darley, C. F., and Tinklenberg, J. R., 1974, Marijuana and memory, in: *Marijuana: Effects on Human Behavior* (L. L. Miller, ed.), Academic Press, New York.

Deahl, M., 1991, Cannabis and memory loss, *British Journal of Addiction* **86:**249–252.

Dornbush, R. L., 1974, Marijuana and memory: Effects of smoking on storage, *Transactions of the New York Academy of Sciences* **36:**94–100.

Edwards, C., Gard, P. R., Handley, S. L., Hunter, M., and Whittington, R. M., 1982, Distalgesic and ethanol impaired function, *Lancet* **1982:**384.

Edwards, J. A., Wesnes, K., Warburton, D. M., and Gale, A., 1985, Evidence of more rapid stimulus evaluation following cigarette smoking, *Addictive Behaviors* **10:**113–126.

Eliany, M., Giesbrecht, N., Nelson, M., Wellman, B., and Wortley, S., eds., 1990, *National Alcohol and Other Drugs Survey (1989). Highlights Report,* Health and Welfare Canada, Ottawa.

Ellinwood, E. H., and Heatherly, D. G., 1985, Benzodiazepines, the popular minor tranquilizers: Dynamics of effect on driving skills, *Accident Analysis and Prevention* **17:**283–290.

Ferraro, D. P., 1980, Acute effects of marijuana on human memory and cognition, in: *Marijuana Research Findings: 1980,* NIDA Research Monograph, No. 31, DHHS Publication No. ADM 80-1001, R. C. Petersen, ed.), pp. 98–119, US Government Printing Office, Washington, DC.

Fields, S., and Fullerton, J., 1975, Influence of heroin addiction on neuropsychological functioning, *Journal of Consulting and Clinical Psychology* **43:**114.

Fischman, M. W., 1984, The behavioral pharmacology of cocaine in humans, in: Cocaine: *Pharmacology, Effects, and Treatment of Abuse,* NIDA Research Monograph, No. 50, DHHS Publication No. ADM 84-1326 (J. Grabowski, ed.), pp. 72–91, U.S. Government Printing Office, Washington, DC.

Fornazzari, L., Wilkinson, D. A., Kapur, B. M., and Carlen, P. L., 1983, Cerebellar, cortical, and functional impairment in toluene abusers, *Acta Neurologica Scandinavica* **67:**319–329.

Franck, D. H., 1983, "If you drink, don't drive" motto now applies to hangovers as well, *Journal of the American Medical Association* **250:**1657–1658.

Frankenhaeuser, M., Myrsten, A., Post, B., and Johansson, G., 1971, Behavioural and physiological effects of cigarette smoking in a monotonous situation, *Psychopharmacologia* **22:**1-7.

Frith, C. D., and Done, D. J., 1983, Stereotyped responding by schizophrenic patients on a two-choice guessing task, *Psychological Medicine* **13:**779–786.

Gawin, F. H., and Kleber, H. D., 1986, Abstinence symptomatology and psychiatric diagnosis in chronic cocaine abusers: Clinical observations, *Archives of General Psychiatry* **43:**107–113.

Ghoneim, M. M,. Mewaldt, S. P., Berie, J. L., and Hinrichs, J. V., 1981, Memory and performance effects of single and 3-week administration of diazepam, *Psychopharmacology* **73:**147–151.

Ghoneim, M. M., Mewaldt, S. P., and Hinrichs, J. V., 1984, Dose-response analysis of the behavioral effects of diazepam, II: Psychomotor performance, cognition and mood, *Psychopharmacology* **82:**296-300.

Ghoneim, M. M., Mewaldt, S. P., and Thatcher, J. W., 1975, The effect of diazepam and fentanyl on mental, psychomotor and electroencephalographic functions and their rate of recovery, *Psychopharmacologia* **44:**61–66.

Goodwin, D. W., Hill, S. Y., Hopper, S., and Viesselman, J. O., 1975, Alcoholic blackouts and Korsakoff's syndrome, in: *Alcohol Intoxication and Withdrawal, Experimental studies II* (M. M. Gross, ed.), pp. 585–593, Plenum Press, New York.

Gottschalk, L. A., 1977, Effects of certain benzodiazepine derivatives on disorganization of thought as manifested in speech, *Current Therapeutic Research* **21:**192-206.

Grant, I., Adams, K. M., Carlin, A. S., Rennick, P. M., Judd, L. L., and Schoof, K., 1978, The collaborative neuropsychological study of polydrug users, *Archives of General Psychiatry* **35:**1063–1074.

Grant, I., Rochford, J., Fleming, T., and Stunkard, H., 1973, A neuropsychological assessment of the effects of moderate marihuana use, *Journal of Nervous and Mental Disease* **156:**278–280.

Guerra, D., Solé, A., Camí, J., and Tobeña, A., 1987, Neuropsychological performance in opiate addicts after rapid detoxification, *Drug and Alcohol Dependence* **20:**261–270.

Harper, C. G., Kril, J. J., and Holloway, R. L., 1985, Brain atrophy in chronic alcoholics: A pathological study, *British Medical Journal* **290:**501-504.

Hartman, D. E., 1988, *Neuropsychological Toxicology: Identification and Assessment of Human Neurotoxic Syndromes,* Pergamon Press, New York.

Hatsukami, D. K., Hughes, J. R., Pickens, R. W., and Svikis, D., 1984, Tobacco withdrawal symptoms: An experimental analysis, *Psychopharmacology* **84:**231–236.

Heimstra, N. W., Bancroft, N. R., and DeKock, A. R., 1967, Effects of smoking upon sustained performance in a simulated driving task, *Annals of the New York Academy of Sciences* **142:**295–307.

Hendler, N., Cimini, C., Ma, T., and Long, D., 1980, A comparison of cognitive impairment due to benzodiazepines and to narcotics, *American Journal of Psychiatry* **137:**828–830.

Henningfield, J., 1987, Tobacco dependence: Behavioral pharmacological basis for nicotine replacement, Presented at the 95th Annual Convention of the American Psychological Association, New York.

Herning, R. I., Hooker, W. D., and Jones, R. T., 1987, Cocaine effects on electroencephalographic cognitive event-related potentials and performance, *Electroencephalography and Clinical Neurophysiology* **66:**34–42.

Hindmarch, I., Kerr, J. S., and Sherwood, N., 1990, Effects of nicotine gum on psychomotor performance in smokers and non-smokers, *Psychopharmacology* **100:**535–541.

Hinrichs, J. V., Mewaldt, S. P., Ghoneim, M. M., and Berie, J. L., 1982, Diazepam and learning: Assessment of acquisition deficits, *Pharmacology, Biochemistry, & Behavior* **17:**165–170.

Hooker, W. D., and Jones, R. T., 1987, Increased susceptibility to memory intrusions and the Stroop interference effect during acute marijuana intoxication. *Psychopharmacology* **91:**20–24.

Hughes, J. R., Higgins, S. T., and Hatsukami, D., 1988, Effects of abstinence from tobacco: A critical review, in: *Research Advances in Alcohol and Drug Problems,* Vol. 10 (L. T. Kozlowski, H. M. Annis, H. D. Cappell, F. B. Glaser, M. S. Goodstadt, Y. Israel, H. Kalant, E. M. Sellers, and E. R. Vingilis, eds.), Plenum Press, New York.

Huntley, M. S., 1974, Effects of alcohol, uncertainty, and novelty upon response selection, *Psychopharmacologia* **39:**259–266.

International Narcotics Control Board, 1991, Narcotic drugs: Estimated world requirements for 1991,

Statistics for 1989, United Nations Publication, 1990: Sales No. E/F/S.90.XI.4, United Nations, New York.

Jackson, J. H., 1931–1932, Selected writings of John Hughlings Jackson, *American Journal of Psychiatry* **133:**384–388.

Judd, L. L., and Grant, I., 1975, Brain dysfunction in chronic sedative users, *Journal of Psychedelic Drugs* **7:**143–149.

Karvinen, E., Miettinen, M., and Ahlman, K., 1962, Physical performance during hangover, *Quarterly Journal of Studies on Alcohol* **23:**208–215.

Kelly, M., Myrsten, A., Neri, A., and Rydberg, U., 1970, Effects and after-effects of alcohol on physiological and psychological functions in man: A controlled study, *Blutalkohol* **7:**422–436.

Khantzian, E. J., Mack, J. F., and Schatzberg, A. F., 1974, Heroin use as an attempt to cope: Clinical observations, *American Journal of Psychiatry* **131:**160–164.

Kiplinger, G. F., Sokol, G., and Rodda, B. E., 1974, Effect of combined alcohol and propoxyphene on human performance, *Archives Internationales de Pharmacodynamie* **212:**175–180.

Kleinknecht, R. A., and Donaldson, D. A., 1975, A review of the effects of diazepam on cognitive and psychomotor performance, *Journal of Nervous and Mental Disease* **161:**399–411.

Kramer, L. D., Locke, G. E., Ogunyemi, A., and Nelson, L., 1990, Cocaine-related seizures in adults, *American Journal of Drug and Alcohol Abuse* **16:**307–317.

Kvalseth, T. O., 1977, Effects of marijuana on human reaction time and motor control, *Perceptual and Motor Skills* **45:**935–939.

Lamberty, G. J., Beckwith, B. E., Petros, T. V., and Ross, A. R., 1990, Posttrial treatment with ethanol enhances recall of prose narratives, *Physiology & Behavior* **48:**653-658.

Lezak, M. D., 1983, *Neuropsychological Assessment,* Oxford University Press, New York.

Linnoila, M., and Hakkinen, S., 1974, Effects of diazepam and codeine alone and in combination with alcohol on simulated driving, *Clinical Pharmacology and Therapeutics* **15:**368–373.

Lishman, W. A., 1986, Alcoholic dementia: A hypothesis, *Lancet* 1986(1):1184–1186.

Lister, R. G., 1985, The amnesic action of benzodiazepines in man, *Neuroscience & Biobehavioral Reviews* **9:**87–94.

Lister, R. G., and File, S. E., 1984, The nature of lorazepam-induced amnesia, *Psychopharmacology* **83:**183–187.

Lucki, I., Rickels, K., and Geller, A. M., 1985, Psychomotor performance following the long-term use of benzodiazepines, *Psychopharmacology Bulletin* **21:**93-96.

Luria, A. R., 1973, The frontal lobes and the regulation of behavior, in: *Psychophysiology of the Frontal Lobes* (K. H. Pribram and A. R. Luria, eds.), pp. 3–26, Academic Press, New York.

Mackworth, N., 1950, Researches in the measurement of human performance, MRC. Special Report No. 268, Her Majesty's Stationery Office, London.

Mangan, G. L., 1982, The effects of cigarette smoking on vigilance performance, *Journal of General Psychiatry* **106:**77–83.

Manschreck, T. C., Schneyer, M. L., Weisstein, C. C., Laughery, J., Rosenthal, J., Celada, T., and Berner, J., 1990, Freebase cocaine and memory, *Comprehensive Psychiatry* **31:**369–375.

Marusarz, T. Z., and Koh, S. D., 1980, Contextual effects on the short-term memory retrieval of schizophrenic young adults, *Journal of Abnormal Psychology* **89:**683–696.

Meade, T. W., and Wald, N. J., 1977, Cigarette smoking patterns during the working day, *British Journal of Preventive and Social Medicine* **31:**25–29.

Mendhiratta, S. S., Varma, V. K., Dang, R., Malhotra, A. K., Das, K., and Nehra, R., 1988, Cannabis and cognitive functions: A re-evaluation study, *British Journal of Addiction* **83:**749–753.

Modell, J. G., and Mountz, J. M., 1990, Drinking and flying—the problem of alcohol use by pilots, *New England Journal of Medicine* **323:**455–461.

Mody, C. K., Miller, B. L., McIntyre, H. B., Cobb, S. K., and Goldberg, M. A., 1988, Neurological complications of cocaine abuse, *Neurology* **38:**1189–1193.

Moskowitz, H., and DePry, D., 1968, Differential effect of alcohol on auditory vigilance and divided-attention tasks, *Quarterly Journal of Studies on Alcohol* **29:**54-63.

Moskowitz, H., and Smiley, A., 1982, Effects of chronically administered buspirone and diazepam on driving-related skills performance, *Journal of Clinical Psychiatry* **43:**45–55.

Murray, J. B., 1986, Marijuana's effects on human cognitive functions, psychomotor functions, and personality, *Journal of General Psychology* **113:**23–55.

Musk, A. W., and Shean, R. E., 1986, The treatment of cigarette dependence, *World Health Forum* **7:**86–87.

Myrsten, A., Elgerot, A., and Endgren, B., 1977, Effects of abstinence from tobacco smoking on physiological and psychological arousal levels in habitual smokers, *Psychosomatic Medicine* **39:**25–38.

Negrete, J. C., and Murphy, H. B. M., 1967, Psychological deficit in chewers of coca leaf, *Bulletin on Narcotics* **19:**11–18.

Newhouse, P. A., Belenky, G., Thomas, M., Thorne, D., Sing, H. C., and Fertig, J., 1989, The effects of d-amphetamine on arousal, cognition, and mood after prolonged total sleep deprivation, *Neuropsychopharmacology* **2:**153–164.

Nicholi, A. M., 1984, Cocaine use among the college age group: Biological and psychological effects: Clinical and laboratory research findings, *Journal of American College Health* **32:**258–261.

Nikaido, A. M., Ellinwood, E. H., Heatherly, D. G., and Gupta, S. K., 1990, Age-related increase in CNS sensitivity to benzodiazepines as assessed by task difficulty, *Psychopharmacology* **100:**90–97.

O'Malley, S., Adamse, M., Heaton, R. K., and Gawin, F. H., 1992, Neuropsychological impairment in chronic cocaine abusers, *American Journal of Drug and Alcohol Abuse* **18:**131–144.

Parker, E. S,. and Weingartner, H., 1984, Retrograde facilitation of human memory by drugs, in: *Psychobiology of Cognition* (H. Weingartner and E. S. Parker, eds.), Erlbaum, Hillsdale, NJ.

Parsons, O. A., Butters, N. M., and Nathan, P., eds., 1987, *Neuropsychology of Alcoholism: Implications for Diagnosis and Treatment,* Guilford Press, New York.

Pascual-Leone, A., Dhuna, A., Altafullah, I., and Anderson, D. C., 1990, Cocaine-induced seizures, *Neurology* **40:**404–407.

Peele, S., 1985, *The Meaning of Addiction,* D.C. Heath & Co, Lexington, MA.

Petros, T. V., Kerbel, N., Beckwith, B. E., Sacks, G., and Sarafolean, M., 1985, The effects of alcohol on prose memory, *Physiology and Behavior* **35:**43–46.

Ray, R., Prabhu, G. G., Mohan, D., Nath, L. M., and Neki, J. S., 1978, The association between chronic cannabis use and cognitive functions, *Drug and Alcohol Dependence* **3:**365–368.

Relman, A. S., 1982, Marijuana and health, *New England Journal of Medicine* **306:**603–604.

Resnick, R. B., and Resnick, E. B., 1984, Cocaine abuse and its treatment, *Psychiatric Clinics of North America* **7:**713–728.

Robinson, C. D., and Moskowitz, H., 1985, Methadone maintenance treatment and aspects of skilled performance, in: *Alcohol, Drugs and Traffic Safety* (S. Kaye and G. W. Meier, eds.), pp. 1145–1157, U.S. Department of Transportation, Washington, DC.

Ron, M. A., Acker, W., Shaw, G. K., and Lishman, W. A., 1982, Computerized tomography of the brain in chronic alcoholism: A survey and follow-up study, *Brain* **105:**497–514.

Rounsaville, B. J., Jones, C., Novelly, R. A., and Kleber, H., 1982, Neuropsychological functioning in opiate addicts, *Journal of Nervous and Mental Disease* **170:**209–216.

Schaeffer, J., Andrysiak, T., and Ungerleider, J. T., 1981, Cognition and long-term use of ganja (cannabis), *Science* **213:**465–466.

Schalen, L., Pyykko, I., Korttila, K., Magnusson, M., and Enbom, H., 1988, Effects of intravenously given baribturate and diazepam on eye motor performance in man, *Advances in Oto-Rhino-Laryngology* **42**:260–264.

Scharf, M. B., Fletcher, K., and Graham, J. P., 1988, Comparative amnesic effects of benzodiazepine hypnotic agents, *Journal of Clinical Psychiatry* **49**:134–137.

Schneider, N. G., Jarvik, M. E., and Forsythe, A. B., 1984, Nicotine vs placebo gum in the alleviation of withdrawal during smoking cessation, *Addictive Behaviors* **9**:149–156.

Schwartz, R. H., Gruenewald, P. J., Klitzner, M., and Fedio, P., 1989, Short-term memory impairment in cannabis-dependent adolescents, *American Journal of Diseases of Children* **143**:1214–1219.

Seppälä, T., Leino, T., Linnoila, M., Huttunen, M., and Ylikahri, R., 1976, Effects of hangover on psychomotor skills related to driving: Modification by fructose and glucose, *Acta Pharmacologica et Toxicologica* **38**:209–218.

Shiffman, S. M., 1979, The tobacco withdrawal syndrome, in: *Cigarette Smoking as a Dependence Process,* NIDA Research Monograph, No. 23 (N. A. Krasnegor, ed.), pp. 158–184, U.S. Government Printing Office, Washington, DC.

Shiffman, S. M., 1982, Relapse following smoking cessation: A situational analysis, *Journal of Consulting and Clinical Psychology* **50**:71–86.

Shiffman, S., and Wills, T. A., 1985, *Coping and Substance Use,* Academic Press, Orlando, FL.

Skegg, D. C. G., Richards, S. M., and Doll, R., 1979, Minor tranquilizers and road accidents, *British Medical Journal* **1979**(1):917–919.

Smart, R. G., Adlaf, E. M., and Walsh, G. W., 1991, *The Ontario Student Drug Use Survey: Trends between 1977 and 1991,* Addiction Research Foundation of Ontario, Toronto.

Smith, C. M., and Barnes, G. M., 1983, Signs and symptoms of hangover: Prevalence and relationship to alcohol use in a general adult population, *Drug and Alcohol Dependence* **11**:249–269.

Smith, G. M., Semke, C. W., and Beecher, H. K., 1962, Objective evidence of mental effects of heroin, morphine and placebo in normal subjects, *Journal of Pharmacology and Experimental Therapeutics* **136**:53–58.

Snyder, F. R., and Henningfield, J. E., 1989, Effects of nicotine administration following 12 hours of tobacco deprivation: Assessment on computerized performance tasks, *Psychopharmacology* **97**:17–22.

Spilich, G. J., 1987, Cigarette smoking and memory: Good news and bad news, Presented at the 95th Annual Convention of the American Psychological Association, New York.

Steele, C. M., and Josephs, R. A., 1990, Alcohol myopia: Its prized and dangerous effects, *American Psychologist* **45**:921–933.

Sternberg, S., 1975, Memory scanning: New findings and current controversies, *Quarterly Journal of Experimental Psychology* **27**:1–32.

Strang, J., and Gurling, H., 1989, Computerized tomography and neuropsychological assessment in long-term high-dose heroin addicts, *British Journal of Addiction* **84**:1011–1019.

Sweeney, D. F., 1990, Alcoholic blackouts: Legal implications, *Journal of Substance Abuse Treatment* **7**:155–159.

Tharp, V. K., Rundell, O. H., Lester, B. K., and Williams, H. L., 1974, Alcohol and information processing, *Psychopharmacologia* **40**:33–52.

Tharp, V. K., Rundell, O. H., Lester, B. K., and Williams, H. L., 1975, Alcohol and secobarbital: Effects in information processing, in: *Alcohol Intoxication and Withdrawal, Experimental Studies: Advances in Experimental Medicine and Biology* (M. M. Gross, ed.), pp. 537–552, Plenum Press, New York.

Tinklenberg, J. R., and Taylor, J. L., 1984, Assessments of drug effects on human memory functions, in: *Neuropsychology of Memory* (L. R. Squire and N. Butters, eds.), pp. 213–223, Guilford Press, New York.

Tulving, E., 1983, *Elements of Episodic Memory,* Oxford University Press, New York.

Uddo-Crane, M., 1990, Effects of cocaine use and withdrawal on clinical memory and new learning, *Dissertation Abstracts International* **51**:1008–1009.

United States Department of Health and Human Services (1993), *National Household Survey on Drug Abuse: 1991* (Publication No. SMA 93-1979), U.S.D.H.H.S., Rockville, MD.

United States Secretary of Health, Education and Welfare, 1980, *Marihuana and Health: Eighth Annual Report to the U.S. Congress.* National Institute on Drug Abuse, Rockville, MD.

Varma, V. K., Malhotra, A. K., Dang, R., Das, K., and Nehra, R., 1988, Cannabis and cognitive functions: A prospective study, *Drug and Alcohol Dependence* **21**:147–152.

Victor, M., Adams, R. D., and Collins, G. H., 1989, *The Wernicke–Korsakoff Syndrome and Related Neurological Disorders Due to Alcoholism and Malnutrition,* 2nd ed., F.A. Davis, Philadelphia.

Walker, D. W., Hunter, B. E., Barnes, D. E., and Riley, J. N., 1980, An animal model of alcohol-induced brain damage: A behavioral and anatomical analysis, in: *Cerebral Deficits in Alcoholism* (D. A. Wilkinson, ed.), pp. 123–147, Addiction Research Foundation, Toronto.

Washton, A. M., and Tatarsky, A., 1984, Adverse effects of cocaine abuse, in: *Problems of Drug Dependence, 1983: Proceedings of the 4th Annual Scientific Meeting of the Committee on Problems of Drug Dependence, Inc.,* NIDA Research Monograph, No. 49, DHHS Publication No. ADM 84-1316 (L. S. Harris, ed.), pp. 247–254, U.S. Government Printing Office, Washington, DC.

Weckowicz, T. E., and Janssen, D. V., 1973, Cognitive functions, personality traits, and social values in heavy marijuana smokers and nonsmoker controls, *Journal of Abnormal Psychology* **81**:264–269.

Wesnes, K., and Warburton, D. M., 1978, The effects of cigarette smoking and nicotine tablets upon human attention, in: *Smoking behaviour: Physiological and Psychological Influences* (R. E. Thornton, ed.), p. 131–147, Churchill-Livingston, London.

Wesnes, K., and Warburton, D. M., 1983, Effects of nicotine on stimulus sensitivity and response bias in a visual vigilance task, *Neuropsychobiology* **9**:41–44.

Wesnes, K., and Warburton, D. M., 1984, The effects of cigarettes of varying yield on rapid information processing performance, *Psychopharmacology* **82**:338–342.

Williams, H. L., Rundell, O. H., and Landgrave, T. S., 1981, Dose effects of secobarbital in a Sternberg memory scanning task, *Psychopharmacology* **72**:161-165.

Wittenborn, J. R., 1979, Effects of benzodiazepines on psychomotor performance, *British Journal of Pharmacology* **7**:61S–67S.

Yesavage, J. A., Leirer, V. O., Denari, M., and Hollister, L. E., 1985, Carry-over effects of marijuana intoxication on aircraft pilot performance: A preliminary report, *American Journal of Psychiatry* **142**:1325–1329.

Zapata-Oritz, V., 1976, The chewing of coca leaves in Peru, *International Journal of the Addictions* **5**:287–294.

Zipursky, R. B., Lim, K. O., and Pfefferbaum, A., 1989, MRi study of brain changes with short-term abstinence from alcohol, *Alcoholism: Clinical and Experimental Research* **13**:664–666.

5

Drug Testing Methods and Interpretations of Test Results

BHUSHAN KAPUR

1. INTRODUCTION

As interest increases in employment-related drug testing, the technologies and the interpretive skills of analysts continue to evolve. Although recent literature indicates that significant refinements and modifications to drug testing technology have been made, the complexity of drug effects is so great that many problems exist in interpretation of the test results. The most frequent problems that confront the toxicology laboratory relate to developing technology that can determine how much and when the drug was taken, how long after use the tests are capable of showing positive results, the causes and rates of false positives and false negatives, and how tests can be "beaten" by employees. These problems will be discussed in this chapter, and the various laboratory procedures that are used to combat these problems will be examined.

2. DRUG PROPERTIES: ABSORPTION, DISTRIBUTION, AND ELIMINATION PHASES

Detection of a drug depends largely on the absorption, distribution, and elimination properties of the drug. There are various routes of drug administra-

BHUSHAN KAPUR • Clinical Laboratories, Addiction Research Foundation, Toronto, Ontario M5S 2S1, Canada.

Research Advances in Alcohol and Drug Problems, Volume 11: Drug Testing in the Workplace, edited by Scott Macdonald and Paul M. Roman. Plenum Press, New York, 1994.

tion: oral (drinking; e.g., alcohol), intravenous (injected into a vein; e.g., heroin) and inhalation via smoking (e.g., marijuana), snorting (e.g., cocaine), or sniffing (e.g., glue). Drugs taken orally are usually the slowest to be *absorbed* (i.e., for the drug to reach the brain and other body organs), whereas intravenous routes result in the fastest absorption. Once the absorbed drug enters the bloodstream, it is rapidly *distributed* to the various tissues in the body. The amount of drug stored depends on the quantity, duration of ingestion, and frequency of use.

Some drugs are fat (or lipid) soluble and are deposited in fat tissues. For example, δ^9-tetrahydrocannabinol (THC), the active ingredient in marijuana, is highly fat soluble, resulting in rapid reductions in blood levels of δ^9-THC as the drug is being distributed to the various tissues (Huestis, Henningfield, & Coner, 1992). Some studies have shown that δ^9-THC levels peak and start to decline in half the time it takes to smoke a marijuana "joint." Concentrations are known to fall by almost 90% in the first hour (Chaing & Burnett, 1984; Huestis et al., 1992), suggesting that a higher degree of sophistication in laboratory analysis is needed to detect fat-soluble drugs. Depending on the amount of drug stored, however, detection can be made in the urine for as long as 60 days after last use (Dackis, Pottash, Annitto, & Gold, 1982). Ethanol or ethyl alcohol, the beverage alcohol that is consumed by people, is not fat soluble and is distributed in the total body water (Kalant, 1971). Because blood is mostly made up of water, the presence of alcohol is more easily detectable than that of fat-soluble drugs like δ^9-THC. (The terms *ethanol* and *alcohol* are used interchangeably in this document.)

The absorption and distribution phases are followed by an *elimination* phase. The liver, where the drugs are metabolized as blood circulates through the organ, is the major detoxification center in the body. The metabolites are then excreted into the urine through the kidneys. At the same time, drugs deposited in fat tissues are also slowly released into the bloodstream and metabolized.

Drugs vary in terms of their elimination half-life, which is the time required for the blood levels to decline by 50% (see Table 1). The half-life of a drug is heavily influenced by a variety of factors, including the individual's age, sex, and physical condition as well as clinical status. A compromised liver and concurrent presence of another disease or drug have the potential of enhancing the toxic effects of the drug by slowing down the elimination process. Under different clinical conditions, however, this process may be sped up. Therefore, great variation can be found in the half-lives of the same drug.

Approximately six half-lives are required to eliminate 99% of any drug. Because cocaine's half-life is relatively short, averaging 1 hour (Baselt, 1982, pp. 193–198), only 6 hours are needed for elimination of 99% of the drug. Cocaine's metabolites, though, have a longer half-life and can be detected for a considerably longer period of time through urine drug assays. In contrast, phenobarbital has a half-life of 80 to 120 hours, so that at least 480 hours (or 20 days) are required to eliminate 99% of the drug. Because there is much variation

Table 1
Drug Half-Lives and Approximate Urine Detection Periods

Drug	Half-life[a]	Detection Period[b]
Methamphetamine	12–34 hours	2–3 days
Amphetamine (metabolite)	7–34 hours	
Heroin	60–90 minutes	few minutes
Morphine (metabolite)	1.3–6.7 hours	1–2 days
Phencyclidine (PCP)	7–16 hours	2–3 days
Cocaine	0.5–1.5 hours	a few hours
Benzoylecgonine (metabolite)	5–7 hours	3–5 days
δ^9-Tetrahydrocannabinol	14–38 hours	90% fall in 1 hour (blood)
δ^9-Tetrahydrocannabolic acid (marijuana metabolite in urine)		Depending on use few days to many weeks
Alcohol (Ethanol)	Blood levels fall by an average of 15–18 mg/100 ml/hour	1.5–12 hours depending on the peak blood level. Urine typically positive for an additional 1–2 hours

[a]Information from Baselt (1982).
[b]The detection period is very much dose dependent. The larger the dose, the longer the period the drug/metabolite can be detected in the urine.

in the half-life of different drugs and the absolute amount of drug present can be very small, it is crucial that the appropriate body fluid for analysis is selected for testing.

Elimination of ethanol follows a very different pattern. Its levels decline almost linearly over time, with the average elimination rate being between 15 mg/100 ml to 20 mg/100 ml (0.015% to 0.02%) per hour, although ranges between 10 mg/100 ml to 30 mg/100 ml (0.01% to 0.03%) per hour have also been observed. In the alcoholic patient, the elimination rate is generally higher. In forensic calculations, a rate of 15 mg/100 ml (0.015% per hour) is usually used.

3. TYPES OF TESTING: BLOOD, URINE, AND HAIR SPECIMENS

Blood and urine are the most commonly used fluids in the analysis for drugs. Blood, which is obtained by an invasive procedure, is available only in small quantities, and levels in blood are low. Urine is the preferred sample of choice because it is available in larger volumes, contains the metabolite, and requires less invasive procedures in its collection. Both sampling procedures, however, are limited in their ability, as they determine the *absolute* amount of drug present in the fluid being examined. This quantity is dependent upon the amount of the drug used and when it was last used, as well as the half-life of the drug.

More recently, hair samples have been used by some organizations. There are a number of technical problems, though, that must be overcome before hair can be used as a definitive proof of drug use. For example, it is known that race, age, sex, season of the year, and diet affect the rate at which hair grows; thus, dating is extremely difficult if not impossible. Additionally, such considerations as how soon the drugs appear in the hair, the effects of hair treatments and detergents, adhesion, diffusion, and stability of drugs in the hair are only a few of the technological problems faced by researchers in the area (Bailey, 1989; Henderson, Harkey, Zhour, & Jones, 1992; Koren, Klein, Forman, & Graham, 1992). An advisory committee of Society of Forensic Toxicology (1992) has reported that "because of these deficiencies, results of hair analysis alone do not constitute sufficient evidence of drug use for application in the workplace." All existing technologies at the moment are limited in terms of determining how much or when the drug was consumed.

Various body fluids e.g., sweat, saliva, blood, and urine have been used for alcohol analysis. Breath, though not a body fluid, is commonly used by law enforcement authorities. Although a number of variables (Jones, 1978) can affect breath/blood ratio, a 2100:1 alveolar breath:blood conversion ratio has been used and accepted for Breathalyzers (Harger, Raney, Bridwell, & Ketchel, 1950). Breath testing equipment calibrated with this conversion factor, however, consistently underestimate actual blood alcohol concentrations (O'Neill, Williams, & Dubowski, 1983). Accuracy of breath analysis results is subject to various instrumental and biological factors (Dubowski, 1975; Simpson, 1987). Potential errors in breath analysis can also be caused by the presence of residual alcohol in the mouth. Immediately after drinking there is enough alcohol vapor in the mouth to give artificially high concentrations on breath analysis. Generally this effect disappears 20 minutes after drinking, but high values for as long as 45 minutes have been reported (Payne, Hill, & King, 1966).

Although both blood and saliva concentrations reflect the current blood alcohol concentration (BAC), blood sampling generally is used in hospitals to assess the patient in the casualty wards. In programs requiring monitoring of alcohol use, urine is probably the sample of choice (Peachey & Kapur, 1986). Urine alcohol concentration, which represents the average blood alcohol concentration between voiding, has the potential of producing positive results in cases where blood may be negative.

4. MEASURING IMPAIRMENT

Except for alcohol, the degree to which a person is influenced or impaired by a drug at the time of the test cannot be determined. Correlations between positive blood levels and degree of impairment are usually stronger than those between urine levels and degree of impairment; however, neither blood or urine tests are sufficiently accurate. Human studies using marijuana and cocaine have shown that a "perceived high" is reached after the drug concentration has peaked in the blood (Chaing & Barnett, 1984). Generally, blood can only show positive results for a short time after drug consumption, whereas urine can be positive for a few days to weeks after last use. For example, metabolites of δ^9-THC (active ingredient in marijuana) that are lipid soluble can be detected in the urine from a few days to many weeks after use, depending on the drug habit of the user (Dackis et al., 1982). Excretion of the drug in urine and its concentrations are also affected by several factors, such as dilution and pH (acidity) of the urine. I have seen many cases where a strong positive urine sample for cannabinoids was found in the morning, a borderline positive in the afternoon, and a strong positive again the next morning. Similar observations have also been made for phenobarbital.

From a positive urine test we cannot determine the form in which the drug was originally taken, nor when and how much was taken. For example, crack, impure cocaine powder, or cocaine paste (which can be smoked, inhaled, injected, or chewed) all give the same result in the urine test. The consumption of poppy seeds have been reported to give positive results for opiate use because some seeds have been known to be contaminated with opium derivatives (Selavka, 1991). Similarly, consumption of herbal coca tea has resulted in positive results for cocaine use. These incidents clearly illustrate the difficulties involved in measuring impairment with urine results. The problem of interpreting urine test results is one of the major bases of concern for restricting their use in the employment setting.

There is no threshold for alcohol effects on performance or motor vehicle crash risk. Although the effects of alcohol on impairment and crash risk appear more dramatically above 80 mg/100 ml (0.08%), a review of literature (Moskowitz & Robinson, 1988; Snyder, 1991) suggests that impairment may be observed at levels as low as 15 mg/100 ml (0.015%). It is not possible to specify a level above which *all* drivers are dangerous and below which they are safe or at "normal" risk (Snyder, 1991).

Legal BAC levels differ in different countries. Some even have more than one legal limit over which the driver of a vehicle is considered as impaired. Some European countries have 50 mg/100 ml (0.05%) others have 80 mg/100 ml (0.08%) as their legal limits. In the United States, the legal limits in individual states vary between 80 mg/100 ml (0.08%) and 100 mg/100 ml (0.10%), but employees who are regulated by the Department of Transportation have a BAC legal limit of 40 mg/100 ml (0.04%). In Canada there are also two limits; BAC levels above 50 mg/100 ml (0.05%) call for suspension of driving privileges, and persons with levels above 80 mg/100 ml (0.08%) are subject to criminal charges.

5. URINE TESTING METHODS

Urine is the most commonly used fluid for drug screening (Miners, Nykodym, & Samerdyke-Traband, 1987). The methods most commonly used in toxicology laboratories are immunoassay, chromatographic, and chromatography coupled with mass spectrometry. These methods vary considerably with respect to their validity and reliability (Rothstein, 1985–1986). Thin-layer chromatography is the least expensive, valid, and reliable method. Gas chromatography coupled with mass spectrometry is considered as nearly perfect (Decresce et al., 1989), but this technology requires highly trained technologists and the most expensive equipment. Figure 1 summarizes these methods.

Immunoassays (EIA, EMIT, and FPIA)

Immunoassay methods are used for preliminary (i.e., initial) screening. Because these methods are based on an antibody-antigen reaction, small amounts of the drug or metabolite(s) can be detected. Antibodies specific to a particular drug are produced by injecting laboratory animals with the drug. These antibodies are then tagged with markers, such as an enzyme (enzyme immunoassay, or EIA), radio isotope (radioimmunoassay, or RIA), or a fluorescence (fluorescence polarization immunoassay, or FPIA) label. Reagents containing these labeled antibodies can then be introduced into urine samples, and if the specific drug being tested for is found, a reaction will occur. RIA is the oldest immunoassay method used to detect drugs. The major drawback of this method is that it requires a separation step and generates radioactive waste; it also requires special equipment to measure radioactivity.

Immunoassays typically are designed for a *class* of drugs. Thus, their specificity (the ability to detect the presence of a specific drug) is not very good, as substances that have similar chemical structures will "cross-react" and give a false positive reaction. For example, the immunoassay method for cannabinoids was developed to detect the carboxylic acid metabolite of δ^9-THC. Yet Rollins, Jennison, and Jones (1990) showed that nonsteroidal anti-inflammatory drugs, ibuprofen (a nonprescription drug in Canada), and naproxyn can give random or sporadic false positives for cannabinoids. Codeine will also give a positive reaction for the morphine (a metabolic product of heroin use) immunoassay, and many antihistamines that are available over the counter may yield positive reactions for amphetamines. Although some reagent manufacturers claim to have overcome many of these cross-reactivity problems, immunoassays are considered good screening tests only if the initial positive is confirmed by a different method.

Urine drug assay kits have been available in North America for several years. More recently, single and multiple test kits designed for home and on-site

1. IMMUNOASSAYS:

Enzyme Immunoassay (EIA)
Enzyme Multiplied Immunoassay Technique (EMIT)
Fluorescence Polarisation Immunoassay (FPIA)
Radio Immunoassay (RIA)

2. CHROMATOGRAPHIC METHODS:

Thin-Layer Chromatography (TLC)
Liquid Chromatography (HPLC)
Gas Chromatography (GC)

3. CHROMATOGRAPHY-MASS SPECTROMETRY:

Gas Chromatography–Mass Spectrometry (GC-MS)
Liquid Chromatography–Mass Spectrometry (HPLC-MS)

Figure 1. Common Drug Testing Methods.

immunoassays have also been introduced. These kits generally carry a cautionary disclaimer that positive test results must be confirmed by the reference gas chromatography/mass spectrometry method. When used in the nonlaboratory environment, they are prone to procedural inaccuracies, poor quality control, abuse, and misinterpretations; therefore, they are not recommended for testing in the workplace. The risk of labeling a person with a false positive is high without confirmatory analysis. In addition, confirmation analysis is generally very expensive when an individual sample is being tested. Figure 2 summarizes the advantages and disadvantages of immunoassay testing.

Chromatographic Methods

Separation of a mixture is the main outcome of the chromatographic method. For illustrative purposes, if one were to put a drop of ink on a blotting paper and hold the tip of the paper in water, one would observe the water rising into the paper. After a period of time and under the right conditions, the single ink spot would separate into many compounds (spots) of different colors (blue ink is a mixture of many dyes). This process, where a mixture of substances is separated in a stationary medium (filter paper), is called chromatography. Processes used in the analysis of drugs include thin-layer, gas, and liquid chromatography, as well as a combination of gas or liquid chromatography with mass spectrometry.

Thin-Layer Chromatography (TLC). TLC is most similar to the ink-separation example. This method requires extensive sample preparation and technical expertise on the part of the analyst, but it is inexpensive and very powerful if used properly. With the exception of cannabis, which requires separate sample

ADVANTAGES

1. Screening tests can be done quickly because automation and batch processing are possible.
2. Technologists doing routine clinical chemistry testing can be easily trained.
3. Detection limits are very low and can be tailored to meet the programs' screening requirements. For example, lower detection thresholds can be raised to eliminate positives resulting from passive inhalation of marijuana smoke.
4. Immunoassays are relatively inexpensive, although the single test kits can be very expensive when quality assurance and quality control samples are included.
5. Immunoassays do not require a specialized laboratory. Most clinical laboratories have automated instruments to do the procedures.

DISADVANTAGES

1. Although the tests are useful for detecting classes of drugs, specificity for individual drugs is weak.
2. Because the antibody is generated from laboratory animals, there can be a lot-to-lot or batch-to-batch variation in the antibody reagents.
3. Results must be confirmed by a non-immunoassay method.
4. A radioactive isotope is used in RIA that requires compliance with special licensing procedures, use of gamma counters to measure radioactivity, and disposal of the radioactive waste.
5. Only a single drug class can be tested for at one time.

Figure 2. Advantages and Disadvantages of Immunoassays.

preparation, a large number of drugs (e.g., cocaine, amphetamine, codeine, and morphine) can be screened at the same time. By combining different TLC systems a high degree of specificity can be obtained, although the training of the analyst is crucial because of the subjectivity involved in interpreting the results. To identify positive TLC "spots," the technologist looks for the drugs and or their metabolite patterns. In the laboratory of the Addiction Research Foundation in Ontario, a trained technologist can identify as many as 40 different drugs.

Gas Chromatography (GC). Similar to TLC, GC requires extensive sample preparation. The sample to be analyzed is introduced into a narrow bore (capillary) column with a syringe. The column, which sits inside an oven, is flushed with a carrier gas (e.g., helium or nitrogen). A mixture of substances introduced into the carrier gas is then volatilized, and the individual components of the mixture migrate through the column at different speeds. Detection takes place at the end of the heated column and is generally a destructive process. Very often the substance to be analyzed is "derivatized" to make it volatile or to change its chromatographic characteristics.

High-Performance Liquid Chromatography (HPLC). In contrast to GC, HPLC uses a liquid under high pressure, rather than a gas, to flush the column. (Thus, this technology is sometimes referred to as high-pressure liquid chromatography.) Typically, the column operates at room or slightly above room temperature. This method is generally used for substances that are difficult to volatilize (e.g., steroids) or are heat labile (e.g., benzodiazepines). The two major differences between GC and HPLC are as follows:

1. GC is a destructive method (it destroys or burns the chemical in its detector to generate the signal), whereas HPLC detection takes advantage of the electronic or chemical structure of the compound.
2. The mobile phase in GC is gas; in HPLC, it is liquid. Consequently, less sample preparation is needed for HPLC. This method also results in high specificity, but it is slower and less sensitive (i.e., unable to detect low levels) than GC.

Gas Chromatography/Mass Spectrometry (GC/MS)

GC/MS is a combination of two sophisticated technologies; gas chromatography (GC) and mass spectrometry (MS). GC physically separates (chromatographs or purifies) the compound, and MS fragments it so that a fingerprint of the chemical (or drug) can be obtained. Although sample preparation is extensive, when the methods are used together the combination is regarded as the "gold standard" by most authorities. This combination is sensitive, is specific, and can identify all types of drugs in any body fluid. Furthermore, assay sensitivity can be enhanced by treating the test substance with reagents. HPLC coupled with MS is the method of choice for substances that are difficult to volatilize (e.g., steroids).

Given the higher costs associated with GC/MS, urine samples are usually tested in batches for broad classes of drugs by immunoassays, and positive screens are later subjected to confirmation by this more expensive technique. This is the most common approach used in employment drug screening programs and is recommended by the National Institute of Drug Abuse (NIDA; 1988) in the United States. Figure 3 is a summary of the advantages and disadvantages of each method of chromatographic drug testing, and Figure 4 summarizes the advantages and disadvantages of all methods of testing.

Procedures for Alcohol Testing

Since the introduction of the micro method for alcohol analysis in blood by Widmark (1922), many new methods and modifications have been introduced. The distillation/oxidation methods are generally *nonspecific* for ethanol (Jain & Cravey, 1974a, b), whereas biochemical (spectrophotometric; Redetzki & Dees, 1976) methods using alcohol dehydrogenase (ADH) obtained from yeast and gas chromatographic (Jain, 1971) methods that are currently used, are specific for ethanol. Radiative attenuation energy technique (Cary, Whitter, & Johnson, 1984) and those using alcohol oxidase method are nonspecific and will detect not

ADVANTAGES

All the chromatographic methods are specific and sensitive and can screen a large number of drugs at the same time.

TLC:	• Negligible capital outlay is needed.
GC:	• The procedure can be automated.
GC-MS:	• This is the "gold standard" test.
	• Computerized identification of fingerprint patterns makes identification easy.
	• The procedure can be automated.
	• This is currently the preferred method for defense in the legal system.
HPLC:	• Of the chromatographic procedures, this has the easiest sample preparation requirements.
	• The procedure can be automated.

DISADVANTAGES

All chromatographic methods are labor-intensive and require highly trained staff. Although all the chromatographic methods are specific, confirmation is still desirable.

TLC:	• Interpretation is subjective; hence, training and experience in interpretation capabilities of the technologist are crucial.
GC-MS:	• Equipment costs are the highest, ranging from \$120,000 to \$200,000 depending on the degree of sophistication required.
	• Because of the complexity of the instrument, highly trained operators and technologists are required.
HPLC-GC:	• Equipment costs are high, ranging between \$25,000 and \$60,000 depending on the type of detector and automation selected.

Figure 3. Summary of Chromatographic Methods.

only ethanol but also other alcohols. The recently introduced alcohol dipstick (Kapur & Israel, 1985), based on the ADH enzyme system, not only is specific for ethanol but also is sensitive and does not require instrumentation. It can be used for the detection of ethanol in all body fluids and can provide semiquantitative results in ranges of pharmacological-toxicological interest. The alcohol dipsticks, currently being made in the laboratories of the Addiction Research Foundation in Ontario, are being used in many alcohol treatment programs (as well as in a number of laboratories) as a screening device.

Breath can be analyzed by using a variety of instruments. Most of the instruments used today detect ethanol by using thermal conductivity, colorimetry, fuel cell, infrared, or gas chromatography techniques. Typically in most countries, local statutes define the instrument and method that can be used for evidentiary purposes. A variety of breath analysis instruments, at prices ranging from \$100 to \$1,000, are available to do the test. These instruments are compact and portable. The Canadian law enforcement authorities use the breath analysis ALERT which can give a "pass" or "fail" result as a roadside alcohol screening device. Those who fail are generally subjected to a Borkenstein breath analysis instrument to measure the BAC before any charges are laid. Many devices are available to preserve the breath sample for later analysis if a "breathalyser" is not available immediately. In forensic laboratories, gas chromatography (in North America) or biochemical procedures (in many European countries) are used to analyze biological samples.

Blood samples that cannot be analyzed soon after collection should be taken with sodium fluoride (NaF) as a preservative (Winek & Paul, 1983). Alcohol dehydrogenase (ADH), the enzyme responsible for the oxidation of alcohol, is also present in red blood cells and will slowly metabolize the alcohol, causing its concentration to drop if the preservative is not added. Large amounts of alcohol can be produced in vitro in the urine samples of diabetic patients if samples are not processed immediately.

	EMIT FPIA	RIA	TLC	HPCL	GC-MS
Ease of sample preparation	√	√		√	
Less highly trained technologists required	√	√			
Limited equipment required	√	√	√		
Low detection limits	√	√	√	√	√
Adjustable lower threshold	√	√			
Highly specific and sensitive			√	√	√
Computerized identification possible					√
Screen for several drugs at a time			√	√	√
Procedures can be automated	√	√		√	√
Special atomic energy license		√			
Confirmation of results	√	√	√	√	
Interpretation is not subjective	√	√		√	√

Figure 4. Advantages of All Testing Methods.

6. INTERPRETATIONS OF TEST RESULTS

False Negatives

A positive or negative result is highly dependent on the sensitivity of the drug detection method. A false negative occurs when the drug is present but is not found because the detection limit of the method used is too high or the absolute quantity of the drug in the specimen is too low. Large amounts of fluids consumed prior to obtaining a sample for analysis can affect detection of drugs in urine samples by causing dilution. Although the absolute amount of drug or metabolite excreted may be the same over a period of time, the final concentration per milliliter will be reduced and may cause a false negative result. Acidity levels in the urine may also affect the excretion of the drug into the urine. In some cases elimination is enhanced, whereas in other cases the drug is reabsorbed.

Several measures can be used to decrease the likelihood of obtaining a false negative result. First, the sensitivity of the method can be enhanced by analyzing for the drug's metabolites. Heroin use, for example, is determined by the presence of its metabolite, morphine. Increasing the specimen volume used for analysis or treating it with chemicals can also make laboratory methods more sensitive. Studies at the Addiction Research Foundation have shown that one 5 mg dose of diazepam is usually detectable for 3 or 4 days. When improved methods are utilized, however, sensitivity can be increased such that the same dose can be detected for up to 20 days. One important drawback of such high sensitivities is that estimates of when the drug was taken are far less accurate.

False Positives

A false positive occurs when results show that the drug is present, when in fact it is not. False positive tests are obtained if an interfering drug or substance is present in the biological fluid and it cross-reacts with the reagents. As discussed in the earlier section on immunoassays, an initially positive test should always be confirmed with a non-immunoassay method. A confirmed positive finding implies only that the urine sample contains the detected drug, nothing more.

Sometimes false positives are attributable to such ingested substances as asthma or allergy medications (Privacy Commissioner of Canada, 1990). Some authors have suggested that employees subject to drug screening refrain from using popular over-the-counter medications, such as Alka-Seltzer Plus and Sudafed, because they have caused false positives (Potter & Orfali, 1990). Some natural substances, such as herbal teas and poppy seeds, can also give positive responses to screens; these may be true positives but need to be distinguished from those resulting from illegal drug use. In other instances, false positives have been caused by mistakes or sabotage in the chain of custody for urine samples.

7. COMMON ADULTERATION METHODS

Switching "dirty" urine for "clean" urine is the most common way to fool a drug screening system. A number of entrepreneurs have attempted to help individuals bypass urine specimen inspection by providing drug-free urine. For example, a company in Florida has a catchy slogan—"Pee for Pleasure"—and sells lyophilized (freeze-dried) urine samples through newspaper and magazine advertisements. Hiding condoms containing clean urine on the body or inside the vagina is another common trick. Recently, a patient at the Addiction Research Foundation (ARF) was caught when a glass bottle that fell into the toilet bowl was discovered by the supervising nurse. This bottle, as was later discovered, had been sealed with a thin plastic wrap and inserted into the patient's urethra.

Others have attempted to substitute apple juice and tea samples for analysis. The clinical laboratory at the ARF has come across several examples of attempted urine adulteration. One recent patient, when she was confronted with an apple-juice sample, told us that she had been on a special juice diet. Patients have been known to add everything from bleach and liquid soap to eye drops and many other household products, hoping that their drug use will be masked. Others may hide a masking substance under their fingernails and release it into the urine specimen. Another method is to poke a small hole into the container with a pin so that the sample leaks out by the time it reaches the laboratory.

Because addition of table salt (sodium chloride) or bleach to the urine is a common practice, many laboratories routinely test for sodium and chlorine in the sample. Liquid soap and crystalline drain cleaners that are strong alkaline products containing sodium hydroxide (NaOH) are also used to adulterate the urine sample; these contaminators can be detected by checking for high levels of pH in the urine sample. Alkalizing or acidifying the urine pH in vivo can also change the excretion pattern of some drugs, including amphetamines, barbiturates, and PCP.

Water loading (drinking large amounts of water prior to voiding) poses an interesting challenge to the testing laboratories. Specific gravity has been used to detect dilution; however, the measurement range is limited, and my colleagues and I have not found it useful in our laboratory. Checking creatinine levels on random urine samples has also been studied as a possible water-loading detection method, but without much success.

Drug using patients clearly are very resourceful, and their ingenuity should not be underestimated. In order to reduce the opportunities for specimen contamination, some workplaces require that employees undergo testing with direct supervision. Another technique used to detect any sample adulteration is to take the temperature of the sample. If taken within 1 minute of voiding, the temperature range of samples is between 36.5 °F and 34 °F, reflecting the inner body core temperature. It is very difficult to achieve this narrow temperature range when hiding a condom filled with urine under the armpit or adding water from a tap or toilet bowl to the urine sample. The temperature must be measured immediately after the sample is taken, since it drops rapidly.

8. LABORATORY PROCEDURAL AND SECURITY STANDARDS

It is important that a laboratory drug testing facility have qualified individuals who follow a specific set of laboratory procedures and meet certain security standards. Laboratory management personnel must have specific documented qualifications in analytical forensic toxicology in order to carry out the analysis of urine samples for drug testing (Kwong, Chamberlain, Frederick, Kapur, & Sunshine, 1988; NIDA, 1988). A schematic flow chart from sample collection to the final disposition of results is shown in Figure 5.

The laboratory should be secure at all times, and access should be limited to authorized individuals only. The laboratory should establish security measures to guarantee that specimens are properly received, documented, processed, and stored. Documentation of chain of custody procedures should include specimen receipt, results during storage, and final disposition of specimen. The laboratory must also comply with any governmental license requirements, be inspected routinely, keep appropriate documentation and procedural manuals, and use properly certified equipment.

Urine specimens should be inspected immediately upon arrival to the laboratory in order to ensure that they have not been tampered with during delivery. Specimens should also be stored in a secure refrigeration unit if they are not tested within 7 days of arrival at the laboratory. The storage temperature should not exceed 6 °C; long-term storage must occur at −20 °C to ensure that positive urine specimens will be available for any retest during administrative or disciplinary proceedings. The laboratory will be required to maintain any specimen under legal challenge for an indefinite period.

9. INITIAL AND CONFIRMATORY TESTING REQUIREMENTS

Specimens can be processed in batches for either initial or confirmatory tests. Every batch should contain an appropriate number of standards for calibrating the instrument and a minimum of two or 10% specimen controls, whichever

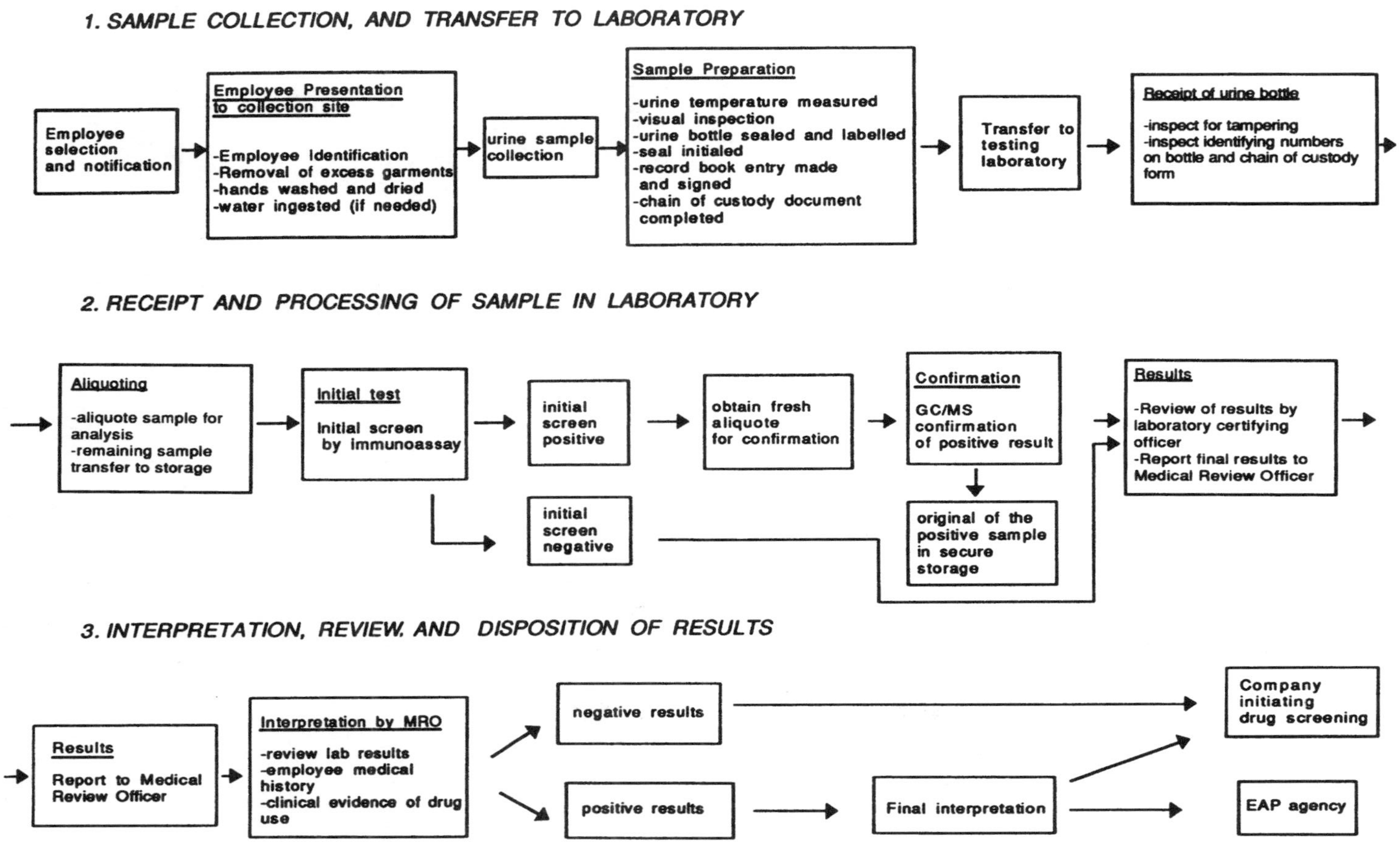

Figure 5. Schematic Representation of the Drug Testing Process.

THC metabolite	100 ng/ml
Cocaine metabolite	300 ng/ml
Opiate metabolites*	300 ng/ml
Phencyclidine	25 ng/ml
Amphetamines	1000 ng/ml

*25 ng/ml if immunoassay is specific for free morphine

Figure 6. Negative Cutoff Levels for Initial Tests.

is higher. Both quality control and blind performance test samples should appear as ordinary samples to the laboratory analyst.

The *initial* (screening) test consists of an immunoassay technique that meets the requirement for commercial distribution and eliminates negative urine specimens from further consideration. The initial cutoff levels for five drugs or classes of drugs are depicted in Figure 6. These should be used when screening a specimen to determine whether it is negative.

In the event of an identified positive on the initial test, a *confirmatory* test, where a second analytical procedure is used to identify the presence of a specific drug or metabolite, should be performed. The confirmatory test on a new aliquot of the sample must employ a different technique and chemical principle from that of the initial test. At present, gas chromatography/mass spectrometry (GC/MS) is the recommended confirmation method. The cutoff concentrations for different drugs are listed in Figure 7.

10. SUMMARY AND CONCLUSION

Major issues related to drug testing were discussed in this chapter. For example, drug testing techniques are not sophisticated enough to measure impairment from drug use. It is also very difficult to determine from the laboratory

THC metabolites*		15 ng/ml
Cocaine metabolites**		150 ng/ml
Opiates:	Morphine	300 ng/ml
	Codeine	300 ng/ml
Phencylidine		25 ng/ml
Amphetamines:	Amphetamine	500 ng/ml
	Methamphetamine	500 ng/ml

*THC metabolite is 11-nor-delta-9-THC Carboxylic Acid
**Cocaine metabolite is benzoylecgonine.

Figure 7. Cutoff Levels for Confirmatory Tests.

results how much of and when the drug was taken. The most sophisticated drug testing approach is gas chromatography in combination with mass spectrometry.

Despite the existence of sophisticated drug testing methods, incorrect test results can still arise. A number of techniques can be employed to reduce the likelihood of obtaining erroneous results. Patients have been known to adulterate urine samples to avoid drug detection; again, various techniques can be employed to detect any adulterated samples.

Only qualified individuals and laboratories that meet certain security standards should be employed for drug testing. Finally, specific initial and confirmatory testing requirements should be met.

REFERENCES

Bailey, D. N., 1989, Editorial: Drug screening in an unconventional matrix: hair analysis, *Journal of American Medical Association,* December 15, **262**(23):3331.

Baselt, R. C., 1982, *Disposition of Toxic Drugs and Chemicals in Man* 2nd Ed. Biomedical Publications, Davis, CA.

Cary, P. L., Whitter, P. D., and Johnson, C. A., 1984, Abbott radiative energy attenuation method for quantifying ethanol evaluated and compared with gas-liquid chromatography and Du Pont ACA, *Clinical Chemistry* **30**:1867–1870.

Chaing, C. N., and Barnett, G., 1984, Marijuana effect and delta-9-tetrahydrocannabinol plasma level, *Clinical Pharmacology and Therapeutics* **36**:234–238.

Chaing, C. N., and Hawks, R. L., 1986, Implications of drug levels in body fluids: basic concepts, urine testing for drugs of abuse, in: NIDA Research Monograph, No. 73 (R. L. Hawks and C. N. Chaing, eds.), pp. 62–83, U.S. Government Printing Office, Washington, DC.

Dackis, C. A., Pottash, A. L. C., Annitto, W., and Gold, M., 1982, Persistence of urinary marijuana levels after supervised abstinence, *Am. J. Psychiatry* **139**:1196–1198.

Decresce, R. P., Lifshitz, M. S., Ambre, J., Mazura, A. C., Tilson, J. E., and Cochran, K. M., 1989, *Drug Testing in the Workplace,* American Society of Clinical Pathologists, Chicago.

Dubowski, K. M., 1975, Studies in breath-alcohol analysis: biological factors, *Z. Rechtmedizin* **76**:93–117.

Harger, R. N., Raney, B. B., Bridwell, E. G., and Ketchel, M. F., 1950, The partition ratio of alcohol between air and water, urine and blood; estimation and identification of alcohol in those liquids from analysis of air equilibrated with them, *J. Biol. Chem.* **183**:197–213.

Henderson, G. L., Harkey, M. R., Zhou, C., and Jones, R. T., 1992, Cocaine and metabolite concentrations in the hair of South American coca chewers, *J. Anal. Toxicol.* **16**:199–201.

Huestis, M. A., Henningfield, J. E., and Cone, E. J., 1992, Blood cannabinoids: 1. Absorption of THC and formation of 11-OH-THC and THCCOOH during and after smoking marijuana, *J. Anal. Toxicol.* **16**:276–282.

Jain, N. C., 1971, Direct blood injection method for gas chromatographic determination of alcohols and other volatile compounds, *Clinical Chemistry* **17**:82–85.

Jain, N. C., and Cravey, R. H., 1974, Analysis of alcohol, I: A review of chemical and infrared methods, *J. Chrom. Sci.* **10**:257–262.

Jain, N. C., and Cravey, R. H., 1974, Analysis of alcohol, II: A review of gas chromatographic methods, *J. Chrom. Sci.* **10**:263–267.

Jones, A. W., 1978, Variability of the blood: breath alcohol ratio in vivo, *J. Stud. Alc.* **39**:1931–1939.

Kalant, H., 1971, Absorption, diffusion, distribution and elimination of ethanol, in: *Effects of Biological Membranes: The biology of alcoholism* (B. Kissin and H. Begleiter, eds.), pp. 1–62, Plenum Press, New York.

Kapur, B. M., and Israel, Y., 1985, Alcohol dipstick—A rapid method for analysis of ethanol in body fluids, in: *Early Identification of Alcohol Abuse,* NIAAA Research Monograph No. 17 (N. C. Chang and H. M., Chao, eds.), pp. 310–320, National Institute on Alcohol Abuse and Alcoholism, Rockville, MD.

Koren, G., Klein, J., Forman, R., and Graham, K., 1992, Hair analysis of cocaine—differentiation between systemic exposure and external contamination, *J. Clin. Pharmacol.* **32:**671–675.

Kwong, T., Chamberlain, R. T., Frederick, D. L., Kapur, B. M., and Sunshine, I., 1988, Critical issues in urinalysis of abused substances: Report of the substance-abuse testing committee, *Clinical Chemistry* **34:**605–632.

Miners, I. A., Nykodym, N., and Samerdyke-Traband, D. M., 1987, Put drug detection to the test, *Personnel Journal* **66:**90–97.

Moskowitz, H., and Robinson, C. D., 1988, Effects of low doses of alcohol on driving-related skills: A review of the evidence, Publication No. DOT HS 807 280, U.S. Department of Transportation, Washington DC.

National Institute on Drug Abuse, 1988, Mandatory guidelines for federal workplace drug testing programs: Final guidelines, *Federal Register* **53:**11970–11989.

O'Neill, B., Williams, A. F., and Dubowski, K. M., 1983, Variability in blood alcohol concentrations, *J. Stud. Alc.* **44:**222–230.

Payne, J. P., Hill, D. W., and King, N. W., 1966, Observations on distribution of alcohol in blood, breath and urine, *Br. Med. J.* **1:**196–202.

Peachey, P., and Kapur, B. M., 1986, Monitoring drinking behavior with the alcohol dipstick during treatment, *Alc. Clin. Expr. Res.* **10:**663–666.

Potter, B. A., and Orfali, J. S., 1990, *Drug Testing at Work: A Guide for Employers and Employees,* Ronin Publishing, Berkeley, CA.

The Privacy Commissioner of Canada, 1990, *Drug Testing and Privacy,* Ministry of Supply and Services, Ottawa, Ontario.

Redetzki, H. M., and Dees, W. L., 1976, Comparison of four kits for enzymatic determination of ethanol in blood, *Clinical Chemistry* **22:**83–86.

Rollins, D. E., Jennison, T. A., and Jones, G., 1990, Investigation of interference by nonsteroidal anti-inflammatory drugs in urine tests for abused drugs, *Clinical Chemistry* **36:**602–606.

Rothstein, M. A., 1985–86, Screening workers for drugs: A legal and ethical framework, *Employee Relations Law Journal* **11:**422–437.

Selavka, C. M., 1991, Poppy seed streusel spoils opiate differentiation guidelines, *Forensic Urine Drug Testing* September:4–5.

Simpson, G., 1987, Accuracy and precision of breath-alcohol measurements for a random subject in the postabsorptive state, *Clinical Chemistry* **32:**261–268.

Snyder, M. B., 1991, *Lower alcohol levels, driver impairment and crash risk,* Auto and Traffic Safety, National Highway Traffic Safety Administration, US Department of Transport, Washington DC, Vol 1, No. 1, Summer 1991.

ToxTalk, 1992, Society of Forensic Toxicology Advisory Committee on Analysis of Hair for Drugs of Abuse, *Revised Consensus Opinion on Applicability of Hair Analysis for Drugs of Abuse,* **16**(4):3.

Widmark, E. M. P., 1922, Eine mikromethode zur bestimmung von aethylalkohol im blut, *Biochemische Zeitschrift* **131:**473–484.

Winek, C. L., and Paul, L. J., 1983, Effect of short-term storage conditions on alcohol concentration in blood from living human subjects, *Clinical Chemistry* **29:**1959–1960.

6

The Impact and Effectiveness of Drug Testing Programs in the Workplace

SCOTT MACDONALD and SAMANTHA WELLS

1. INTRODUCTION

In this chapter the impact and effectiveness of drug testing programs in the workplace (sometimes referred to as drug screening programs) are examined. It will become clear in this review that few scientific evaluations have been conducted to assess the impact of screening programs; therefore, much of this chapter focuses on our speculations about possible impacts. For the purpose of evaluating the effectiveness of screening programs, the objectives of screening and the critical assumptions underlying these objectives are assessed. A primary focus of this chapter is what happens to companies when drug screening programs are initiated. Because screening programs can be implemented in a number of different ways, the answer is largely dependent on the type of program and how it is implemented. These variations in types of screening programs and their possible differential impacts are explored. Prior to exploring these issues, an examination of the history and extent of drug testing programs is provided. This historical perspective is useful for understanding why these programs were initiated and how prevalent they are today.

SCOTT MACDONALD and SAMANTHA WELLS • Social Evaluation and Research, Addiction Research Foundation, London, Ontario N6G 4X8, Canada. The views expressed in this document are those of the authors and do not necessarily reflect those of the Addiction Research Foundation.

Research Advances in Alcohol and Drug Problems, Volume 11: Drug Testing in the Workplace, edited by Scott Macdonald and Paul M. Roman. Plenum Press, New York, 1994.

2. HISTORY AND EXTENT OF DRUG TESTING PROGRAMS

Drug testing first appeared in the United States during the 1960s and early 1970s when the Department of Defense used urinalysis to screen military personnel returning from Vietnam. Treatment programs used tests as part of the rehabilitation of those with dependency problems. The 1980s saw a massive increase in the use of drug testing programs following the development of more reliable technology for testing and heightened awareness about the apparent high rates of drug use among certain populations (i.e., military personnel). The highly publicized occurrence of a fatal aircraft carrier accident that involved drugs served to intensify fear about the harmful effects of workplace drug use. After the U.S. Navy implemented testing of personnel in 1982, private companies began to inquire about the legalities of employee screening, and some (e.g., Greyhound Corporation) initiated screening of employees and job applicants.

The late 1980s saw important legislative developments in the United States that opened the doors to widespread implementation of drug screening programs. President Reagan signed an executive order in 1986 promoting the establishment of a drug-free federal workplace. In addition, the Anti-Drug Abuse Act was passed, and a statement of guidelines for federal employee drug testing programs was enacted. The U.S. Department of Transportation adopted a policy to implement random drug screening programs in aviation, rail, mass transit, trucking, and pipelines ("DOT Adopts," 1989). By 1995, the U.S. Coast Guard hopes to achieve bilateral agreements with European countries and Canada to execute mandatory drug testing in all forms of transport and pipeline operations (Glass, 1992).

Drug testing programs have become increasingly prevalent in the United States; in 1986, about 25% of the largest 500 companies had such programs (Mani & Burns, 1986). A study conducted by the American Management Association in 1986 indicated that out of more than 1,000 companies surveyed, 20% had drug testing programs (Cornish, 1988). In 1987, 49% of 364 respondents from a *Fortune* survey of the top 1,000 companies in the United States reported having preemployment screening. Between 1988 and 1990, the percentage of companies of all sizes with screening programs increased from 3.2% to 4.4% (International Labor Office, 1991).

The prevalence of drug screening programs varies largely by the characteristics of companies. A 1988 survey of medium- and large-sized corporations in the United States indicated that manufacturing firms and companies in the utility and transportation sectors were most likely to have drug testing programs; companies in banking, insurance, or other financial services were less likely to have such programs (Axel, 1989). Also, companies with screening tended to be relatively large, with a substantial work force and several work sites (Axel,

1989). The most common type of testing used in the United States was preemployment screening (92%), followed by probable-cause testing (77%; Cornish, 1988). Of the companies with screening, 12% used periodic screening, and only 8% tested randomly (Cornish, 1988).

Although most studies indicate an overall increase in the percentage of companies with drug screening programs since the early 1980s, it is notable that a proportion of companies in the United States have abandoned their programs. In a survey of 145,000 U.S. businesses that had screening programs in 1988, only two thirds had such programs in 1990 (Hayghe, 1991). This reduction is largely attributable to the discontinuation of programs among smaller companies.

Few studies have been conducted on the prevalence of drug screening programs in Canada, but most of these indicate that drug testing programs are less prevalent there than in the United States. In 1990, about 19.5% of federally regulated Canadian transportation companies with 100 or more employees had drug screening programs, and 14.5% had alcohol screening programs (Macdonald & Dooley, 1991). Within the transportation sector, drug screening was most common in rail firms (50%), followed by airports (33%) and bus (23%), truck (21%), and airline companies (17%). Legislation in Canada is pending for mandatory screening in federally regulated transportation companies. Employees in hazardous working conditions were most likely to be tested; 80% of companies with screening tested such employees. The most common type of screening program was preemployment testing (81%), followed by periodic (44%) and postaccident screening (36%; Macdonald & Dooley, 1991). These and other types of drug testing and their impact on the workplace are described in the following section.

Unfortunately, the extent of testing programs in Europe is largely unknown, but they are believed to be much less prevalent than in North America. As yet, no legislation mandating drug screening programs is known to have been enacted in any of the European countries.

3. IMPACT OF TESTING PROGRAMS

As yet, little research focusing on the impact of testing programs has been conducted. In this section, variables related to the impact of drug testing are examined and possible impacts of these programs are presented, including both anticipated and unanticipated consequences. These impacts include effects of drug testing on drug use, legal and ethical issues, employee morale, and productivity in the workplace. Two important variables are related to the impact of drug screening: the type of screening program, and the consequences of a positive test.

Types of Testing Programs

The following is a list of the several types of screening programs implemented in workplaces (Decresce et al., 1989; Macdonald & Dooley, 1991; Stennett-Brewer, 1988):

- *Preemployment testing.* Job applicants are tested for drugs before employment.
- *Random testing.* Employees are tested on a random basis; each employee has an equal chance of being selected for a test. This usually involves testing employees without cause or notice.
- *Periodic testing.* Employees are tested for drugs on a predetermined timetable, usually at a yearly medical checkup.
- *Probable-cause testing.* Employees are tested after a job accident, after a period of decreased job performance, or when obvious behavioral symptoms of drug use are displayed (slurred speech, red eyes, etc.).
- *Reasonable suspicion.* Employees are tested after they have displayed various behavioral symptoms, such as lateness or high absenteeism. The grounds for tests for reasonable suspicion are less rigorous than for probable-cause screening.
- *Posttreatment testing.* Employees are tested after having received some form of treatment for alcohol or drug use problems.
- *Upon transfer or promotion.* Employees are tested after being transferred or promoted to another position.
- *Voluntary testing.* Employees may choose to be tested, but it is not a formal requirement of work.

Preemployment testing is the most common and widely accepted type of screening (Osterloh & Becker, 1990). Employers are least likely to face union resistance and liability problems when preemployment screening is used, because employers have no obligation to satisfy the demands of nonemployees (who are not yet members of a union; Fay, 1991; Osterloh & Becker, 1990). Because preemployment screening is used for the purpose of preventing drug users from obtaining employment, one might expect a slow decrease to occur over time in the proportion of drug users in the workplace; a rapid decrease in drug use would not be expected, because existing employees could still cause problems. One shortcoming of preemployment screening is that people could abstain from drug use when applying for work, but start reusing drugs thereafter.

With *random testing,* either all or a portion of the employees at a work site can be tested on a given day. Among the various types of screening programs, random screening has generated the most resistance and controversy (Decresce et al., 1989; Osterloh & Becker, 1990; Stennett-Brewer, 1988). Labor unions and civil rights organizations have severely criticized this approach for infringing upon the privacy of individuals and allowing the potential for abuse of employees (Decresce et al., 1989). Critics argue that random screening promotes "feelings of insecurity, oppression, and anxiety in employees," which in turn could produce low productivity (Segal, 1989). Random screening programs have also been criticized for being inefficient and costly (Osterloh & Becker, 1990). Nonetheless, random screening is sometimes supported for not singling out individuals for suspicious behavior in the workplace (DuPont, 1990). Because each employee has an equal chance of being tested, individuals who are selected for a drug test are not at risk of being labeled by supervisors or fellow employees as being possible drug users. Notably, random testing has been touted as the most effective deterrent against drug use (Fay, 1991).

Periodic testing usually involves testing employees according to a predetermined timetable, such as at a yearly medical examination or upon return from a layoff or lengthy illness. Typically employees are provided with advance notice as to when the tests will take place (Decresce et al., 1989). This form of testing, though more likely to withstand legal challenges, may permit drug users to avoid detection by abstaining from drugs for an appropriate duration before the tests are administered (Decresce et al., 1989). Those who are truly addicted and have severe drug problems will be less able to abstain, however, even with the knowledge that they will be tested.

There are two types of *probable-cause testing*. The first type, known as *postaccident testing,* involves screening employees who have been involved in industrial accidents or injuries. The second type involves testing employees who show behavioral signs of alcohol or drug use problems. A growing number of companies require testing after *all* industrial accidents (Decresce et al., 1989). With postaccident testing, no evidence is needed to indicate that employees involved in an accident were impaired. Legal problems do not usually arise with this type of screening, because employers are responsible for ensuring safety in the workplace and therefore have a right—and sometimes a responsibility—to investigate the cause of accidents (Decresce et al., 1989). A possible impact of this approach is that employees might be reluctant to report minor accidents and injuries for fear of being tested (Jones, 1990; Segal, 1989). Some employers have attempted to address this problem by confining testing to cases where accidents involve carelessness (Decresce et al., 1989).

For the second type of probable-cause testing, supervisors must be trained to recognize behavioral symptoms of alcohol or drug use problems. Researchers argue that this type of screening is likely to survive legal challenges because individuals are not tested unless sufficient evidence indicates that they are using drugs at work (Decresce et al., 1989; Segal, 1989; Stennett-Brewer, 1988; Tyson & Vaughn, 1987). A problem with this approach is that supervisors must focus on behavioral symptoms of use rather than work problems. Such symptoms could be misdiagnosed, leading to singling out and labeling of individuals who may not be drug users (DuPont, 1990). Another criticism is that supervisors could abuse their discretion and harass certain employees (Segal, 1989).

Probable impacts of *reasonable-suspicion testing* are very similar to those of probable-cause screening, where supervisors also identify behavioral problems. Criticisms of reasonable suspicion testing are stronger, however, because the criteria used to determine whether employees should be tested are less stringent. This type of testing has been severely criticized because possible symptoms of drug and alcohol dependency problems (e.g., lateness or absenteeism) are often symptoms of other problems, such as depression or stress.

Other types of screening are much less prevalent in the workplace. *Post-treatment testing* can be used to monitor the alcohol or drug use behavior of individuals who previously tested positive and have received treatment. This type of testing is intended to deter identified users from continuing to use alcohol or drugs. Screening in cases where employees have been transferred or promoted is not widely used, and little is known about its consequences. Finally, voluntary screening is also not widely used, and little is known about its impact on the workplace.

Consequences of Positive Tests

There are three typical consequences for those job applicants or employees who test positive. With preemployment screening, the job applicant usually is not hired; with other types of screening, the employee either is fired or is provided with various types of treatment or rehabilitation services.

Differential impacts can result depending on the actions taken by the employer once an employee has been identified as a drug user. Clearly, the ramifications from both the employee's and employer's perspectives of dismissing existing employees are quite different from those for providing treatment. Dismissal implies that drug screening is governed by a punitive enforcement model of drug use, and it is grounded on somewhat moralistic and pragmatic principles. One shortcoming of this approach is that when the employee is dismissed, the employer must hire and train a new employee. Also, the dismissed employee may have difficulty obtaining new employment and may not receive treatment if a drug problem exists.

The treatment option is more analogous to a constructive-confrontational model first used with so-called employee assistance programs. It is suggestive of a more humanitarian approach to dealing with drug problems among employees. This approach might be considered less effective in terms of reducing drug problems in the workplace, though, because treatment is not 100% effective in combating drug problems. Although different types of treatment are associated with different success rates, no single treatment or combination of treatments could be considered perfect for all patients with alcohol problems (see Holden et al., 1991, for a review).

Other Impacts

Concern has been expressed by some researchers that testing programs may have serious negative impacts on the workplace. In one study, the perceptions of college juniors regarding their desire to work at companies with and without preemployment drug testing were examined (Crant & Bateman, 1990); Potential job applicants indicated more positive attitudes towards and likely intentions to apply for jobs with companies that did not have testing. Possible reasons for these results are that companies with testing are more likely to be viewed as mistrusting employees and as invading personal privacy. Hence, one possible impact of screening is a decline in the total number of job applicants, including users *and* nonusers.

Other researchers have argued that drug testing programs can produce a reduction in employee morale (International Labor Office, 1991; Maltby, 1987; O'Keefe, 1987; Rothman, 1988; Rothstein, 1989; Weeks, 1987), which in turn could relate to lower productivity levels. Drug screening could also undermine labor-management relations, impede employee recruitment, and promote litigation (Rothstein, 1991, as cited in Smithers Institute, 1992). If mass screening is implemented, some companies in high-drug-use localities might have difficulty finding qualified drug-free applicants, especially at times when the labor market pool is diminishing (Smithers Institute, 1992).

Another area rarely considered is the impact of drug screening on society as a whole. Some have suggested that widespread mandatory screening may encourage covert behavior and possibly escalate crime rates (Ellis, 1988; International Labor Office, 1991). For example, detected drug users might increase their drug intake as a result of being fired, which may cause them to engage in criminal activity to pay for drugs (Ellis, 1988). Additionally, drug screening has also been linked to the creation of a black market for clean urine (Rothman, 1988).

4. THE EFFECTIVENESS OF TESTING PROGRAMS

The effectiveness of drug screening programs is measured by the extent to which their objectives are achieved. For the purpose of evaluating the effectiveness of screening, the major objectives are described below.

Objectives of Drug Testing in the Workplace

The most commonly cited objective of drug testing proponents is to reduce industrial accidents by employees in the workplace. The use of many drugs and alcohol causes reductions in motor coordination and perceptual abilities (see Chapter 4). Therefore, it is commonly argued that if drug use in the workplace can be eliminated, especially for those in safety-sensitive positions, accidents will be reduced.

A second objective is to reduce drug- and alcohol-related problems in the workplace associated with low productivity, such as absenteeism, tardiness, and turnover (Addiction Research Foundation, 1990). If drug-positive employees are fired or not hired, costs associated with company health care plans might be reduced, because heavy drug and alcohol users are considered likely to use such programs (Walsh & Hawks, 1986). This rationale also has been used by some companies in the United States that have adopted employment policies prohibiting tobacco use on and/or off the job. If drug-positive employees are given treatment, some have suggested that screening can be used to facilitate their recovery, thus improving their health.

A third objective behind drug testing in the workplace is to reduce the widespread use of illicit drugs in society. This purpose has been clearly articulated in U.S. governmental documents: "Because 70% of all drug users are employed, the workplace may be the most strategic point in society from which to combat the scourge of drugs" (Office of National Drug Control Policy, 1990, p. 1). Constitutional safeguards in many industrialized countries, such as rights to privacy and due process, can be bypassed through government regulation or agreements between employers and employees. Such measures can make drug screening in the workplace a very powerful detection tool for drug use in society. It is argued that drug testing programs provide a means to reducing drug use in society through specific and general deterrence. *Specific* deterrence refers to the identification of individual drug users and intervention by punishment (e.g., dismissal) or treatment. Accordingly, the apprehended user would be less likely to continue using drugs for fear of losing his or her employment. *General* deterrence refers to the process where users who have not been caught are deterred by the threat of being caught.

Some employers adopt testing programs simply because they have been legislated to do so, and hence they do not have any specific objectives. For example, in the United States, certain federal government transportation employees are required to undergo mandatory drug screening (Heller & Robinson, 1991; Kaplan & Williams, 1988). The U.S. government is also introducing legislation mandating carriers from Canada and other countries landing in the United States to conduct testing.

The Effect of Alcohol and Drugs on Work Performance

The validity of justifications for drug testing depends on the main arguments employers use for adopting programs. The two major objectives—reducing the risk of industrial accidents and reducing performance problems—are based on the assumption that drug users are more likely to experience these outcomes. Much of the evidence suggesting that use of drugs is associated with increased industrial accidents and decreased performance has been inferred from laboratory studies that show motor coordination and perceptual abilities decrease with the ingestion of many drugs. This laboratory evidence was reviewed extensively in Chapter 4.

Although drugs may directly cause performance deficits in laboratory situations, it is possible that drug use in the workplace is not prevalent or serious enough to cause such problems. Markus (1992) examined the percentage of employees testing positive for alcohol and various types of drugs in several workplace settings; employees were most likely to test positive for alcohol (4.53%), THC (3.63%), and benzodiazepines (2.09%; see Chapter 1). The results of this study suggest that drug and alcohol usage is very prevalent in the workplace.

In Chapter 1, studies that examined the relationship between alcohol/drug use and accidents and/or work performance were reviewed. Some of this evidence showed that alcohol and drug users are at a higher risk of having on-the-job accidents and/or performance problems. The methodology of and accuracy of conclusions drawn from many of these studies, however, have been vigorously challenged (Horgan, 1990a, b). One problem is that several types of drugs are often combined into one category; users are simply compared with nonusers, making it difficult to arrive at conclusions regarding the relative risk of one particular drug. Another shortcoming of most of these studies is that they do not distinguish between moderate and heavy users; high rates of accidents and productivity problems are likely to be found most among the heaviest users. This implies that the overall relationships found in these studies might be more attributable to accident rates and productivity problems among a minority of heavy users. Also, such studies may produce inconclusive results, because many researchers do not draw a distinction between post and current use of drugs.

Another limitation of these studies is that they do not provide conclusive evidence that drug use is causally related to performance problems. Because drug users differ from nonusers in many respects, it is difficult to conclude that drug use, rather than some other confounding characteristic, is the actual cause of performance problems. For example, higher rates of involuntary separation found in some studies might be explained by a tendency of drug involvement to be related to "facets of a lifestyle reflecting other possible deviant attitudes and behaviors besides drug use" that might be considered undesirable to an employer (Sheridan & Winkler, 1989, p. 133). Sociocultural and demographic factors that also accompany drug use (e.g., age, gender, or race) may be more important predictors of workplace problems (Horgan, 1990a). Drug users also may be more likely than nonusers to be risk takers, which could explain a higher rate of job-related problems (Macdonald & Dooley, 1991; Newcomb, 1988).

Studies Comparing Drug-Positive and Drug-Negative Employees. Studies that assess differences between drug positives (those testing positive for drug use) and drug negatives (those testing negative for drug use) in terms of workplace problems are the most relevant studies to use when assessing the effectiveness of drug screening in the workplace. Whereas most studies focus primarily on the impact of alcohol on workplace problems those using drug testing for identification focus on the impact of drug use. Such studies do not rely on self-reported data, which are often biased because users do not always admit to their habits. Also, because drug testing is used to identify drug users, results regarding differences between drug-positive and drug-negative groups in terms of accident rates and work performance problems provide more accurate information about whether drug testing programs actually prevent or reduce workplace problems.

A number of researchers have compared workplace accidents and performance problems of drug-positive and drug-negative employees. These studies were usually conducted in settings where preemployment drug testing results had no bearing on subsequent hiring or job termination decisions. Several studies employing drug testing to assess the work performance and accident rates of drug users and nonusers are displayed in Table 1.

In terms of job accidents, Zwerling, Ryan, and Orav (1990) found that those testing positive for marijuana or cocaine were significantly more likely to have reportable accidents and work injuries. In a subsequent study, the same subjects were followed up after 2 years of employment, and risks of adverse outcomes were found to have declined among drug positives after the first year (Ryan, Zwerling, & Jones, 1992). In a longitudinal study of 5,465 job applicants, Normand, Salyards, and Mahoney (1990) failed to find significant differences between drug positives and negatives in terms of job accidents or injuries. Crouch, Webb, Peterson, Buller, and Rollins (1989) also failed to find differences in accidents for drug-positive and drug-negative groups, but their results were inconclusive as a result of small sample sizes. Because few studies have explored the role of drugs in work accidents, definitive conclusions cannot be drawn.

These findings suggest that the relationship between drug use (with the exceptions of alcohol dependence and impairment by alcohol) and on-the-job accidents has not been empirically established, although some studies indicate a weak relationship. Therefore, it follows that the effectiveness of drug testing programs in reducing possible drug-related accidents is also scientifically unproven. For studies that show drug use to be related to occupational accidents, it is not clear whether drug use is the primary cause. Showing that drug use is a cause of on-the-job accidents, however, is a minimal requirement for assessing the effectiveness of programs.

The determination of drug use as a cause of accidents cannot be made by analysis of a single accident. Although very large single accidents (e.g., train crashes or shipwrecks where the conductor or captain has shown evidence of drug use) have received great publicity and outrage by the public, definitive conclusions that drugs actually caused these accidents cannot always be made. Only the examination of the proportion of drug users involved in accidents compared to the proportion of users not involved in accidents, using cohort or case control studies and controlling for potential confounding variables, can one establish convincing empirical evidence that drug use causes accidents.

With respect to job performance problems (e.g., absenteeism and turnover rates), those testing positive and negative in preemployment drug tests also have been compared (Blank & Fenton, 1989; Normand & Salyards, 1989, Sheridan & Winkler, 1989). Normand and Salyards' study (1989) of applicants to the U.S. Postal Service found that involuntary separation (i.e., employer-initiated employment termination) and job absenteeism rates were higher among the groups that tested positive than among those who tested negative for drugs. Blank and Fenton's study (1989) of 482 U.S. Navy recruits revealed that users of marijuana were significantly more likely than others to separate from the Navy after $2^1/_2$ years. This study is inconclusive, however, because differences in turnover may have been attributable to spurious factors; recruits testing positive sometimes had to undergo subsequent drug tests, and positive test results often resulted in being discharged (Normand et al., 1990). Sheridan and Winkler (1989) found similar rates of absenteeism among positives and negatives but noted some significant differences between the two groups within certain subgroups of employees.

A study of employees at a power company indicated that drug positives had significantly more sick hours and unexcused absences compared to a control group (Crouch et al., 1989); interestingly, however, the costs of medical insurance benefits were higher for the control group than for the drug positives. In another study, use of cannabis, barbiturates, cocaine, and nicotine among 5,465 job applicants was found to be related to high absenteeism and involuntary turnover rates (Normand et al., 1990). Zwerling et al. (1990) also found that marijuana-positive applicants had significantly higher absences, disciplinary charges, and involuntary turnover compared to negatives. In this study, cocaine positives had significantly higher absences only (Zwerling et al., 1990). Contrary findings were found by Parish (1989), who determined that 11 drug-negative employees were fired during the study, but no drug positives were fired. Significant differences were not found between drug positives and drug negatives for job performance variables (Parish, 1989). These latter findings were deemed

Table 1
Empirical Studies on the Relationship between Alcohol or Drug Use and Workplace Problems

Author/Date	Research Questions[a]	Type of Study/ Description	Groups
Blank and Fenton (1989)	What are the attrition patterns of marijuana positive and marijuana negatives and how do they differ?	2 groups; postmeasurement design. Navy recruits were tested for marijuana use. Those testing positive were recruited but given a stern warning regarding drug use. Both groups were followed up for attrition.	1,052 Navy recruits: (1) positive for marijuana use; (2) negative for marijuana use.
Crouch et al. (1989)	What is the difference in absenteeism, medical expenses, and on-the-job accidents between those testing positive and those testing negative?	2 groups; postmeasurement design	Utah Power and Light Co. employees: (1) 12 tested positive for drug use; (2) 47 control subjects (frequency matched).
Normand and Salyards (1989)	What is the difference in absenteeism and turnover between drug-positive and drug-negative applicants on preemployment tests?	2 groups; postmeasurement design. All job applicants were tested for drugs. The employer was never made aware of the results.	U.S. Postal Service employees: (1) 354 tested positive; (2) 3,866 tested negative.
Normand et al. (1990)	What is the difference in the absenteeism and turnover rates between drug-positive and drug-negative employees on preemployment tests?	2 groups; postmeasurement design. All job applicants were tested for drugs.	U.S. Postal Service employees: (1) 395 tested positive; (2) 4,001 tested negative.

(continued)

Table 1 (*Continued*)

Drugs Investigated	Dependent Measures	Results	Comments
Marijuana	Attrition	• 57% of the marijuana positives were retained, compared to 81% of the marijuana negatives. • No statistical tests.	14% of the marijuana positives were discharged for alcohol or drug use.
Amphetamines, barbiturates, benzodiazepines, cannabinoids, cocaine, ethanol, methadone, narcotics, and phencyclidine	Absenteeism, on-the-job accidents	• The drug positives had significantly ($p < .05$) more sick hours (75 hr) and unexcused absences (64 hr) compared to the control group (56 hr and 19 hr, respectively). • Medical expenses were higher for the control group. • Results were inconclusive for accidents.	
Amphetamines, barbiturates, benzodiazepine, cannabinoids, cocaine, methadone, opiates, and phencyclidine	Job absences, voluntary turnover	• Mean absence rate was 45% higher for those testing positive ($p < .05$). • Those testing positive were 1.5 times likely to be involuntarily separated (i.e., employer-initiated employment termination). • No difference between groups for overall turnover. • Those testing positive for cocaine had higher rates of absenteeism and turnover than those testing positive for marijuana.	
Marijuana, cocaine, and other commonly tested drugs	Absenteeism, turnover, injuries, and accidents	• Drug positives had a mean absence rate of 6.63%, compared to 4.16% for negatives ($p < .01$). • Drug positives had a 47% higher rate of involuntary turnover than negatives.	

(*continued*)

Table 1 (*Continued*)

Author/Date	Research Questions[a]	Type of Study/ Description	Groups
Parish (1989)	Do drug-positive employees differ from drug-negative employees in terms of their job performance?	The work performances of drug-negative and drug-positive employees hired over a 6-month period at a large hospital were compared.	(1) Drug-positive employees; (2) drug negative employees
Sheridan and Winkler (1989)	What is the difference in the absenteeism rates of drug-positive and drug-negative employees?	2 groups; postmeasurement design	Georgia Power employees: (1) 62 positive versus 401 negatives for 1986; (2) 54 positives versus 312 negatives for 1987.
Zwerling et al. (1990)	What is the difference between drug-positive and drug-negative employees in a variety of performance measures?	2 groups; postmeasurement design. Preemployment tests were conducted but had no impact on hiring decisions.	4.964 U.S. Postal Service employees: (1) 198 positive for marijuana; (2) 55 positive for cocaine; (3) 5 positive for other drugs; (4) 229 negative.

[a]In many of these papers, authors explored other research questions. The research questions listed here are those that are relevant to this chapter and are not stated in the exact words of the original author(s).

tentative, however, because of the low power of statistical tests used in the study (Normand et al., 1990).

The results of the studies discussed above suggest that preemployment drug screening programs might be moderately successful in reducing performance problems in the workplace. There are several methodological limitations of the aforementioned studies, though, that emphasize the tentative nature of their

Table 1 *(Continued)*

Drugs Investigated	Dependent Measures	Results	Comments
		• No difference between groups for overall turnover. • No significant differences between groups were found for injuries or accidents.	
Barbiturates, opiates, benzodiazepines, propoxyphene, meperidine, marijuana, amphetamines, cocaine, phencyclidine, and phenothiazines	Job performance variables: job retention, supervisor evaluations, and reasons for termination	• No relationship was found between drug use and job performance.	
Cannabinoids, cocaine, and other drugs	Demotions, absenteeism	• For both years, the positives did not significantly differ from the workforce or negatives in terms of demotions. • For both years, positives had similar rates of absenteeism to negatives, but within some job-classification subgroups significant differences occurred.	
Cannabinoids, cocaine, and other nontherapeutic drugs	Voluntary turnover, involuntary turnover, accidents, injuries, discipline, and absence	• Those who tested positive for marijuana had significantly ($p < .05$) increased risk of accidents, injuries, discipline, absences, and involuntary turnover compared to negatives. • Cocaine positives had significantly increased risk of injuries and absences only, and those positive for other drugs had significantly increased risk of discipline only.	Study controlled for age, sex, smoking, race and job classification.

results. One shortcoming of studies using preemployment testing is that nothing can be said about the effectiveness of other types of screening programs, such as periodic or probable-cause screening. Each study was conducted at one workplace location; this means that the results for each are only generalizable to the type of industry and geographic area in which it was conducted (Zwerling et al., 1992). Drug use prevalence is likely to vary by industry and geographic area, which also limits the generalizability of study results (Zwerling et al., 1990).

Other factors are also important. The type and amount of a drug consumed, the frequency and method of usage, and the degree of addiction are critical factors in assessing accident/performance risk. These factors have been rarely investigated; in fact, most of them cannot be assessed through testing. Furthermore, the drugs discussed above do not include the large variety of over-the-counter and prescription drugs that also might affect performance and job safety (see Klein, 1972). Therefore, the true extent to which drug use is a significant factor in workplace accidents and performance deficits is largely undetermined.

Table 2
Empirical Studies on the Effectiveness of Drug Screening Programs

Author/Date	Study Objectives	Type of Study/ Description	Groups
Needleman and Romberg (1989)	How has the percentage of confirmed positives for four drugs of abuse changed among U.S. Navy and Marine Corps personnel?	Four groups; data generated by the Navy Drug Screening Laboratory are reviewed and compared.	(1) Navy recruits; (2) Navy service school members; (3) Marine Corps recruits; (4) Marine Corps service school members.
Osborne et al. (1990)	How has the proportion of employees testing positive changed after implementation of a drug screening program?	One group; monthly measurements for 12 months	Employees from a nuclear power facility
Taggart (1989)	(1) How does the percentage of work force testing positive change over time with screening? (2) How does the frequency of accidents change over time with screening?	One group; yearly measurements for 5 years	Employees from Southern Pacific Railroad

Outcome Studies on the Effectiveness of Testing Programs

As mentioned at the outset of this chapter, the effectiveness of drug testing programs is determined by the extent to which their objectives are achieved. In this section, each testing objective discussed earlier is evaluated in terms of the extent to which it is being met. Table 2 summarizes empirical studies on the effectiveness of drug screening programs, but it does not include the findings of company reports—often cited in magazines and journal articles—where sufficient details regarding research methods and results were unobtainable.

Table 2 *(Continued)*

Drugs Investigated	Dependent Measures	Results	Comments
Marijuana, cocaine, amphetamines, and opiates	Percentage of confirmed positives	• The positive marijuana rate declined significantly among the four groups between 1983 and 1988. • The positive cocaine rate increased among all four groups. • The amphetamine and opiate confirmed positive rates remained fairly constant.	
Amphetamines, cocaine, and marijuana	Percentage testing positive	• For employees, the percentage testing positive dropped from 3% to 1%. • For contractors, the percentage testing positive remained constant.	
Marijuana, cocaine, alcohol, and other unspecified drugs	Personal injury accidents	• The percentage of positive tests dropped from about 22% in 1989 to 6% in 1988. • The number of personal injuries dropped from 2,234 to 322, and the number of train accidents attributable to human failure dropped from 911 to 54, over a 5-year period.	The drop in personal injury accidents cannot be attributed to drug screening, because several rival events (track improvements, risk reduction programs, etc.) occurred simultaneously (see Jones, 1990).

Two major objectives of drug screening are to reduce industrial accidents and to reduce performance problems in the workplace (e.g., absenteeism and turnover). Some studies have indicated that the frequency of industrial accidents and performance problems has been reduced considerably following the implementation of drug screening programs. According to Osterloh and Becker (1990), General Motors reported that absenteeism was reduced by more than 40%, disciplinary actions dropped by 50%, and accidents fell by 50% after the implementation of drug screening programs. An article in *Time* reported that since a drug screening program was implemented at an electric utility, absenteeism dropped by 25% and medical claims rose by only 6%, compared with 23% in previous years (Castro, Beaty, & Dolan, 1986).

Many studies have been severely criticized for attributing reductions in accident rates and improvement in productivity to drug screening without accounting for the influence of other program developments (Eichler, Goldberg, Kier, & Allen, 1988; Jones, 1990; Sheridan & Winkler, 1989). For example, a study conducted at the Southern Pacific Railway reported that the number of personal injuries on the railroad dropped from 2,234 to 322, and the number of train accidents attributable to human failure dropped from 911 to 54, in the 5-year period following the institution of a random drug screening program (Taggart, 1989). Massive engineering improvements in the tracking system, the implementation of crew risk reduction programs, the expansion of training programs, and other safety improvements, however, occurred simultaneously with the use of the drug screening program (Jones, 1990). These measures may have accounted for the majority, if not all, of the reported reductions in accidents, injuries, and productivity problems.

Studies discussed earlier demonstrating that drug-positive employees have more performance problems than drug-negative employees add credence to the argument that screening programs might reduce such problems. With screening, employers would typically hire only drug-negative applicants and fire or rehabilitate drug-positive employees; therefore, workplace problems could be reduced by eliminating those who test positive. As shown earlier, though, research comparing the work performance of drug-negative and drug-positive employees is inconclusive. Some studies do indicate that drug-positive employees suffer from more work performance problems than drug-negative employees (McDaniel, 1989; Normand & Salyards, 1989; Normand et al., 1990; Sheridan & Winkler, 1989). In contrast, other studies suggest that minimal differences exist between the two groups in terms of work performance and on-the-job accident rates (Clinical Chemistry News, 1989; Parish, 1989).

Companies often wish to reduce the costs associated with drug and alcohol use. Walsh and Gust (1986) report that alcohol and drug abuse costs amount to approximately $100 billion in lost productivity per year. Normand et al. (1990) estimated that the U.S. Postal Service could save roughly $4,000,000 in productivity costs in the first year of screening. Notably, however, Horgan (1990a) observed that in the Normand et al. (1990) study the influence of such other variables as race, age, and gender were not controlled. Hence, confounding variables may obscure such estimates.

Another major objective of drug screening is, by reducing drug use in the workplace, to reduce drug use in society as a whole. Some companies have noted reductions in the percentage of employees who test positive over subsequent years of screening (Needleman & Romberg, 1989; Osborne et al., 1990; Willette, 1986). According to Willette (1986), the U.S. Navy reported that after drug screening was implemented, positive test results dropped steadily from 48% to less than 5%. Similarly, in a study conducted by Needleman and Romberg (1989), the positive marijuana rate declined significantly among U.S. Navy and Marine Corps recruits and service school members between 1983 and 1988. One possible explanation for this reduction might be that drug users seeking employment are less likely to apply to employers with screening. It could also be argued that users employed better methods for beating the tests. Some authors have suggested accordingly that casual users of drugs may be more likely to test positive than heavier users, because the latter group has learned how to beat the tests (Weiss & Millman, 1989). In addition, it may be that drug testing programs are implemented when unions are at their weakest; if so, employees may resist using drugs in fear of being laid off or fired (Osterloh & Becker, 1990).

In summary, it appears that evidence is inconclusive, not only that drug use is related to work performance problems and work accidents, but also that drug screening programs actually reduce such work performance problems. Too few empirical studies on the effectiveness of drug screening programs exist at this time to prove that programs are effective in reducing drug use among employees, accidents and performance problems in the workplace, or drug problems in society as a whole.

5. CONCLUSION

This chapter has touched upon a wide variety of issues related to the impact and effectiveness of drug screening programs. Knowledge about the impact of drug use on job performance and the impact and effectiveness of drug screening programs in the workplace is limited because research in these areas is sparse and lacking in terms of scientific rigor. The empirical evidence is most conclusive that on-the-job alcohol impairment is likely related to accidents and performance problems in the workplace. Research studies on drug use and performance problems as a whole are methodologically weaker than studies of alcohol and similar problems. Research is inconclusive as to whether drug use is related to work accidents. It is suggestive that drug use is related to performance problems;

however, this finding should be treated with caution because of the methodological weaknesses of the studies. Clearly the laboratory setting is very different from the workplace, and a better understanding of the relationship between alcohol and/or drug use and workplace behavior is needed.

In terms of evaluating the effectiveness of drug screening programs, evidence is also inconclusive. It has not been determined that the objectives of screening programs are being met, because studies on the effectiveness of screening programs are few in number and most of them have severe methodological shortcomings. In addition, there may be negative consequences of drug screening that have not been empirically examined; clearly, this area has not been adequately researched. There is a great need for sophisticated empirical studies investigating (a) the relationship between drug use and workplace performance and accidents; (b) the extent to which drug screening programs reduce drug use, occupational accidents, and performance problems; and (c) the extent to which drug screening programs have a negative impact on the workplace. Information obtained from such studies would permit more decisive conclusions to be drawn about the impact and effectiveness of drug screening programs.

REFERENCES

Addiction Research Foundation, 1990, *Employment-Related Drug Screening,* Toronto.

Axel, H., 1989, Characteristics of firms with drugs testing programs, in: *Drugs in the Workplace: Research and Evaluation Data,* NIDA Research Monograph, no. 91, U.S. Government Printing Office, Washington, DC.

Blank, D., and Fenton, J., 1989, Early employment testing for marijuana: Demographic and employee retention patterns, in: *Drugs in the Workplace: Research and Evaluation Data,* NIDA Research Monograph, no. 91, U.S. Government Printing Office, Washington, DC.

Castro, J., Beaty, J., and Dolan, B., 1986, Battling the enemy within, *Time* (March 17), pp. 52–61.

Cornish, C. M., 1988, Overview of drug use and drug testing, in: *Drugs and Alcohol in the Workplace: Testing and Privacy,* pp. 33–50, Callaghan and Company, Wilmette, IL.

Crant, J. M., and Bateman, T. S., 1990, An experimental test of the impact of drug-testing programs on potential job applicants' attitudes and intentions, *Journal of Applied Psychology* **75:**127–131.

Crouch, D., Webb, D., Peterson, L., Buller, P., and Rollins, D., 1989, A critical evaluation of the Utah Power and Light Company's substance abuse management program: Absenteeism, accidents and costs, in: *Drugs in the Workplace: Research and Evaluation Data,* NIDA Research Monograph, no. 91, U.S. Government Printing Office, Washington, DC.

Decresce, R. P., Lifshitz, M. S., Ambre, J., Mazura, A. C., Tilson, J. E., and Cochran, K. M., 1989, *Drug Testing in the Workplace,* American Society of Clinical Pathologists, Chicago, IL.

DuPont, R. L., 1990, Mandatory random testing needs to be undertaken at the worksite, in: *Controversies in the Addictions Field,* vol. 1. R. C. Engs, ed., pp. 105–111, Kendall/Hunt Publishing Company, Dubuque, IA.

Eichler, S., Goldberg, C. M., Kier, L. E., and Allen, J. P., 1988, *Operation "Red Block": Case Study of a Peer Prevention Substance Abuse Program for Railroad Industry Personnel,* Institute for Human Resources, Rockville, MD.

Ellis, D., 1988, Urine testing—A critical appraisal, *Canadian Journal of Criminology* **30**:261–271.

Fay, J., 1991, *Drug Testing*, Butterworth-Heinemann, Stoneham, MA.

Glass, J., 1992, USCG puts drug testing on hold, *Lloyds List*, July 21.

Hayghe, H. V., 1991, Anti-drug programs in the workplace: Are they here to stay? *Monthly Labor Review* **114**:26–29.

Heller, D., and Robinson, A., 1991, *Substance Abuse in the Workforce*, Ontario Ministry of Labor, Toronto.

Horgan, J., 1990a, Test Negative: A Look at the "Evidence" Justifying Illicit-Drug Tests, *Scientific American*, March 18, p. 22.

Horgan, J., 1990b, Your analysis is faulty, *New Republic*, April, pp. 33–35.

Jones, J. P., 1990, Drug testing did not reduce Southern Pacific's accident rate, *Forensic Urine Drug Testing* (June):2–4.

Kaplan, E., and Williams, L. G., 1988, Will employees' rights be the first casualty of the war on drugs? *Kansas Law Review* **36**:755–785.

Klein, K. E., 1972, Prediction of flight safety hazards from drug induced performance decrements with alcohol as reference substance, *Aeronautical Medicine* **43**:1207–1214.

Lederman, S., and Metz, B., 1960, Les accidents du travail et l'alcool, *Population* **15**:301–316.

Macdonald, S., and Dooley, S., 1991, The nature and extent of EAPs and drug screening programs in Canadian transportation companies, *Employee Assistance Quarterly* **6**:23–40.

Maltby, L. L., 1987, Why drug testing is a bad idea, *Inc.* June, pp. 152–153.

Markus, W., 1992, Questionnaire results tabulated, *Forensic Urine Drug Testing*, December, p. 5.

Masi, D. A., and Burns, L. E., 1986, Urinalysis testing and EAPs, *EAP Digest* **6**:37–43.

McDaniel, M., 1989, Does pre-employment drug use predict on-the-job suitability? in: *Drugs in the Workplace: Research and Evaluation Data*, NIDA Research Monograph, no. 91, U.S. Government Printing Office, Washington, DC.

Needleman, S. B., and Romberg, R. W., 1989, Comparison of drug abuse in different military populations, *Journal of Forensic Science* **34**:848–857.

Newcomb, M. D., 1988, *Drug Use in the Workplace*, Auburn House, Dover, MA.

Normand, J., and Salyards, S. D., 1989, An empirical evaluation of preemployment drug testing in the United States Postal Service: Interim report of findings, in: *Drugs in the Workplace: Research and Evaluation Data*, NIDA Research Monograph, no. 91, U.S. Government Printing Office, Washington, DC.

Normand, J., Salyards, S. D., and Mahoney, J. J., 1990, An evaluation of pre-employment drug testing, *Journal of Applied Psychology* **75**:629–639.

Occupational Safety and Health Reporter, 1989, DOT adopts final rule implementing drug testing for up to 4 million workers, *Occupational Safety and Health Reporter* **19**:1261–1262.

Office of National Drug Control Policy, 1990, *Building a Drug-Free Workforce*, Office of National Drug Control Policy, Washington, DC.

O'Keefe, A. M., 1987, The case against drug testing, *Psychology Today*, June, pp. 34–38.

Osterloh, J., and Becker, C. E., 1990, Chemical dependency and drug testing in the workplace, *West J. Med.* **152**:506–513.

Papoz, L., Weill, J., L'Hoste, J., Chich, Y., Got, C., and Goehrs, Y., 1986, Biological markers of alcohol intake among 4,796 subjects in accidents, *British Medical Journal* **292**:1234–1237.

Parish, D. C., 1989, Relation of the pre-employment drug testing result to employment status: A one year follow-up, *Journal of General Internal Medicine* **4**:44–47.

Pell, S., and D'Alonzo, C., 1970, Sickness absenteeism of alcoholics, *Journal of Occupational Medicine* **12**:198–210.

Potter, B. A., and Orfali, J. S., 1990, *Drug Testing at Work: A Guide for Employers and Employees*, Ronin Publishing, Berkeley, CA.

Rothman, M., 1988, Random drug testing in the workplace: Implications for human resource management, *Business Horizons,* March/April, pp. 23–27.

Rothstein, M. A., 1989, Medical screening and employment law: A note of caution and some observations, *Employment Testing* **3:**363–369.

Ryan, J., Zwerling, C., and Jones, M., 1992, The effectiveness of preemployment drug screening in the prediction of employment outcome, *Journal of Medicine* **34:**1057–1063.

Segal, J. A., 1989, How reasonable is your suspicion? *Personnel Administrator,* December, pp. 103–104.

Shain, M., 1982, Alcohol, drugs and safety: An updated perspective on problems and their management in the workplace, *Accident Analysis and Prevention* **14:**239–246.

Sheridan, J., and Winkler, H., 1989, An evaluation of drug testing in the workplace, in: *Drugs in the Workplace: Research and Evaluation Data,* NIDA Research Monograph, No. 91, U.S. Government Printing Office, Washington, DC.

Smithers Institute, 1992, *Report on Workplace Substance Abuse Policy,* Cornell University, Ithaca, New York.

Stennett-Brewer, L., 1988, Employer drug testing: Legal issues—interview with Karen Hawley Henry, J.D., *Employee Assistance Quarterly* **4:**57–70.

Taggart, R., 1989, Results of the drug testing program at Southern Pacific Railroad, in: *Drugs in the Workplace: Research and Evaluation Data,* NIDA Research Monograph, No. 91, U.S. Government Printing Office, Washington, DC.

Tyson, P., and Vaughn, A. V., 1987, Drug testing in the workplace, *Occupational Health and Safety,* April, pp. 24–36.

Walsh, J. M., and Gust, S. W., 1986, Drug abuse in the workplace, *Seminars in Occupational Medicine* **1:**237–241.

Walsh, J. M., and Hawks, R. L., 1986, Q & A: Employee drug screening [leaflet], National Institute on Drug Abuse, U.S. Department of Health and Human Services, Rockville, MD.

Weeks, J. L., 1987, Eight problems examined that point out serious inadequacies in testing for drug abuse, *Mining Engineering* **39:**999–1002.

Weiss, C., and Millman, R., 1989, Alcohol and drug abuse in the workplace in broad perspective, *Bulletin of the New York Academy of Medicine* **65:**173–184.

Willette, R. E., 1986, Drug testing programs, in: *Urine Testing for Drugs of Abuse,* NIDA Research Monograph, no. 73, U.S. Government Printing Office, Washington, DC.

Winkler, H., and Sheridan, J., 1989, An examination of behavior related to drug use at Georgia Power Company, Presented at the National Institute on Drug Abuse Conference on Drugs in the Workplace: Research and Evaluation Data, Bethesda, MD.

Zwerling, C., Ryan, J., and Orav, E. J., 1990, The efficacy of pre-employment drug screening for marijuana and cocaine in predicting employment outcome, *Journal of the American Medical Association* **264:**2639–2643.

Zwerling, C., Ryan, J., and Orav, E. J., Costs and benefits of preemployment drug screening, *Journal of the American Medical Association* **267:**91–93.

7

Evaluation Approaches for Cost-Effectiveness and Effectiveness of Drug Testing Programs

JOAN A. MARSHMAN

In the current economic climate, one question increasingly dominates decision making about expenditures: What are we getting for our money? This is a critical question for all types of decision makers—private and public sector, large operations and small—and a concern for members of the general public who variously wear the hats of consumer, investor, and taxpayer. It is no less a concern in drug abuse programming than in other areas, as evidenced by the remarks of the Hon. Charles B. Rangel, Chairman of the U.S. House of Representatives Select Committee on Narcotics Abuse and Control (Rangel, 1990, p. 23): "We need economists and business people to evaluate what we are doing, and at least to give us ideas as to where we should be going in order to come up with better approaches to the problem. . . . We need the benefit of . . . guidance as to how to do a better job [with the resources] we have now." When these concerns focus on employees' drug use, three types of questions are important:

1. Should we be using scarce resources to take action against employees' drug use?
2. If we take action, should that action include drug testing?
3. If we include drug testing, which approach to drug testing should we use? Should we randomly test all employees, or only employees who

JOAN A. MARSHMAN • Addiction Research Foundation, Toronto, Ontario M4S 2S1, Canada.

Research Advances in Alcohol and Drug Problems, Volume 11: Drug Testing in the Workplace, edited by Scott Macdonald and Paul M. Roman. Plenum Press, New York, 1994.

have been involved in workplace accidents; all job applicants, or just applicants to whom we propose to make job offers? Moreover, should we buy a comprehensive testing program contract, or should we organize urine collection and medical review of results in-house and buy laboratory testing services only?

In most North American workplaces, the first question is virtually rhetorical. Because of the regulatory environment, community norms, company values, collective agreements, and/or occupational safety concerns, employers do allocate resources to "action" against employees' drug use. Such action commonly includes provision of extended health care insurance to cover substance use treatment and rehabilitation (as well as substance-related use of general health services), employee assistance programs (EAPs), and the processes of dismissing substance-using employees and recruiting and training their replacements. Much of the variability among employers lies in the magnitude of the resources allocated and the balance in their objectives between (a) resolving drug-related problems and (b) preventing such problems by deterrence of drug use.

Thus, the second and third questions are the focus of more active and widespread discussion and debate (e.g., Faley, 1988). Their importance is reflected in Wish's comment (1990) that "a 100% increase in risk for absenteeism from 3% (for non-users) to 6% (for drug users) may not justify the varied costs involved in establishing a drug screening program" (p. 2677). And though the questions may be voiced most often by employers, the answers are relevant also to employees, who are affected both directly by the testing process itself and indirectly by employers' testing-related costs. They are also important to public policymakers, because public policy development concerning workplace drug testing should take into account both the effectiveness and the relative costs of the policy alternatives.

Cost-benefit analysis (CBA) addresses the question of whether the benefits of action (specifically, drug testing) against employees' drug use, measured in dollars (or other monetary units), equal or exceed its costs.* The second and third questions, though, are also amenable to cost-effectiveness analysis (CEA). The term *cost-effective* is used colloquially to indicate that a course of action or

*Traditionally, CBA compares the total of all costs (C) to the total monetary value (B) of all tangible benefits (i.e., elements of outcome) from the perspective of society. The North American literature on economic evaluation of substance use programs, however, is dominated by a somewhat narrower approach, cost-offset analysis (COA). COAs can be viewed as CBAs from a limited perspective. They typically include costs (C) of an intervention (e.g., treatment) from the perspective of the insurer or employer. These costs are compared with the saving or benefit (B) that accrues to the insurer or employer as a result of the intervention (e.g., reduction in the employees' use of health services in the posttreatment period). The result of CBA or COA is typically expressed as the difference ($B - C$).

program[†] imposes an acceptably low cost for the amount of effect it generates. Low, however, is a relative term; it has meaning only when two or more programs are compared. Accordingly, as noted by Drummond, Stoddart, and Torrance (1987) the CEA question is best expressed in its incremental form: What are the additional costs that one program imposes relative to another, compared with the additional effect it delivers, or vice versa?

Thus, CEA can be used to address the second question above when the analysis compares the company's "action" program with and without a drug testing component—or, often, the company's old program versus its new program. When applied to the third question, the comparison is between alternative versions of the drug testing process. Although the programs or processes being compared may have several types of effects, CEA (unlike CBA) compares each as if it was the sole effect produced.[‡]

The purpose of this chapter is to examine the use of cost-effectiveness analysis in addressing these important issues. The CEA approach presented is commonly used in evaluation of health programs, reflecting the position that drug testing is a drug abuse prevention strategy based on principles of deterrence and early detection/intervention. The chapter should assist the reader to appreciate the potential contributions of CEA to drug testing program evaluation, and to appraise more critically both proposals for assessing the cost-effectiveness of drug testing programs and the reported results of such program evaluations.

1. COST-EFFECTIVENESS ANALYSIS (CEA)

It follows from the incremental cost-effectiveness question that one workplace anti-drug program can be deemed more cost-effective than a second when (a) the first program is more effective than the second but also has a higher cost,

[†]In this chapter the term *program* is used, along with *course of action*, to denote a set of processes. A drug testing process can be considered as one of the component processes of the human resources management program. Other component processes might include, but are not restricted to, training of supervisors to detect substance-impaired workers, provision of addiction treatment services under an employer-paid general health services plan, an employee assistance program, counseling of drug users by an occupational health department, reassignment of test-positive employees to non-safety-sensitive positions, employee retraining, and processes for dehiring known or suspected drug users or refusal of employment to test-positive job applicants. A schematic representation of a human resources management program is presented in Figure 1.

[‡]In some program evaluations using the CEA approach, comparison of the alternative programs is made along several dimensions of effect. In that case the effects selected for measurement should be potentially achievable to the same extent through the alternative programs (Drummond et al., 1987, p. 74). The analysis considers each effect separately, as if each was the sole effect produced (i.e., there is no integration of the measured effects into a global measure of benefit).

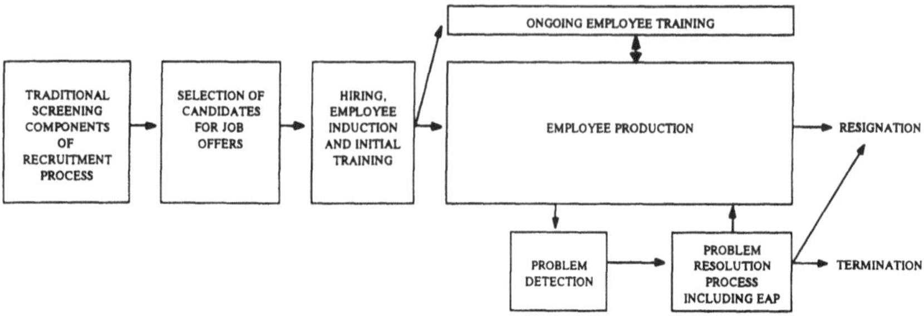

Figure 1. Human Resource Management Program in the Absence of Drug Testing.

and the extra cost per extra unit effect is judged acceptable to the decision maker; (b) the first program is less effective than the second, but also has a lower cost, and the extra cost per extra unit effect of the second is judged unacceptable by the decision maker; or (c) the first program is at least equally effective as the second and also has a lower cost, so that the first has a lower average cost per unit effect (Doubilet, Weinstein, & McNeil, 1986). Accordingly, the result of the analysis is expressed as the difference in cost of two programs divided by the difference in their effect (or the inverse).* When the two programs are equally effective, the CEA result in commonly expressed as the comparison of their mean costs per unit effect.*

For example, the human resources management program in a workplace operating without a drug testing process (i.e., the "old" program) might be represented functionally by Figure 1. This program's processes could be considered generic—used to prevent and resolve employee problems whether the latter are associated with drug use or not. If a process of random drug testing for employees were then introduced to create the "new" program, positive drug test results could be considered problems to be addressed via these same generic processes. This new program would impose extra costs on the employer and be expected to produce extra effects. The extra costs would include not only costs of the drug testing process itself, but also the downstream costs of the problem-resolution process (potentially including treatment and/or rehabilitation) for test-positive employees who would not have been labeled as problems under the old program. The extra benefits of the new program might include increases in the number of drug-free employees and productivity, as well as reductions in workplace accidents, employee turnover, and employee theft (i.e., tangible effects), and improved employee morale and quality of life (i.e., intangible effects). Each of these program effects might be considered a separate basis for CEA.

*i.e., $[(C_1 - C_2)]/(E_1 - E_2)]$ or its reciprocal, where C and E represent cost and effect, respectively.
*i.e., (C_1/E) versus (C_2/E).

This example serves to emphasize the importance of clearly defining the programs being compared in a cost-effectiveness analysis, not only to ensure accurate understanding of the cost-generating processes, but also to ensure selection of the most relevant program effect(s).

2. PROGRAM EFFECTIVENESS

Selecting Program Effects as a Basis for Evaluation

In principle, the effectiveness of a workplace drug testing program might be assessed consistent with the program's objectives, using any of a wide spectrum of measured effects. In reality, there is considerable confusion about the objective(s) of workplace drug testing (Robinson, 1989).

Table 1 presents a "menu" of objectives (and subobjectives) toward which a hypothetical program might be directed. Corresponding to each objective is a set of program effects or outcomes that might be considered in planning an evaluation of the program's effectiveness and/or cost-effectiveness. Many of these are currently used by employers in the evaluation of their EAPs (Houts, 1991), ranging from detection rate of drug-using employees (e.g., Cangianelli, 1989) through rates of employee turnover, absenteeism, lateness, product defects, or workplace accidents (e.g., Crouch, Webb, Bullers, & Rollins, 1989; Sheridan & Winkler, 1989; Zwerling, Ryan, & Orav, 1992).

In general, CEAs will be useful for management decision making and/or public policy formulation if they are based on outcomes that are:

- consistent with the objectives established for the action programs under consideration;
- causally attributable to these programs;
- meaningful and highly valued by the (major) decision-making or stakeholder group(s);
- relevant for virtually all members of the programs' target group, whether that target group is a single category of individuals (e.g., job applicants, current employees, or employees involved in workplace accidents), or a mix of such categories;
- detectable/measurable by valid and reliable methods in the relevant program setting(s);
- relatively nonresponsive to conditions or events that are independent of the programs under evaluation; and
- potentially achievable to the same extent through the alternative processes.

Table 1
Some Hypothetical Workplace Drug Testing Objectives and Potential Effects of Drug Testing Programs

Objectives of the Drug Testing Program	Examples of Relevant Program Effects
To identify substance-using current/potential employees so as to	• Number or proportion of current/potential employees identified as substance users
a. provide an objective basis for mandatory referral for treatment/rehabilitation	• Number or proportion of substance-using employees referred to EAP on a mandatory basis • Number or proportion of substance-using job applicants referred for treatment/rehabilitation
b. prevent their further drug use, and thereby	• Number or proportion of test-positive employees/job applicants engaged successfully in a treatment/rehabilitation process • Proportion of test-positive employees/job applicants testing negative in repeated follow-up tests
(i) enhance the quality of life of the newly drug-free employees/job applicants and their families	• Quality-of-life measurement of the treated employees/job applicants and their families
(ii) reduce the prevalence of substance use and/or the extent of use in the community, and the associated cost burden to the community	• Community prevalence of substance use • Extent (i.e., quantity × frequency) of substance use in the community • Economic costs of substance use to the community
(iii) prevent the onset of drug use among currently drug-free employees	• Incidence of substance use in the employee group • Prevalence of substance use in the employee population
(iv) prevent productivity losses	• Employee absenteeism rates • Employee error rates; product flaw rates
(v) prevent workplace accidents and other incidents	• Prevalence of workplace accidents and other incidents • Costs of workplace accidents and other incidents, including property damage, personal injury, administrative and disciplinary actions, and legal actions
(vi) prevent/minimize cost increases for employer-paid health and disability benefits	• Cost of employer-paid health insurance premiums • Cost of self-insured disability benefits
(vii) prevent drug-related employee turnover	• Employee turnover rates • Costs of dehiring, hiring, and training
c. deter substance use among potential job applicants, and thereby reduce the prevalence and/or extent of drug use in the potential applicant pool and the associated cost burden to the community.	• Prevalence of substance use in the potential applicant pool • Extent (quantity × frequency) of use in the potential applicant pool • Economic costs to the community of substance use attributable to the potential applicant pool

When these criteria are applied, it is clear that some outcomes in Table 1 are not ideal as effectiveness measures. Consider, for example, measuring the number (or proportion) of positive urine tests, or the number (or proportion) of individuals identified as drug users (e.g., Cangianelli, 1989; Taggart, 1989). Such program effects might be entirely consistent with the objective to identify the presence of drugs in urine samples of current (or potential) employees, or to identify substance-using current (or potential) employees. They also meet the criteria of being relevant for all urine samples (or individuals) tested, attributable to the testing process per se, resulting from the application of valid and reliable detection methods, and subject to change as a function of changing test methods.

Positive urine samples in and of themselves are not ordinarily meaningful, although they might be if the program is *pro forma* (i.e., its ultimate objective is merely to provide documentary evidence of compliance with legislative or regulatory requirements). Their use can be criticized on several bases, including the following:

- A single positive urine test does not have a definitive meaning; it merely reflects recent use of a drug, perhaps by a casual user, perhaps by a compulsive drug abuser (Wish, 1990).
- A positive test result does not indicate impairment of performance or fitness for work, which may be influenced by a host of factors (e.g., tolerance to the drug, personality, environment, and work demands; Heller & Robinson, 1991, pp. 37–39).
- Detection alone, without subsequent discontinuation of drug use, is of little value (Osterloh & Becker, 1990).

Therefore, unless the positive urine test result or the labeling of the employee is coupled with some subsequent action—including assessment of drug use behaviors and, as appropriate, disciplinary action, job reassignment, counseling, or referral for treatment—there is no basis for assuming that it will have a positively valued effect on drug use, productivity, workplace accident rates, health service utilization, or employees' quality of life. Hence, in most workplace situations, neither a positive laboratory result for an urine sample nor labeling of an employee as a drug user, in isolation from subsequent action process(es), is an appropriate basis for CEA of anti-drug programs.

Analogously, consider for a moment the drug testing of job applicants (i.e., potential employees). Suppose that job offers were withheld from test-positive individuals who were otherwise qualified (i.e., the process of drug testing was coupled with an exclusionary hiring process). In this case the more relevant effect for program evaluation might be the number of test-positive employees avoided. A company might anticipate that avoidance of such employees would reduce its risk of drug-related lost productivity, workplace accidents, and high health service insurance rates. This inference, however, requires knowledge that the types of drug users identified by such testing actually contribute disproportionately to these problems in similar workplaces (see Chapter 6 for a review).

Also in the realm of preemployment testing, it is not valid to assume that rejection of test-positive job candidates decreases drug use in the potential job applicant pool, or in the larger community. A reduction in the proportion of test-positive candidates over time may suggest a reduction in drug use in the community, but it also may reflect merely a self-selection process among job applicants (i.e., drug users may refrain from applying as it becomes known that applicants will be tested and rejected if they test positive).

Readers of evaluation reports often assume that a reported result is generalizable to other settings, or that a reported effect is a valid proxy for some other effect that they wish to achieve. Instead of engaging in such wishful thinking, managers and policymakers should critically assess reported (or proposed) drug testing outcomes in relation to their own settings and their own employee populations.

Measuring Program Effectiveness

As emphasized previously, determination of cost-effectiveness involves a comparison of two programs, frequently an old (or baseline) program versus a new program (created by addition of drug testing) in a specific workplace (e.g., Taggart, 1989). Over the short term (i.e., several months to a year), many factors that could affect program outcomes are likely to remain constant (e.g., the types of employee groups or job applicants, job roles, physical plant, work processes, and social norms of the community). Under these conditions a real difference in effect produced by a drug testing process is more likely to be detectable, and the size of the difference accurately estimated. In contrast, when programs are compared across multiple workplaces or widely varying time periods (e.g., Bray, Marsden, Rachal, & Peterson, 1990), differences in these factors may result in failure to detect real differences between programs, inferences of a difference when none really exists, or over- or underestimation of the size of the difference.

Cost-effectiveness evaluations based on "old" versus "new" programs in a single work site, though, are vulnerable to other types of methodological problems. One such problem arises from the erroneous assumption that when there was no drug testing, there was no problem resolution of employee drug use. Particularly in work settings with an EAP, it is inevitable that some drug-using employees are identified as poor performers, accident prone, or excessively absent and are referred for assistance via the EAP, with resulting reduction or elimination of their drug use (e.g., Roman, 1989; Sheridan & Winkler, 1989). In such cases, the erroneous zero-effect assumption for the old program would result in overestimation of the difference between old and new programs (i.e., the effectiveness of the added drug testing process).

Another potential error arises from the assumption that an identified drug user is equivalent in the two programs. It is tempting to think that the difference between programs (e.g., in accident rate or absenteeism costs) can be estimated as the difference in number of users identified. As noted by Morgan (1988), however, drug-using employees referred to an EAP (in the absence of drug testing) because of performance deficits are more likely to be regular and/or heavy users. Therefore, the workplace impact per identified user, as well as the number of users identified, might be quite different under the two programs.

Further, this difference between users identified by EAP and by drug testing may vary over time, being more pronounced in the earlier months of a drug testing program and diminishing as drug users learn strategies to avoid detection (e.g., abstaining for a requisite pretest period, or substitution or dilution of urine; Cangianelli, 1989; Coombs & Ryan, 1990; Henriksson, 1991). If such avoidance behaviors became widespread, only those unable to abstain (e.g., heavier, drug-dependent users) or those completely indifferent to the consequences of their use would be identified by the drug testing process. Therefore, over time, drug users identified under the old and new programs might become quite similar.

Another potential error in old-versus-new program comparisons is too brief a measurement period for the old program. This is a particularly important consideration when drug testing is introduced in response to a perceived increase in drug use. In this situation, the period immediately preceding the introduction of the testing process might indeed have had unusually high numbers of drug-using employees identified, disciplined, or referred for treatment/rehabilitation. These numbers, however, might be only temporary artifacts reflecting, for example, unusual alertness and diligence on the part of supervisors or security personnel following specialized training. Alternatively, these pretest numbers might reflect a real but short-lived increase in employees' drug use—the result of temporarily lowered drug prices or reduced community drug enforcement activity—that would return to earlier levels whether or not a drug testing process was introduced. The result of this error would be overestimation of the effectiveness of drug testing.

Overestimation of drug testing effectiveness could also arise from too brief a measurement period for the new program. It is quite likely that, for the initial period of a new drug testing program, some drug-using employees would abstain from drug use. As they learned from coworkers' experience how to avoid detection, though, they would probably revert to their previous drug use practices.

Finally, measurement of drug testing effects over longer periods (e.g., over several years) may be vulnerable to error from evolutionary change in the drug testing technologies themselves. For example, in their study of preemployment drug screening, Zwerling, Ryan, and Orav (1990) encountered a change in drug testing technology for cocaine—a shift from thin-layer chromatography to the more sensitive immunoassay screening method (see Blaze-Temple, 1992). Analogously, other changes in the workplace introduced during the evaluation period (e.g., changes in supervisory practices), may confound the effects of drug testing programs (e.g., Sheridan & Winkler, 1989).

Examples of Reported Program Effectiveness

Several of the methodological issues raised in previous sections are reflected in literature reports of drug testing programs. Three examples are presented here as illustrations.

The widely cited U.S. Navy experience with drug testing highlights the issue of comparability of employee groups in "old" versus "new" programs. As typically reported by proponents of drug testing, the navy reduced its personnel's test-positive rate from 48% in 1981 to less than 5% by 1989 (e.g., Lesher, 1990; Osterloh & Becker, 1990) following its introduction of drug testing. The casual reader of such reports (unlike the U.S. Navy itself) is likely to infer, incorrectly, that this difference is a measure of change in drug use behavior as a result of the drug testing process per se. Drug testing, however, was only one component of the navy's "zero tolerance" response to drug use (e.g., Cangianelli, 1989). Therefore, the difference in test-positive rates must realistically be attributed to the composite effect of all elements of the navy program together with changes that occurred in the general U.S. population. Several factors that might have contributed to the observed decrease are the following:

- Drug-using naval personnel who were willing to comply with new zero-tolerance policy might voluntarily have accessed the navy's enhanced treatment/rehabilitation services prior to producing a positive test.
- Drug-using naval personnel who were unwilling to adopt the long-term drug-free life-style expected under navy policy might have voluntarily resigned or retired prior to producing a positive test.
- Because the U.S. adolescent/young adult population, the pool from which recruits are drawn, showed a decline in marijuana use over the course of the 1980s, the potential applicant pool probably contained fewer drug users (Bray et al., 1990); further, some drug users in the potential applicant pool might have selected other career options when faced with the new zero-tolerance policy.
- As drug testing became more widespread during the 1980s, drug users became better informed about strategies for avoiding detection, so that the rate of false negative results probably increased.

A second illustration of methodological issues in measuring program effectiveness comes from the drug testing experience of the U.S. Federal Railroad Administration. In their analysis, Moody, Andrenyak, Wilkins, and Rollins (1990) highlighted the findings that positive test results for accident-involved personnel are not a valid proxy for drug-caused workplace accidents, and that the extent of causal linkage between positive test results and accidents varies among drug classes. Overall, alcohol or drug use was causally linked in approximately one third of positive events. Cannabinoids, the most commonly detected drug group, were causally linked to only 5 of the 22 cannabinoid-positive accidents assessed, whereas cocaine and ethanol were causally linked to 3 of 4 accidents assessed.

Undoubtedly, many factors contributed to these differences. One probable factor is the much slower clearance of cannabinoids from the body (e.g., Heller & Robinson, 1991). Because of slower clearance, cannabinoids can be detected in urine for weeks after last use, long after concentrations in brain tissue have fallen below levels that would alter performance, and long after either cocaine or alcohol would be detected. Another possible contributing factor is the nature of the impairment produced by cannabinoids, cocaine, and alcohol. Regardless of the mechanistic basis, it is clear that the results of CEA for this program would be quite different depending on whether accident causation or drug detection rates were used in the evaluation.

The nonequivalence of positive drug testing results and adverse employment outcomes is highlighted also by Zwerling et al. (1990) in their report on preemployment drug screening as a predictor of employment outcome. Although preemployment test-positive status for marijuana or cocaine was associated with adverse employment outcomes, the risk of such outcomes was much lower than suggested by conventional wisdom. Further, the two drugs were quite different in types of outcomes and risk levels. These results underscore the fact that test-positive preemployment status cannot be assumed to be a uniformly valid proxy for problems in the workplace.

3. PROGRAM COSTS

Thus far this chapter has focused on program effects and their measurement. It has emphasized the importance of critically examining drug testing evaluation reports and proposals to ensure the appropriateness of both the type(s) of effects measured and the measurement processes. Now the focus shifts to the types of costs to be considered in CEA and the measurement of these costs.

Fundamental to this discussion is the definition of program costs. From a societal perspective, the cost of a program is the total cost of all the resources used up in production of the measured effect(s). Although costs and effectiveness are equally important for CEA, costs have generally been treated less rigorously than effectiveness in program evaluations. Typically, costs have been addressed after effectiveness assessment, when managers or public policymakers want to place the program's effectiveness into a value-for-money context. This has often meant the use of cost information, collected for other purposes (e.g., Crouch et al., 1989; Sheridan & Winkler, 1989; Zwerling et al., 1992), that was less than ideal for CEA.

Ideally, evaluators anticipate the need for analysis of costs at the design stage of the evaluation. This permits them to consider the adequacy of existing cost data for CEA purposes, to define supplementary data collection needs, and to integrate the collection of data concerning resources use with collection of outcome data (Drummond & Stoddart, 1984). Given the gap between this ideal and usual practice, managers and policymakers concerned with cost-effectiveness of drug testing should carefully examine reported or proposed program costing in terms of the following questions, which have been adapted from Drummond et al. (1987):

- From whose perspective are the costs considered, and is this perspective appropriate to the decision-making needs?
- Are all of the relevant costs considered?
- Are the costs measured by appropriate methods?
- Is adjustment made for differences in timing of costs?
- Is a sensitivity analysis included?

Costs from Whose Perspective?

It is typically the employer who introduces drug testing into the workplace and pays the drug testing bills. Therefore, it is commonly assumed that the employer's perspective on drug testing program costs is the only appropriate one.

It may indeed be the most relevant perspective for particular decision-making contexts, as in the following hypothetical example. Suppose that the effectiveness of a drug testing program was defined in terms of the number of test-positive employees reassigned to non-safety-sensitive positions. Suppose further that such reassignment did not alter employee productivity, and that it occurred without prejudice to the test-positive employees' compensation, job security, opportunities for advancement, or seniority rights. Suppose also that this outcome was achieved without use of retraining, generic counseling, EAP services, treatment/rehabilitation services, or termination, as well as without altering the employment situation of any other employee. If this hypothetical program is compared with a nontesting program, the extra costs incurred are limited to the costs of the drug testing process (including medical review and reporting to the employer) and the costs of reassigning these employees to their new position. Because these costs are borne exclusively by the employer, they would constitute the total extra cost of the drug testing program from the employer's perspective. In this case, the additional cost from society's perspective would be zero.

In contrast, suppose that the effectiveness of the drug testing program was defined in terms of the number of employees successfully treated for drug use problems. Suppose further that the process leading to this outcome included several types of action downstream from the drug testing per se: referral of test-positive employees to the workplace EAP, use of employer-paid treatment/rehabilitation services that require patients' copayment, use of vacation time for treatment, and use of self-help/mutual support services as part of aftercare. In this case, program cost estimates would differ depending on whose perspective was taken: the employer's, the drug-using employees', or society's. The drug testing and referral processes and treatment/rehabilitation service utilization would be costs from the perspective of the employer, but not the employees; treatment copayments, vacation time used for treatment, out-of-pocket expenses (e.g., transportation to treatment and self-help sessions), and personal time used by employees to participate in self-help groups would be costs from the perspective of the employees, but not the employer; and costs from the perspective of society would include both of these subsets plus the cost of the self-help group resources used. In order to ensure that all costs relevant to a particular perspective are being considered, it is often helpful to identify all the cost elements associated with each of the program processes and the stakeholder(s) to whom each of the costs accrues.

Any of these perspectives may be addressed using CEA, but the appropriate perspective(s) will be determined by the nature of the decision(s) to be made. Thus, the employer who is considering expansion of a drug testing program to another work site would undoubtedly wish a cost estimate from his or her own perspective but might not be concerned with the employees' or the societal perspectives. In contrast, union leaders negotiating the program's expansion to the new work site would be particularly interested in costs to the employees, and the legislator or regulator considering mandatory industrywide testing might need cost estimates from all three perspectives (employer, employee, and society). Therefore, decision makers should critically examine the costing perspective(s) adopted in CEA reports or proposals. They should ensure that the cost elements included are consistent with the perspectives selected and that CEA results from the most relevant perspectives are taken into account in their decision making.

What Are the Relevant Costs?

It was noted above that costs can be defined as resources used up in producing the program effects and that various costs are borne by the employer, employee, and society. It is also important to recognize that costs are incurred not only in the actual conduct of the component processes (e.g., personnel time, materials, and fees), but also in providing the work-site infrastructure for these processes (e.g., building space, heat and light, management activity, and support services). Other overhead costs of drug testing recognized in the literature are associated with labor negotiations and litigation (Henriksson, 1991), and employee theft and sabotage (e.g., Rothstein, 1989). Because the total of these overhead costs may be substantial, it is essential that they be incorporated into cost estimates (e.g., see Crouch et al., 1989).

Overall Program Costs. When programs with and without a drug testing component are being compared using CEA, the "extra cost" imposed by the introduction of drug testing is the difference in total cost of the two programs.* This difference is the net result of differences in the types of resources used, the quantities of those resources, and the cost per unit resources.

Suppose the effectiveness of the programs being evaluated is defined as the number of detected employees who stop their drug use and continue their employment. Then the problem-detection box in Figure 1 would include all of the workplace's generic actions/activities that result in detection of drug use, such as the following:

- supervisor observation
- regular employee performance reviews
- monitoring of individual or team production records
- monitoring of product defects or errors
- time-sheet monitoring for employee lateness and absenteeism
- monitoring of incident/accident and employee illness reports

Analogously, the problem-resolution box in Figure 1 would include all of the generic actions taken when a drug-using employee is detected, including the following:

- disciplinary action
- supervisor referral to the workplace EAP
- EAP counseling and referral to specialized services
- use of drug treatment services, including specialized assessment, specific treatment/rehabilitation services, self-help groups, and treatment aftercare
- posttreatment EAP counseling to facilitate and support reentry to the workplace
- preparation of the documentation concerning these actions/services

Typically, these generic processes continue when a drug testing process is added to the human resources management program. After addition of drug

*i.e., $(C_1 - C_2)$.

testing, however, the problem-resolution box would also include actions taken uniquely in response to positive drug testing results, such as the following:

- interviews to inform employees of their positive test results and discuss options for action
- test-linked referral to the workplace EAP
- reassignment of test-positive employees to non-safety-sensitive positions
- posttreatment supplementary drug testing program to deter and detect relapse
- disciplinary actions uniquely associated with the positive test results
- preparation of the documentation specifically linked to these actions

Finally, both programs would include the generic processes of employee training, termination, and resignation, all of which involve the use of resources. Therefore, the total cost of each program would include that part of generic activity costs attributable to identified drug users, plus the entire cost of its drug-specific activities.

When the difference in cost of the two programs is calculated, however, costs that are truly identical offset each other. It is therefore unnecessary to estimate the cost of processes that are known to remain constant in their resource use under the two program conditions. For example, suppose that in both the old and new programs, the same number (*X*) of drug-using employees was detected by generic activities (e.g., supervisor observation), but that an additional number (*Y*) of drug-using employees is detected by the new drug testing process. If all other conditions remain the same, CEA would not require cost estimates for the generic processes. This assumes, however, that the programs were identical not only in the number of supervisor-identified drug-using employees, but also in those employees' resulting use of resources in the problem-resolution, training, reassignment, resignation, and termination processes. Clearly this condition would not be met if, with the introduction of the drug testing process, supervisors changed their behavior (e.g., by reducing their rates of referral of drug users to the EAP). Nor would the condition be met if drug-using employees began to resign to avoid being detected by the testing process.

Generally, evaluators should begin their program costing by identifying all contributing processes and the resources used in them. Particular resource elements can be deleted when they are shown to be constant for the programs being compared, or to represent negligibly small costs.

Cost of the Drug Testing Process Per Se. The drug testing process itself provides a useful focus for examining both direct operating and overhead costs. As discussed in Chapter 5, this process can be viewed as comprising three phases:

- sample collection, storage, and transport (i.e., sample generation)

- laboratory processing
- interpretation, review, and disposition of laboratory results

Traditionally, laboratory test fees were based on a clinical facilities model and covered laboratory processing only. In other words, testing fees were based on assumptions that an adequately large, properly preserved, and secure sample was received by the laboratory, and that the laboratory's output was a report to the ordering physician identifying the presence/absence or concentration of the chemical entity or entities identified in the order. Many laboratories continue to quote fee schedules based on this limited service model.

In contrast, some so-called total service packages include virtually the entire continuum of drug testing services: random selection of employees to be tested, supervised urine collection in a mobile facility, drug screening and confirmation of positive screening results, medical review of test-positive employees/applicants, and provision of expert medical opinion of the test results for the employer and in any subsequent (quasi-)legal proceedings. In work sites subject to externally mandated testing, the usual management question is not which of these functions will be included in the testing process, because all functions are typically prescribed (U.S. Department of Health and Human Services, 1988; Health and Welfare Canada, 1990), but rather which will be done in-house rather than purchased from an external supplier.

The employer who opts to purchase service for laboratory processing only implicitly opts for in-house sample generation (i.e., collection, storage, and transportation of urine samples). The costs to that employer will include not only laboratory billings but also "internal" costs associated with these other functions. Operating costs for sample generation might include the cost of personnel time for urine collection*, sealing, labeling, and logging samples; and secure storage transportation charges; overhead costs might include training and supervision costs for personnel engaged in urine collection and washroom maintenance, as well as capital costs associated with modification (or construction) of washroom and storage facilities to meet regulatory requirements.

Analogously, an employer might opt to purchase the services of a medical review officer as part of a comprehensive laboratory testing package. Alternatively, a workplace's internal physician, if appropriately trained, might provide those interpretation and review services. In the latter case, direct operating costs to the employer would include physician and perhaps secretarial time, and perhaps also increased telephone, facsimile transmission, and/or courier service utilization. Overhead costs to the employer might include specialized physician training and continuing education, a specialized reference library, and a larger

*Sample packaging materials (i.e., bottles, seals, labels, forms, and shipping containers) constitute a cost to the program, whether purchased directly or provided by the testing laboratory and included in the laboratory's fees.

space allocation to the corporate health unit to accommodate additional secretarial services and file space.

It follows from these examples that a cost estimate for a program's drug testing process, based solely on a laboratory's testing fee schedule, might be quite misleading. Therefore, evaluation proposals and reports should ensure that both operating and overhead components have been appropriately included in cost estimates.

Are Costs Appropriately Measured?

Drummond et al. (1987) recommended that costs for CEA studies of health programs be determined in accordance with generally accepted cost accounting principles (e.g., see Horngren, 1982). Thus, total program cost would be determined ideally by calculating the cost of each type of resource used (i.e., the number of units used multiplied by cost per unit) and summing across all types of resources. The reader is referred to the sources just cited for detailing costing procedures.

It was noted in the earlier section on cost perspectives that the costing process should be anticipated at the design stage of the evaluation, so that existing cost data can be explored for their adequacy for CEA and appropriate new data needs can be defined. Management information for generic process activity (e.g., EAP, human resource management, security) is often inadequate for CEA purposes, either because records are not maintained in a way that permits measurement of total or drug-related workload or because overhead costs are not reflected in departmental expenditure records. Therefore, it may be necessary to generate different types of workload or activity data and overhead-adjusted total costs for these service departments as a basis for estimating overhead-adjusted unit costs.

Is Adjustment Made for Difference in Timing of Costs?

When costs (or benefits) from different time periods are compared, it is customary to discount those incurred in the later period(s) in order to express all components in constant units (i.e., present-value calculation). This is particularly important in old-versus-new program comparisons, because costs and effects are likely to be distributed over two or more years.

Different discount rates may be justified in different program contexts. In evaluation of publicly funded programs, the rate typically used is similar to the return on government bonds (i.e., the so-called social rate of time preference). An alternative for private sector program evaluation is the real (i.e., inflation-adjusted) rate of return that would have been realized had the resources been put to an alternative use (Drummond et al., 1987). In their recent study of employee testing in the Utah Power and Light Company, Crouch et al. (1989) used a discount rate of 8%, whereas Zwerling et al. (1992) used a basic discount rate of 5% in their study of preemployment drug screening in the U.S. Postal Service.

Why Include a Sensitivity Analysis?

It is always tempting to treat a quantitative result (e.g., extra cost per extra unit effect) as if it were a precise and accurate measure. The fact is that even the most carefully generated CEA result incorporates error contributions from its underlying assumptions and measurement processes. Further, if the programs being evaluated were to be applied in other settings, environmental and process differences would contribute to somewhat different results.

As a means of formally recognizing such factors, economic evaluators usually incorporate a sensitivity analysis in their studies (i.e., they repeat their calculations using alternative assumptions and cost estimates). Typically they select alternative values for those factors that are the most vulnerable to error or change and that might be expected to have a relatively large impact on the final result. For example, in their sensitivity analysis, Zwerling et al. (1992) varied the discount rate from 0% to 7.5%, and the prevalence of test-positive samples from 0.4% to 20%. If the resulting change in the cost-effectiveness ratio is relatively small, then the original result can be used with some confidence by a wide range of decision makers. If the change in ratio is quite large, however, then the decision maker must carefully assess the nature and extent of the shifts in terms of the decision at hand.

4. USE OF CEA VERSUS CBA IN THE ECONOMIC EVALUATION OF DRUG TESTING PROGRAMS

To date, economic evaluations of workplace drug testing programs have focused largely on cost-benefit analysis (CBA) or the more limited cost-offset analysis (COA) rather than CEA. Crouch et al. (1989) undertook CBA evaluation of the Utah Power and Light Company's substance abuse management program, which included drug testing as well as an EAP and insured health services. Using a case control design, they estimated costs associated with program planning, site preparation, legal fees, computer setup, urine testing, EAP's grievance procedures, and quality assurance procedures. The total of these costs was compared with the potential savings from decreased vehicle accidents, reduced absenteeism, and reduced employee turnover. When the benefit period of the program was projected to 5 and 10 years, with discounting at 8%, the drug testing program was found to yield considerable financial savings. It is important to note that this report is a preliminary evaluation, however, based on the profiles of only 12 test-positive employees.

Zwerling et al. (1992) also used the CBA model in their evaluation of preemployment drug testing in the U.S. Postal Service. They estimated benefits as costs potentially avoidable through preemployment drug testing, based on the employment experience of a cohort of 2,533 postal workers. These workers experienced drug testing at the time of hiring, but the test results were not revealed to them or to their supervisors. Included in the accounting of benefits were reductions in rates of absenteeism, accidents, injuries, and turnover. Program costs included drug screening and confirmation of positive results, as well as recruitment and training of employees to replace screened-out applicants. The reported results, based primarily on estimates for the first year, indicated a potential net saving, but the magnitude of the saving was relatively small, and it was transformed to an estimated net loss when different assumptions were used in the sensitivity analysis. Therefore, the authors cautioned employers to examine their own industry's experience carefully before adopting a drug testing policy with the expectation of a net saving.

In these studies, the CBA question clearly was addressed from the employers' perspective, thus becoming effectively a cost-offset question of whether the drug testing program was a good financial decision for the employer. This is quite different to the incremental CEA question, formulated from the employer's perspective, that might be posed in a comparison of old and new programs: What was the extra cost of drug testing, to the employer, for each extra unit of effect achieved (e.g., for each drug-using employee avoided, for each percentage-point reduction in absenteeism, or for each unit increase in production rate)?

It is hardly surprising that to date the CBA (or COA) model for economic evaluation has been dominant, for the following reasons:

- The employer's return on program investment has been an issue of particular concern and one that is addressed directly via CBA. Further, the CBA (but not the CEA) model facilitates comparison of a drug testing program with alternative uses of employer resources that would yield quite different types of effects (e.g., a program to update production technology or to improve employee training).
- It is usually anticipated that drug testing programs will produce several effects or outcomes, and CBA permits incorporation of multiple effects into a single composite result, whereas CEA requires calculation of a separate cost-effectiveness ratio for each.
- Because there is considerable confusion about the objectives of workplace testing, evaluators are reluctant to select one effect as the sole or primary basis for CEA. This problem, which is particularly difficult when neither program is superior on all CEA bases, is circumvented when CBA is used.

- Given the relatively short history of workplace drug testing, few workplaces have had the opportunity to compare alternative testing programs.

As noted previously, however, the introduction of drug testing can be viewed as an initiative to produce an incremental change in effectiveness in the human resources management program, and is clearly amenable to CEA. Further, the use of CEA analysis obviates the need to assess the benefits of the drug testing process in dollar terms.

Two examples of testing cited in the Cornell/Smithers Report (1992) apply CEA principles to drug testing programs, although they appear to have methodological limitations. Their measure of effect (number of positive urine tests) is not an ideal measure, for reasons discussed above. Further, the program comparison was based on mean cost per positive test—$77,000 in the public-sector example, and more than $20,000 in a private-sector example—an approach that apparently assumes zero cost and zero effect for the baseline program. The inappropriateness of this assumption for the public-sector case is clear from the report's notation that approximately one third of the 73 test-positive employees discharged were already candidates for discharge prior to testing, presumably because they had been identified as problems by the baseline program. It appears that in these examples, the more appropriate effectiveness measure would have between the number of drug-using employees identified and dismissed. Accordingly, the incremental CEA result would have been the additional cost to the employer (or other party) per additional drug-using employee identified and dismissed.

Given that CEA is a relevant model for economic evaluation of drug testing programs, under what circumstances should it be considered? It seems likely that CEA will become increasingly used when one or more of the following conditions occur:

- Employers have become committed to a specific objective (or set of objectives) for employee and/or applicant drug testing and want to make an informed selection between alternative programs.
- The cost and/or effect difference(s) between the alternative programs is (are) probably large enough to be managerially significant.
- It is desirable to assess the difference in costs of the alternative programs relative to the difference in outcome from multiple perspectives (typically the employer, the employees, and society).

As decision makers give increasing attention to these issues in the 1990s, the CEA model of evaluation will be used more frequently.

REFERENCES

Blaze-Temple, D., 1992, Drug testing in the Australian workplace: Overview of the issues, *Drug and Alcohol Review* **2:**59–73.

Bray, R. M., Marsden, M. E., Rachal, J. V., and Peterson, M. R., 1990, Drug and alcohol use in the military workplace: Findings from the 1988 Worldwide Survey, in: *Drugs in the Workplace: Research and Evaluation Data,* vol. II, NIDA Research Monograph, No. 100 (S. W. Gust, J. M. Walsh, L. B. Thomas, and D. J. Crouch, eds.), pp. 25–43, U.S. Government Printing Office, Washington, DC.

Cangianelli, L. A., 1989, The effects of a drug testing program in the Navy, in: *Problems of Drug Dependence, 1989; Proceedings of the 51st Annual Scientific Meeting, of the Committee on Drug Dependence, Inc.,* NIDA Research Monograph, No. 95 (L. S. Harris, ed.), pp. 211–217, U.S. Government Printing Office, Washington, DC.

Coombs, R. H. and Ryan, F. J.,1990, Drug Testing Effectiveness in Identifying and Preventing Drug Use, *Am. J. Drug Alcohol Abuse* **16:**173–184.

Cornell/Smithers Report, 1992, *Drug testing: Cost and effect,* **1:**1–4.

Crouch, D. J., Webb, D. O., Buller, P. F. and Rollins, D. E., 1989, A critical evaluation of the Utah Power and Light Company's substance abuse management program: Absenteeism, accidents and costs, in: *Drugs in the Workplace: Research and Evaluation Data,* NIDA Research Monograph, No. 91 (S. W. Gust and J. M. Walsh, eds.), pp. 169–193, U.S. Government Printing Office, Washington, DC.

Doubilet, P., Weinstein, M. C., and McNeil, B. J., 1986, Use and misuse of the term "cost effective" in medicine, *New England Journal of Medicine,* **314:**253–256.

Drummond, M. F., and Stoddart G. L., 1984, Economic analysis and clinical trials, *Controlled Clinical Trials* **5:**115–128.

Drummond, M. F., Stoddart, G. L., and Torrance, G. W., 1987, *Methods for the Economic Evaluation of Health Care Programs,* Oxford University Press, Toronto.

Faley, R. H., Kleiman, L. S., and Wall, P. S., 1988, Drug testing in public and private-sector workplaces: Technical and legal issues, *Journal of Business and Psychology* **3:**154–186.

Health and Welfare Canada, 1990, *Canadian Laboratory Standards for Drug Screening in the Workplace* (Catalogue No. H42-2/23-1990), Ministry of Supply and Services, Ottawa.

Heller, D., and Robinson, A. E., 1991, *Substance Abuse in the Workforce: A Review Document to Provide Background Information as an Aid to Public Discussion and Policy Development,* Ontario Ministry of Labor, Toronto.

Henriksson, L. E., 1991, The unconvincing case for drug testing, *Canadian Public Policy,* **17:**183–196.

Horngren, C. T., 1982, *Accounting: A Managerial Emphasis,* Prentice-Hall, Englewood Cliffs, NJ.

Houts, L. M., 1991, Survey of the current status of cost-savings evaluations in employee assistance programs, *Employee Assistance Quarterly* **7:**57–72.

Lesher, R. L., 1990, Statement of the U.S. Chamber of Commerce, in: *The Impact of Drugs on American Business and the American Economy: Hearing before the Select Committee on Narcotics Abuse and Control,* House of Representatives, 101st Congress, 2nd Session, October 3, 1990, SCNAC–101–2–13, Washington, D.C.

Moody, D. E., Andrenyak, D. M., Wilkins, D. G., and Rollins, D. E., 1990, Mandatory post-accident drug and alcohol testing for the Federal Railroad Administration: A comparison of results for two consecutive years, in: *Drugs in the Workplace: Research and Evaluation Data,* vol. II, NIDA Research Monograph, No. 100 (S. W. Gust, J. M. Walsh, L. B. Thomas, and D. J. Crouch, eds), pp. 79–96, U.S. Government Printing Office, Washington, DC.

Morgan, J. P., 1988, The "scientific" justification for urine drug testing, *The University of Kansas Law Review* **36:**683–697.

Osterloh, J. D., and Becker, C. E., 1990, Chemical dependency and drug testing in the workplace, *Western Journal of Medicine* **152:**506–513.

Rangel, Charles B., 1990, *The Impact of Drugs on American Business and the American Economy: Hearing Before the Select Committee on Narcotics Abuse and Control,* House of Representatives 101st Congress, 2nd Session, October 3, 1990, SCNAC–101–2–13, p. 23, Washington, DC.

Robinson, A. E., 1989, Drug use testing: The Canadian scene *Journal of Forensic Sciences* **34:**1422–1432.

Roman, P. M., 1989, The use of EAPs in dealing with drug abuse in the workplace, in: *Drugs in the Workplace: Research and Evaluation Data* (S. N. Gust and J. M. Walsh, eds.), NIDA Research Monograph, No. 91, pp. 271–285, U.S. Government Printing Office, Washington, DC.

Rothstein, M. A., 1989, Medical Screening and Employment Law: A note of caution and some observations, *Employment Testing* **3:**363–369.

Sheridan, J., and Winkler, H., 1989, An evaluation of drug testing in the workplace, in: Drugs in the Workplace: Research and Evaluation Data, NIDA Research Monograph, No. 91, (S. W. Gust, and J. M. Walsh, eds.), pp. 195–216, U.S. Government Printing Office, Washington, DC.

Taggert, R. W., 1989, Results of the drug testing program at Southern Pacific Railroad, in: *Drugs in the Workplace: Research and Evaluation Data,* NIDA Research Monograph, No. 91 (S. W. Gust, and J. M. Walsh, eds.), pp. 97–108, U.S. Government Printing Office, Washington, DC.

U.S. Department of Health and Human Services, 1988, Mandatory guidelines for Federal workplace drug testing programs, *Federal Register* **53:**11970–11989.

Wish, E. D., 1990, Preemployment drug screening, *Journal of the American Medical Association* **264:**2676–2677.

Zwerling, C., Ryan, J., and Orav, E. J., 1990, The efficacy of preemployment drug screening for marijuana and cocaine in predicting employment outcome, *Journal of the American Medical Association* **264:**2639–2643.

Zwerling, C., Ryan, J., and Orav, E. J., 1992, Costs and benefits of preemployment drug screening, *Journal of the American Medical Association* **267:**91–93.

8

Some Legal Aspects of Drug Testing in the Canadian Workplace

Human Rights, Collective Bargaining and Labor Arbitration, and the Canadian Charter of Rights and Freedoms

MONIQUE PINSONNEAULT

In recent years, the use of drugs by workers has become a major concern for employers. Canadian and American studies show that a certain percentage of workers use drugs, and that the use of some drugs can lead to industrial accidents (see Chapter 1). In some cases, authors have argued that drug testing has reduced accidents in the workplace (Bickis, Carter, Dobson, & Lees, 1987; Dupont, 1990; Kaplan, Langevin, & Ross, 1988). It is not surprising, therefore, that some employers have resorted to drug testing in the selection and monitoring of employees. The implementation of drug testing by employers, however, can infringe workers' rights under the law.

This chapter focuses on whether it is lawful for Canadian employers to require workers to undergo drug tests. It considers first whether drug testing can lead to discrimination under federal and provincial human rights legislation that recognizes the dignity, worth, and equality of every person. It then considers how the Canadian Charter of Rights and Freedoms,* which guarantees funda-

*Part 1 of the Constitution Act, 1982, being Schedule B of the Canada Act 1982 (U.K.), 1982, c. 11. Hereinafter called "the Charter."

MONIQUE PINSONNEAULT • Attorney, Auckland, New Zealand.

Research Advances in Alcohol and Drug Problems, Volume 11: Drug Testing in the Workplace, edited by Scott Macdonald and Paul M. Roman. Plenum Press, New York, 1994.

mental rights and freedoms to individuals, applies to drug testing in the workplace. Finally, it deals with issues arising from the negotiation, implementation, application, and interpretation of drug testing programs covering unionized employees. The human rights legislation, collective bargaining and labor arbitration affecting unionized employees, and the Charter can combine to constrain the formulation and implementation of drug testing in the workplace.

1. HUMAN RIGHTS

The main question relating to human rights legislation is whether the performance of drug testing and the use of testing results could lead to discrimination based on handicap.* Courts and tribunals have not yet had to deal with this issue; therefore, one can only resort to the current legislation and its interpretation to answer this question.

Canadian federal, provincial, and territorial human rights laws protect workers against discrimination in employment based on grounds such as handicap. In addition, most Canadian jurisdictions have enacted provisions stipulating that employers cannot make any oral or written inquiry concerning a prohibited ground of discrimination. Most human rights legislation provides for an exception to the foregoing where there is a bona fide occupational requirement, but in some instances, employers have the duty to accommodate handicapped workers.

To understand how these principles of human rights legislation apply to drug testing, an analysis of the following concepts is required: handicap; bona fide occupational requirement; employers' duty to accommodate; and remedies for discriminatory action by employers.

Handicap

It is first necessary to determine whether drug addiction or use can be considered to be a handicap under human rights legislation. There is no common definition of *handicap* in the legislation; where it is defined, however, the wording is general enough to include a broad range of diseases and impairments. The definitions are meant to encompass any handicap, including those only within the perception (or belief) of others. The federal statute† is the only legislation that defines the term *handicap* by expressly including previous or existing depen-

*In this chapter, the application of the human rights legislation will only be addressed with respect to discrimination based on handicap. The reason is that this chapter discusses the right of employers to resort to drug testing in order to ensure that the workers' health status or condition is suitable for the work to be performed. It is possible, however, although less likely, that drug testing gives rise to complaints alleging discrimination based on other prohibited grounds (e.g., sex or age).

†Canadian Human Rights Act, R.C.S. 1985, C. H-6, section 25.

dence on alcohol or a drug. Outside federal legislation, an important question is whether a drug user will be considered as having a handicap, either mental or physical. Although such question has not been answered by the courts and tribunals, it seems likely that where the use of drugs has reached the point of dependence and/or constitutes an illness, it will come within the legal definition of a handicap. Medical and/or scientific evidence would be required to prove dependence or illness.

Whether social or casual use of drugs (as opposed to drug addiction) could amount to a handicap must also be examined. Although this issue has not yet been considered in Canadian jurisprudence, one could contend that social or casual use of drugs should not be seen as a handicap because it does not constitute either a disease or a physical or mental impairment. But in dealing with this issue, one must remember that human rights legislation is broad enough to encompass discrimination based on a perception or belief that a person has a handicap. Based on this principle, it is arguable that social or casual users of drugs could be considered to be handicapped in instances where they are believed to be addicted to drugs. For example, if a worker who is a casual drug user tests positive for drugs, an employer might conclude based upon the test that the user is drug addicted. In such a case, the worker would be perceived as having a handicap and would be protected by human rights legislation. If the employer believed that the worker was a casual or social user, however, the latter's condition would not amount to a handicap, and discrimination could not be alleged regarding an action taken by the employer against worker. Consequently, it appears that an individual testing positive to drugs would not always be entitled to the protection of the human rights laws.

Although this interpretation is based on general principles established by the legislation and the jurisprudence, the current statutes (except the federal act), do not provide a clear answer as to whether drug use and drug addiction constitute a handicap. Current legislation needs to be improved to clarify these issues.

Bona Fide Occupational Requirement

Canadian human rights legislation makes discrimination in employment unlawful, except when it is based on a bona fide occupational requirement. Such requirement can be defined as a rule, policy, or working condition that is legitimate and reasonable, considering all the relevant aspects of its implementation and application. Employers can use this as a defense in cases where a requirement discriminates directly on a prohibited ground such as handicap.

The Supreme Court of Canada, in a number of decisions, has held that a bona fide occupational requirement must be imposed honestly and in good faith and must be objectively related to the performance of a certain work or occupation, in the sense that it is reasonably necessary to assure the safe, efficient, and economical performance of the job.* From these decisions and other cases, it emerges that three important elements must be taken into account in the assessment of bona fide occupational requirement. First, one must look at the requirements of the work with regard to the tasks to be performed. Second, the capacity of a worker must also be assessed objectively.† Third, the assessment of the ability and qualifications of a handicapped worker must be conducted on an individual basis and not by reference to a group of people with the same handicap.

In what circumstances would the performance of drug testing to ensure that workers are free from drug use problems and can perform their work safely and properly constitute a bona fide occupational requirement? To justify drug testing, an employer must first show that drug addiction or drug problems entail or, may entail, a significant reduction in the workers' capacity to perform the essential tasks of their jobs safely and productively. Because safety is usually the primary reason to test for drugs, it is arguable that drug testing constitutes a bona fide requirement in most safety-sensitive positions (e.g., nuclear plant workers, train conductors, airline pilots, bus drivers). Adequate performance of work is the second reason to test for drugs. Where objective facts lead employers to believe that job performance is adversely affected by drug addiction or drug use, drug testing should be considered a bona fide occupational requirement. In either case, the procedures and methods involved in drug testing must be scientifically reliable.

An argument against the legitimacy of drug testing as a bona fide requirement is that the link between testing positive and the capacity to do a job may be tenuous. A positive test result does not necessarily imply that the worker is a drug addict; depending on the drug and dosage, a positive result indicates that the worker has used a given drug in the hours, days, or even weeks prior to the test (see Chapter 5). As well, the use of drugs may not necessarily mean that a worker is at increased risk of industrial accidents and performance problems.

The meaning to be given to a positive drug test is particularly important in jobs where the workers' and the public's health and safety are at stake. For such jobs, the solution perhaps lies in the creation of refutable legal presumptions. For example, legislation could presume that some workers (e.g., those seeking or working in safety-sensitive positions) who test positive for drugs are a safety risk and should be denied access to work in such positions until further test results are negative.

**Ontario Human Rights Commission v. Etobicoke* (1982) 1 S.C.R. 202; *Bhinder v. C.N.* (1985) 2 S.C.R. 561; and *Quebec (Commission des droits de la personne) v. Brossard (Town of)* (1988) 2 S.C.R. 279.

†On the individual assessment of an employee with alcohol abuse problems, see *Niles v. Canadian National Railways*, 91 C.L.L.C. 17018.

The predetermined positions to which the legal presumption could apply should be selected taking into account the health and safety risk that drug use problems may entail for the worker using drugs, his or her coworkers, and the public. This would raise the question of when a risk is important enough to prevent a worker with drug use problems from performing a certain job. Commentators, courts, tribunals, and some human rights commissions agree that the safety risk has to be real to be a component of a bona fide occupational requirement. To assess the risk involved, courts and tribunals have compared the risk posed by a "normal" person to the risk posed by a handicapped individual; they have found that the safety risk posed by the latter has to be greater than that posed by the former. In addition, the risk factor has to be considered in relation to the worker's condition or handicap, not the condition of people with the same handicap.

The question of when drug testing and being free of drug use problems constitute a bona fide occupational requirement cannot be solved easily. Legal guidelines on this issue are necessary to clarify and improve the current legislation.

The Duty to Accommodate

Where a discriminatory rule can be justified as a bona fide occupational requirement, employers do not have a duty to accommodate affected employees unless the law requires them to do so.

A different approach is taken in cases of adverse effect discrimination, where the law can be interpreted as such.* Adverse effect discrimination arises

> where an employer, for genuine business reasons, adopts a rule or standard which is on its face neutral, and which will apply equally to all employees, but which has a discriminatory effect upon a prohibited ground on an employee or a group of employees in that it imposes, because of some special characteristics of the employee or group, obligations, penalties, or restrictive conditions not imposed on other members of the workforce.†

In cases of adverse effect discrimination, the bona fide requirement will be upheld, but the employer will have to accommodate the affected employee to the point of undue hardship to the business,‡ which has been defined to mean that an employer has "to take such steps as may be reasonable to accommodate without undue interference in the operation of the employer's business and without undue

***Central Alberta Dairy Pool v. Alberta Human Rights Commission,* (1990) 33 C.C.E.L. 1 (S.C.C.).
†*Ontario Human Rights Commission and O'Malley v. Simpsons Sears Limited.* (1985) 2 S.C.R. 536.
‡See *Bhinder v. C.N.* (1985) 2 S.C.R. 561; *Ontario Human Rights Commission and O'Malley v. Simpsons Sears Limited.* (1985) 2 S.C.R. 536; and *Central Alberta Dairy Pool v. Alberta Human Rights Commission* (1990) 33 C.C.E.L. 1 (S.C.C.).

expense to the employer."* One could assume that factors to be considered include financial costs, the disruption of the collective agreement, the size of the employer's operations, and the nature of any safety risks.

Adverse effect discrimination relating to drug testing might occur in a case where a worker who is required to give a blood sample for a drug test cannot do so for religious reasons. In such a case, reasonable accommodation would mean finding other ways to ensure that the worker is fit to perform his or her work safely and efficiently.

Where employers have the legal duty to accommodate workers with a handicap, how would the duty to accommodate apply to employees having drug use or addiction problems? Reasonable accommodation can take different forms: time for treatment, therapy, rest periods, or leaves of absence for extended treatment. Accommodation might also include job restructuring, part-time or modified work schedules, and reassignment of work.

The duty to accommodate might also vary depending on whether the workers are current employees or prospective employees. Although current employees are entitled to reasonable accommodation, it is doubtful that employers should bear the burden of accommodating and rehabilitating prospective employees with drug use problems. Referring them to hospitals, clinics, or institutions where they could get treatment should suffice.

"Reasonable accommodation" and "undue hardship" are very general and imprecise concepts. It is difficult to determine their scope. More clarity in the law would certainly provide workers and employers with a better understanding of their rights and obligations.

Remedies

Although Canadian human rights laws vary from one jurisdiction to another, all statutes provide for a right to compensation to workers who are discriminated against. They also oblige the employer to make available to the victim the privilege, opportunity, or right that was denied as the result of an illegal practice. Under these statutes, a board of inquiry, a human rights board or tribunal, or a court may recommend or award compensatory and/or punitive damages to the worker and order such action to be taken as would rectify the harm caused to the worker. Some statutes provide for the right to obtain an injunction to restrain a person from depriving or restricting any individual from the enjoyment of a right under the human rights legislation. The reinstatement of a dismissed employee can also be ordered when the legislation expressly or implicitly permits this.

How would the foregoing principles apply to complaints involving drug testing? Workers might be denied employment or discharged from employment

**Ontario Human Rights Commission and O'Malley v. Simpsons Sears Limited* (1985) 2 S.C.R. 536.

based on their refusal to undergo a drug test, or on the results of a test. In such cases, human rights boards, tribunals, and courts will accept formal complaints from workers where drug use is found to be a handicap, the employer's requirement does not constitute a bona fide occupational requirement, and the duty to accommodate workers has not been fulfilled. If workers succeed, they have a right to damages and the right to be reinstated or to be offered the job that they were unjustly refused.

In conclusion, it can be said that all the questions raised by drug testing in the workplace cannot be answered with certainty by the current human rights legislation. The principles are very general and do not specifically deal with the issues raised by drug testing. This is not to say that the present legislation must be entirely rejected; the solution lies in the clarification of current law by enacting more specific guidelines for drug testing.

2. COLLECTIVE BARGAINING AND LABOR ARBITRATION

Currently, there are no provisions for drug testing in most collective agreements. Regardless of this, there are some relevant questions to be addressed: whether unions and employers have the power to bargain on this issue, whether employers can unilaterally implement a drug testing program, and how boards of arbitration are likely to decide on grievances relating to drug testing.

Collective Bargaining

Under Canadian legislation, once a trade union is certified or recognized as a bargaining agent, it has the exclusive power to bargain directly with the employer for the purpose of reaching a collective agreement applying to the employees included in the bargaining unit. The employer is then precluded from bargaining with any other person or organization on behalf of the employees: "There is no room left for private negotiation between employer and employee."*

In Canadian legislation, *collective agreement* is defined as a written document concerning terms and conditions of employment. Hence, legislation makes it lawful for unions and employers to negotiate working conditions regarding drug testing: who to test, how and by whom the test should be done, and what to do with the results are all potentially issues for collective bargaining.

**Syndicat catholique des employes de magasins de Quebec Inc. v. Compagnie Paquet Ltd.*, (1959) S.C.R. 206, at 212. See also *Canadian Pacific Railway Co. v. Zambri*, (1962) S.C.R. 609, at 624; *McGavin Toastmaster Limited v. Ainscough*, (1976) 1 S.C.R. 718, at 725; *General Motors v. Brunet*, (1977) 2 S.C.R. 537 at 549; and *Association internationale des debardeurs v. Association des employes maritimes*, (1979) 1 S.C.R. 120, at 127, 128.

The Labor Arbitration Perspective

Whenever a conflict arises between the union, the employees, and the employer on the application or the interpretation of a collective agreement, labor arbitrators have the statutory authority to decide upon any grievance filed by any of them. The collective agreement is the fundamental source of arbitrators' jurisdiction, and statutes are a secondary source to which they can resort to render a decision where relevant to solving a case. Labor arbitrators also have the jurisdiction to consider the Canadian Charter of Rights and Freedoms in deciding upon grievances where a collective agreement constitutes government action. In a recent case, the Supreme Court found that the labor arbitrator had the right to consider whether a provision for mandatory retirement in a collective agreement was void under the Charter.*

In the exercise of their powers, labor arbitrators can grant various remedies to resolve grievances. They generally have the power, granted by the statutes and by collective agreements, to award damages, to amend the decision of the employer in disciplinary matters, to reinstate a dismissed employee, and to make any order that might be appropriate or necessary to enforce the terms of the collective agreement and the law.

How are labor arbitrators likely to deal with the problems raised by drug testing? The first part of the following discussion deals with the unilateral implementation of a drug testing program by an employer whose employees are unionized. The second part deals with the grounds on which labor arbitrators have allowed or are likely to allow employers to require unionized employees to undergo a drug test. As Canadian arbitrators have not often had the opportunity of deciding upon these issues, some American labor arbitration cases on drug testing will be used to provide material for the discussion.

Implementation of a Drug Testing Program. Subject to certain limitations, it is part of the employers' management rights to introduce programs or policies covering unionized employees. In the leading case dealing with this issue, it was held that among other criteria, such programs (a) must not be inconsistent with the collective agreement and (b) must not be unreasonable.† How would these criteria apply to the implementation of a drug testing program?

Consistency of the Program With Collective Agreement. This limitation forces an arbitrator to compare the drug testing program with any relevant provision of the collective agreement to ensure that the program does not contradict the collective agreement. If the program conflicts with an express or general provision of the collective agreement, it will be declared to be contrary to the collec-

**Douglas/Kwantlen Faculty Assn. v. Douglas College*. (1990) 3 S.C.R. 570; appeal from (1988) 2 W.W.R. 718, 21 B.C.L.R. (2d) 175 (B.C. C.A.).

†*Re Lumber and Sawmill Workers' Union and KVP Co. Ltd.* (1965) 16 L.A.C. 73 (J. B. Robinson).

tive agreement and therefore unenforceable.* Deciding whether a program conflicts with the collective agreement, however, can present difficulties and lead to a subjective decision in cases where the provisions of the collective agreement are general and/or leave room for uncertainty. Legal guidelines on drug testing would help avoid this.

Reasonableness of a Program. The requirement of reasonableness means that a program must not indirectly undermine the collective agreement. Reasonableness is also related to the rationale of the program and to the means employed to achieve the objective of the program.†

In assessing the reasonableness of a drug testing program, arbitrators need to balance employers' management rights and employees' privacy rights.‡ They have to consider the extent to which drug testing is necessary to protect the employer's interests in (a) carrying out its operations safely and efficiently and (b) protecting the health and safety of the employees and the public. In assessing this, at least one of the following issues will presumably be raised: employee off-duty conduct, safety and efficiency of the workplace, and procedures and methods of testing.

Employees and unions argue that a problem arising with the implementation of a drug testing program is that such a requirement would have the effect of regulating the conduct of employees while off-duty by detecting drug use outside the workplace and outside working hours. This argument is based on the fact that not all drug tests show that the person who tests positive for drugs was either impaired or under the influence of drugs at the moment the sample was taken. A drug test may be positive as a result of drug consumption hours, days, or weeks before the test. In response to this, employers would claim that the arbitral jurisprudence acknowledges that an employer should normally have a say in an employee's off-duty conduct regarding drug use if that conduct has or may have a demonstrable adverse effect on the employee's safety and performance, on the safety of other employees and the public, and on the company's business.§ Employers would contend that in most cases, the reason for an employer to require drug testing is to allow the rational determination of whether there has been recent drug use, and to assess whether there is a possibility of future

*On medical examination, see *Re Corporation of the City of London* and *Canadian Union of Public Employees* (1983) 9 L.A.C. (3d) 262 (B. A. Langille); and *Re City of Toronto* and *Canadian Union of Public Employees* (1984) 16 L.A.C. (3d) 384 (M. G. Picher).

†On the reasonableness of a medical examination program, see *Re Fraser Valley Milk Producers Co-operative Association (Dairyland Foods)* and *International Association of Machinists*, 9 L.A.C. (4th) 36 (D. R. Munroe).

‡The arbitral jurisprudence has developed a right to privacy for employees.

§On medical examination and health status of employees, see D. J. M. Brown and C. M. Beatty, *Canadian Labour Arbitration*, 3d ed. (Aurora, Ontario, Canada Law Book, 1988), at 7–20 ff.

impairment while on the job as a result of subsequent use. Such contention would probably gain the approval of an arbitrator, especially in a workplace where employees are working in safety-sensitive positions (e.g., in refinery process plants, petro-chemical plants, nuclear plants, and transportation industries).* Indeed, in such cases, employers need the ability to rely on evidence of recent drug use to prevent future unsafe performance of work. For instance, a program providing for drug testing of employees involved in work-related accidents may be designed to ensure safety in the workplace by precluding future injuries and accidents.†

Further, one could maintain that safety considerations involving the nature of the industry and work environment and/or any evidence of a widespread drug problem within the work areas could outweigh intrusions into employees' privacy and justify random drug testing. Unions and employees would certainly respond by saying that random testing encroaches upon the employees' privacy and dignity. It is not clear which argument is correct, because the arbitral jurisprudence has not yet determined criteria to assess the reasonableness of a random testing program.

The reasonableness of a drug testing program would also depend on the procedures and methods involved. The modes of obtaining the biological samples from workers should respect their privacy. The chain of custody (i.e., the identification, storage, preservation, and transport of the biological samples) and the methods of testing the samples should be accurate and reliable. Methods of testing should be scientifically acceptable. Labor arbitrators have not yet set specific standards regarding procedures and methods of drug testing.

The arbitral jurisprudence on the reasonableness of a drug testing program is still in an embryonic stage, and the outcome of such a case is unpredictable.‡ Employees' and employers' interests would be better safeguarded if legislation set out basic guidelines regarding drug testing in the workplace.

Requirement to Undergo a Drug Test. According to the jurisprudence, employers must rely upon some clear contractual§ or legislative basis to be able to require an employee to undergo a medical examination‖ or test. There is an exception to this principle where employers have reasonable grounds to require a

*See *Transport Provost Inc.* and *Syndicat des travailleurs de l'energie et de la chimie* (1991) T.A. 1005.

†*Re Morton Thiokol Inc.* and *International Association of Machinists & Aerospace Workers* (1989) 93 L.A. 434 (A. D. Allen, Jr.) (USA).

‡See *Re Provincial-American Truck Transporters* and *Teamsters Union*, (1991) 18 L.A.C. (4th) 412, in which the arbitrator held, without considering the safety reasons for testing, that the drug testing policy was analogous to employees searches to prevent theft by employees and was unreasonable.

§On medical examination, see *Catelli* and *Syndicat international des travailleurs de la boulangerie, confiserie et du tabac d'Amerique*. (1985) T.A. 306 (M. Gravel); *Cite de Dorval* and *Association des Pompiers de Dorval* (1984) T.A. 455 (J. Laberge).

‖On medical examination, see D. J. M. Brown and D. M. Beatty, *Canadian Labour Arbitration*, 3d ed. (Aurora, Ontario, Canada Law Book. 1988), at 7–52.

medical examination or test. This section discusses the grounds on which employers should be allowed to require unionized employees to undergo a drug test.

Contractual Terms. Contractual terms may be contained in a collective agreement or in an individual agreement. The terms can be general or express.

Most current collective agreements do not contain provisions on drug testing. Nevertheless, the requirement that an employee undergo a drug test can be seen as implicit in the general terms of a collective agreement (e.g., those related to health and safety of employees and others,* or to management rights). Where a collective agreement authorizes drug testing in general terms, the employer can carry out drug testing so long as he or she does not act in a malicious or arbitrary manner.† If a collective agreement contains a specific clause on drug testing, however, the employer's requirement must be within the boundaries of the provision.

The obligation to undergo a drug test can also be part of an individual agreement signed by an employee under particular circumstances. Such agreement could, for example, be signed by an employee who admits being a drug user or who is found to be one because of positive drug test results. Where such agreement exists, the employee has the obligation to undergo a drug test that falls within the framework of the agreement.‡

Requirement Based on Reasonable Grounds. Reasonable grounds constitute a limited exception to the employees' right of freedom from physical intrusion.§ A reasonable ground exists where an employer needs (a) to be satisfied about the fitness of employees to carry out efficiently and safely the tasks to which they are assigned or will be assigned, and (b) to protect the health and safety of employees and the public.

There is a long-established principle in labor arbitration to the effect that an employer may set, as a qualification for continued employment, the condition that an employee be physically and mentally fit to perform efficiently and safely the tasks he or she is to undertake, and that in appropriate cases, employers can discharge, suspend, or alter the employment status of employees who have ceased to meet this qualification.‖ Drug testing constitutes a legitimate requirement where it can be demonstrated that it allows an employer to ensure employ-

**Hospital Reine-Elizabeth* and *Syndicat national des employes de l'Hopital Reine-Elizabeth* (May 17, 1989) DTE 89T-1132 (L. B. Courtemanche).

†*Syndicat des postiers du Canada* and *Societe canadienne des postes* (5 April 1990) DTE 90T-928 (A. Rousseau).

‡*Re Canadian National Railway Co.* and *United Transportation Union.* (1989) 6 L.A.C. (4th) 381 (M. G. Picher).

§*Re Canadian National Railway Co.* and *United Transportation Union.* (1989) 6 L.A.C. (4th) 381 (M. G. Picher).

‖*Re Niagara Regional Board of Commissioners of Police and Niagara Region Police Association* (1975) 9 L.A.C. (2d) 272 (K. P. Swan), at 273.

ees' fitness to work safely and efficiently. This would be the case for most safety-sensitive positions.

The protection of employees' health and safety could also constitute a reasonable motive for requiring them to submit to a drug test. Positive drug test results can show that there is a risk to the health and safety of the employee and or of his or her coworkers arising from the employee's drug problem. If the safety risk is real, greater than normal, or significant,* drug testing would be justified.

Public safety can also constitute a legitimate ground for drug testing. In the course of their operations, employers have the duty to maintain public safety; to fulfill this duty, employers whose activities affect the lives and safety of others must be able to conduct drug testing to ensure that their employees are physically and mentally qualified to perform their work safely.† This applies to many industries, including the transportation industry,‡ nuclear plants, hospitals,§ and refineries.

Procedures and Methods. The procedures and methods involved in drug testing should be such as to warrant the accuracy and reliability of the results. Inappropriate procedures and methods may undermine the legitimacy of a requirement related to drug testing. A drug test must meet rigorous standards relating to the collection of biological samples, the chain-of-custody procedures, the methods of testing, and the qualifications of the technician responsible for it.‖ Arbitrators have not yet established what procedures and methods are acceptable.

Other Grounds for Testing. Arbitrators could, in some circumstances, rely upon such other grounds as past practice,# statutory law, and the "obey now, grieve later" principle** to rule on the employers' right to require their employees to submit to a drug test. A discussion of these grounds is beyond the scope of this chapter.††

*See D. J. M. Brown and D. M. Beatty, *Canadian Labour Arbitration*, 3d ed. (Aurora, Ontario, Canada Law Book, 1988), at 7–48.

†See *Canadian Pacific Limited* and *United Transportation Union*, Canadian Railway Office of Arbitration, Case No. 1703 (M. G. Picher).

‡On drug testing by bus companies, see *Mayflower Contract Services* and *Laborers' International Union of North America* (1989) 91 L.A. 1353 (D. J. Petersen) (USA); *Cleveland Board of Education* and *Teamsters* (1988) 90-1 ARB 3356 (G. W. Van Pelt) (Labour Arbitration Awards) (USA).

§*Hopital Reine-Elizabeth* and *Syndicat national des employes de l'Hopital Reine-Elizabeth* (17 May 1989) DTE No. 89T-1132 (L. B. Courtemanche).

‖See *Canadian Pacific Limited* and *United Transportation Union*, Canadian Railway Office of Arbitration, Case No. 1703 (M. G. Picher).

#"Past practice" consists of a particular conduct mutually accepted by the parties to the collective agreement over an extended period of time.

**The rule "obey now, grieve later" is to the effect that an employee must first obey the order given by his or her employer or one of its representatives, file a grievance later on if he or she believes that the order was contrary to the collective agreement.

††See D. J. M. Brown and D. M. Beatty, *Canadian Labour Arbitration*, 3d ed. (Aurora, Ontario, Canada Law Book, 1988).

In conclusion, it can be said that the arbitral jurisprudence on drug testing is still developing. No coherent and consistent principles or rules have yet been established, and the outcome of a case is often unpredictable. The enactment of legislation on drug testing in the workplace would help to improve this situation.

3. THE CANADIAN CHARTER OF RIGHTS AND FREEDOMS

The Charter guarantees certain fundamental rights and freedoms, including the right to liberty and security of the person (section 7) and the right to be secure against unreasonable search and seizure (section 8). In the context of drug testing in the workplace, two main questions normally arise. The first is whether the Charter applies to individual employment contracts and collective agreements; the second is whether legislation on drug testing, if enacted in Canada, would be in accordance with the principles enshrined in the Charter. This question takes on particular importance because of the need for legislation on drug testing. Indeed, the current law is ill equipped to address the issues raised by drug testing in the workplace.* The imprecision and uncertainty of the current law support the need for new legislation providing for more certainty, predictability, and clarity; legislation should clearly define the rights, obligations, and liabilities of parties that engage in drug testing.

The Application of the Charter to Individual Employment Contracts and to Collective Agreements

Section 32 of the Charter provides that the Charter applies to the Parliament and government of Canada and to the legislature and government of each province in respect of all matters within their authority. The Supreme Court of Canada has held that the Charter does not apply to private parties when no exercise of governmental power or reliance upon governmental action in involved.† Therefore, the Charter does not apply to private litigants, such as an employee and a private employer. The Charter would apply, however, if private litigants rely upon a right given by a statute, regulation, order, by-law, or regulation of a government entity. Moreover, the Charter does not apply to a collective agreement between two private parties, although it does apply to a collective agreement that is an act of the legislative, executive, or administrative branch of the government.‡

*See sections 1 and 2 of this chapter.

†*Retail, Wholesale and Department Store Union, Local 580, et al. v. Dolphin Delivery et al.* (1986) 2 S.C.R. 573; *McKinney v. University of Guelph* (1990) 3 S.C.R. 230.

‡See, for instance, *Douglas/Kwantlen Faculty Association v. Douglas College* (1990) 3 S.C.R. 570; appeal from (1988) 2 W.W.R. 718, 21 B.C.L.R. (2d) 175 (B.C. C.A.).

It follows that, as between employees and private employers, the Charter could not be invoked to challenge any act or decision of an employer related to drug testing, unless the act or decision (or the collective agreement on which it was based), constituted an act of the legislative, executive, or administrative branch of government.

The Legality of Legislation on Drug Testing under the Charter

If legislation on drug testing in the workplace was enacted in Canada, would such legislation comply with the Charter? The right to liberty and security of the person (section 7) and the right to be secured against unreasonable search and seizure (section 8) are the principal rights that could be infringed by legislation that permits drug testing.* Under section 1 of the Charter, these rights are subject to such reasonable limits, prescribed by law, as can be demonstrably justified in a free and democratic society. Further, section 33 provides that any law or provision of a law can, by specific enactment, be exempted from the application of section 2 and sections 7 through 15. Legislation authorizing drug testing in the workplace could contain such an exemption; if this was the case, drug testing conducted under the legislation could not be challenged under the Charter. Because the Charter's rights and freedoms are so fundamental, however, governments vary rarely resort to section 33. Therefore, it is unlikely that section 33 would be invoked in legislation on drug testing. Such legislation, though, would still need to comply with section 1 of the charter.

An analytical framework to determine the legality of legislation under section 1 of the Charter has been developed by the Supreme Court of Canada.† The analysis comprises two steps. First, it is necessary to determine whether the legislation limits a right or a freedom guaranteed by the Charter. Second, where the legislation limits a right or a freedom, it is necessary to assess whether the limit is valid under section 1 of the *Charter.*

Limitation of a Right Guaranteed by the Charter. As noted above, at least two fundamental rights could be infringed by legislation authorizing drug testing: the right to be secure against unreasonable search and seizure (section 8) and the right to liberty and security of the person except in accordance with the principles of fundamental justice (section 7). Despite the fact that the content of sections 7 and 8 has mainly been discussed in cases dealing with criminal law, the Supreme Court of Canada has never suggested that sections 7 and 8 would not protect intrusions in administrative procedures. It is contended that the rights provided

*An analysis of whether section 15 of the Charter, which deals with equality rights (equality before the law without discrimination based on mental or physical disability, etc.), could be infringed by legislation on drug testing is beyond the scope of this chapter.

†See *R. v. Big M Drug Mart Ltd.*, (1985) 1 S.C.R. 295; and *R. v. Oakes*, (1986) 1 S.C.R. 103.

for in sections 7 and 8 are general enough to encompass intrusions in administrative procedures as well as criminal ones.

Search and Seizure. The purpose of section 8 is to protect the right of privacy. The search of a person's property without his or her consent is against the right of privacy;* so is the inspection of his or her body and its orifices. Likewise, the taking of a blood sample without the consent of the individual constitutes unreasonable seizure and, therefore, violates section 8.† The analysis of a biological sample to detect drugs is considered the same as a search.‡ Thus, a logical conclusion is that drug testing can infringe the right against unreasonable search and seizure in two ways: by actually taking a blood sample or other biological specimen, or by analyzing or testing a biological sample.

Liberty and Security. The concept of liberty provided for by section 7 envisages the absence of constraints or external interference of a nature such as in an unreasonable search. Consequently, it is likely that drug testing would interfere with the right to liberty where a biological sample is taken from a person's body without consent. When voluntary consent is obtained, however, section 7 cannot be violated.

The right to security provided by section 7 protects a person's physical and mental integrity, including control over his or her body and mind. Such a right would be violated, for example, by the collection of a urine sample for drug testing.§ Hence, drug testing can infringe or limit the right to security, except when it is in accordance with the principles of fundamental justice. This exception is discussed later in this chapter.

Because drug testing could infringe or limit some rights guaranteed by the Charter, an assessment has to be made of whether such an infringement or limit is permitted by the Charter.

Validity of the Limit or Infringement in Legislation on Drug Testing. The second step of the analytical framework proposed by the Supreme Court of Canada, as it could apply to legislation on drug testing, has two parts. The first part asks whether legislation on drug testing is within the exception specified in section 7 (conformity with the principles of fundamental justice) and within the limitation in section 8 (reasonableness). The second part asks whether legislation on drug testing could represent "reasonable limits prescribed by law as can be demonstrably justified in a free and democratic society" under section 1. The concept of "principles of fundamental justice" used in section 7 will be dealt with first. The limitation of reasonableness established by section 8 will be dealt with next while analyzing section 1, in which this limitation is present.

**Hunter v. Southam Inc.*, (1984) 2 S.C.R. 145; *R. v. Genest* (1989) 1 S.C.R. 59.
†*R. v. Dyment* (1988) 2 S.C.R. 417.
‡*National Treasury Employees Union et al. v. Von Raab*, (1989) 109 U.S. S. Ct. 1384.
§*Re Dion v. R.* (1987) 30 C.C.C. (3d) 108 (Que. S.C.).

The Principles of Fundamental Justice. If the government interferes with the right to security or liberty of the person in regulating drug testing, section 7 of the Charter requires such interference to conform with the "principles of fundamental justice." This term qualifies the section 7 rights and imposes a requirement to assess the procedural fairness as well as the substance of legislation that would deprive a person of these rights.* The substance and procedures must be in accordance with the basic principles that govern the justice system. They must be fair and in harmony with the values and legal principles of the society, as well as with societal interests.

The substance and procedures of legislation on drug testing could conform to these principles. Legislation on drug testing should satisfy three primary conditions related to the substance. First, the objective of legislation should be legitimate; the performance of drug testing for the purpose of protecting the health and safety of workers and the general public by preventing accidents and injuries is legitimate. Second, there should be no risk of damage to worker's well-being. The performance of drug testing does not generally involve a clear risk of damage to the physical and mental well-being of workers. Neither pricking by a needle to obtain a blood sample nor the collection of a urine sample, most would agree, presents a risk of damage to the physical or mental integrity of the person. Third, the worker's consent should be required before a drug test is performed, thereby giving the worker a right to make a choice as to whether he or she will submit to the test.

There are several ways to ensure that the procedures of legislation on drug testing comply with the principles of fundamental justice. First, legislation should require that drug testing be performed by people with expertise in approved hospitals, laboratories, or health institutions. This would secure higher standards and greater adequacy and reliability in the results. Legislation should also provide for the right of workers to have their biological samples retested. Second, legislation should provide for chain-of-custody procedures aiming to maintain control and accountability from initial collection of biological samples to final disposition—at each stage in handling, testing, storing, and reporting results. For example, the collection of biological samples should respect the dignity of workers. Third, a timetable should be established in legislation for such events as reporting the results of a drug test, having a sample retested, or taking any action following the results of a test. This is important to avoid undue delays and to allow workers and employers to obtain the necessary information to make appropriate decisions in each particular case. Fourth, legislation should provide adequate recourse, remedies, and penalties.

Section 1 of the Charter. In a section 1 analysis, it is necessary to determine whether the limit to the guaranteed rights and freedoms (a) is prescribed by law,

**Re B.C. Motor Vehicle.* (1985) 2 S.C.R. 486, at 512 and 499.

(b) is a reasonable limit, and (c) can be demonstrably justified in a free and democratic society.

At least two features of the "prescribed by law" requirement have been suggested by the courts. The first one is that the limit must have the force of law (i.e., the limit must be expressed in a regulation, statute, or civil or common law). The second feature is that a limit on a right or freedom must be specific. This is based on the view that the law cannot be uncertain, because citizens must be able to foresee the consequences of their actions.* With respect to the first feature, legislation on drug testing would have the force of law by being passed as law by the federal or a provincial Parliament. With respect to the second, legislation on drug testing should be specific enough if it provides for precise rules regarding all the important aspects of drug testing (i.e., when, by whom, how, and under what circumstances drug testing can be performed, and the kinds of remedies and penalties available in the case of wrongdoing by a party).

As noted above, according to the Supreme Court of Canada a limit is legitimate under section 1 if the purposes of the legislation, the means to attain the purposes, and the effects of the limit are reasonable and demonstrably justified in a free and democratic society.† The Supreme Court has set two main criteria that must be satisfied to establish that a limit is lawful. The first focuses on the importance of the objective: the measures responsible for a limit on a Charter right or freedom must be of sufficient importance to warrant overriding a constitutionally protected right or freedom, and the objective must relate to concerns that are pressing and substantial in the society. The second criterion requires the means chosen to attain the purposes to be reasonable and demonstrably justified.

Would legislation on drug testing satisfy these two criteria? The primary objective of legislation on drug testing should be to provide for the protection of the health and safety of workers and the general public; the ancillary objective is safe and proper performance of work. Do these objectives relate to concerns that are pressing and substantial in the society?

The primary objective of protecting health and safety obviously relates to concerns that are pressing and substantial. First, drug testing in the workplace possibly can help to prevent or decrease the risk of accidents and injuries, and can thereby protect the health and safety of workers and the public. Second, the importance of the health and safety of workers and citizens is recognized by the Charter under the right to security provided in section 7; the right to security

**Reference Re ss. 193 and 195.1(1)(c) of the Criminal Code (Man.).* (1990) 1 S.C.R. 1123.

†In some subsequent cases, the Supreme Court of Canada applied or formulated the requirements of section 1 in a slightly different manner. It appears that the model established in *Oakes,* however, has remained the basic framework to determine whether a limitation of a right or freedom guaranteed by the Charter is justifiable under section 1.

comprises the protection of one's physical and mental integrity. Third, the history of Canadian legislation shows that health and safety of workers and the public in general has always been of substantial concern in Canadian society. Examples of these concerns are legislation on occupational health and safety and the statutory obligation to use seat belts in motor vehicles. Consequently, where the nature of the work being performed affects the health and safety of employees and the public (e.g., in safety-sensitive positions), drug testing would likely be considered legitimate.

The ancillary objective, safe and proper performance of work, also relates to important concerns in the society. Safe and proper performance of work has always been an implied part of any employment contract. Further, the law imposes a duty on workers to perform their work safely (occupational health and safety law) and properly (common law). Moreover, under the common law, employers have always had the obligation to select employees who can perform their work safely and adequately. For these reasons, one would be justified in concluding that the objective of legislation on drug testing would be important enough to limit a protected right.

According to the second criterion established by the Supreme Court of Canada, the means to attain the objective of legislation must be reasonable and demonstrably justified. Legislation is reasonable and demonstrably justified when it meets the three components of the so-called proportionality test established by the Supreme Court: (a) the measures adopted must be designed to achieve the objective and they must not be arbitrary or unfair; (b) the means should impair as little as possible the protected right or freedom; and (c) there must be a proportionality between the effects of the measures and the objective. Would legislation on drug testing meet the proportionality test?

The first component of the test can be satisfied if drug testing can reasonably be expected to increase the health and safety of workers and to improve proper performance of work. With respect to the second component of the proportionality test, it is possible to say that drug testing would impair "as little as possible" the rights guaranteed by the Charter. This rests on two bases. The first is that there is no less intrusive measure than drug testing to achieve the objective (i.e., protecting health and safety by detecting drug use) with any likelihood. Other methods include training supervisors to recognize such signs or symptoms of drug use as blurred eyes, coordination problems, rapid change of mood, and absenteeism problems. Such symptoms are not always present, however, and even if they are, they can be difficult to detect. The second basis is that legislation would seek to circumscribe drug testing in order to avoid as much as possible intrusion into worker's fundamental rights. This could be done by prescribing clear requirements and specifications on when, by whom, how, and under what circumstances drug testing can be performed. For instance, legislation should provide that only some workers, such as those working or seeking work in safety-sensitive positions and other predetermined positions, can be tested for drugs in specific circumstances.

The third component of the proportionality test requires that the effects of the measures should not be so deleterious as to outweigh the objective of the measures. If the protection of the health and safety of workers and citizens was the primary objective of legislation on drug testing, it would outweigh restrictions caused by the measures (i.e., drug testing). This is because the protection of people's health and safety is guaranteed by the Charter under the right to security (section 7). Such protection is more important than one's right to freedom from drug testing in certain specific circumstances. In conclusion, if the aforementioned conditions discussed in this chapter can be met, legislation on drug testing would be in accordance with the principles of the Charter.

REFERENCES

Bickis, V., Carter, D., Dobson, D., and Lees, R., 1987, Policy study: Drug impairment and drug testing in the workplace, in: *Occupational Health Centre,* Queens University, Kingston, Ontario 4–17.

Canada Labour Code, R.S.C., 1985 C.L-2, 3.36(1).

DuPont, R. L. 1990, Mandatory random testing needs to be undertaken at the worksite, in: *Controversies in the Addiction's Field,* (R. C. Engs, ed.), pp. 105–111.

Kaplan, E. S., Langevin, J. B., and Ross, R. A., 1988, Drug and alcohol testing in the workplace: The employers perspective, *William Mitchell Law Review,* **14**:365.

9

Constitutional and Statutory Treatment of Drug Testing in the United States

RISA L. LIEBERWITZ

1. INTRODUCTION

Drug testing brings together two worlds normally viewed as unrelated in the treatment of rights and responsibilities: the workplace and criminal law enforcement. Testing for the presence of metabolites consistent with illegal drug use is a highly intrusive search of a person. Given the invasion of privacy resulting from any search of a person or place, the Fourth Amendment to the U.S. Constitution prohibits government from conducting searches without a warrant issued by a court upon a showing of probable cause. Broadening the power of an employer to search employees through drug testing must draw comparisons with government searches under the Fourth Amendment. Such a comparison raises questions about society's vision of the workplace, including employee rights and the scope of employer power. Should the government use methods of criminal law enforcement when acting as an employer? Should private employers be able to assume a police power by using these same enforcement methods against employees? What restrictions and obligations should be placed on employers who test employees for drugs? Is there any justification for the loss of privacy of employees subjected to sweeping drug testing?

This chapter will explore the legal issues raised by drug testing through

---

RISA L. LIEBERWITZ • New York State School of Industrial and Labor Relations, Cornell University, Ithaca, New York 14853-3901. The author would like to thank David S. Bahn for his help in the development of this chapter.

Research Advances in Alcohol and Drug Problems, Volume 11: Drug Testing in the Workplace, edited by Scott Macdonald and Paul M. Roman. Plenum Press, New York, 1994.

analysis of judicial decisions that have addressed challenges to such testing as an illegal search under the Fourth Amendment or under a state constitution. The U.S. Supreme Court set the stage for current constitutional treatment of employee drug testing in its two 1989 decisions on the issue, *Skinner v. Railway Labor Executives' Association* and *National Treasury Employees Union v. Von Raab.* These decisions have been interpreted by the lower federal courts as establishing the constitutional validity of a broad range of drug testing by government employers or by private employers testing under government mandate or authorization. This chapter will explore the issues underlying the legal reasoning of the federal courts by setting forth the development of legal doctrine applied to drug testing, followed by a critique of the decisions. As will be discussed, Fourth Amendment challenges to drug testing may be raised only against governmentally conducted or authorized drug testing, as the amendment does not apply to searches by private employers acting independently of governmental requirements or authorization. Thus, the critique of the judicial treatment of drug testing will include an analysis of the tension in U.S. legal doctrine between rights in the public and private sectors.

2. FOURTH AMENDMENT PRINCIPLES

The Fourth Amendment protects individuals against unreasonable searches and seizures conducted by the government. This straightforward statement embodies a number of complicated concepts—the nature of governmental action as differentiated from nongovernmental or private conduct, the definition of a search or seizure, and the content of the concept of reasonableness. The logical starting point for exploring these concepts is the text of the Fourth Amendment:

> The right of the people to be secure in their persons, houses, papers, and effects, against unreasonable searches and seizures, shall not be violated, and no Warrants shall issue, but upon probable cause, supported by Oath or affirmation, and particularly describing the place to be searched, and the persons or things to be seized.

Though the text does not explicitly limit Fourth Amendment restrictions to governmentally conducted or authorized searches,* the U.S. Supreme Court has required a finding of state action before triggering an individual's protection under the Fourth Amendment and other provisions in the Bill of Rights and the Fourteenth Amendment (*Civil Rights Cases,* 1883). This public/private distinction is a central issue in drug testing, given private employers' role in instituting

*This article will refer to searches, though the constitutional treatment of both searches and seizures involve similar concepts. Also, the references to drug tests refer to urinalysis drug tests.

testing programs, as well as the role of the government in testing its own employees and in requiring regulated private industries (e.g., the transportation industry) to implement drug testing programs. As a result, drug testing by federal, state, or local governments of public employees and governmentally authorized or mandated drug testing by private employers is covered under the Fourth Amendment, but drug testing carried out by private employers on their own initiative is not subject to the amendment's limitations.* This dual treatment of individual rights has been the target of much criticism and, as will be discussed, is at the heart of the Supreme Court's dilution of Fourth Amendment rights for employees in general.

The Fourth Amendment covers searches or seizures of persons, houses, papers, and effects. Underlying this scope of protection, and the Fourth Amendment in general, is the value placed on privacy. Faced with historically evolving types of searches, the Supreme Court has found that governmental conduct is a search or seizure covered by the Fourth Amendment if an individual has a reasonable expectation of privacy in the area searched or the property or information seized. Thus, the Court has found that wiretapping of a public telephone in a phone booth on the street is a search, as individuals have a reasonable expectation of privacy in such telephone conversations (*Katz v. United States,* 1967). The Court has also held that bodily intrusions such as taking blood (*Schmerber v. California,* 1966) are searches. In its recent drug testing cases, the Court held that a urinalysis drug test required by governmental regulations is a search, given the societal value of privacy attached to the bodily function of urination.

Perhaps the most difficult issue within Fourth Amendment analysis is the concept of a "reasonable" search. Again, the restriction on government to conduct only reasonable searches and seizures is based on the value of protecting individuals' privacy. The Fourth Amendment may thus be seen as an attempt to weigh the government's interest in carrying out its police power against society's and individuals' interests in protecting a sphere of privacy from governmental intrusion. Under the conventional interpretation, the Fourth Amendment strikes a balance by defining reasonableness primarily in terms of the clause that requires the government to obtain a warrant, issued by an impartial magistrate upon a showing of probable cause, prior to conducting the search (Amsterdam, 1974; Strossen, 1988). Probable cause may defined as existing facts or circumstances on which to base a belief that evidence is to be found in the place to be searched, closer to a "more-likely-than-not standard than a hunch or suspicion" (Slobogin, 1991). The focus on the warrant clause thus places specific limitations on government's initiation of a search. Even after a warrant is issued, the reasonable-

*The Fourth Amendment applies to the federal government and by incorporation into the Fourteenth Amendment, to state governments (*Mapp v. Ohio,* 1961).

ness requirement provides further restrictions on the government to conduct the search in a reasonable manner (Amsterdam, 1974).

As Fourth Amendment interpretations have been developed by the Supreme Court, this conventional interpretation has been limited by exceptions to the warrant requirement and, on a more fundamental level, by the Court's shift away from using the warrant clause as the touchstone of reasonableness toward applying an ad hoc balancing test that may find searches reasonable even when supported by neither a warrant nor probable cause. Certain exceptions to the warrant requirement were developed in the context of criminal law enforcement, finding warrantless searches reasonable in exigent circumstances, such as searches incident to arrest (*Chimel v. California,* 1969), arrests and searches made by police in "hot pursuit" of a criminal suspect (*Warden v. Hayden,* 1967), or searches of automobiles that might be moved (*Carroll v. United States,* 1925). In each of these situations, however, probable cause is required. The suspension of the warrant requirement has been justified by the need to avoid losing the suspect or evidence in the time required to obtain a warrant.

The Supreme Court has approved other warrantless searches, however, that include a suspension of the requirement of probable cause as well. These exceptions to the probable cause requirement have been made for searches in the civil context, in the setting of criminal law enforcement, and in an area that may be labeled as quasi-criminal. In the civil context, the Supreme Court first suspended the probable cause requirement for "routine" administrative inspections of buildings to enforce housing codes or other similar regulatory laws (*Camara v. Municipal Court,* 1967). Given the nature of such searches, which are focused on inspecting a geographic area (e.g., all buildings on a block), neither a warrant nor any individualized evidence of suspected illegal activity is required. In the criminal enforcement setting, the Court has found that warrantless "pat-down" searches do not violate the Fourth Amendment when a police officer has "reasonable suspicion" that an individual is armed and may use the weapon against the officer or another person. This reduction of probable cause to reasonable suspicion is based on the safety factor, as well as the limited nature of the search of a pat-down of outer clothing (*Terry v. Ohio,* 1968). Reasonable suspicion is a quantum of evidence lower than probable cause, but still based on "specific and articulable facts, rather than on a hunch" (Slobogin, 1991).

The category of warrantless searches on less than probable cause, which may be labeled quasi-criminal, falls primarily in the area of enforcement of immigration laws (Wright, 1984). The Court has upheld roving border patrol stops and inspections of vehicles and passengers upon reasonable suspicion (*United States v. Brignoni-Ponce,* 1975), as well as border patrol detentions at permanent checkpoints without any individualized suspicion of illegal conduct (*United States v. Martinez-Fuerte,* 1976). Outside of immigration enforcement, the Court has upheld suspicionless highway sobriety-checkpoint stops (*Michigan*

Department of State Police v. Sitz, 1990). In these vehicle-stop cases, the Court has emphasized the limited nature of the intrusion and the deterrence rationale underlying the stops (Cornish & Louria, 1991).

Each suspension of the probable cause requirement in the cases of administrative inspections, the frisking of individuals, and vehicle stops has been accompanied by the Court's application of an ad hoc balancing test, to the exclusion of the warrant clause. Rather than determining the reasonableness of a search by applying the warrant clause requirements, the Court has shifted to a generalized balancing of governmental interests against individual privacy interests. In applying the balancing test, the Court has placed a heavy emphasis on the government's interests while discounting the intrusion on privacy (Slobogin, 1991; Strossen, 1988).

3. EXPANSION OF THE BALANCING TEST

The categorization of searches into criminal, civil, and quasi-criminal contexts has been done in this discussion to show the scope of the Supreme Court's willingness to suspend the warrant requirement and lower the probable cause threshold of evidence across a range of criminal and civil cases. This division, however, is problematic in a number of ways. First, the Fourth Amendment itself does not identify differences in treatment of criminal and civil cases. Additionally, this approach of drawing lines that supposedly represent separate spheres of society is artificial and, as will be discussed further, false. The Supreme Court has relied on this civil/criminal dichotomy to expand the use of its balancing test to searches, including urinalysis drug tests, by non–law enforcement agents.

Three Supreme Court cases preceded the Court's decisions in *Skinner* and *Von Raab,* setting the stage for the drug testing cases by extending the use of ad hoc balancing to searches of areas that normally would be viewed as carrying a strong expectation of privacy. In each case the Court justified a warrantless search, without probable cause, of traditionally private areas by focusing on the goal of a search to fulfill "special needs beyond the normal need of law enforcement."

In *New Jersey v. T.L.O.* (1985), *O'Connor v. Ortega* (1987), and *Griffin v. Wisconsin* (1987), the Supreme Court expanded its use of ad hoc balancing beyond the earlier exceptions of administrative searches, limited pat-down searches, and border patrol automobile stops to uphold even more intrusive searches of a high school student's purse, a public employee's desk, and a probationer's home. Examination of each case will reveal the Court's reliance on a false dichotomy between criminal and civil searches.

In *T.L.O.*, a high school assistant vice principal searched a student's purse after a teacher discovered the student smoking in the school lavatory. The search revealed not only cigarettes but rolling papers, marijuana, and other material consistent with marijuana dealing. This evidence was given to the police, to whom the student (identified in the case as T.L.O.) confessed that she had been selling marijuana at school. The evidence from the search and the confession were used to convict T.L.O. on delinquency charges in juvenile court.

While concluding that the Fourth Amendment applies to searches by non–law enforcement officials, the Court found that the warrant and probable cause requirements were unsuitable for the school setting. Instead, the "legality of a search of a student should depend simply on the reasonableness, under all the circumstances, of the search." Reasonableness would be measured by balancing the "individual's legitimate expectations of privacy and personal security . . . [against] the government's need for effective methods to deal with breaches of the public order." In this case, the majority's conclusion that the school official's search of the purse was reasonable was justified by focusing almost exclusively on the initial evidence of reasonable suspicion of T.L.O.'s violation of school rules and subsequent evidence of illegal drug dealing. Justice Blackmun concurred, based on his view that the school setting presented "exceptional circumstances in which special needs beyond the normal need for law enforcement" justified substituting a balancing test for traditional warrant and probable cause requirements.

This phrasing of the "special needs" test reappears in *O'Connor v. Ortega* and *Griffin v. Wisconsin* to uphold warrantless searches without probable cause. In *O'Connor,* the Court upheld a public employer's search of the office, including the desk and files, of Dr. Ortega, a psychiatrist and chief of professional education at the state hospital. The search was conducted as part of an investigation into suspected misconduct by Ortega in managing the residency program, including possible coercion of residents to contribute toward purchase of a computer and allegations that Ortega had sexually harassed employees. The plurality opinion applied the ad hoc balancing test to determine that the search was reasonable under all the circumstances, based on the finding that Ortega had a lowered expectation of privacy at work regarding searches by his employer, an expectation that was outweighed the public employer's "need for supervision, control, and the efficient operation of the workplace." The plurality also relied on its finding of reasonable suspicion, while disclaiming any holding that individualized suspicion is mandated under its balancing test of reasonableness.

Most significant in the Court's expanded use of its ad hoc balancing test is the continually reiterated distinction between searches by law enforcement officials and those conducted by others, such as government employers in *O'Connor* and school officials in *T.L.O.* The *O'Connor* plurality highlighted this distinction in three ways. First, the plurality found that public employees have a lowered expectation of privacy with regard to searches by the government acting as employer, as opposed to searches by police. The Court majority also suspended the warrant requirement for workplace searches by the public employer because such searches usually seek work-related information, rather than evidence of criminal activity. Finally, the Court used the distinction between searches by police and other government officials to apply its ad hoc balancing test instead of the probable cause requirement. Because of the public employer's "special needs, beyond the normal need for law enforcement," the general standard of reasonableness was seen as constitutionally sufficient.

O'Connor is particularly significant in setting the stage for the Supreme Court's drug testing cases, given the parallels of the workplace contexts. The *O'Connor* Court expanded the special-needs exception to the workplace to suspend the warrant and probable cause requirements, assessing the constitutionality of the search by the public employer under its balancing test of reasonableness. Further, the line drawn between searches by law enforcement officials and other government agents foreshadows the Court's treatment of drug testing by employers.

In its final special-needs decision prior to *Skinner* and *Von Raab,* the Court continued to harden the dichotomy between constitutional standards for searches by police and those by non–law enforcement officials. The most startling aspect of *Griffin v. Wisconsin,* however, is that the Court drew this distinction in direct contradiction to the facts of the case. In *Griffin,* the Court upheld a warrantless search without probable cause of a probationer's home by state probation officers accompanied by police officers, based on a tip that the probationer, Griffin, might have a gun in his house. A gun was found and used as evidence in Griffin's felony trial and conviction. The Court concluded that the search was reasonable, based on the state's "special need" of supervising probationers.

In *T.L.O., O'Connor,* and *Griffin,* the Supreme Court went a long way toward establishing a two-tiered system of Fourth Amendment rights; one for criminal law enforcement by police, and one for searches by non–law enforcement government officials. After these cases, it appears that searches by police will be analyzed from the starting point of the warrant clause, with the issue being whether the search fits into an exception to the requirements of a warrant and probable cause. Searches by non–law enforcement officials where the Court finds "special needs," though, will be judged under a general standard of reasonableness through the ad hoc balancing test.

This dichotomy is a false one, as the reality of these three cases demonstrates. In fact, in each case, the searches sought evidence that could be used in criminal enforcement proceedings. In *T.L.O.*, the evidence was used by the police to obtain a confession and to convict T.L.O. on juvenile delinquency charges. In *O'Connor,* the public employer searched for evidence that could have been proof of potential criminal conduct, including extortion and fraud. In

Griffin, the search was the basis for Griffin's subsequent felony conviction. Thus, in each case, the Court relied on the dichotomy under the special-needs test to allow non–law enforcement government agencies to use intrusive law enforcement means of gathering evidence without either a warrant or probable cause. With the drug testing cases, the Supreme Court further hardened its criminal/noncriminal search dichotomy, focusing attention on public employers and agencies as non–law enforcement personnel with special needs to deter illegal drug use by employees.

4. THE SUPREME COURT ON DRUG TESTING

Current workplace drug testing is conducted by employers either in response to government mandates or by employer choice. President Ronald Reagan's Executive Order No. 12,564 (1986) required federal executive branch agencies to develop plans to achieve a "drug-free workplace," including testing agency employees and applicants for illegal drug use. A number of federal agencies, including the Department of Transportation, the Department of Defense, and the Federal Aviation Administration, have also adopted regulations requiring private employers regulated by the agency to conduct drug testing of applicants and employees at the private-sector workplace (Cairns & Grady, 1990; Christian & Barber, 1990). Congress enacted an appropriations bill for the Department of Transportation in 1991 that included provisions requiring both drug and alcohol testing of "safety-sensitive" employees in the aviation, railroad, commercial motor vehicle, and mass transit industries (P.L. 102-143, 1991).

Many private-sector employers have voluntarily chosen to implement drug testing programs, encouraged by economic studies asserting great financial losses from employee substance abuse and the federal Drug-Free Workplace Act of 1988, which requires federal contractors to certify that they have a drug-free workplace in order to receive federal funds (though the act does not mandate drug testing; Cairns & Grady, 1990; Cornish & Louria, 1991). Finally, state and local governments have also engaged in drug testing of applicants and employees (Cornish & Louria, 1991).

Whether drug testing is carried out through legislative mandate (as opposed to private employer initiative) determines whether the Fourth Amendment is applicable. Given the requirement of state action, only drug testing by a government agency or official, or by a private employer under government mandate or authorization, will be subject to a Fourth Amendment challenge. Drug testing implemented at a private employer's initiative is free from Fourth Amendment scrutiny. Thus, millions of employees in private industry will have no federal constitutional claim regarding workplace drug testing—nor is it likely that these employees will be able to challenge drug testing under their state constitutions, which generally require state action as well. As will be discussed, these employees must determine if their state has enacted legislation regulating private-sector workplace drug testing, or they must rely on collective bargaining for protection in unionized workplaces.

Employees who work for federal, state, or local governments, or who are tested in private industry under government regulations, can raise Fourth Amendment challenges to workplace drug testing. As a result of the Supreme Court's 1989 decisions in *Skinner* and *Von Raab,* however, these employees may be left with little more protection than private-sector employees outside Fourth Amendment protection. In both cases (decided the same day), the Court applied its ad hoc balancing test to open the door to wide-scale governmentally mandated or authorized drug testing based on neither a warrant nor any individualized suspicion of drug use.

In *Skinner,* the Court reviewed the constitutionality of Federal Railroad Administration (FRA) regulations, adopted in 1985, that mandated railroad companies to conduct blood and urine alcohol and drug tests of employees involved in a train accident resulting in death, property damage over a specified amount, or release of hazardous material accompanied by evacuation or reportable injury. The FRA regulations also authorize railroad companies to require employees to take breath and urine tests for certain rule violations and in cases where at least two supervisors find reasonable suspicion that an employee is impaired by alcohol or a controlled substance. *Von Raab* involved a Fourth Amendment challenge to the U.S. Customs Service's 1986 implementation of a drug testing requirement as a condition for promotion to positions that involved drug interdiction, carrying firearms, or handling classified material. *Skinner* and *Von Raab* thus presented the Court with Fourth Amendment issues of drug testing by private employers pursuant to government mandate and authorization, and by a government agency of its own employees.

The analysis is similar in both cases, with *Skinner* substituting the balancing test for warrant and probable cause requirements, and with *Von Raab* further lowering the quantum of evidence needed to support drug testing. The Court concluded that a urinalysis drug test is a search, as the collection and analysis of a urine sample invades the reasonable expectation of privacy of the employee. From this point, though, the Court majority abandoned traditional Fourth Amendment analysis, explicitly relegating warrant and probable cause requirements to criminal law enforcement. Instead, the Court once again found that "special needs beyond the normal need for law enforcement" justify "balanc[ing] the governmental and privacy interests to assess the practicality of the warrant and probable cause requirements in the particular context." In *Skinner,* the Court found special needs in safety concerns of the railroads; in *Von Raab,* the special needs were the Customs Service's interests in deterring drug use by employees in the targeted positions and lowering the possibility of bribing such employees.

Predictably, in both cases a majority of the Court applied the balancing test to conclude that drug testing was a reasonable search under the Fourth Amendment. What is striking in the Court's reasoning is its dismissal of the employees' privacy interests as "minimal"—in contrast to the Court's view of the "compelling" nature of the government's interests—despite the fact that drug tests would be performed without any prior evidence of drug use by any employee. The Court is untroubled by the lack of any individualized evidence, stating that "where the privacy interests implicated by the search are minimal, and where an important governmental interest furthered by the intrusion would be placed in jeopardy by a requirement of individualized suspicion, a search may be reasonable despite the absence of such suspicion."

How did a majority of the Court strike this "balance"? The initial step of deepening the divide between the criminal and civil contexts is crucial, emphasizing that probable cause is relevant for criminal investigations, but "may be unhelpful in analyzing the reasonableness of routine administrative functions, especially where the Government seeks to *prevent* the development of hazardous conditions or to detect violations that rarely generate articulable grounds for searching any particular place or persons." The focus on the constitutional viability of "preventive" searches in the noncriminal context thus permits the Court to find drug testing reasonable, even without individualized suspicion, because the deterrence rationale renders irrelevant actual detection of drug use (Cornish & Louria, 1991). This reasoning, though, requires the Court to carve out a category of searches separate from traditional Fourth Amendment analysis in criminal law enforcement, as preventive searches are directly at odds with the purpose of the Fourth Amendment to prohibit government from engaging in sweeping searches in hopes of turning up some evidence (Cornish & Louria, 1991).

The Court's separation of criminal law enforcement from other contexts is flawed on a theoretical and factual basis. As the *Skinner* dissent states:

> The majority today completes the process begun in *T.L.O.* of eliminating altogether the probable cause requirement for civil searches—those undertaken for reasons "beyond the normal need for law enforcement." . . . By its terms, however, the Fourth Amendment—unlike the Fifth and Sixth—does not confine its protections to either criminal or civil actions.

Given the application of the Fourth Amendment to both criminal and civil contexts, the dissent objects to the majority's description of the warrant and probable cause requirements as simply "impracticable." Further, the Court majority not only rejected the probable cause requirement but also concluded that neither reasonable suspicion nor even any evidence of individualized suspicion of drug use or impairment was constitutionally required for the drug testing. In *Von Raab*, there was even less evidence, given the Customs Service's admission that there was no basis to conclude that drug use was a problem by agency employees in general.

The Court's shift to supporting searches without individualized suspicion not only continued the slide begun in *T.L.O.* but also represented a qualitative change in constitutional analysis, given the intrusiveness of the drug test. As the *Skinner* dissent identified, the Court, for the first time, had upheld a suspicionless search of a person's body. The searches in *T.L.O.*, *O'Connor,* and *Griffin* were of places or objects, based on some level of individualized suspicion. By contrast, in *Skinner* and *Von Raab,* no evidence existed to support searches of a person involving a bodily function subjectively and objectively recognized as extremely private.

The Court relied on the workplace context to sharpen further the criminal/civil dichotomy, based on the view that the employees had a lowered expectation of privacy flowing from both the non–law enforcement purpose and the employment setting of the drug testing. In both cases the Court found the employees' privacy interests to be minimal, given the general restrictions to which the employees "consent" in employment, as well as their specific employment in the regulated railroad industry or in an agency that is the "Nation's first line of defense" against drug importation.

As in *T.L.O.*, *O'Connor,* and *Griffin,* the criminal/civil distinction is also factually flawed. In *Skinner,* the dissent noted that the FRA regulations provide that blood and urine samples may be subpoenaed by outside parties, which "appear[s] to invite criminal prosecutors to obtain the . . . samples drawn by the FRA and use them as the basis of criminal investigations and trials." The Customs Service regulations provide that test results may be given to other agencies only with the employee's consent; although this regulation does provide some division between the criminal and civil contexts, the drug testing draws on criminal law enforcement procedures to discover evidence of controlled substance use by employees of an agency charged with illegal drug interdiction. Thus, drug testing by the Customs Service itself intertwines the criminal and civil contexts, as the Customs Service argued to the Supreme Court when it stated: "If a law enforcement agency and its employees do not take the law seriously, neither will the public on which the agency's effectiveness depends" (*NTEU v. Von Raab,* dissent by Justice Scalia).

5. THE FEDERAL COURTS AFTER *SKINNER* AND *VON RAAB*

The Supreme Court's drug testing decisions put in place the constitutional analysis to support sweeping drug testing programs by government employers of their employees and by private-sector employers testing under governmental regulations. The lower federal courts have focused on certain principles from *Skinner* and *Von Raab* to establish approval for wide-scale programs instituting preemployment, postaccident, reasonable suspicion, and random drug testing.

The special-needs test, separating government actions as criminal law enforcer from its actions as employer or industry regulator, has been central to the lower courts' analysis (*Bluestein v. Skinner,* 1990; *NTEU v. Yeutter,* 1990). Additionally, in finding special needs for the drug tests beyond the normal need for law enforcement, the courts have relied on the Supreme Court's rejection of a requirement of individualized suspicion of drug use, and particularly the *Von Raab* position freeing the government from demonstrating a basis for believing that drug use is a general problem at the workplace (*Harmon v. Thornburgh,* 1989; *Taylor v. O'Grady,* 1989).

The lower courts have developed the Supreme Court's special-needs concept and ad hoc balancing test primarily in terms of the nature of particular job categories. This approach has been central to the analysis of random drug testing programs, which were not at issue in *Skinner* and *Von Raab.* The courts have not viewed random drug testing as qualitatively different from other types of drug testing without individualized suspicion, despite the surprise nature of random testing, which is performed in the absence of a triggering event, unlike preemployment or postaccident testing. The courts have instead viewed random testing as flowing logically from *Skinner* and *Von Raab* and have upheld such testing based on government assertions of special needs of safety, security, or integrity interests tied to deterring illegal drug use by employees in certain job categories.

Based on *Skinner*'s emphasis on government interests in safety, the lower federal courts have consistently upheld random drug testing programs of employees in jobs tied to transportation, either in the private transportation industry or as drivers or pilots employed by a government agency. The federal Circuit Court of Appeals for the District of Columbia has been active in this area, rejecting Fourth Amendment challenges to programs of the Department of Transportation (*AFGE v. Skinner,* 1989) and the Department of Agriculture's Food and Nutrition Service (*NTEU v. Yeutter,* 1990) for random drug testing of motor vehicle operators who transport passengers. This court has also upheld random drug testing of employees who work in the transportation field in jobs other than drivers or pilots, including U.S. Army civilian air traffic controllers, aviation mechanics, aircraft attendants, Federal Aviation Administration (FAA) aircraft mechanics, and FRA hazardous material inspectors (*AFGE v. Skinner,* 1989; *NFFE v. Cheney,* 1989).

The Ninth Circuit Court of Appeals relied on the government's interest in safety to uphold federal agency regulations mandating random drug testing of millions of employees in private industry; in one case, FAA regulations requiring random testing of airline personnel in the private commercial aviation industry (*Bluestein v. Skinner,* 1990), and in another case, Federal Highway Administration regulations requiring random testing of commercial motor vehicle operators (*Department of Transportation v. Teamsters,* 1991). The Ninth Circuit has also upheld federally mandated random drug testing in nontransportation industries under a safety rationale, including employees working in natural gas and hazardous-liquid pipeline operations (*IBEW v. Skinner,* 1990).

Although broadly defining the government's interest in safety, some courts have drawn distinctions among occupations within fields such as transportation and health care, invalidating random drug testing of employees where there was an insufficient relation between those employees' jobs and the asserted safety rationale. Thus, one federal circuit upheld a regional transit authority's random drug testing program for employees in safety-sensitive positions, but not for maintenance custodians (*Transport Workers' Union, Local 234 v. Southeastern Pennsylvania Transportation Authority,* 1989). A federal district court recently upheld random testing of Veterans Administration health professionals who have direct contact with patients, perform diagnostic testing or therapeutic work, or prepare and disseminate drugs, but found such testing unconstitutional for other employees, including safety and occupational health specialists, electricians, and elevator mechanics (*AFGE v. Derwinski,* 1991).

The courts have also held that the government's special need for security supports random drug testing of federal government employees in jobs requiring secret or top-secret security clearances, without proof that an employee's job duties actually involve access to secret or top-secret government documents (*AFGE v. Skinner,* 1989; *Harmon v. Thornburgh,* 1989; *Hartness v. Bush,* 1990). The government interest in security has been scrutinized more closely in cases where the drug testing program covers employees without such a security clearance and who are not closely tied to drug enforcement activities.

The courts have been influenced on this issue by the Supreme Court's remand to the lower federal court in *Von Raab* for clarification of the category of employees who would be tested on the basis of handling classified material, approving testing only for employees likely to gain access to sensitive information. Thus, the D.C. Circuit Court found random drug testing of all Department of Justice criminal prosecutors and employees with access to grand jury proceedings unconstitutional. The circuit court concluded that although a security interest would exist for a category of Justice Department employees limited to those "closely tied to the enforcement of federal drug laws," the current scope of the program was overly broad (*Harmon v. Thornburgh,* 1989). This same circuit, however, upheld a preemployment drug testing program for all Department of Justice attorney positions, finding that applicants have a lower expectation of privacy than current employees (*Willner v. Thornburgh,* 1991).

A recent decision in the D.C. federal district court held that neither security nor safety interests justified random drug testing of Department of Human Services motor vehicle operators who neither carry passengers nor have access to classified information (*AFGE v. Sullivan,* 1992). A similar concern with overly broad assertion of security and safety interests led the Seventh Circuit to invalidate annual drug tests of county correctional officers who did not have regular access to prisoners or firearms, or the opportunity to smuggle drugs into prisons (*Taylor v. O'Grady,* 1989).

The courts may be willing to reject a generalized assertion of a special need to protect the "integrity" of a government function or a private industry. Thus, random drug tests of army civilian laboratory employees have been found unconstitutional (*NFFE v. Cheney,* 1989). Assertions of integrity, however, have been found adequate to support random testing of employees tied to drug enforcement, including Army civilian drug counselors (*NFFE v. Cheney,* 1989). The Seventh Circuit recently held that the government's interest in safety and integrity was sufficient to uphold a state random drug testing program for employees in the horse racing industry, including jockeys and parade marshals (*Dimeo v. Griffin,* 1991).

The federal court decisions upholding random drug testing have important common characteristics. As in *Skinner* and *Von Raab,* the government's asserted "special needs" are often accepted without proof of a drug problem in the public or private workplace and without scrutiny of actual job functions. As a result, broad job categories of employees in the transportation industry may be subject to random testing, without evidence of an employee's drug use, drug use in the workplace, or the relation between the particular job and the safety of other employees or the public. Similarly, assertions of security interests are unquestioningly accepted for employees working in the areas of criminal drug enforcement or drug counseling, without evidence that such employees are more susceptible to corruption or blackmail than other employees.

Courts that find the government interest sufficient to support random testing also conclude that the employee privacy interest is minimal, based on the nature of employment in regulated industries or in "sensitive" government positions. This superficial approach not only permits an intrusive search without evidence of individualized suspicion under traditional Fourth Amendment standards, but without actual evidence supporting the government's interest under the ad hoc balancing test of reasonableness. This approach also misleadingly targets illegal drug use as the sole or primary basis for safety or security problems, ignoring other important issues related to workplace safety and security—including alcohol use and employees' emotional problems (e.g., clinical depression)—that can affect work performance, as well as employer responsibilities for creating a safe workplace ("Marital Problems," 1990; Sonnenstuhl, Trice, Staudenmeier, & Steele, 1987).

The artificial dichotomy between searches for criminal law enforcement purposes and workplace searches continues in the lower courts. Federal courts recognize that drug testing reveals evidence of drug metabolites, which may be consistent with either on-duty or off-duty drug use. Courts upholding suspicionless drug testing on the basis of the government's assertion of a special need beyond the normal needs of law enforcement (e.g., safety or security) find that evidence of off-duty illegal drug use is relevant. Where special needs for suspicionless drug testing are not found, though, the courts have limited testing to drug tests based on reasonable suspicion of on-duty drug use or impairment. Under this analysis, the courts explicitly recognize that testing for off-duty drug use is a criminal law enforcement function, subject to traditional Fourth Amendment requirements (*AFGE v. Sullivan,* 1990; *NTEU v. Yeutter,* 1990).

6. DRUG TESTING UNDER STATE LAWS

At the state level, drug testing issues have been litigated through challenges under state constitutions, state statutes, or common law. As most state constitutions have been interpreted to require state action, private employees generally must look to statutory regulations or common-law causes of actions for relief. More than twenty states have enacted legislation regulating drug testing for public or private employees located within the state (Cairns & Grady, 1990). State statutory language echoes federal constitutional language, focusing on the quantum of evidence required for testing and procedural protections for employees subject to drug testing. Following the pattern of the federal courts' approach to constitutional challenges to drug testing under governmental regulations, state laws distinguish between preemployment testing and random testing of current employees according to occupation.

Most states with statutes regulating applicant testing are limited primarily to providing such procedural protections as required notice to applicants of testing, confirmation tests of positive test results, and confidentiality of results.* Even the few states with comprehensive statutory regulation of drug testing follow the federal courts' pattern of providing broad freedom to employers to condition initial employment on negative drug test results. For example, Maine and Vermont impose probable cause requirements for testing of current employees in many jobs, but permit employers to conduct general applicant drug testing (Morgan, Lewis, & Bockius, 1991).

State regulation of testing of current employees varies across jurisdictions, with some states imposing a requirement of probable cause or reasonable suspicion of illegal drug use.† The definition of reasonable suspicion may vary as well, with Minnesota, for example, broadly defining reasonable suspicion to include postaccident testing (Morgan, Lewis, & Bockius, 1991). Additionally, even states with such evidentiary requirements usually provide exceptions for

*See, e.g., statutes in Connecticut, Florida, Kansas, Maine, Maryland, Minnesota, Montana, and Vermont (discussed in Morgan, Lewis, & Bockius, 1991).

†See, e.g., statutes in Connecticut, Iowa, Kansas, Maine, Minnesota, Montana, Rhode Island, and Vermont (discussed in Morgan, Lewis, & Bockius, 1991).

random testing in circumstances involving safety-sensitive positions or where testing is required or authorized under federal law.* In general, states will be limited in any regulation of drug testing where federal requirements preempt the states from restricting the scope of federal drug testing regulations.† Finally, some states specifically provide the right to employers to conduct drug testing of applicants and employees on a broad basis.‡

Private employees also have attempted to challenge drug testing by private employers through individual lawsuits raising such claims as wrongful discharge in violation of public policy, invasion of privacy, or defamation. Many of these lawsuits have been unsuccessful.§ Private employees in unionized settings, though, may achieve limits on drug testing of current employees, which is a mandatory subject of bargaining (*Johnson-Bateman Co.*, 1989).‖

Thus, at the state level, legislation follows federal patterns of regulating along occupational lines. States may interpret their own constitutions, however, to provide greater protection than does the Fourth Amendment. The possibility of state constitutional protection will apply primarily to drug testing of employees who work for state or local governments. Though the states do not appear likely to set a general trend toward broader constitutional protection, there are several state court decisions that demonstrate the potential for liberal interpretation of state constitutions. In a recent example of such independent action, the highest state court in Massachusetts held that random drug testing of Boston police officers violated the state constitution's prohibition against unreasonable searches and seizures, in light of the lack of evidence of an illegal drug use problem in the police department (*Guiney v. Police Commissioner,* 1991).

Prior to the U.S. Supreme Court drug testing decisions, the highest state court in New York held that required drug tests of all probationary teachers prior to granting tenure violated the prohibitions against unreasonable searches and

*See, e.g., statutes in Connecticut, Iowa, Maine, Minnesota, and Vermont (discussed in Morgan, Lewis, & Bockius, 1991).

†For example, the FRA regulations upheld in *Skinner* (1989) preempt state laws on the same subject matter and supersede collective bargaining agreements or arbitration awards. The Washington State Supreme Court has held that Nuclear Regulatory Commission drug testing rules preempt a challenge under the state constitution to drug testing in a nuclear plant (*Alverado v. Washington Pub. Power Supply Sys.*, 1988). The recent Omnibus Transportation Employee Testing Act of 1991, included in the Department of Transportation Appropriations Act, includes provisions preempting inconsistent state or local laws.

‡See, e.g., statutes in Maryland, Nebraska, and Utah (discussed in Morgan, Lewis, & Bockius, 1991).

§See, e.g., cases in Connecticut, Michigan, New Jersey, Ohio, Pennsylvania, Texas, and Wyoming (discussed in Morgan, Lewis, & Bockius, 1991). See also, discussions of cases in Cairns and Grady (1990) and Christian and Barber (1990).

‖As noted above, federal regulations may explicitly supersede conflicting collective bargaining provisions and arbitration awards (Crain, 1989; *Skinner,* 1989).

seizures in the federal and state constitutions (*Patchogue-Medford Congress of Teachers v. Board of Education,* 1987). The court significantly limited the effect of this holding in a subsequent decision, finding that random drug testing of police officers in the New York City Police Department's Organized Crime Control Bureau was constitutional (*Caruso v. Ward,* 1988).

In contrast to other states, several appellate state courts in California have held that the state constitutional right of privacy applies to private conduct as well as governmental action. One appellate court relied on the state constitutional right of privacy to find that a private railroad company breached an implied contractual covenant of good faith and fair dealing by discharging a computer programmer who refused to undergo a random drug test (*Luck v. Southern Pacific Transportation Co.,* 1990). Another court found that a private employee could challenge his discharge for refusal to take a random drug test, as a violation of public policy established by the state constitutional right of privacy (*Semore v. Pool,* 1990).

7. ANALYSIS AND IMPLICATIONS

As a result of federal employee drug testing, federal regulations applied to private industry, the federal government's encouragement of private-sector employer initiatives, and drug testing of state and local government employees, millions of public- and private-sector employees are currently subjected to drug testing (Cornish & Louria, 1991). Faced with constitutional challenges to governmentally mandated or authorized drug testing, the Supreme Court has applied its ad hoc balancing test to complete its creation of a two-tiered system of Fourth Amendment rights—the first tier providing protection under traditional Fourth Amendment standards for criminal law enforcement searches, and the second reducing the analysis to a generalized determination of reasonableness for searches fulfilling "special needs beyond the normal need for law enforcement." After *Skinner* and *Von Raab,* the lower courts have focused on the Supreme Court's development of "special needs" according to a context defined by the goal of the search; that is, whether the search furthers criminal law enforcement or other governmental purposes. The lower courts have applied this focus on non–law enforcement goals broadly to define "special needs" in the workplace, upholding sweeping random drug testing of public and private employees.

The evolution of this dichotomous approach to the Fourth Amendment can be traced from the Court's initial use of the balancing test in 1967 for administrative searches, subsequently applied to pat-down searches, border patrol stops, and sobriety-checkpoint stops. In applying the balancing test to determine reasonableness under such circumstances, the Court justified the exception to the warrant clause requirements by the context of the search and the limited intrusion involved as a result of the nature and scope of the search. The development and application of the balancing test of reasonableness was significantly expanded with the Court's articulation of the special-needs concept in *New Jersey v. T.L.O.*, *O'Connor v. Ortega*, and *Griffin v. Wisconsin*. With these cases, context became all important, defined in terms of the initial goals of the search, its location, and the official who conducts it. Although these searches of a purse, an office, and a home were not limited intrusions, the contexts of the school, the workplace, and the probation relationship created the "special needs" that made a warrant and probable cause "impracticable."

In *Skinner* and *Von Raab*, the Court took the special-needs concept and the balancing test to their ultimate extension. As the *Skinner* dissent identifies, prior to these cases, the Court had applied the special-needs balancing test only for searches of places or possessions upon individualized suspicion. With the drug testing cases, the Court upheld searches involving a personal bodily function, based on neither a warrant nor any quantum of evidence of individualized or even general drug use in the workplace. The context of the workplace and the goal of drug deterrence were seen as all important, leading the Court to substitute the balancing test for traditional Fourth Amendment standards. Further, in applying the balancing test itself, the Court accepted at face value the heavy weight of the asserted governmental interests while devaluing the employees' privacy interests. The Court relied on the employment context as a basis for inflating the government's interests in conducting a suspicionless search and reducing the employees' expectation of privacy in the act of urination.

The Court also focused on the employment context as establishing the non–law enforcement goals of safety and integrity to support suspicionless drug testing. As in the prior special-needs cases, though, this dichotomy between criminal and civil searches is theoretically and actually flawed: The Fourth Amendment does not carve out a civil search exception. Further, in each of the special need cases, the line drawn between law enforcement and non–law enforcement goals may be crossed by the use of the evidence or the nature of the agency conducting the search.

The use of the criminal/civil dichotomy has devastating effects on Fourth Amendment rights. As a result of this focus on the goals of the search, nonpolice government officials may constitutionally use invasive law enforcement means without fulfilling Fourth Amendment requirements. This singular focus on goals ignores the value of privacy underlying the Fourth Amendment, which protects individuals from intrusive searches unless the government has a warrant based on probable cause (Cornish & Louria, 1991).

The Supreme Court's drug testing cases have a further ironic twist. The Court held that governmentally mandated or authorized drug testing by private-sector employers creates state action, thereby extending Fourth Amendment protections to private-sector employees. Although this seemingly expands the scope of employees protected by the Fourth Amendment, the ad hoc balancing test applied in *Skinner* and *Von Raab* simultaneously leaves both public- and private-sector employees with almost no constitutional protection from unreasonable searches and seizures. Further, the Court's holdings result in constitutional sanction for government mandates of private use of law enforcement means (Cornish & Louria, 1991). In the case of drug testing, the reach of this power is felt away from the workplace as well, as drug testing may provide evidence consistent with off-duty or on-duty drug use.

The combined effect of the context of the workplace and the goal of deterrence of illegal drug use may be the keys to explaining the Court's expansion of the special-needs balancing test. In *O'Connor, Skinner,* and *Von Raab,* the Court explicitly found that the employment setting, particularly in certain industries, diminishes societal recognition of employees' expectation of privacy. Additionally, the *Skinner* dissent observes that the Court, "swept away by society's obsession with stopping the scourge of illegal drugs . . . succumbs to . . . popular pressures" in upholding the searches. The dissent concludes: "The immediate victims of the majority's constitutional timorousness will be those railroad workers whose bodily fluids the Government may now forcible collect and analyze. But ultimately, today's decision will reduce the privacy all citizens may enjoy, for . . . principles of law, once bent, do not snap back easily."

REFERENCES

AFGE v. Derwinski, 777 F.Supp. 1493 (N.D. Cal. 1991).

AFGE v. Skinner, 885 F.2d 884 (D.C. Cir. 1989), cert. denied, 110 S.Ct. 1960 (1990).

AFGE v. Sullivan, 744 F.Supp. 294 (D.D.C. 1990).

AFGE v. Sullivan, 7 IER 353 (D.D.C. 1992).

Alverado v. Washington Pub. Power Supply Sys., 111 Wash.2d 424, 759 P.2d 427 (Wash. 1988), cert. denied, 490 U.S. 1004 (1989).

Amsterdam, A., 1974, Perspectives on the fourth amendment, *Minnesota Law Review* **58:**350.

Bluestein v. Skinner, 908 F.2d 451 (9th Cir. 1990), cert. denied, 111 S.Ct. 954 (1991).

Cairns, S. S., and Grady, C. V., 1990, Drug testing in the workplace: A reasoned approach for private employers, *George Mason University Law Review* **12:**491.

Camara v. Municipal Court, 387 U.S. 523 (1967).

Carroll v. United States, 267 U.S. 132 (1925).

Caruso v. Ward, 72 N.Y.2d 432, 530 N.E.2d 850 (N.Y. 1988).

Chimel v. California, 395 U.S. 752 (1969).

Christian, B. J., and Barber, J., 1990, Employee drug testing in the transportation industry: Private initiatives and government imperatives, *George Mason University Law Review* **12:**561.

Civil Rights Cases, 109 U.S. 3 (1883).

Cornish, C. M., and Louria, D. B., 1991, Employment drug testing, preventive searches, and the future of privacy, *William and Mary Law Review* **33:**95.

Crain, M., 1989, Expanded employee drug-detection programs and the public good: Big brother at the bargaining table, *New York University Law Review* **64:**1286.

Daily Labor Report, 1990, Marital problems affect more workers than substance abuse, executives say, **16:**A–2.
Department of Transportation v. Teamsters, 932 F.2d 1292 (9th Cir. 1991).
Dimeo v. Griffin, 943 F.2d 679 (7th Cir. 1991).
Drug-Free Workplace Act of 1988, 41 U.S.C. Sec. 701 (1989).
Executive Order No. 12,564, Drug-Free Federal Workplace, 1986, 5 U.S.C. Sec. 7301.
Griffin v. Wisconsin, 483 U.S. 863 (1987).
Guiney v. Police Commissioner, 411 Mass. 328, 582 N.E.2d 523 (Mass. 1991).
Harmon v. Thornburgh, 878 F.2d 484 (D.C. Cir. 1989), cert. denied, 110 S.Ct. 865 (1990).
Hartness v. Bush, 919 F.2d 170 (D.C. Cir. 1990), cert. denied, 111 S.Ct. 2890 (1991).
IBEW v. Skinner, 913 F.2d 1454 (9th Cir. 1990).
Johnson-Bateman Co., 295 N.L.R.B. No. 26 (1989).
Katz v. United States, 389 U.S. 347 (1967).
Luck v. Southern Pacific Transportation Co., 218 Cal.App.3d 1, 267 Cal. Rptr. 618 (Cal. Ct.App.1st, 1990), pet. to rev. denied (Cal. S.Ct. 1990), cert. denied (1990).
Mapp v. Ohio, 367 U.S. 643 (1961).
Michigan Department of State Police v. Sitz, 110 S.Ct. 2481 (1990).
Morgan, Lewis & Bockius, 1991, State-by-state drug and alcohol testing survey, *William and Mary Law Review* **33:**189.
National Treasury Employees Union v. Von Raab, 489 U.S. 656 (1989).
New Jersey v. T.L.O., 469 U.S. 325 (1985).
NFFE v. Cheney, 884 F.2d 603 (D.C. Cir. 1989), cert. denied, 110 S.Ct. 864 (1990).
NTEU v. Yeutter, 918 F.2d 968 (D.C. Cir. 1990).
O'Connor v. Ortega, 480 U.S. 709 (1987).
Omnibus Transportation Employee Testing Act of 1991, Title V of the Department of Transportation and Related Agencies Appropriations Act, 1992, P.L. 102-143.
Patchogue-Medford Congress of Teachers v. Board of Education of the Patchogue-Medford Union Free School District, 70 N.Y.2d 57, 510 N.E.2d 325 (N.Y. 1987).
Schmerber v. California, 384 U.S. 757 (1966).
Semore v. Pool, 217 Cal.App.3d 1087, 266 Cal.Rptr. 280 (Cal. Ct. App. 4th, 1990), pet. to rev. denied (Cal. S.Ct. 1990).
Skinner v. Railway Labor Executives' Association, 489 U.S. 602 (1989).
Slobogin, C., 1991, The world without a Fourth Amendment, *UCLA Law Review* **39:**1.
Strossen, N., 1988, The Fourth Amendment in the balance: Accurately setting the scales through the least intrusive alternative analysis, *New York University Law Review* **63:**1173.
Sonnenstuhl, W. J., Trice, H. M., Staudenmeier, W. J., and Steele, P., 1987, Employee assistance and drug testing: Fairness and injustice in the workplace, *Nova Law Review* **11:**709.
Taylor v. O'Grady, 888 F.2d 1189 (7th Cir. 1989).
Terry v. Ohio, 392 U.S. 1 (1968).
Transport Workers' Union, Local 234 v. Southeastern Pennsylvania Transportation Authority, 884 F.2d 709 (3d Cir. 1989).
United States v. Brignoni-Ponce, 422 U.S. 873 (1975).
United States v. Martinez-Fuerte, 428 U.S. 543 (1976).
Warden v. Hayden, 387 U.S. 294 (1967).
Willner v. Thornburgh, 928 F.2d 1185 (D.C. Cir. 1991).
Wright, R. F., 1984, The civil and criminal methodologies of the Fourth Amendment, *Yale Law Journal* **93:**1127.

LEGAL ISSUES

10

Arbitration of Drug Testing Disputes

TIA SCHNEIDER DENENBERG and R. V. DENENBERG

1. INTRODUCTION

The forensic laboratory has assumed a pivotal role in the employment relationship in the United States; job tenure often hinges upon the analysis of body fluids. When the results of urine or blood tests for drugs are introduced as evidence in workplace disciplinary disputes, the central issue typically is whether the test result, or the result in combination with other evidence, provides just cause for discharge or suspension. The arbitrator is required to resolve a host of factual, technical, and due process questions. Although constitutional and legal precepts have some bearing on such disputes, the arbitrator's primary task is to decide whether, in light of all the circumstances, the discipline is a reasonable exercise of managerial prerogative. In so doing, arbitrators apply the "law of the shop," which includes written collective bargaining agreements (union-management contracts) and unwritten customary practices.

The cases reviewed in this chapter, illustrating issues that typically arise in drug testing disputes, may serve as a guide in workplace policy formation, whether or not an arbitration forum is invoked or a union is involved. Discernible in the opinions is a broad theme: The desire to combat drug abuse does not justify arbitrary punishment or sacrifice of the standards of fairness that customarily have governed the employment relationship. By and large, the arbitration process has helped ensure that chemical impairment is addressed within a framework of principled rule application.

TIA SCHNEIDER DENENBERG and R. V. DENENBERG • Denenberg Associates, Red Hook, New York 12571

Research Advances in Alcohol and Drug Problems, Volume 11: Drug Testing in the Workplace, edited by Scott Macdonald and Paul M. Roman. Plenum Press, New York, 1994.

2. THE OCCASION FOR TESTING

A threshold issue in any dispute is likely to be: Was it proper to administer a test to the grievant in the first place? This question entails an examination of the principle of selection that governs the testing program (usually urinalysis for a short list of illegal substances). Testing is conducted either with "reasonable suspicion" (which is also termed "for cause") or without such cause or suspicion. Reasonable-suspicion testing occurs only when there is some basis for believing that a specific individual is impaired by chemicals. It is often incident-driven, in the sense that the urinalysis is triggered by an accident or other event. Testing without reasonable suspicion is conducted as a matter of routine among a class of employees, even though there may be no indication that any particular individual is affected by drugs. It may be divided into two subcategories: periodic testing and unscheduled ("surprise" or "unannounced") testing (see Chapter 6 for details).

Testing without Reasonable Suspicion

A barrier to random testing, some arbitrators have held, is the "just cause" provision of contracts. One such ruling was delivered in a case where the contract stipulated that the employer "will not discharge or discipline an employee without just cause." Implicit in the provision, an arbitrator found, was a presumption of innocence and protection against compulsory self-incrimination:

> When an employee is required to undergo urinalysis for a drug or alcohol test without probable cause or reasonable suspicion, he is required to give evidence against himself. He must prove his innocence before any discipline has ever been imposed. The rule of random testing is contrary to the normal and customary rule of discipline that an employee is presumed to be innocent of the particular offense. (Caraway, 1988)

Also repugnant to the just-cause provision, the arbitrator held, was the likelihood that random testing would sweep casual users into the disciplinary net, as well as habitual users who might be impaired on the job.

In some contracts, testing is expressly limited to cases of reasonable suspicion. An arbitrator held that a contract clause defining the grounds for testing professional athletes precluded a random testing program unilaterally imposed by the commissioner of pro football. The employers (i.e., team owners) contended that the program was an exercise of residual disciplinary authority, invested in the commissioner, that transcended the contractual definitions. But the arbitrator held that the "commissioner's rule-making authority was supplanted, in certain respects, by specific agreement language . . . which established clear procedures concerning . . . testing" (Kasher, 1986). The arbitrator noted that the player's association had consistently resisted suggestions in bargaining to include "unscheduled" analyses. The decision suggests that employers may not shift to a random basis by relying on an assertion of inherent management rights despite a specific contractual requirement for reasonable suspicion.

If the collective bargaining agreement lacks a provision on testing, arbitrators nevertheless may find random urinalysis a violation of more general contractual restraints or of the basic principle that employer rules must be reasonable. One such restraint, an arbitrator decided, was a contract clause stipulating that "all new rules will be subject to negotiation" with the union. The employer, a trucking firm, added testing unilaterally to each driver's annual physical examination, arguing the necessity of complying with U.S. Department of Transportation prohibitions against driving while "under the influence" of impairing substances. In the years before testing, the arbitrator observed, the company had never been cited for non-compliance: "It hardly appears necessary for any rules to be issued to cause further compliance . . . . There has not been any triggering activity by the employees and it appears to me there has not been any negotiation either" (Feldman, 1987).

Although employers have sometimes insisted that unique safety problems in their industry warrant random testing, arbitrators have carefully weighed the worker's interest in privacy against the employer's assertion of special needs, even when employers produce hazardous material (e.g., in the nuclear power industry). A manufacturer of U.S. Army munitions ordered urinalysis for certain drugs (but not alcohol) every six months; names were chosen randomly by computer. The arbitrator determined that random testing was insupportable because of its "highly intrusive nature," although, given the presence of explosives, "the threshold inquiry for requiring employees to take drug tests [for cause] is correspondingly low" (Heinsz, 1987).

Random testing of office and clerical employees at a nuclear power plant was also disallowed by an arbitrator, who saw a conflict with the contract. Employees who tested positive were to be placed on disability status and denied access to the facility until they could furnish "proof of rehabilitation and negative urine samples." The employer pointed out that the clericals enjoyed unescorted access to areas that were sensitive and subject to close government regulation. The arbitrator was more impressed by contract language "which provides that the company has accepted the obligation to promote the welfare of the employees by maintaining conditions of employment that are equitable, reasonable and fair." He took note of the elaborate safeguards that were already in place:

> The intrusiveness of the testing, the nature of the work performed by the affected employees, the location of the work, the record of the employees, the current effective monitoring procedures, and the low probability that the test would prevent work impairment due to drugs persuade me that the rule requiring a drug screen . . . is not reasonable. (Fraser, 1988)

In all three cases discussed immediately above—involving trucking, munitions, and nuclear power—federal regulation of the industry was pervasive. Yet the arbitrator in each case rejected the notion that the employer was constrained to adopt the specific type of testing regimen it had promulgated. Although the arbitrators evidently accepted that the regulations called for careful measures to prevent employees from working while impaired, they doubted that random testing had to be among them or that employers were relieved of the obligation to conform to the contract.

Reasonable Suspicion Testing

Although reasonable suspicion testing tends to survive arbitral scrutiny more readily than random testing, the latter also may be invalidated because of a conflict with the contract. An arbitrator ruled that discharging employees if they refused a management order to submit to a drug test negated the contractual requirement that discipline "shall be based upon just and sufficient cause." The burden of proof was improperly transferred from the employer to the employee, in the arbitrator's opinion. "To unilaterally require the employee to take a test . . . or be suspended or discharged is requiring the employee to prove his innocence before the employer decided to assess a penalty." The arbitrator suggested that the employer concentrate on "observing overt behavior or conduct of the employee relative to his job" (Kagel, 1987).

Testing for cause may violate the contract if the group of employees liable to be tested has been arbitrarily targeted. For example, a municipal transit agency announced that employees would be tested if supervisors had a "reasonable belief" the employee was "under the influence" of alcohol or drugs. The policy was premised upon a need to ensure that employees who performed safety-critical jobs or came into contact with the public were not impaired. Yet all members of the bargaining unit were candidates for testing, even though some (such as clericals) performed no safety-sensitive or public-related work, and non–bargaining unit members in safety-sensitive or public-related positions (such as security/law enforcement personnel) were not covered by the testing program. To focus exclusively on the bargaining unit members, the union argued, violated a contract clause stating that "management . . . recognizes its responsibility to treat employees fairly and equitably." The arbitrator agreed that "if safety and dealing with the public are the distinguishing criteria then it does not follow that the procedure should be based on bargaining unit membership . . . . Procedures leading to testing should be directed at distinguishing factors which cut across all bargaining units as well as management" (Concepcion, 1986).

Arbitrators are often invited to scrutinize the selection process for suspect motives. They may be urged to find that the decision to test a given employee was capricious, discriminatory, retaliatory, or driven by a desire to intimidate. A complete catalog of impermissible motives would also include race or gender discrimination, animus toward union activists, and the desire to purge the work force of "whistle-blowers." Some employees have contended that they were tested because they exposed safety problems at nuclear plants and similarly critical facilities (Boals, 1986; "The Nuclear Dilemma," Washington Post, 1986). Motives are most likely to be questioned when supervisors enjoy relatively unfettered discretion to select employees for testing, particularly because the mere act of ordering the test may stigmatize an employee, even if the results are negative.

Definition of Cause for a Test

What constitutes cause to single out an employee for testing? In its most basic form, it has been described aptly as "some quantum of individualized suspicion . . . some articulable basis . . . for believing that a specific person has been affected by drugs" (Lorrora v. City of Chattanooga, 1986). U.S. Federal Aviation Administration regulations take a similar, if more elaborate, approach by stating that a decision to test "must be based on a reasonable and articulable belief that the employee is using a prohibited drug on the basis of specific, contemporaneous physical, behavioral, or performance indicators of probable drug use" (Department of Transportation, 1988). Emphasis on articulation rules out testing based on mere hunches or other inexpressible feelings, which cannot be objectively evaluated.

It is not at all certain, however, that a supervisor could distinguish indicators linked to prohibited drugs from those linked to legal substances, prescription drugs (including steroids), or other causes. Some corporate medical directors have argued that only a physician can competently evaluate ostensibly drug-induced symptoms—and make the decision to test—because endocrine disorders or psychiatric illnesses may be at the root of unusual behavior. Medical directors have also called attention to various conditions, not readily identifiable by the layman, that mimic the effects of drugs, including "depression, diabetic acidosis and effects of certain workplace toxins (such as carbon disulfide and various hydrocarbon solvents). Although not often recognized adequately, another example is chronic sleep deprivation secondary to shift work (a problem of increasing magnitude)" (C. E. Curtis, 1988; see also Cornell/Smithers Report, 1992).

Given that it often will be necessary to justify the decision later, the approval of a lawyer may be sought. Under a private-sector testing agreement between players and owners in the National Basketball Association, an official who formerly served as an assistant U.S. attorney and deputy police commissioner of New York City was charged with determining whether sufficient evidence exists to order a drug test ("Loyd and Wiggins," New York Times, 1987). The decision maker was qualified, by virtue of his background, to exercise quasi-prosecutorial discretion. Employers lacking such in-house prosecutors are likely to be less scrupulous, although specially prepared supervisors may be designated to review proposed drug tests. The Federal Aviation Administration, for example, mandated the following practice: "At least two of the employees's supervisors, one of whom is trained in detection of the possible symptoms of drug use, shall substantiate and concur in the decision to test an employee who is reasonably suspected of drug use" (Department of Transportation, 1988).

Most often, the decision to test is made by a regular line manager applying a written policy. Typical is a policy providing that reasonable suspicion "shall include, but not be limited to, management's personal observation of an employee's appearance, behavior, or speech" (National Report on Substance Abuse, 1987). Purely statistical indicators, such as excessive absenteeism or tardiness, would be unlikely to qualify as reasonable suspicion under such a formula. An arbitrator declared invalid a company policy mandating testing of any employee involved in an industrial accident requiring treatment by a doctor. The policy, the arbitrator concluded, "is on its face arbitrary and only one step away from constituting random testing. No consideration is given to the seriousness of the accident and/or injuries sustained. No consideration is given to fault" (R. L. Ross, 1988). Nor, ruled another arbitrator, does a past history of drug use justify testing if the contract permits it only in case of a "reasonable possibility of injury." The arbitrator asserted that "some individualized showing must be made that there is a reasonable chance that the theoretical potential for injury may actually be realized in the concrete circumstances which then exist" (L. Katz, 1986).

Of course, when there is palpable evidence of impairment or poor performance, body fluid analysis is less essential. Keen observation by supervisors of an employee's behavior is often enough to convince an arbitrator that an employee was not functioning normally. In cases involving the nation's primary drug, alcohol—which has a much longer history in arbitration—proving impairment has not always required the results of a medical test (blood alcohol concentration). The "unsteady gait" and other well-known signs, attested by lay witnesses, are considered highly probative and valued as corroboration, even when a blood test is in evidence.

Bizarre behavior is a common reason for administering a drug test. In one case, the grievant "made leaping or dancing" motions and "claimed to be a gazelle—all in the presence of customers." The arbitrator held that employer "took reasonable steps in ordering the grievant to submit to testing to determine whether any chemical accounted for her behavior" (McKay, 1986). In another case, the grievant had fallen asleep several times during his shift and had to be shaken awake repeatedly; he also seemed disoriented. The arbitrator concluded that the "grievant's behavior on the day in question—sleeping on the job, incoherence, and difficulty in walking—would suggest that something was wrong and that whatever it was could be drug-related" (Staudohar, 1989). In another case, a "last chance agreement" between an employer and a chemically dependent employee conditioned reinstatement on willingness to submit to a test "at any time." The arbitrator held that the requirement was enforceable even in nonworking hours, "since the purpose is not merely the capacity of the individual to perform his work adequately but his overall physical condition" (Daniel, 1987).

Secondhand Information

In some instances, employers have ordered tests without benefit of firsthand information; they have acted on the basis of reports relayed by coworkers, members of the public, or undercover informers. Some of these sources may be anonymous. Is testing based on such secondhand information valid?

Being identified by a coworker as drug user has been rejected by an arbitrator as a basis for urinalysis of a long-term employee with a good performance record. The grievant, who had been employed for 10 years as a bus driver, was included on a list of employees who purportedly were involved with drugs. The list was spontaneously supplied to management by two other employees. The arbitrator emphasized the vagueness of the allegations: "All the company had were alleged and totally unsubstantiated rumors about a potential drug problem at an undefined time and in an undefined place and under undefined circumstances. The company never made any independent investigation to verify or find support for these allegations" (Goodman, 1987). The arbitrator also called attention to the possibilities for abuse inherent in a denunciation of one employee by another. An investigation prior to ordering a test, he wrote, might have revealed ulterior motives, such as

> a junior employee seeking to hold his job over a senior employee in periods of layoff, an employee seeking to cause harm to another because of issues wholly unrelated to the job, an employee seeking to endear himself to management, [or] a union steward seeking to get rid of an employee because of the employee's feelings about the union. (Goodman, 1987)

An anonymous tip sometimes can be leveraged into something more substantial. In a nuclear power plant, the employer received a tip about an employee who had a poor work record and who had previously been accused of marijuana use. The employee submitted to a test, registered positive, and was discharged. The arbitrator upheld the discharge, finding that the employer relied on the totality of the circumstances, including an acknowledgement by the employee (once the latter was confronted) of marijuana use. As is often true, the nature of the work site was an important factor for the arbitrator: "We cannot ignore the context. Obviously, the operation of a nuclear facility requires the company to be extra careful" (Abrams, 1989).

Anonymous telephone calls from customers have been held to be inadequate reason to administer a test, unless they lead to other evidence. In a case involving a California utility company, the arbitrator remarked: "A drug test is too intrusive an invasion of privacy to be conducted on the basis of an anonymous call . . . . [If supervisors] had found a basis on which to order a drug test for grievant—independent of the informant's call—there would have been proper cause to order the test" (Alleyne, 1987). Responding to the customer tip, company officials found the grievant placid and red-eyed. But the arbitrator commented: "There was no evidence indicating that a calm and placid manner was out of character for grievant, and it is doubtful that red eyes, in an air polluted environment like Los Angeles, would alone be a basis for a drug test" (Alleyne, 1987).

In another case, redness of eyes did qualify as a suspicious condition, at least in combination with another untoward circumstance: lagging well behind schedule on a bus route. A supervisor boarded the bus being driven by the grievant and noticed, according to the arbitrator,

> that she was abnormal in her [unusually rapid side-to-side] head movements, exaggerating them, and that her speech was slurred and eyes red. Considering that she was running 20 minutes late (the other drivers were 6–10 minutes late) and was acting strangely, [the supervisor] was certainly justified in asking her to submit to testing. (Baroni, 1987)

Refusal to Submit to Testing

A well-established arbitral maxim holds that an employee must "obey now and grieve later" when faced with an order from a superior that he or she considers wrong. Where it seems appropriate, this rule is often applied without modification in drug testing cases, although the outcome may be influenced by other factors. Illustrative is the case of a warehouse worker who refused a test after sustaining a back injury and was discharged. Although the union argued that he should have been offered medical treatment rather than screening, the arbitrator found that the obey-now principle was applicable: "If he was not under the influence of any drugs he had nothing to fear" (Wies, 1987).

In a similar case, the grievant, an employee of a machinery manufacturer, refused to be tested despite wobbling and staggering toward her work station. The arbitrator found that other employees had been discharged for similar refusals, that the testing requirement was posted throughout the workplace, and that the grievant had been repeatedly warned that she would be discharged if she refused. The arbitrator concluded that the grievant's adamancy was a missed opportunity to dispel doubt: "Clearly, all parties are better served by obtaining medical verification of a suspected condition" (J. B. Katz, 1981).

Several features of this pair of cases are worth noting. In both the employer had good reason to suspect drugs, because the grievants had manifest dysfunctions: a back injury in one case and subnormal motor coordination in the other (both also had a known history of drug involvement). Nevertheless, the cases had different outcomes. Critical to each was the adequacy of the warning the grievant had received before refusing the test. The arbitrator found that the manufacturing worker had been adequately warned and thus properly discharged, but the warehouse worker was reinstated (without back pay) because the arbitrator believed that "the employee who is about to lose his job for refusing to obey an order from his supervisor must be made aware of such danger. . . . The grievant's supervisor . . . failed to explicitly forewarn him of the grave consequences of his disobedient behavior" (Wies, 1987).

Another arbitrator concluded that mere refusal to submit to a test, standing alone, did not amount to adequate grounds for a discharge because the company rules did not specify that discharge was the inevitable consequence of refusal. "At best," the arbitrator wrote, "the company is entitled to draw an adverse inference from an employee's decision to decline any testing, provided the employee is forewarned that such an adverse inference will be drawn" (Concepcion, 1984).

The rationale for the obey-now rule traditionally has been that output could not be allowed to suffer while employees turned the workplace into a debating society. But an order to take a test is not an order to perform work, nor is it based on the exigencies of the production process. Unquestioning obedience, therefore, may not be demanded by the circumstances. One arbitrator has commented that

> the urinalysis directive . . . does not directly implicate the company's production or any related work. Where a directive is outside the mainstream of the employer's operation, the non-complying employee may run the risk of discipline if the directive is ultimately found to be valid. However, where the directive is found to be invalid, the employee's non-compliance will be considered justified and no discipline may be imposed. (L. Katz, 1986)

In another case, a charge of insubordination for refusal to submit to a routine screen was not sustained because the arbitrator concluded that the employer failed to show either that drugs menaced the plant or that the individuals targeted displayed any signs of drug use. The arbitrator wrote that "forcing them to take such a test is an invasion of privacy and unwarranted requirement to furnish confidential medical information . . . . I find that the refusal to take the drug screen was a reasonable protest against the invasion of privacy" (Warns, 1986).

Humiliation and Embarrassment

It has been remarked that direct observation of urination by a "collection site person" trespasses against strongly held cultural values. The U.S. Supreme Court, for example, noted that collection methods "require employees to perform an excretory function traditionally shielded by great privacy." Whether an undue intrusion on personal space has taken place depends on the specific circumstances, according to an arbitrator: "The most that can be said is that under certain circumstance, it may be unacceptable" (McKay, 1986).

Acutely aware that an individual's dignity may be injured by micturition monitoring, arbitrators have adopted a standard similar to the "shock-the-conscience" test developed in constitutional adjudication. One arbitrator, appalled by the conditions under which a grievant had been required to give his specimen, stated: "Surely there must be a better way than requiring the employee to urinate into a container in full view of a total stranger . . . . Something must be done to avoid this disregard of one's personal dignity" (Goodman, 1987). In a case involving mine workers, an arbitrator declared unreasonable a substance abuse policy that called for observation if "there is some reason to believe that the employee has the means to alter or substitute the specimen." The arbitrator explained that if "a possibility exists that the circumstances might provide a means of altering a urine sample, then the circumstances or location should be changed rather than requiring observation for urination" (Stoltenberg, 1988).

An asserted inability to urinate because of embarrassment—to which jocular terms like "bashful kidney syndrome" or "pee-fritis" are sometimes attached—has been less persuasive than modesty as an explanation for refusing to provide a urinalysis sample. A customer service representative at a utility company was discharged when he failed to provide a sample despite drinking water over a period of hours. The arbitrator did not credit his "claims that he was nervous and could not urinate during any of the five attempts made in the presence of the company's medical director . . . . As the bladder filled the physical need to relieve the pressure would seem to overcome any emotional inhibition" (Simpkins, 1989).

3. CHAIN OF CUSTODY AND LABORATORY ANALYSIS

Because a grievant may face the workplace counterpart of "capital punishment" on the basis of a test report alone, arbitrators carefully assess the accuracy, reliability, and diligence of the analysts supplying the critical item of evidence. Although efforts at standardization are under way, the care with which samples or specimens are handled, the qualifications of the laboratory technicians and supervisors, and their scientific thoroughness are often challenged.

Integrity of the Sample

As a threshold matter, there may be a disagreement about the integrity of the urine sample at issue. Did it emanate from the grievant charged with misconduct? Was it properly handled and secured all times? Assuring an unbroken chain of custody begins with verified sample-taking. It is always possible that the contents of the jar may be bogus, adulterated, or diluted. Indeed, the low rates of positives in some testing programs may be partly attributable to cheating. Employers often go to great lengths to thwart subterfuge. Monitors are told to watch for "unusual circumstances, behavior or appearance . . . for example, excessive liquid splashing, no liquid splashing, sound of opening container, sound of pouring of liquid, paper noise, very short or very long time spent in restroom/stall" (Pacific Gas and Electric Company, 1990).

Sample tampering is a common reason for discharge. In a return-to-work agreement, a hospital laundry employee pledged to complete treatment for cocaine dependency and accept "random bodily fluid sampling to verify her continued drug-free condition" for a year. Shortly before reinstatement, she provided a treatment center with a sample. Having spilled some of the urine accidentally, according to the employee, she accepted another woman's offer of supposedly "clean" urine to mix with her own, enabling the jar to be filled completely. The sample tested positive for methadone. The employee was discharged on the ground that she had violated the agreement and falsified a medical record. The arbitrator wrote:

> The union maintains that . . . if anything, the dishonesty was de minimis . . . for, surely, she would not have substituted another's urine except upon assurance that her urine was clean and that the donor's urine was clean. I do not agree with the union regarding the nature of the act. The substitution was clearly a dishonest act . . . . The grievant took a qualified gamble in accepting the urine substitution. She gambled it would be clean. It was not. The ante in this case was the employer's trust, and the grievant lost it. (A. R. Rothstein, 1986)

The arbitrator was unconvinced by the purported reason for the substitution. The grievant said that she feared that an insufficiency would be taken by the counselor as an admission that her urine was "dirty." The arbitrator pointed out that it was more likely that the counselor would have simply asked the grievant to return later to give the sample.

Postcollection Handling

Lapses in the chain of custody can occur immediately after the sample is taken—for example, when the grievant and the monitor or supervisor fail to remain with the jar until it is properly labeled, sealed, placed in the shipping container, and dispatched to the laboratory. Deficiencies in the handling of samples by the laboratory also may occur. Myriad jars are processed, creating opportunities for analytical mistakes or clerical errors. When the handling of the sample is in doubt, arbitrators have sometimes applied a relatively relaxed standard of "due care," as illustrated by this arbitral comment:

> It is my conviction that the company exercised all due care, from securing the sample and placing the proper identification on it. Additionally, it was protected with care to the laboratory where it was tested. If a greater requirement were placed on the process of securing and testing samples of this type it might well . . . become impossible to carry out. (Boner, 1985)

But in other cases, arbitrators have demanded a detailed history of the jar in question:

> Although [company and laboratory officials] all testified in general as to the procedure used by the company for the testing and delivery of urine samples from the plant to the [laboratory], there was scant specific evidence as to the handling of the grievant's urine samples. There were no witnesses or documentary evidence of receipts or other business records as to the chain of custody for each of the samples and tests of the grievant. (Heinsz, 1987)

Record-keeping discrepancies resulting in dubious chronologies can lead to reinstatement:

> It would stretch the bounds of credulity to suggest a drug screen was performed by [the laboratory] on the grievant's specimen on the very same day it was being refrigerated at [another] facility. . . . Beyond a reasonable doubt the specimen tested . . . was positive for marijuana[;] however, there remains the overriding question as to whether it was the grievant's original and/or authentic specimen from beginning to end. (Speroff, 1987)

Grievant-Initiated Tests

In some cases, the grievant has offered to supply his or her own urinalysis to counter the report from the employer's laboratory. It is then typically the grievant who bears the burden of establishing the identity and integrity of the sample. Comparing a grievant-initiated test result with the result of the employer-ordered test, an arbitrator commented that he was being asked to "accept a test of an unobserved urine sample which was in [the grievent's] sole custody as superior to the observed urine sample obtained by the company for which the chain of custody by disinterested parties was firmly established" (Brisco, 1987).

In another case, a grievant discharged for allegedly smoking marijuana in a company parking lot had her urine and blood tested by a laboratory, and she submitted the results as evidence. While opining that "their probative value is limited," owing to doubts about the chain of custody and proximity to the parking lot events, the arbitrator did "look favorably upon the fact that grievant, of her own volition, arranged for the drug testing in an effort to clear herself. Her actions were consistent with her strong stance at hearing that she does not smoke marijuana and did not do so on the date in question" (Goldstein, 1987). The grievant was reinstated with full back pay.

Laboratory Performance

After the propriety of the sample handling has been assured, there remains the essential matter of analytical accuracy. Even when sound in principle, the technology for analyzing a body fluid may be applied incorrectly. Experts have urged employers to assess carefully a laboratory's quality control system before contracting for services and to monitor performance by submitting trial samples periodically for blind testing (Hansen et al., 1985). Since 1988, drug testing laboratories providing services to the federal government have been subject to a certification program governed by guidelines of the National Institute on Drug Abuse (NIDA) and requiring internal quality control standards as well as external proficiency testing (Department of Health and Human Services, 1988). The guidelines call for six cycles of performance testing each year; unless at least 90% of the test samples are correctly identified, the laboratory's certification may be revoked. Some employers use only NIDA-certified laboratories. Results from such laboratories presumably will have more credibility than those from other facilities.

It may be advisable nonetheless for employers to verify independently the performance of the accuracy of the laboratories on whose reports they depend. The certification of some laboratories has been revoked at least temporarily because of errors. Arbitrators have acknowledged the need for thorough review of laboratory practices:

> The reliability of all drug determinations, whether by immunoassay or Gas Chromatography/Mass Spectrometry, depend upon many factors, such as the certainty of specimen identification; specimen storage; handling; preparation; proper cleaning and calibration of testing instruments and hardware; preparation and storage of test reagents; and the qualification and training of laboratory personnel performing the tests and interpreting the results . . . . Care should be taken to base termination decisions upon dual or multiple testing results. (Baroni, 1987)

Direct testimony by laboratory representatives is not necessary to authenticate a report, some arbitrators have decided, provided that the laboratory appears to be qualified by reputation or certification and its record keeping is adequate. An affidavit or other document detailing the tests performed might be sufficient.

The admissibility of laboratory records, standing alone, was challenged in a mining industry case. The union contended that admitting the records without the testimony of laboratory personnel amounted to reliance on hearsay evidence. The arbitrator chose to regard the disputed documents as records kept in the ordinary course of business and therefore as entitled to due weight:

> While it may be true that the records could have been more professionally offered and received had a representative of [the laboratory] been called to testify, I cannot deny company's right to place certain business records before the arbitrator . . . . This is not to say that union could not have offered expert testimony for the purpose of challenging the subject lab tests; but for whatever reason, it could not do so. Thus, it

> must be held that grievant was given a fair and reasonable opportunity to defend against the charges made out against him and to rebut any and all arguments advanced by company. (Nicholas, 1987)

The adversarial imbalance that marked the case—the union presented no technical witness to dispute the laboratory report—is characteristic of many arbitrations. "For whatever reason," typically expense, the grievant often lacks the ability to dispute the technical evidence with expert opinion. As a practical matter, the playing field may be far from level.

Some arbitrators, insisting upon a rigorous standard of proof when laboratory reports are challenged, have taken the view that the reports are indeed hearsay and not to be presumed reliable. In the case of a railroad brakeman whose urine tested positive for marijuana during a physical examination, an arbitrator declared that "if written hearsay laboratory reports are challenged, [the employer] must provide evidence from a credible source that the tests were conducted in accordance with acceptable scientific procedures. Bare assertions regarding the reputation or pedigree of the testing laboratory are not sufficient for that purpose" (Eischen, 1989).

Another arbitrator held that the employer's burden of proof included "the obligation to make available, by testimony and written records, complete details of the testing" (Schwartz, 1986). Reinstating a motorcycle patrolman who was discharged on the basis of a positive urinalysis for cocaine, an obviously exasperated arbitrator remarked upon the "difficulty [of] reviewing and making sense out of some of the evidence that was produced by the laboratory" (Bairstow, 1988). The arbitrator noted the absence of quality control documents and slipshod practices that included undated or altered records.

At the very least, it has been held, employers have a duty to disclose the actual laboratory report to the affected employee as soon as possible. A bus operator was reinstated with full back pay, in part because the employer merely communicated the results of a urine test for alcohol but denied him access to the report. The arbitrator decided that the grievant should have been "put in a position at the earliest opportunity to counter the central evidentiary basis for the discharge penalty. This is actually a matter of notice and fair hearing which is at the heart of due process" (Yarowsky, 1987). In addition, employers have been faulted for failing to disclose that a urine sample, ostensibly taken for purposes of medical diagnosis, also was used for a disciplinary purpose: screening for illegal drugs.

Evaluation of Analytical Methods

Arbitrators are often called upon to evaluate the specific methods that were used to analyze the sample being offered in evidence against the grievant. One issue typically will be whether the initial test that registered positive was confirmed by another test based on a different chemical method. The importance of the confirmation step for the immunoassay technique used in screening was underscored by a forensic journal report.

> Biological samples such as urine are complex chemical mixtures. As such, there is no absolute guarantee that the drug antibodies [in an immunoassay] will not bind with another similar compound; or that another substance will not trigger a false positive. Thus the results are always suspect to some degree . . . . [Yet] unconfirmed immunochemical testing is being used to influence hiring, firing, and disciplinary actions. ("Workplace Alcohol Testing," Employee Testing and the Law, 1986).

Drugs that appear commonly on employment screens (i.e., marijuana, opiates, cocaine, amphetamines, and PCP) may produce a false positive in an unconfirmed immunoassay, owing to the possibility of "cross-reactivity" (Battelle Human Affairs Research Centers, 1988).

A survey by CompuChem Laboratories of North Carolina found that forensic experts expressed strong preferences about which combinations of analytical methods—such as immunoassay, radio immunoassay, thin-layer chromatography (TLC), and gas chromatography/mass spectrometry (GC/MS)—should be used for initial detection and for confirmation. Often, these preferences varied with the type of drug in question. In contrast, arbitrators who were surveyed had a difficult time discerning differences in the reliability of various combinations that were rated by the forensic experts, such as immunoassay confirmed by GC/MS. The study concluded that arbitrators "have little understanding of the differences in accuracy among commonly used analytical methods." In fact, 61% of those who heard a case involving urinalysis could not recall which methods were used to analyze the sample (Hoyt, Finnigan, Nee, Shults, & Butler, 1987).

Some arbitrators, however, have voiced a preference for the best available technology, drawing a sharp distinction between expensive and inexpensive tests:

> The so-called "$10 tests" appear to be inherently unreliable. If that were the only test the company intended to administer, it would be extremely questionable whether the underlying order [to submit to the test] would be valid. However, the so-called $100 test (GC/MS) is a reliable indicator of the presence of drug metabolites . . . . Thus, a directive to submit to urinalysis would not appear to be invalid due to the claimed unreliability of the testing. (L. Katz, 1986)

The contract itself may furnish a standard for assessing the adequacy of the analytical method. A county firefighter with seven years of seniority was discharged when his urine registered positive for cocaine. The contract called for the employer to be "guided by the most recent research in toxicology" and to conduct a "second test." Although confirmatory tests were performed, the original sample was used; the union contended that a second sample should have been analyzed. The arbitrator found that "there was no meeting of the minds on this point in negotiations, as the union officials deemed the language to mean two sample specimens" (Boals, 1990). That and various technical violations of the agreement meant that the discharge had to be overturned.

Commonly at issue is the proper threshold for a positive result. Not all positives are alike. A laboratory typically predetermines the minimum concentration of a drug—known as the "decision" or "cutoff" level—that will cause the urine to be reported as positive. A relatively high decision level helps avoid false positives attributable to "background noise" (spurious chemical reactions in the urine).

The decision level may be changed abruptly in the course of a testing program. For example, the decision level could be raised from 25 ng/ml (nanograms per milliliter) to 75 ng/ml to preclude an argument that the result was attributable to passive inhalation of marijuana smoked by others. (A nanogram is a billionth of a gram, or one 28-billionth of an ounce.) Some testing programs have set the level as high as 100 or even 200 ng/ml. A "positive" result thus may vary substantially from one employer to another, and also from time to time within the same testing program. Such variability demonstrates that "positive" is not a threshold determined by objective scientific criteria—such as correlation with impairment—but the result of an administrative decision by the laboratory and the employer. A study undertaken for the U.S. Nuclear Regulatory Commission noted that

> There is no literature explicitly focused on establishing cut-off levels for urine test programs. Cut-off levels used by business and by [the Department of Defense] in existing urine screening programs have been established on the basis of laboratory studies, policy considerations, legal defensibility and implementation factors. (Battelle Human Affairs Research Centers, 1988)

In other words, cutoffs are largely based on convenience. Raising the cutoff means that fewer subjects register positive; lowering the level increases the proportion of positives.

Arbitrators may find themselves faced with having to decide whether a positive at a given level provides just cause for discharge, even though they are aware that a similar concentration would not count as a positive if the grievant worked for another employer, if the employer had contracted with a different laboratory, or if the test had been performed at an earlier time. The unstable cutoff level is often troubling. In a case which turned upon a positive urinalysis for cocaine, an arbitrator complained about the "bewildering maze of laboratory procedures, analytical approaches, and [lack of] . . . agreement on a specific numerical standard universally applied in reputable laboratories through the United States" (Bairstow, 1988). In another case, the arbitrator deplored the casual manner in which the cutoffs for urinalysis were determined, noting that "an occupational nurse, who admittedly had absolutely no training or experience in drug testing and its ramifications, not only chose the laboratory to do the testing, but set the ground rules for the 'levels' to be considered" (Draznin, 1987). A signal advantage of testing protocols negotiated by the collective bargaining parties (see below) is that they eliminate disputes about cutoff levels.

4. PROVING JUST CAUSE

The limitations of the urinalysis result as evidence is often emphasized by experts who may be called upon to testify in arbitration. For example, Kurt Dubowski of the University of Oklahoma, an experienced forensic toxicologist, has explained that

> drug-induced, intoxication, impairment, or other effects on a person at any given time cannot be established or even validly presumed from a urine test result, or a series of such results. These limitations arise from the nature of urinary drug excretion, which is often in the form of pharmacologically inactive drug metabolites, from the well-documented absence of correspondence between drug effects on the person and urine concentrations of psychoactive drugs, and from the low correlations of the variables. (Dubowski, 1987)

Job Relevance

Owing to the difficulty of relating urinalysis results to impairment, the relevance to the job is often a key issue. By and large, arbitrators have regarded off-duty misconduct, including lawbreaking, as beyond the reach of the employer's disciplinary powers, unless the misconduct has a direct bearing on the employment relationship. Arbitral thinking on this question has been summarized as follows:

> The employer must . . . demonstrate that there is a valid nexus between the off-duty misconduct and the status of the grievant as an employee. The decisions indicate that this may be accomplished by showing that the misconduct has damaged the employer's business or will do so if the employee is reinstated; that fellow employees would refuse to work with the offender or would be exposed to danger from the offender; and/or that the nature of the misconduct is disqualifying, in that it is incompatible with the duties of the employee's job classification (Hill et al., 1986).

In a typical alcohol intoxication case, the grievant is charged with being under the influence of ethanol while on the job, a violation of workplace rules. A test result—blood alcohol concentration—may be introduced into evidence to substantiate the charge that the grievant was chemically impaired while at work. In such cases, the job relevance is clear; the impairment is temporally related to the offender's duties. But the most common form of drug testing, urinalysis for cannabinoids (marijuana), reaches far back in time, searching for possible drug use during periods when the employee was off duty. To that extent, urinalysis is much less closely linked to traditionally disciplinable conduct. Urinalysis fights the presumption that the employer's sole concern is performance and fitness while at work. "The fact that employment-related testing threatens the jobs of millions of persons who are not manifestly bad workers," observes a drug policy expert, "fuels much of the opposition to employee testing" (Kleiman, 1992).

In a case concerning the positive urinalysis result of a bus driver, the arbitrator observed that upholding a discharge on the basis of a the positive alone "would defy all arbitral wisdom to the effect that proven employee misconduct, and not private misconduct (without a nexus to the job), must be presented to sustain a termination" (Goodman, 1987). Indeed, if tangible relevance is not required, an employee is terminable for using impairing substances at any time, a premise that would have significant consequences if applied to alcohol, the most pervasive chemical threat to workplace safety:

> A company rule prohibiting all marijuana usage off the job would not be a reasonable rule. Society tolerates off-the-job consumption of alcoholic beverages, and no company rule makes all consumption of alcohol off the job a dischargeable offense, without considering its effect on job performance.
>
> Job-related alcohol problems are more numerous and more serious than job-related drug problems. Increasingly, alcohol consumption off the job having an effect on job performance is treated as an illness requiring treatment. Illegal drug usage off the job, having an effect on job performance, is not treated as an illness, even though drug addition is no less an illness because the drug is illegally possessed and consumed (Alleyne, 1987).

In the System

The boundary between off-duty and on-duty drug use becomes blurred when workplace policies contemplate discipline of employees who have drugs "in their system," as determined through urinalysis or from other evidence. A penalty is assessed for registering positive, even though what is in the system may be metabolic waste products that are not psychoactive. Such an infraction is sometimes termed a "presence violation." Some arbitrators have endorsed the in-the-system concept, reasoning that what is detectable should be punishable:

> The effect of our grievant's off the job indulgence in marijuana was to introduce cannabinoid metabolites into his system which were retained over a period of time and remained as a detectable level of drugs while on the job. Notwithstanding the union "correlation" argument, the presence of drugs on the job must be recognized as a potential cause of serious emergency and cannot be ignored. Therefore, this type of off the job behavior is not beyond the control of the company (Milentz, 1987).

This line of reasoning erases the distinction between active and inert chemicals, and assumes that the latter can give rise to an emergency—an assumption that, in a sense, repeals the laws of pharmacodynamics. Other arbitrators, wary of such assumptions, have been reluctant to uphold summary discharge for in-the-system offenses unless the employee suffered actual impairment while working. For example, an arbitrator criticized a testing program promulgated by a utility company:

> The fundamental premise of the plan is a fallacy. It equates "in the system" with "under the influence" or "impairment." This is simply not so . . . . [The company's expert witness] stated the test identifies the "risk of impairment." This is word salad. The test tells you nothing about the nature, degree, or scope of the risk . . . . I cannot imagine an arbitrator sustaining discipline on grounds the employee might have stolen the goods, might have been insubordinate, might have been late to work. This is totally inconsistent with the concept of "just cause." (Babiskin, 1985)

In some instances, use of drugs has been defined in such a way that off-duty use is included, and the rule has been upheld because of special circumstances. A refinery, for example, prohibited "use (including drug use as evidenced by laboratory tests), possession, distribution or sale of drugs" (Grimes, 1987). This provision replaced a prohibition against being "under the influence" while at work. The arbitrator recognized that the change obscured the difference between use and impairment, as well as extending the employer's oversight to off-duty hours. He nevertheless upheld the discharge of an employee who tested positive for marijuana, in part because he was a "continuous drug user" and worked with explosive gases. "If the grievant were in another line of work, perhaps packing shoe boxes, his off-duty marijuana might not matter" (Grimes, 1987).

The Question of Intent

A commonly advanced argument is that punishing the mere act of registering positive ignores the element of intent and that the possibility of inadvertent inhalation or ingestion must be considered. The theoretical cogency of this argument was accepted by an arbitrator in the case of a transit agency mechanic who claimed his positive urinalysis for cocaine resulted from drinking Health Inca Tea, an herbal preparation (known as "over-the-counter cocaine") that for a time was legally for sale (Siegel et al., 1986):

> The record is devoid of any bargaining history with respect to the policy which would indicate that the drafters intended that the procedures . . . cover all circumstances surrounding use, including unintentional use . . . . Although the possibility of an employee unintentionally ingesting a controlled substance for which (s)he has tested positively is remote, that possibility exists, and an employee's due process rights must be preserved in such circumstances. (J. Ross, 1988)

In the end, the arbitrator discounted the grievant's explanation, in part because the employee had unconvincingly invoked accidental exposure as an explanation for one of two previous cannabinoid positives.

Grievants frequently claim that a positive resulted from passive inhalation of ambient marijuana smoke. Experiments with passive inhalation generally have produced urine concentrations that were less than 20 ng/ml and thus not likely to be detected on workplace tests; other explanations must be sought for positives at higher levels. Moreover, the high smoke densities typical of experimental conditions are unlikely to be reproduced elsewhere. Yet some arbitrators have felt unable to rule out passive inhalation as an explanation for a positive as long as the "phenomenon of passive inhalation remains controversial in the scientific literature . . . . The scientific concerns being increasingly expressed about the serious health hazards of secondary exposure to carcinogens . . . suggest that passive inhalation has to be taken seriously as a possible source of a nonsmoker's positive test" (Jones, 1988). The credibility of the grievant, rather than technical considerations, appears to be the decisive factor.

Under the Influence

If a urinalysis positive is relied upon as the sole or primary piece of evidence against the grievant, a question arises: Does the test result itself amount to just cause for discipline? The collective bargaining agreement, as interpreted by the arbitrator, could provide a reference point for deciding the disciplinary significance of the result.

An arbitrator upheld the discharge of a truck driver with 8 years' service who registered positive for marijuana. The test was ordered because the driver seemed "sullen and withdrawn," as well as uncoordinated, after returning from a funeral leave occasioned by the sudden death of his brother. In the urinalysis, the cutoff had been set at 100 ng/ml. The contract stated: "An employee may be discharged for . . . being under the influence of drugs . . . . The employer may request an employee to take a medical test to determine whether he was under the influence of . . . drugs." The union argued that the positive did not demonstrate the grievant was under the influence. The arbitrator held that

> the contract says the test results can be used to conclude that an employee is under the influence of drugs. The union's mistake is assuming that "under the influence of drugs" has a precise scientific meaning that is incorporated in the contract . . . . I cannot interpret the contract to authorize discharge only upon a type of proof that exceeds present scientific capabilities. (Cooper, 1986)

In another case involving a 100 ng/ml decision level, the arbitrator was less certain about the meaning of that value. A shipyard workers' union had challenged a testing program that regarded the employee as presumptively under the influence if he or she registered positive at an immunoassay level above 100 ng/ml, and conclusively under the influence if the result were confirmed by GC/MS. After listening to a debate among technical experts, the arbitrator concluded as follows:

> I have no quarrel with the 100 ng threshold level. My quarrel is with the company's conclusion that a level of 100 ng . . . if confirmed by the laboratory GC/MS test, means that the employee is "under the influence." . . . The evidence in this case does

> not conclusively show that a recording of 100 ng in the urine, if confirmed, is synonymous with any mental or physical impairment. (Schmertz, 1986)

The arbitrator resolved the dilemma by allowing the employer to declare a result of 100 ng/ml in itself a violation of company rules, whether or not that level proved anything about the employee's condition. The arbitrator did not "consider it unreasonable for the company to deem . . . 100 ng . . . a prohibited or an unacceptable level of the drug, and to conclude that such a level *may* cause impairment or *may* result in being under the influence". The arbitrator called for "some additional due process protection" all the same, and he ordered that the company physician

> shall also examine the affected employee physically for the presence or lack of presence of other symptoms of drug and alcohol use . . . [including] a test of reflexes, examination of eyes, gait, general demeanor, breath and condition of speech. . . . [The results of the examination] shall be made a part of the official record of any disciplinary action imposed on and/or counseling required of the affected employee and shall be available if the matter is grieved or arbitrated.

Another employer of marine craftsmen, taking its cue from the shipyard decision, modified its testing policy to remove the presumption of impairment and substitute the concept of a "prohibited level." That policy, too, was upheld in arbitration, although the arbitrator felt moved to "caution the parties to exercise the procedures under the plan with great care and concern for those affected" (Rothschild, 1986).

It is interesting to note that whereas the arbitrator in the original shipyard case doubted that the employer could rely upon a 100 ng/ml positive to establish impairment, the arbitrator in the trucker's case deemed such a result to be sufficient proof. The reasoning of the latter arbitrator seems to be that if the contract allows the employer to request a test, then the test results must have meaning for the disciplinary proceedings, even if they have no such meaning for scientists. Of course, the contract did not mention marijuana specifically; the framers might have been alluding to tests (e.g., for blood alcohol concentration) that scientists generally accept as an index of impairment.

The contrasting decision in the shipyard case not to accept the test result as proof of impairment suggests that arbitrators may be left with such deep reservations about the significance of a test result standing in isolation that corroboration will be demanded. The issue then is likely to be whether the totality of the evidence, not the test result alone, justifies discipline. Evidence of impairment is particularly significant when the employer claims the right to impose summary discharge. An arbitrator ruled that a municipal bus driver who tested positive for marijuana could not be discharged for that alone, because "the grievant's demeanor and physical appearance were normal, and no field sobriety test was deemed necessary" (Rappaport, 1989). Another bus driver was also reinstated, despite registering positive at a level of 75 ng/ml, because the arbitrator could find little else amiss: "There is a void of any evidence to suggest that grievant engaged in any misconduct related to his job, to the performance of his job, or to his commitment to providing safe passage for customers" (Goodman, 1987).

Evidence of satisfactory dexterity was a factor in an arbitrator's decision to reduce a suspension from 7 months to only 14 days and to award the grievant back pay. The grievant, a 15-year employee, had tested positive for marijuana (at 31 ng/ml) when he applied for a promotion to crane operator. Accepting that the marijuana was used off duty, the arbitrator concluded that the grievant's "success on the hands-on manual test . . . and the absence of any testimony describing job impairment indicate that his drug usage has been minimal" (Strasshofer, 1990).

An accident is sometimes regarded as corroborative evidence for a positive test result. Yet the mere fact that an accident occurred, an arbitrator concluded in the case of a crane-switch operator, did not demonstrate that the grievant was impaired. "It is undisputed that the grievant operated the switch engine for over 3 hours including approximately 15 stops and starts without incident. That level of work performance evidences that the grievant was not under the influence of a behavior modifying drug" (Clarke, 1985). In the related case of a forklift operator who tested positive, the arbitrator took into consideration that the grievant had a better overall safety record than his predecessor in the job. The grievant "had no accidents during his three months on the job even though he was working double shifts part of the time" (Fullmer, 1988).

Joint Protocols

Few employment policies are as contentious as drug testing. To minimize disputes, over technical issues at least, some collective bargaining partners have agreed to joint testing protocols. Given the uncertainties surrounding arbitration, negotiating a joint protocol would seem to offer many advantages. It defines the occasions on which the employee may be tested and determines the significance of the result for the subject's employment status. It may specify the substances to be detected, the cutoffs that define a positive result, the proper chain of custody, the analytical methods, and the laboratory to which the analysis will be entrusted. Possible penalties or treatment options are spelled out. Bargaining also presents an opportunity to review the cost-effectiveness of testing, and to consider less complex—and therefore less brittle—alternative strategies for dealing with substance abuse (M. A. Rothstein, 1991).

A common outcome of bargaining is an agreement to permit testing for cause only, coupled with progressive discipline rather than summary discharge. Practical opportunities for recovery are provided. An example is the agreement negotiated by California's Bay Area Rapid Transit Authority and the Service Employees International Union in 1990. It authorized reasonable-suspicion and postaccident testing but allowed an employee to divulge a substance abuse problem and opt for rehabilitation, covered by the employer's insurance, when faced with a demand to submit to a test; during rehabilitation, the employee is unpaid but continues to accrue vacation time and sick leave. Undergoing rehabilitation precludes discipline (National Report on Substance Abuse, 1990). Such creative agreements demonstrate that there is considerable scope for freely bargained, consensual substance abuse policies (Denenberg & Denenberg, 1991).

REFERENCES

Abrams, R., 1989, Georgia Power Co., *Daily Labor Report,* No. 167 (August 30, 1989).

Alleyne, R., 1987, Southern California Gas Co., *Labor Arbitration Reports* **89:**393.

Babiskin, W., 1985, Niagara Mohawk Power Corporation And OBEW, Sys. Council U-11, unpublished, 54.

Bairstow, F., 1988, City of Miami and Fraternal Order of Police, 18–19, unpublished.

Baroni, B. J., 1987, Metropolitan Transit Authority, Houston, *Labor Arbitration Reports* **89:**129.

Battelle Human Affairs Research Centers, 1988, *Fitness for Duty in the Nuclear Power Industry: A Review of the Technical Issues,* 5.

Boals, B., 1990, Metropolitan Dade County, *Labor Arbitration in Government* (February, 1982), **20**(2):4258.

Boner, P. J., 1985, Union Oil Company of California, *Labor Arbitration Reports* **87:**297.

Brisco, C., 1987, Valvoline Oil Company, *Labor Arbitration Reports* **89:**209.

Bureau of National Affairs, Inc., 1986, *Alcohol and Drugs in the Workplace: Costs, Controls and Controversies,* Special Report, 108.

Caraway, J. F., 1988, Vulcan Materials Co., *Labor Arbitration Reports* **90:**1161.

Clarke, J., 1985, Georgia-Pacific Corp., *Labor Arbitration Reports,* **86:**411.

Concepcion, D., 1984, Reynolds Electrical and Engineering Co., *American Arbitration Association,* Sum of Lab. Arb. Awards, **303**(10).

Concepcion, D., 1986, Bay Area Rapid Transit District, *Labor Arbitration Reports,* **88:**1.

Cooper, L., 1986, Roadway Express Inc., *Labor Arbitration Reports* **87:**224.

Cornell/Smithers Report, 1992, The Fatigue Factor, Cornell University School of Industrial Relations, Ithaca, NY (January, 1992).

Curtis, C. E., 1988, Westinghouse Electric Corporation, communication with the author.

Daniel, W. P., 1987, Kaydon Corp., *Labor Arbitration Reports* **89:**377.

Denenberg, T. S., and Denenberg, R. V., 1991, Alcohol and Other Drugs: Issues in Arbitration, BNA Books, Washington, D.C.

Department of Health and Human Services, 1988, Mandatory Guidelines for Federal Workplace Drug Testing Programs, Federal Register (April 11, 1988), 53.

Department of Transportation, 1988, Federal Aviation Administration, Appendix 1-Drug Testing Program **14**(1):1, **121**(1):469.

Draznin, J., 1987, ITT Barton Instruments, Co., *Labor Arbitration Reports* **89:**1196.

Dubowski, K. (1987), Drug Testing: Scientific Perspectives, *Nova Law Review* **11:**528.

Eastern District of Tennessee, 1986, Lovvorn v. City of Chattanooga, **647:**875.

Eischen, D., 1989, Louisiana and Arkansas Railway Company and United Transportation Union, unpublished arbitration, 5.

Employee Testing and the Law, 1986, November, Workplace Alcohol Testing: Cost-Effective, (November, 1986), 8.

Feldman, M. J., 1987, Hobart Corporation, *Labor Arbitration Reports* **88:**905.

Fraser, B., 1988, Boston Edison Company, *American Arbitration Association,* Sum. Lab. Arb. Awards, **363**(1), Quotations are from pages in unpublished manuscript version.

Fullmer, J. A., 1988, Stanadyne, Western Division, *Labor Arbitration Reports* **91:**993.

Goldstein, E. H., 1987, Modine Manufacturing Company, *Labor Arbitration Reports* **90:**189.

Goodman, D., 1987, Trailways, Inc., *Labor Arbitration Reports* **88:**1073.

Grimes, J. A., 1987, Marathon Petroleum Co., *Labor Arbitration Reports* **89:**716.

Hansen, H. J., Caudill and Boone, 1985, Crisis in drug testing, *Journal of the American Medical Association* **253:**2382.

Heinsz, T. J., 1987, Day & Zimmerman, Inc., *Labor Arbitration Reports* **88:**1001.

Hill, M. et al., 1986, Discipline and discharge for off-duty misconduct: What are the arbitral standards?, Proceeding of the National Academy of Arbitrators, 152.

Hoyt, Finnigan, Nee, Shults, and Butler, 1987. Drug testing in the workplace: Are methods legally defensible, A survey of experts, arbitrators, and testing laboratories, *Journal of the American Medical Association* **258:**504.

Jones, E. A., 1988, Southern California Rapid Transit District and United Transportation Union, unpublished, 40.

Kagel, S., 1987, Boise Cascade Corp., unpublished.

Kasher, R., 1986, National Football League Players Association and National Football League Management Council, unpublished.

Katz, J. B., 1981, American Standard, *Labor Arbitration Reports,* **77:**1085.

Katz, L., 1986, Boston Edison Company and Utility Workers Union, Local 387, *American Arbitration Association,* Case No. 1130–1520–85, unpublished.

Kleiman, M., 1992, *Against Excess: Drug Policy for Results,* Basic Books, New York.

McKay, G. R., 1986, Union Plaza Hotel, *Labor Arbitration Reports* **88:**528, 531.

Milentz, C. R., 1987, Texas City Refining, *Labor Arbitration Reports* **89:**1159.

National Report on Substance Abuse, 1987 BNA, Inc., Washington, D.C. (January 7, 1987) 5.

National Report on Substance Abuse, 1990 BNA, Inc., Washington, D.C. (May 23, 1990) 4.

New York Times, 1987, Lloyd and Wiggins of Rockets Banned for Drug Use (January 14, 1987).

Nicholas, S. J., 1987, Jim Walter Resources, Inc., *Labor Arbitration Reports* **90:**367.

Pacific Gas and Electric Company, 1990, Diablo Canyon (California) Power Plant Fitness for Duty Program, Pacific Gas and Electric Company, Attachment I.

Poisonlab, Inc., 1989, Drug Testing Services for Business and Industry (September, 1989), 19.

Rappaport, L., 1989, Southeastern Pennsylvania Transit Authority, *Labor Arbitration in Government,* **19:**4185.

Ross, J., 1988, Washington Metropolitan Area Transit Authority and Local Union 689, Amalgamated Transit Union, unpublished, 5.

Ross, R. L., 1988, Stone Container Corp., *Labor Arbitration Reports* **91:**1186.

Rothschild, P. W., 1986, Hopeman Brothers, Inc., *Labor Arbitration Reports* **88:**373.

Rothstein, A. R., 1986, Alta Bates Hospital, *Labor Arbitration Reports* **87:**719.

Rothstein, M. A., 1991, Arbitration in the Employer Welfare State, Proceedings of the National Academy of Arbitrators, 94.

Schmertz, E., 1986, Bath Iron Works Corporation, unpublished.

Schwarz, M., 1986, Wappingers Central School District, New York, unpublished.

Siegel, R. et al., 1986, Cocaine in Herbal Tea, *Journal of the American Medical Association* **255:**40.

Simpkins, J., 1989, Philadelphia Gas Works, *American Arbitration Association,* Summary of Labor Arbitrations Awards, **364**(7).

Speroff, B. J., 1987, Phoenix Transit System, *Labor Arbitration Reports* **89:**973.

Staudohar, P., 1989, Owens-Brockway, *Labor Arbitration Reports,* Sum. of Lab. Arb. Awards, **365**(4).

Stoltenberg, C. F., 1988, Sharples Coal Corp, *Labor Arbitration Reports* **91:**1065.
Strasshofer, R., 1990, Toledo Edison, Co., *American Arbitration Association,* Summary of Labor Arbitration Awards, **372**(1).
Warns, M., 1986, Gem City Chem, Inc., *Labor Arbitration Reports* **86:**1023.
Washington Post, 1986, The Nuclear Dilemma: Safety and the Drug Issue (May 5, 1986).
Wies, E. M., 1987, Sanford Corporation, *Labor Arbitration Reports* **89:**968.
Yarowsky, S., 1987, Regional Transportation District, *Labor Arbitration Reports* **90:**27.

11

Behavioral Tests to Assess Performance

BARBARA BUTLER and DAVID TRANTER

1. INTRODUCTION

As company policies on alcohol and drugs in the workplace are being developed, there has been considerable controversy about the use of drug and/or alcohol testing as a method to identify employees who have used illicit drugs or misused alcohol and/or licit medications in contravention of the policy. Proponents of substance testing tie it to their concern for employee and public safety, and to the impacts that the use/misuse of these drugs could have on workplace performance. They argue that this type of testing is an effective deterrent to the use of drugs or alcohol, and a good method of identifying employees who may have a problem or may have contravened company policies in this area. Opponents argue that a positive urine test simply confirms use of a particular drug in the recent past, but not whether the individual was impaired in any way at the time of the test. They suggested that if the real concern is safety and on-the-job performance, there should be other, less intrusive methods of identifying impaired individuals so that they can be moved out of a job prior before their performance jeopardizes safety for themselves, coworkers, or the public.

Underlying this debate is the increasing recognition that human functions can be altered by drugs in various ways and to varying degrees. Beyond the physiological and biochemical changes they bring about, aspects such as behavior, personality, and performance are also affected. In the area of occupational performance, different skills are needed for different jobs, and the disturbance of

---

BARBARA BUTLER and DAVID TRANTER • Barbara Butler & Associates, Inc., Toronto, Ontario M5R 2S1, Canada.

Research Advances in Alcohol and Drug Problems, Volume 11: Drug Testing in the Workplace, edited by Scott Macdonald and Paul M. Roman. Plenum Press, New York, 1994.

any of these functions can result in a decrease in accuracy, efficiency, productivity, worker safety, and job satisfaction.

Drug effects on workplace performance have been a focus of recent research, largely as a result of increasing concern about workplace safety and productivity. But because performance can be affected by numerous other factors that are not drug related, such as fatigue and stress, interest has been drawn to performance testing as a way of identifying impairment from any source. In view of the controversy associated with body fluid testing, performance-based tests have been proposed as a more attractive alternative, one that provides a less invasive method of identifying performance decrements with potentially more job relevance.

The question that must be addressed about the various forms of performance testing currently being developed and/or marketed as effective "fitness for duty" tests is whether they are sufficiently job related to meet employers' needs in addressing workplace alcohol and drug use while providing opponents to substance testing with a less invasive approach to the issue. A critical consideration is the specific goal of the testing program. When making decisions in this area, the employer must resolve if a generic measure of performance is acceptable, or if a more focused measurement tied directly to the required job skills is preferable. Employers must also decide whether impairment from any source at all needs to be assessed (e.g., fatigue, illness, drugs), or if their concerns are focused strictly on confirming the use of a banned substance in the context of a work rule violation. Considerations such as these go into selecting what type or types of tests can actually be used effectively to meet workplace goals. They also lead to an entire other set of questions concerning what to do if an individual fails to pass a test.

Within the context of this book on drug testing, performance testing will be examined in this chapter as to its potential application in the workplace as an alternative to using body fluid testing to identify possible impairment by drugs or alcohol. The intent is to present objectively the most recent information on procedures and devices that are in use or are currently being testing in the laboratory or field, and to assess their advantages and limitations, as well as their potential utility as part of a workplace drug and alcohol policy.

One qualification to this review should be established up front. Originally, performance testing programs for drug or alcohol impairment were for the most part not developed for general use in the workplace. The potential to transfer the basic principles of these tests to the workplace may well exist, however, and it is presently being explored with great interest by a number of product development centers. The key is to understand the strengths and weaknesses of each test, and to be clear on the intended results of the chosen method in the context of each company's specific needs. To this end, there are a number of criteria that should be used to determine the extent to which a test can be considered both practical and effective:

- *Sensitivity.* The extent to which a performance test can accurately measure very small changes in performance. For example, a highly sensitive test is able to detect impairment that might be related to very low alcohol levels.
- *Reliability.* The extent to which a test can measure the same factors in the same manner from one test to the next. Reliability is a measure of the test's ability to reproduce the same results in the same situation with the same individual. A test that is highly reliable shows very little error *within* tests administered.
- *Specificity.* The ability of a test to detect specific drug types and distinguish them from other factors that might affect performance, such as fatigue or depression.
- *Validity.* The extent to which the test measures what it is specifically designed to measure. A test is valid if it measures only those variables that the test is designed to measure and not other extraneous factors.
- *Ease of use.* The extent to which it is easy to set up and administer the test and interpret the results, as well as such attributes as the user-friendliness and portability. This is an important factor, as a good test should be fairly simple, inexpensive, and nonintimidating to use.

These factors are evaluated in this review of performance testing programs, which begins with the more direct approach of observing behavior and detecting impairment by comparing the observed behavior with normal unimpaired behavior using previously established criterion based on "drug-free" population data are applied equally to all tested individuals to determine whether they may currently be impaired. An alternative approach, which requires the use of standardized tests comparing an individual's baseline scores with their current state, will be examined in the context of computerized performance tests, which are now being considered for workplace settings. One specific field application of these tests, in the form of in-vehicle detectors of impaired driving, is examined.

2. DRUG EVALUATION AND CLASSIFICATION (DEC) PROGRAM

This drug-use identification program is an extension of the performance-based testing found in the standardized field sobriety tests used by Canadian and American police forces. It originated with Los Angeles Police Department (LAPD) traffic enforcement officers who recognized their need for specialized training when dealing with the growing incidence of driving impairment by drugs other than alcohol. Because a reading of blood alcohol content was typically the only measure of impairment to confirm suspicion from the field sobriety tests, drivers impaired by other drugs frequently escaped detection and prosecution.

Therefore, this program is particularly useful if the suspect is obviously impaired and the blood alcohol level does not account for the impairment. It consists of a rigorous training program that allows officers to recognize the signs and symptoms of seven drug categories (hallucinogens, cannabis, phencyclidine, depressants, stimulants, narcotic analgesics, and inhalants) through classroom instruction and field certification. The standardized, systematic process allows the officer to examine a person suspected of impaired driving or another alcohol- or drug-related offense by doing the following:

- assessing general appearance, behavior, and medical and drug use history through an interview
- measuring objective physiological symptoms for signs of substance use (eyes/pupils, vital signs, muscle tone)
- conducting a battery of behavioral tests designed to assess psychomotor performance, the ability to follow and remember instructions, and divided attention (similar to field sobriety tests)

The integrated findings become the basis of the opinion of the drug recognition technician (DRT) as to whether the suspect is impaired, whether the impairment is drug related, and what categories of drugs are responsible (Gates & Page, 1989). In all cases, urine and/or blood analysis is used to corroborate the DRT's opinion when impairment by drugs is suspected as a result of their analysis. The process is not a means of determining exactly what drug(s) the suspect has ingested; it simply permits the presence of drugs to be narrowed down to certain broad categories. Therefore, it is not a substitute for a chemical test, which is the last step in the process that must be conducted to provide the scientific evidence to corroborate the suspicion (NHTSA, 1991).

The DEC program has had a number of scientific validations and field reviews and is now being used in law enforcement throughout the United States with a high degree of acceptance and success (R. C. Mayer, NHTSA, personal communication, 1992). It is being extended to the prison systems and the workplace in varying forms. The advantage this program has over the field sobriety performance tests is its higher degree of specificity—in being better able to establish the possible source of impairment, and the drug categories themselves. The more complex program is not as easy to administer, however, needing highly trained professionals, the right equipment, and at least 20 minutes of time. Reliability could also vary with the skills of the administering officers.

Officers involved in its original development see clear potential for the use of the DEC program in the workplace in a "reasonable cause" situation to identify performance decrements that may be attributable to drug and alcohol impairment and to confirm drug or alcohol use. They have developed training program for supervisors based on the DEC principles, and it is being used successfully in an increasing number of U.S. workplaces (T. Page, Drug Alcohol Training Associates, personal communication, 1992). Management and supervisory personnel receive detailed training about specific signs and symptoms of the drugs of abuse and, within their ongoing performance management role, receive training for reasonable-cause or reasonable-suspicion referrals on the basis of the proven DEC techniques in documenting, assessing, and constructively confronting an employee who is suspected of impairment.

One of the biggest concerns about a supervisor's role in the implementation of a company drug and alcohol program is that he or she will either ignore or cover up a problem because of insufficient knowledge of alcohol and drug use signs or effects, or will make arbitrary referrals, particularly where it leads to a drug test. This type of program would be a very useful supervisory training tool for any company drug and alcohol program, whether drug testing is involved or not. In addition, it is a useful method of minimizing any perception of arbitrariness in decisions around identification and referral for a reasonable-cause drug test. It provides a stronger justification for taking the sample, in the form of an articulate and credible reason for believing the impairment is the direct result of drug use. Training on the signs of use for the seven categories of drugs will minimize expense and the volume of sample needed for analysis. A drug test will only provide evidence of use; the physical exam will answer questions about impairment. Overall, this type of performance-based program provides an opportunity for better assessment of the possible cause of a performance problem before the decision to request a specimen for testing is made, but if impairment by drugs is suspected it is not a substitute for a drug test, which provides the confirmatory information.

3. COMPUTERIZED IMPAIRMENT TESTS

Background

Computerized performance tests have been used for the past 30 years as a method of measuring an individual's ability to perform specific tasks. Much of the research in this area evolved from the initial efforts of the U.S. Air Force and NASA in the 1960s (Jex, 1987; Koonce, 1984). Computer tests were initially developed by these groups to select individuals who were particularly well suited to perform under conditions of high stress, such as unusual and difficult flying conditions.

With the advent of the compact, high-speed personal computer, computerized performance testing may have appeal in many more areas of the private sector. Conceptually, it is relatively easy to take an ordinary personal computer and, with the right software, turn it into a performance testing device. With growing pressures for employers to develop alcohol and drug policies and to minimize liabilities associated with safety risks in the workplace, these devices are becoming increasingly available on the commercial market to employers who want to test whether their employees are impaired and possibly unfit to perform their jobs. A number of the computerized performance tests under development may be sufficiently sensitive to determine whether an individual's ability to perform certain tasks is impaired in some way. The tasks that they test may not be directly related to the job the employee actually performs, however, and this is a key issue to be resolved when deciding whether to use these tests in a workplace setting.

Some individuals have proposed that computerized tests can be used as a simple, fairly effective first measure in detecting performance decrements that may be caused by drug or alcohol use, in addition to other possible causes of impairment. They note that the tests are generally easy to administer and are objective, in that the computer measures the same variables using the same procedure every time, producing a score based specifically on these variables. Other behavioral tests can be subjective in that they rely on an observer's impressions when judging impairment. Therefore, an increasing number of companies with employees in safety-sensitive positions are considering computerized testing as a way to measure an employee's ability to do the job safely.

Measuring whether an employee is fit to operate a vehicle or a complicated piece of machinery, however, is in fact a very difficult task, even when using a computer. This is because several factors combine to create an interactive process that influences an individual's ability to perform a given task (Thar, 1991). The key factors are as follows:

- *Biological.* The presence or absence of specific chemicals in the body can influence the way an individual normally operates. For example, alcohol is one element that alters normal body chemistry such that the ability to perform even simple tasks can be adversely affected.
- *Physiological.* Physical stress also affects the body's ability to perform tasks. For example, fatigue can influence many different areas of physical functioning. Most people have experienced how difficult it can be to concentrate when very tired.
- *Psychological.* An individual's psychological state of mind can often influence how simple operations are performed. Factors such as depression can contribute to one's motivational state and ability to carry out basic tasks successfully.

- *Social.* Social factors can also play a role. For example, extreme social stress (e.g., being recently evicted from one's home) can in turn influence how well one performs in the job. Here, external social pressures contribute to the individual's task performance.
- *Environmental.* External environmental stressors also contribute to performance impairment. Factors such as temperature or noise can be a strong force in influencing behavior or body function.

Given that so many factors contribute to human behavior, it is extremely difficult to develop a computer test that can determine the specific reason an individual has become impaired, and even more difficult to narrow this focus and determine whether impairment is a result of drug or alcohol use. Without other kinds of supporting evidence, it is hard to determine whether an individual's low performance score might be the result of alcohol use or of other causes, such as physical illness or fatigue.

Computerized testing devices can measure only an employee's ability to perform a particular task as compared to an established performance standard, which is usually considered as general "fitness for duty." On their own, these tests may not be capable of specifically determining drug and alcohol impairment, although research is under way with some of them to refine this skill. Generally, computerized tests qualify individuals as being fit for duty if they can demonstrate that their ability to perform the test is within their normal range of behavior and therefore not impaired as the result of *any* of the above factors. The various forms of computer testing are discussed below, followed by an evaluation of their advantages and limitations and a description of tests currently available (or under research or field trial).

Generic Performance Tests

Because many factors contribute to one's ability to perform, it is not surprising that performance can be defined and measured in a wide variety of ways. In the context of technological applications, countless tests have been devised over the years to measure many different aspects of performance. Some of the more common performance tests include the following:

- *Sensory/perceptual ability tests.* These tests include measures of the ability to detect or discriminate different stimuli. For example, a sensory perception test might require subjects to observe a screen and indicate the point at which they observe a steady light beginning to flicker.
- *Motor ability tests.* These tests generally examine the subject's gross or fine motor capabilities, measuring such factors as balance and dexterity. An example would be to require the subject to press a series of buttons as

quickly as possible. This test measures the subject's ability to coordinate movement for a preselected task.

- *Psychomotor skill tests*. These tests measure motor ability as well as basic cognitive functions. A measure such as the hand-eye coordination test is sensitive to psychomotor skill. Another test might require the subject to follow a quickly moving object around the computer screen. This test measures the subject's ability to track a moving object, as well as the speed at which the subject can react to the movement.
- *Learning tests*. These tests examine the subject's ability to perform basic learning skills. For example, the subject would read a passage and answer a number of questions related to it in order to demonstrate his or her understanding of the information presented. Many of these tests are similar in nature to academic tests (e.g., for reading comprehension).
- *Memory tests*. This involves tests such as the delayed recognition test, in which subjects are required to memorize a sequence of digits displayed on the screen and compare them with other series of digits, then indicate whether the two series are similar (Sternberg, 1966), thus measuring the subject's ability to recall and match information.
- *Decision-making tests*. Subjects demonstrate their logical reasoning powers such as in a grammatical reasoning test by, for example, determining whether a statement is true or false. This enables measurement of the subject's ability to make rapid and logical decisions based on the information presented (Baddeley, 1968).

The ability to perform all of the above tests is affected to varying degrees by many factors, including the use of drugs and alcohol. It is impractical to integrate all of them into a large test battery to measure performance impairments in the workplace. To require employees to complete a complex battery of tests regularly would be extremely time-consuming and unrealistic for use in most work settings. Instead, it is necessary to determine first what skills need to be measured in order to provide the most valid and reliable performance assessment.

Again, the employer must decide if measuring general performance is the goal, or if a more focused and specific task-related performance measurement is preferable. The employer also needs to decide whether impairment from any source at all needs to be examined, or if impairment from drugs and alcohol is the priority. Considerations such as these go into selecting what type(s) of tests should actually be utilized to meet policy objectives.

Generic Computer Tests of Performance

Three basic methods of performance measurement using computer technology have been developed for wide use in the workplace. In this section, the discussion of each computer test will be focused on its ability to identify forms of impairment, with a view to assessing advantages and limitations with respect to potential usefulness as part of a workplace safety policy. The discussion will focus specifically on measurement of impairment caused by drugs or alcohol, as this has been the impetus for much of the development work currently under way and provides the context for the available research data.

Reaction Time Test. The reaction time (RT) test is a popular and well-known test that has been used in many work- and non-work-related situations. This test generally involves presenting the subject with a visual or auditory stimulus and requiring that he or she press a button in response to the stimulus as quickly as possible. It is typically very easy to administer.

The difficulty with RT tests is that they provide a very broad measurement of body/motor function behavior and are not particularly sensitive to different types of impairment (Howat, Sleet, & Smith, 1991). Many studies examining RT tests and alcohol influence have found that reaction time was not altered unless the subject was intoxicated with blood alcohol concentration (BAC) levels in excess of 0.08% (Bernheim & Michiels, 1973; Linnoila, Erwin, Ramm, & Cleveland, 1980; Perrine, 1976; Rundell & Williams, 1977). This suggests that RT tests are of limited value for determining performance impairment attributable to alcohol use, because a wide variety of skills become impaired at BAC levels between 0.01% and 0.04% (Moskowitz, 1985; U.S. Transportation Research Board, 1987). Research on reaction time and marijuana use has also been carried out extensively with similar results. Experiments involving simple RT tests tend to show very little, if any, reaction time decrease as a result of large doses of marijuana (Dornbush, Fink, & Freedman, 1971; Kvalseth, 1977; Moskowitz, Harman, & Schapero, 1972).

Although there is evidence that reaction time is influenced by alcohol and/or marijuana, no conclusive evidence exists to suggest that RT tests alone are good measures of performance deficits. Even research examining complex reaction time designs suggests that there is limited evidence to support reaction time as a sensitive indicator of performance impairment (Moskowitz, 1985). Another difficulty with RT tests is that reaction time is highly variable between individuals. Studies of marijuana use indicate that reaction times vary considerably across subjects, even when the subjects have never used marijuana before (Clark, Hughes, & Nakashima, 1970; Rossi, Kuehnle, & Mendelson; 1977). Frequent users of alcohol tend to show relatively less change in reaction time as their BAC levels increase than do less frequent users of alcohol. Therefore, although RT tests are easy to administer, they are generally not sensitive enough to measure impairment, and at best, they can function only as part of a larger test battery.

Critical Tracking Task. The critical tracking task (CTT) test is a psychomotor test that typically requires the subject to correct the unpredictable movement of an object on a computer screen. For example, one CTT device requires the subject to attempt to center a pointer on the screen while the pointer moves about in differing directions. The CTT is a type of hand-eye coordination test, but also a measure of compensatory reaction time (i.e., one's ability to compensate quickly for the changes that the pointer makes). During the test, the pointer movement becomes increasingly difficult to maintain, until eventually the subject loses control of it altogether. This kind of test is analogous to a video game that requires players to keep a car centered on the road as the road twists and turns with increasing and varying difficulty.

Originally designed in the mid-1970s to test the ability of air force pilots to control unstable aircraft, the CTT was found to be sensitive to alcohol use (Klein & Jex, 1975). It was further tested by General Motors and subsequently by NHTSA to examine its value as a preventive mechanism for drunk driving through the use of an interlock device, as discussed later in this chapter (Tennant & Thompson, 1973). Since then, the CTT has been used extensively in research examining the effects of alcohol and drugs on performance. Some research studies have found that a correlation exists among alcohol consumption, the rate of accidents, and CTT scores (Allen, Jex, & Strain, 1984; Allen, Stein, & Jex, 1981). Elsewhere, the CTT has been shown to be sensitive to BAC levels of 0.065% to 0.07% (Burns & Moskowitz, 1980; Moskowitz & Burns, 1981).

Other research, however, has found that although the CTT is sensitive to alcohol, it has limited effectiveness at low to moderate alcohol doses. The CTT accurately detects some subjects who have used moderate to high levels of alcohol, but fails to detect them all. For example, one study demonstrated that the CTT detects only 35% to 40% of subjects with BAC levels of 0.10% (Allen, Stein, Summers, & Cook, 1983), considered the legal level of driving impairment in most U.S. states, and higher than the 0.08% BAC level established in the Canadian criminal code. Another study found that the CTT detected subjects with BAC levels of 0.08% only 34% of the time, and BAC levels of 0.10% to 0.12% approximately 41% of the time (Noy, 1987).

Although the available data are not conclusive, the CTT appears to be more sensitive to drug and alcohol impairment than simple and complex RT tests. The CTT has demonstrated its ability to detect alcohol and marijuana effects when consumption has been at moderate and high levels. As BAC levels decline, though, so does the ability of the CTT to detect drugs and alcohol with any degree of confidence.

Divided Attention Task. Divided attention task (DAT) tests typically require the subject to attend to two simultaneous and conflicting tasks. For example, rather than simply requiring the subject to keep a car on the road, DAT tests require the subject to drive and decide between avoiding an oncoming car and a child darting out onto the street (Mills, 1991). The time taken by the subject to respond to changes from one display to the next is measured. This is a more complicated test than RT tests and CTT tests, and it is felt by some to be more representative of the dilemma of the intoxicated individual because activities such as operating an automobile or heavy machinery often require simultaneous decisions involving competing stimuli. The intoxicated driver generally has more difficulty than a sober individual deciding which stimulus to respond to first.

Studies using the DAT indicate that the device tends to be more sensitive to alcohol use than RT and CTT tests, and sensitive to much lower doses of alcohol and marijuana (Hindmarch, Kerr, & Sherwood, 1991; Mills & Bisgrove, 1983; Mills, Bisgrove, Hill, Ballard, & Stepney, 1986; Moskowitz & Burns, 1971; Perez-Reyes, Hicks, Bumberry, Jeffcoat, & Cook, 1988). Of the three tests that have been described, it would seem that DAT tests are the most sensitive to drug and alcohol impairment. Despite this advantage, the DAT is a much more complicated device to set up and use. This seems to be a fact of life for many performance tests; the more sensitive the device, the more complicated it is to administer.

Computer Tests and Effectiveness Criteria

When the three common types of computerized impairment tests are reviewed in light of the criteria for determining a test's effectiveness, what becomes most evident is that there is no single test presently available that completely fulfills all of the criteria of sensitivity, specificity, reliability, validity, and ease of use. Rather, the tests available can be placed on a continuum of criteria, meeting some requirements while falling short of others. Often, what makes a test strong in one area inevitably makes it less effective in others; for example, it has already been demonstrated that in the tests described above, as a test becomes more sensitive, it typically becomes more difficult to administer.

Generally speaking, computerized impairment tests measure up to the criteria in the following manner:

- *Sensitivity.* There is considerable variation regarding how sensitive computerized tests are to drug and alcohol use, as well as other types of impairment. Based on the research, it appears that the more complicated divided-attention tests tend to be the most sensitive to impairment.
- *Specificity.* All computerized impairment tests have limited specificity, as they are typically unable to determine the cause of impairment. These tests are able to indicate whether the subject likely is impaired but cannot distinguish, for example, whether the subject has performed poorly as a result of drug or alcohol use or other factors (e.g., depression or fatigue).
- *Reliability.* A particular advantage of computerized testing is that the

computer uses the same procedure each and every time for testing a subject. Computer testing is therefore reliable in that it measures the same factors in the same way each and every time.

- *Validity.* All computerized tests can be considered invalid if the aim is to test for impairment resulting from drugs and alcohol specifically, because the tests do not measure these factors directly. Rather, most computerized performance tests measure general performance impairment and can be considered valid only insofar as they detect such general impairments from a wide variety of sources.
- *Ease of Use.* Computerized tests vary considerably in this regard. Tests range from requiring the subject to perform very simple and brief tasks to performing fairly complicated and lengthy procedures.

Overview of Pros and Cons

There are two fundamentally different perspectives brought to the evaluation of the workplace relevance of computer performance tests. One viewpoint is the belief that tests such as DAT and CTT provide valid assessments of impairment and can identify impaired workers based on their preestablished baseline performance record. Another viewpoint is that computerized performance tests have a limited application in the workplace because they are too general in nature to measure job-specific skills, and therefore their relevance is questionable.

Supporters assert that performance is governed by the nervous system and that by testing any aspect of the nervous system (e.g., tracking ability) it is possible to measure overall ability to perform. The central nervous system is a interdependent system that can be compromised in its entirety by one single adversely affected function; therefore, if an individual's reaction time is slower, this is indicative of general deficits in his or her ability to function. Proponents of this stance state that testing such predetermined and fairly general tasks as tracking ability is valid because these measures indicate the nervous system's overall state of functioning.

Furthermore, proponents of tests such as CTT and DAT state that the latter are not intended to be diagnostic or conclusive, nor are they meant to represent sensitive measures of performance. The test's function is not to determine the extent to which a person is impaired or the reason for impairment. Instead, like taking a temperature, they are meant to raise a flag regarding an individual with a potential problem, and to demand clear policies regarding procedures dealing with individuals that fail the test. This might include subsequent measures to determine either the cause of impairment or if the individual is still fit to perform the job.

Detractors contend that computer tests centered around one basic skill have limited value in the workplace because they measure certain tasks that may not resemble the skills required to perform the job successfully. They add that most tests that require subjects to perform a single function run the risk of measuring a skill irrelevant to the actual job. For example, if hand-eye coordination is an important part of a particular job, then it might be useful to test employees regarding this ability. Testing an employee's hand-eye coordination when the job requires vigilance, though, may be completely unnecessary. In order to establish job relevance and better fulfill the criteria of validity, reliability, and sensitivity in the workplace, computerized performance must more directly measure job-specific skills and adhere to good psychometric practice (R. Heron, Transport Canada, personal communication, 1992). One way to do this would be, roughly, to do the following:

- Carry out task analysis in the field to determine the information processing and motor components that are critical to the safe performance of the job.
- Carry out laboratory tests to develop paradigms for measuring the components.
- Develop a testing instrument or procedure (or battery of instruments or procedures) that is psychometrically sound—in other words, that satisfies requisites of reliability, validity, and discriminability, has a good set of norms, and is sensitive to various types of impairment.
- Administer the instrument in the field, testing for validity, operational practicality, acceptability, and so forth.
- Modify as needed and retest regularly.

Proponents of computer testing state that only through this type of rigorous routine can a performance test be established that provides a valid measure of impairment on the job and a legitimate trigger to look more seriously at the cause of impairment. They add that with a generalized testing device, what is being measured is the individual's ability to perform the test itself and nothing else. Other critics of generalized computer tests say that many tests become so automatic that they are not really testing anything after a while; as the test is learned, there is the risk that it may be measuring different cognitive/motor faculties than originally intended.

In considering whether to use computerized testing, employers should understand both sides of the argument. It is not surprising that tests like those that use the CTT and DAT are attractive to many companies. These devices are simple, relatively inexpensive, and very easy to use; the test has already been developed, and companies do not have to go through the time-consuming and expensive process of developing their own. The ease with which one of these tests can be obtained and used, however, has to be weighed against whether it is really testing relevant skills in the workplace and meeting program goals with regard to safety.

Employers must be very clear regarding their specific needs and the true implications of test results, so that resources are not wasted and companies do not relax in a false sense of security regarding safety in the workplace. For example, passing a computer test before driving a transport truck across the country will not necessarily stop the driver from using an impairing substance at some time on the road. Therefore, the test itself will not guarantee safety. All it can do is put the employer on notice that further investigation (e.g., a medical assessment or a drug test) is needed regarding possible impairment of an employee who has failed it when signing on to duty. A safe workplace free of the negative effects of alcohol or drug use can only be reached through the implementation of a comprehensive policy that goes far beyond a simple "sign on to duty" test.

Computerized Impairment Tests Currently Available

There are a number of computerized performance test that are being developed for use in the workplace to measure employee fitness for duty in a wide variety of settings. Each test presented in this section is at a different stage of completion; some are fairly widely available, whereas others are still in the development or field trial stage. For the most part, they are meant to be used by companies on a daily basis for all employees who hold safety-sensitive positions as they sign on to duty. The information presented is subject to change, as the field of computerized impairment testing is a rapidly growing one.

The Readiness Monitor. The Readiness Monitor is the name given to the commercial application of the SEDI (Simulated Evaluation of Drug Impairment) device that was developed by Dr. Ken Mills more than a decade ago (K. Mills, personal communication, 1992) and is marketed through SEDI Corp. in North Carolina. It is a divided-attention test that detects changes in cognitive functioning rather than motor decisions. It was originally developed as a research tool and has been used extensively to measure performance impairment in laboratory settings (Mills & Bisgrove, 1983; Mills et al., 1986; Perez-Reyes et al., 1988; Perez-Reyes et al., 1991). More recently, it has been used to measure directly the effects of alcohol, drugs, and other stresses on performance in the workplace.

The Readiness Monitor requires the subject to observe three computer screens simultaneously and enter his or her responses on one of four buttons. One screen is positioned in the front and center of the subject's field of vision, and the other two screens are located on either side of the middle screen, several inches away. The middle screen displays a numeric value that changes approximately every half second. Below a critical point, the subject is to press the second button; above it, he or she must press the third button. Each peripheral screen displays numeric values as well; if either the left or right display changes from a steady state value to specified critical values, then the subject is required to press the first button (when the left screen changes) or the fourth button (for the right screen).

The device measures the subject's ability to respond to these changes, as well as which changes they respond to. The commercial Readiness Monitor tests individuals for 1 minute and requires 110 decisions during that interval. The stimulus sequence changes with every trial on a random basis so that the likelihood of the patterns being memorized is minimal. Preliminary results of the test indicate that the Readiness Monitor is sensitive to even low drug and alcohol doses. At the time of this writing, it is available for wide commercial use and is currently being tested in various workplace settings to establish a standardized data base for impairment. The company is also working to make the test administration as simple as possible (K. Mills, personal communication, 1992).

Factor 1000. Factor 1000 is a critical tracking test that is one of the simplest tests currently available and can be run on any personal computer with the addition of software and a control panel. The test requires the subject to sit in front of a screen that displays a pointer in the center and, using a control knob, to attempt to keep the pointer centered in the target area as it moves around the screen in an unpredictable manner. As the test continues, the pointer becomes more and more difficult to control; in a relatively short time, it gets out of control and leaves the target area, completing the test.

Employees establish a record of past scores that become a baseline of data against which current scores are compared. If they fail after four tries, Factor 1000 asks them to report to the supervisor immediately. Depending on company policy, after a mandatory break of 10 minutes, the employee may be allowed one more set of four tries. This test indicates the individual's suitability to work by alerting management to the fact that the employee's score is below their regular performance standard on this particular task. Like the other computerized tests, it is non-diagnostic, and follow-up procedures must be established by the company for those that fail the test. Although it seems less sensitive to low doses of drugs and alcohol, some companies have reported that it has contributed to a reduction in accidents (M. Corak, Continuous Improvement Services, personal communication, 1992). This could be a function of the effectiveness of the device, as well as of an associated increase in safety awareness and the need to do the job without impairment, with the test providing a daily reminder.

Essex DELTA. The DELTA, developed by the Essex Corporation, is a more complex performance computer test being used for workplace fitness-for-duty tests and scientific research. Like the other tests, it runs using a personal computer with an added keypad. DELTA is unlike the Readiness Monitor and Factor 1000, however, as it is not just a single test, but rather a battery of 15 different tests that are employed to measure performance impairment. This allows the employer to customize the battery to meet the company's specific workplace requirements.

The DELTA test measures both cognitive and psychomotor performance, and although it consists of several different tasks, it generally takes only a few minutes to do. It allows a lot of flexibility in that it can measure a range of skills, from very simple to quite complicated. Possible tests range from short-term memory measurements to mathematical processing tests to spatial tests. The DELTA also compiles statistics based on several test results and completes complex computations based on the requirements of the company. Currently, there are no critical tracking or divided-attention tests as part of the DELTA battery; most of the tasks focus on mental processing and reaction time. DELTA's advantage is that it is flexible and can be quite specific or very general in focus, depending on the needs of the company. Essex has published results from field studies to demonstrate high reliability and validity (J. Banisch, Essex Corporation, personal communication, 1992).

ARCO PACT. The Atlantic Richfield Company (ARCO) has produced an impairment test called the Performance Assessment Computerized Test (PACT), which is supported by cognitive theory suggesting that the first function to be affected by stress is mental attention. Developers of the device examined a variety of performance tests and selected those that appeared to be the most sensitive measures of ability to direct attention.

The test battery runs on a divided computer screen, with each side containing a separate performance test. An arrow points to the test that is to be taken first. The left side of the screen contains a test that examines the subject's spatial orientation abilities, requiring decisions about the positioning of a stick figure. On the right side of the screen is a logical reasoning task; in this test, the subject is required to respond as quickly as possible to a series of statements about the relationship between two letters that are presented. The two tests were selected for the battery because they are sensitive to two different cognitive functions (spatial orientation and logical reasoning). One of the critical factors that makes PACT sensitive to performance impairment is that it requires the subject to determine which test to take first, based on the direction of the arrow, and then perform the task required. A variety of scores can be obtained, including those for screen selection accuracy, test selection accuracy, and response time.

Like the Factor 1000 test, each subject must establish a personal baseline; performance is then evaluated relative to each subject's personal norm. The entire test takes 2 to 5 minutes to complete. The PACT has been field tested in a variety of work situations, including with truck drivers, security officers, pilots, students, and other populations, and has been tested for its sensitivity to many stresses, including fatigue, alcohol, hypoxia, prescription drugs, and others (ARCO, 1991).

NovaScan. This computerized test battery was developed through Nova Technology, Inc., and, like many of the other computer tests, has its roots in military and space research. It is simple to set up and use, working on any IBM-compatible personal computer. The test typically takes 3 to 5 minutes to complete, and each individual's score is compared with his or her own preestablished baseline. NovaScan is promoted as a refined and more sensitive divided-attention test using attention switching and resource allocation, thus incorporating measurement of a number of processes in addition to individual skills. This requires subjects to view the screen and complete two or more types of tasks in a nearly simultaneous manner. The separate tasks may include hand-eye coordination, spatial orientation, short-term memory, vigilance, or any other skill. The test measures the subject's ability both to complete the specific task and to switch between tasks.

The overall test battery can be altered so that employers can customize the test to reflect skills, symbols, and terminology that are specific to their particular workplace. Every time an employee performs successfully on their test, the computer averages the score into a new baseline, so it is always current and allows for improvements over time on an indefinite basis. If the individual does not meet his or her normal baseline after two tries, the supervisor or test administrator triggers the next appropriate action based on company policy. On the basis of laboratory research, the marketing company asserts that NovaScan is very sensitive to impairment of many types. Validation data indicate that 80% of subjects will be detected by the test at BAC levels of 0.04%, with 100% detection by the time individuals reach 0.08%. Similar sensitivity is expected for marijuana, diazepam, and fatigue, and further research is being conducted in these and other areas (D. P. Bernheisel, Nova Technology, personal communication, 1992).

Tracometer. This device was developed at the Canadian National Research Council as a scientific device for experiments in motor control theory. It was used for a variety of purposes, but as it became clear that performance was affected by alcohol, increasing focus was placed on the device's ability to measure impairment from substances. Its use in detecting the effects of drugs on performance up to now has been with universities and pharmaceutical companies, but its potential for use in the workplace is currently being explored. It is easy to set up and operate, and it consists of a pursuit-tracking task operated using a personal computer. The subject uses a steering wheel to pursue a target (one of five lights) on the display; as the subject aligns the pointer with the lit target, a new target lights up, and this process continues until the test is complete. This generally takes just over 2 minutes.

The Tracometer measures and stores two aspects of performance speed: reaction time (the time taken to decide which way to move when the target lights), and movement time (the time taken to move the pointer in line with the target). Performance accuracy is also measured in terms of errors (movement in the wrong direction) and overshoots (movements across the target). The Tracometer is a validated and accepted test for measuring performance skills in a laboratory setting; it has been found to show a clear effect of alcohol on skilled performance and has shown dose-related effects for other drugs. Research toward application in a workplace setting is now under way, including work by the Canadian government that is described in the next section (Buck, 1992).

4. IN-VEHICLE DETECTORS: IN-FIELD APPLICATION OF COMPUTER TESTS

A significant amount of research has been conducted over the past 20 years to develop an in-vehicle system that would prevent an impaired driver from operating his or her motor vehicle. The devices examined range from breath testers to psychomotor tests, all of which would either prevent a vehicle from starting or alert other drivers and/or the police through alarm systems. The use of performance testing in this situation is reviewed because of its potential relevance to work-related driving tasks, as well as the opportunity to look at a practical application of computer testing devices in the field and, potentially, the workplace. Specifically, this is one of the few situations in which a practical application of computer testing on the job has been assessed and reported. In-vehicle test systems could be used in the workplace in a number of situations: by fleet owners interested in reducing accidents and insurance costs, on commercial and/or public transportation vehicles, on other vehicles driven on site in the course of work (fork lifts, etc.), as a sanctioning option for convicted drunk drivers, and as a monitoring device in any situation where an individual with a past problem must use a company vehicle.

Predriving performance-based tests have included cipher lock systems, in which a driver is required to enter a numerical code in a given length of time; they have shown promise for keeping impaired drivers with relatively high blood alcohol contents off the road (Dingus, Hardee, & Wierwille, 1987). More extensive study has gone into the potential use of more sophisticated devices designed to correlate test performance with blood alcohol level; these tests involve reaction time, divided attention, short-term memory, and/or eye-hand coordination. The devices used are based on the same principles as the computer tests that were reviewed earlier in this chapter. Although none actually measure BAC levels, they could be useful in detecting impairment from drugs, alcohol, or other sources and therefore warrant further review. They may also present a practical tool for performance testing in the workplace in certain instances.

Specific research in this area was undertaken by the U.S. Department of Transportation through the National Highway Transportation Safety Administration, using the Drunk Driving Warning System (DDWS) as a vehicle-mounted system to test driver impairment, activate vehicle alarms, and record relevant data. With similar features to the "sign on to duty" computer tests being proposed for the workplace, the DDWS requires a driver to pass a short steering competency test in order to drive the car (i.e., do his or her job) in a normal manner. If performance does not exceed an established pass level, the driver must wait 10 minutes and try again. There are four chances to pass; if the driver operates the vehicle after a failure, or without taking the test, the emergency lights will flash and the horn will honk at speeds of 10 mph and above, alerting police and other drivers. The alarm system wires are sealed in the factory in a manner that allows detection of any tampering. To ensure that the person taking the test is the one driving, weight systems are installed such that if the driver moves off the seat or opens the door after successfully passing the test, it has to be taken again (thus preventing a sober accomplice from taking the test on the driver's behalf).

To validate the DDWS and obtain a direct correlation between performance test results, blood alcohol content and driving performance, NHTSA commissioned a comprehensive research experiment using the critical tracking task (CTT) measure for further field tests. The CTT was chosen because it showed sufficient BAC discrimination and acceptable false positive levels, and because the hardware required no additional engineering work to integrate it into the DDWS. Similar to the computer tests being assessed for their use in the workplace, the CTT in this instance requires the operator to balance a needle in a steering column-mounted instrument by turning the steering wheel; it becomes harder to balance over time, and eventually the driver is no longer able to control the needle.

The field study concluded that there was no way to know if the CTT and the DDWS were accurate in discriminating the driver's blood alcohol content and effective in preventing alcohol-impaired driving. Although Stein and Allen (1986) concluded that in-vehicle deterrents to drunk driving could be one of the most effective solutions, provided the system used to detect an impaired operator does not also deter a sober driver from normal driving, the U.S. government has abandoned its research in this area, based on the conclusion that practical performance-test-based devices (where performance correlates with BAC level) have not yet been developed. The CTT did not adequately discriminate between sober and impaired drivers at lower BAC levels, and was not very accurate at BACs of 0.05% to 0.08%. NHTSA is now focusing on in-car alcohol breath analyzer interlock systems, instead of computer-based systems, as the former present a practical alternative to the problems associated with Driving While Impaired performance tests.

NHTSA did not shut the door on the possibility of the development of more promising performance tests, however, and specifically noted the potential of the Tracometer for use in this area. The Canadian government's research on the Impairment Warning Device (IWD) is based on the Tracometer, a step-tracking device that involves pursuit tracking rather than the compensatory tracking of the CTT (as described earlier). When designed for in-vehicle use, the IWD has the simplicity of operation of the CTT but appears to be more sensitive to impairment effects, particularly of alcohol, and is more consistent in measuring its influence (Noy, 1987). In Transport Canada studies comparing the accuracy of the two devices with respect to impairment accuracy, the results indicated that the Tracometer was more sensitive than the CTT to the effects of alcohol over a wide range of BAC levels. For example, at BAC levels above 0.10%, the Tracometer failed about 85% of the subjects, whereas the CTT failed only 40%. It was concluded that this clearly confirmed the potential of the Tracometer as a test of alcohol intoxication.

Though the Impairment Warning Device is not commercially available, it shows some real promise. Current research is determining its potential as a deterrent and detection in-vehicle device for commercial drivers, but it will not likely be available for wide use for some time. Researchers believe that although the impetus for current work is the development of drunk-driving countermeasures, the technology can easily be extended to include other applications.

5. OVERALL CONCLUSIONS

With increasing concerns about the impact of drug and alcohol use on human functions and performance, particularly with respect to workplace safety and productivity, companies and governments are trying to develop mechanisms to identify employees whose performance may be impaired by these substances. Drug tests remain a controversial identification method, so performance testing is being proposed as an alternative identification tool for employees whose performance may be impaired by drugs, alcohol, or other factors (fatigue, stress, etc.).

This chapter has reviewed a number of performance tests currently in use or under intensive research and field tests. Although many were not specifically developed for the workplace, the potential to transfer their basic principles was reviewed. The Drug Evaluation and Classification program, which is based in part on commonly used field sobriety performance testing, is being used throughout the United States as a mechanism to identify driving impairment attributable to drugs. There is clear potential for its use in the workplace as a tool to train supervisors to identify performance decrements that may be caused by alcohol or drug use, and as a less intrusive identification method for a reasonable-cause referral for medical assessment or a drug test. The procedure can provide objective confirmation of that assumption and minimize any perception of arbitrariness in decisions about identification and referral.

The other systems examined represent standardized performance tests that objectively measure the subject's response using devices based on reaction time (RT), critical tracking task (CTT) and divided-attention task (DAT) tests. They are all computer based, which gives operators much better control over their administration compared to older versions of the same tests used in psychological laboratories. None of these systems, however, appears to represent an innovative departure from long-standing techniques (Buck, 1992). There are strong emotions on both sides of the argument about using computerized impairment testing. Therefore, employers must be very clear on their specific needs and understand the true implications of test results, so that resources are not wasted and they do not relax in a false sense of security regarding safety in the workplace.

In each case, subjects must reach an appropriate level of performance before the system can be used to detect impairment, and baseline scores must be established while the individuals are not impaired. Although these tests may be able to identify a change in the ability to perform on a particular machine, which would trigger further assessment of the individual's capabilities, they are not yet sensitive enough to measure critical levels of drug or alcohol impairment. In other words, they are meant to raise a flag, not to be diagnostic. Although this may be desirable from the point of view of considerations of privacy, it may also serve to disguise the effect of factors not normally regarded as causing impairment, such as time of day, short-term practice effects (warm-up), and conscious intent on the part of the subject to perform poorly, or at least differently (Buck, 1992).

If companies choose to use this identification technology, they should do so only as part of an overall policy, not as a stand-alone procedure to ensure improved safety conditions. The procedure must be applied in a nondiscriminatory fashion, backed by a comprehensive assessment program to determine the source of impairment and whether the individual is still capable of doing his or her own particular job safely, and have clear provisions for the consequences of either failing a test or refusal to take the test. For example, decisions need to be made as to whether individuals who fail the test will be sent home with pay, sent home without pay, or moved to another job considered less sensitive (assuming there *are* other jobs).

More specifically, if a company policy specifically prohibits the use of or impairment by drugs or alcohol when on duty, it should be recognized that computer tests will only identify individuals who may be candidates for further assessment. In order to determine if the individual was impaired by drugs or alcohol, further tests would be required, which may include a drug or alcohol test. Therefore, computer tests currently available are not necessarily an alternative to drug testing, as they simply identify an employee who *may* be impaired by a substance. Studies are finding that as the technology improves, the ability to detect alcohol and/or drug impairment may be there; it is simply too early to tell with certainty at this point.

Another concern is that the employee who fails may have failed a test of skills that have little to do with those needed to do his or her job; provision for further assessment is then needed. It is not sufficient to show that the subject is impaired on any given performance test if it is not also shown that impairment on the test correlates with impairment on the work task. It has been suggested that to develop a true workplace *performance* testing program, the critical skills must be determined for the specific job at hand, and the tests must be tailored to evaluate the individual's ability to perform those particular skills. One way to go about this would be to identify jobs where testing is needed, isolate the critical skills, select tests thought to measure these skills, and conduct field tests to determine practical application. Some of the devices being developed with a range of test batteries are beginning to address this shortfall.

To this end, Buck (1992) suggests that carrying out an ergonomic task analysis is a desirable preliminary step for any job to ensure the test used is appropriate to the specific conditions of the job, and eliminate the possibility that inefficient or unsafe performance derived from the design of the task being performed, not the specific capabilities of the individual involved. This is reinforced by human rights considerations, which suggest that the tests must be shown to meet a *bona fide* occupational requirement and may be judged discriminatory if the required test is not relevant to the task in question (Webb, 1989).

One example that attempted to focus on particular skills required to do a job (steering a car), was researched intensively by the U.S. government. They concluded that performance-based devices may be feasible for preventing alcohol-impaired driving, provided that they can produce high accuracy at low BACs, as well as minimal individual differences in performance so that universal cutoff scores can be used. It also noted that such a performance-based device might have a collateral benefit of detecting impairment attributable to causes other than alcohol. There were practical problems identified with the critical tracking task used for the field tests; perhaps these could be overcome with further development of more promising performance tests, as is now under way in both Canada and the United States.

Performance testing for workplace impairment is an area of research that is developing and changing rapidly. The field is a growing one that is worth watching, but which demands a significant amount of further work to ensure that devices or recognition programs are job relevant and that the results are valid with respect to the specific workplace testing needs. There continues to be potential for application in the workplace setting, but only where needs are clearly understood and performance testing is used in the context of a comprehensive policy that responds specifically to those needs.

REFERENCES

Allen, R. W. and Jex, H. R., 1972, Visual-motor response of crewman during a simulated 90-day space mission as measured by the critical task battery, NASA SP-281, 239–246.

Allen, R. W., Stein, A. C., and Jex, H. R., 1981, Detecting human operator impairment with a psychomotor task, in: *Proceedings of 17th Annual Manual Conference Control*, JPL, 81–95, 611.

Allen, R. W., Stein, A. C., Summers, L. G. and Cook, M. L., 1983, Drunk driving warning system: Final report, (December, 1983), U.S. Department of Transportation National Highway Administration, Washington, D.C.

Allen, R. W., Jex, H. R. and Stein, A. C., 1984, A cybernetic test for the detection and deterrence of impaired human operators, Systems Technology, Inc., Paper No. 340, IFAC 9th Triennial World Congress, Systems Technology, Hawthorne, CA.

ARCO: Atlantic Richfield Company, 1991, PACT validation status.

Armstrong, S.A., 1992, Traffic Support Services Metropolitan Toronto Police, personal conversation.

Baddeley, A. D., 1968, A three minute reasoning test based on grammatical transformation, *Psychonomic Science* **10:**341.

Banisch, J., 1992, DELTA Product Manager, Essex Corporation, personal conversation.

Bernheim, J., and Michiels, W., 1973, Effects psycho-physiques du diazepam et d'une fiable dose d'alcool chez homme, *Schweiz Med Wochenschr* **103:**863.

Bernheisel, D. P., 1992, Nova Technology Inc., personal conversation.

Buck, L., 1992, Detecting Drug-impaired Behaviour, Unpublished manuscript, Tracometer Inc., Milton, Ontario.

Burns, M., and Moskowitz, H., 1980, Effects of diphenhydramine and alcohol on skills performance, *European Journal of Clinical Pharmacology* **17:**259.

Bureau of Justice Assistance, 1991, Drug Recognition Program Monograph, May, 1991, Bureau of Justice, Washington, D.C.

Clark, L. D., Hughes, R., and Nakashima, E. F., 1970, Behavioral effects of marijuana: Experimental studies, *Archives of General Psychiatry* **23:**193.

Corak, M., 1992, Continuous Improvement Services Inc., re. Factor 1000, personal conversation.

Dingus, T. A., Hardee, H. L., and Wierwille, W. W., 1987, Development of models for on-board detection of driver impairment, *Accident Analysis and Prevention* **19**(4).

Dornbush, R. L., Fink, M., and Freedman, A. M., 1971, Marijuana, memory and perception, *American Journal of Psychiatry* **128:**194.

Gates, D. F., and Page, T. E., 1989, *The Drug Recognition Expert Program: A National Update*, Los Angeles Police Department, Los Angeles, CA.

Heron, R., 1992, Transportation Development Center, Transport Canada, personal conversation.

Hindmarch, I., Kerr, J. S. and Sherwood, N., 1991, The effects of alcohol and other drugs on psychomotor performance and cognitive functions, *Alcohol and Alcoholism* **26**(1)**:**71.

Howat, P., Sleet, D., and Smith, I., 1991, Alcohol and driving: Is the 0.05% blood alcohol concentration limit justified?, *Drug and Alcohol Review,* **10:**151.

Jex, H. R., 1987, The critical instability tracking task: Its background, development and application, Paper No. 344, Systems Technology, Hawthorne, California.

Klein, R. H., and Jex, H. R., 1975, Effects of alcohol on a critical tracking task, *Journal of Studies on Alcohol* **36:**11.

Koonce, J. M., 1984, A brief history of aviation psychology, *Human Factors* **26**(5)**:**499.

Kvalseth, T. O., 1977, Effects of marijuana on human reaction time and motor control, *Perceptual Motor Skills* **45:**935.

Linnoila, M., Erwin, C. W., Ramm, D., Cleveland, W. P., 1980, Effects of age and alcohol on psychomotor performance of men, *Journal of Studies on Alcohol* **41**:488.

Mayer, R. C., 1992, Office of Alcohol and State Programs, NHTSA, personal conversation.

Mills, K. C., 1992, SEDI Corp., personal conversation.

Mills, K., 1991, Behavioral Performance Tests for the Assessment of Substance Abuse in the Workplace, address to 1991 Drug-Free Workplace Conference and Exposition, Anaheim, CA.

Mills, K. C., and Bisgrove, E. Z., Body sway and divided attention performance under the influence of alcohol: Dose-response differences between males and females, *Alcoholism: Clinical and Experimental Research* **7**(4):393.

Mills, K. C., Bisgrove, E. Z., Hill, G., Ballard, F., and Stepney, C., 1986, A Computer Test of Actual and Simulated BAC Impairment, National Institute on Alcohol Abuse and Alcoholism, Small Business Research Grant, Phase 1, 1 R43 AA06522–01, London, Ontario.

Moskowitz, H., 1985, Marihuana and driving, *Accident Analysis and Prevention* **17**:323.

Moskowitz, H., and Burns, M., 1971, Effect of alcohol on the refractory period, *Quarterly Journal of Studies on Alcohol* **32**:782.

Moskowitz, H., and Burns, M., 1981, The effects of alcohol and caffeine in combination on driving-related skills, in: *Alcohol, Drugs, and Traffic Safety* (L. Gildberg, ed.), Almqvist and Wiksell, Stockholm.

Moskowitz, H., Sharma, S., and Schapero, M., 1972, The effects of marihuana upon peripheral vision as a function of the information processing demands upon central vision, *Perceptual Motor Skills* **35**:875.

National Highway Transportation Safety Administration, 1988, Potential for Application of Ignition Interlock Devices to Prohibit Operation of Motor Vehicles by Intoxicated Individuals, A Report to Congress, (May, 1988), U.S. Department of Transportation, Washington, D.C.

National Highway Transportation Safety Administration, 1991, *Drug Evaluation and Classification Program Briefing Paper* (May, 1991), Washington, D.C.

Noy, I., 1987, The tracometer as an intoxication warning device, in: *Proceedings of the Human Factors Society—31st Annual Meeting,* 751.

Page, T., 1992, Drug Alcohol Training Associates Inc., personal conversation, program literature and seminar, Drug-Free Workplace Conference, Chicago.

Perez-Reyes, M., Hicks, R. E., Bumberry, J., Jeffcoat, R., and Cook, E., 1988, Interaction between marihuana and ethanol: Effects on psychomotor performance, *Alcoholism: Clinical and Experimental Research* **12**:268.

Perez-Reyes, M., et al., 1991, The pharmacologic effects of daily marijuana smoking in humans, *Pharmacology Biochemistry & Behavior* **40**:691.

Perrine, M. W., 1976, Alcohol and highway crashes, *Mod Probl Pharmacopsychiat* **11**:22.

Rossi, A. M., Kuehnle, J. C., and Mendelson, J. H., 1977, Effects of marihuana on reaction time and short-term memory in human volunteers, *Pharmacology Biochemistry & Behavior* **6**:37.

Rundell, O. H., and Williams, H. L., 1977, Alcohol, practice and information processing, *Alcohol Tech Rep* **6**:56.

Stein, A. C., and Allen, R. W., 1986, *The Use of In-vehicle Detectors to Reduce Impaired Driving Trips, Alcohol, Accidents and Injuries* (February, 1986), Society of Automotive Engineers, Warrendale, PA.

Sternberg, S., 1966, High-speed scanning in human memory, *Science* **153**:652.

Tennant, J. A., and Thompson, R. R., 1973, A critical tracking task as an alcohol interlock system, SAE paper 730095, presented at the International Automotive Engineering Congress and Exposition, Detroit.

Thar, W., 1991, address to Imperial Oil Limited Workshop on Alcohol and Drug Policy Development.

U.S. Transportation Research Board, 1987, *Zero Alcohol and Other Options: Committee on Benefits and Costs of Alternative Federal Blood Alcohol Concentration Standards for Commercial Vehicle Operators,* National Research Council, Washington, D.C.

Webb, R. D. G., 1989, Ergonomics, rehabilitation and human rights, in: *Rehabilitation and Ergonomics* (F. Poirier, ed.), pp. 48–57, Human Factors Association of Canada, Mississauga, Ontario.

12

Alternatives to Drug Testing

Employee Assistance and Health Promotion Programs

MARTIN SHAIN

1. INTRODUCTION

Whenever possible, we should adopt those methods for preventing and controlling harm to self and others that are least likely to interfere with the enjoyment of personal rights and freedoms. Such is the premise of this chapter. It is adopted for the simple reason that the "principle of the least drastic means" is a fundamental, if often unstated tenet of Western liberal democracy.* As such, it should require no defense as the basis for a discussion concerning different ways of containing or preventing drug abuse and social harm that results from drug abuse. Indeed, the principle of the least drastic means serves as a criterion against which the desirability of various alternatives can be assessed.

This perspective invites the reader to look at drug testing and screening with a view to deciding, if possible, to what extent these procedures *are* the least restrictive means for achieving the objectives claimed for them, assuming we can agree on the legitimacy of the objectives themselves. To provide answers, I will concentrate on two classes of intervention as potential or real alternatives to drug

*For example, in Canada, this principle was articulated by the Supreme Court in *The Queen v. Oakes*, 1 SCR 103 (1986).

MARTIN SHAIN • Workplace Program, Addiction Research Foundation, Toronto, Ontario M5S 2S1, Canada.

Research Advances in Alcohol and Drug Problems, Volume 11: Drug Testing in the Workplace, edited by Scott Macdonald and Paul M. Roman. Plenum Press, New York, 1994.

testing and screening: employee assistance programs (EAPs) and health promotion programs and policies (HPPs). Both types of programs, however, are usefully considered in the context of more comprehensive policies that are directed toward the establishment and maintenance of safe, healthy workplaces. Some attention will be given toward the end of the chapter to comprehensive workplace policies that appear to offer more than the simple combination of existing programs. No consideration will be given to task- or performance-simulation testing as an alternative to drug testing (this is the subject of Chapter 11). The question to be addressed here, then, is the extent to which EAPs, HPPs, and their policy umbrellas achieve—or could achieve—the reasonable objective of minimizing problems associated with substance abuse in the workplace.

The principle object of this inquiry is to determine the extent to which such interventions are viable alternatives to drug testing. It is also worth thinking, however, about the legitimate realm (if any) of drug testing; such a realm is what remains after every other effort has been made to achieve reasonable drug control objectives by less drastic means. To the extent that these objectives remain unmet, drug testing might become a means worth considering for closing the gap between expectation and achievement.

2. THE OBJECTIVES OF DRUG TESTING AND SCREENING

In order to make the following discussion meaningful, it will be necessary to be more precise about the objectives of drug testing and screening. Then, we shall be able to compare these with the objectives of EAPs and HPPs and arrive at some basis for considering such interventions as alternatives to drug testing and screening.

Although opinions may vary concerning the objectives of different forms of drug testing and screening, the following are offered as working accounts of why such measures are used, typically, in practice. Note the absence of any reference to rehabilitation of drug users. Although employers may institute rehabilitative measures (e.g., EAPs), these are not part of the drug testing or screening procedures themselves. The relationship *between* the two forms of intervention will be taken up once it is clear what each seeks to achieve in its own right.

In the following, there is also no discussion of drug testing as a stratagem in the "war against drugs"—that is, as a stratagem directed at the elimination of all (illicit) drug use in society, regardless of its effect on job performance, safety, and personal health. It is beyond the scope of this chapter to discuss the role of drug testing in the workplace in this broader context.

The Objectives of Preemployment Drug Screening

By requiring that some or all potential employees be screened for the use of certain substances before their contracts of employment are confirmed, pre-employment drug screening seeks to:

- exclude users of certain substances from the work force or from certain jobs
- deter the use of such substances among applicants

The Objectives of Random Drug Testing

By instilling in users and potential users of certain drugs the fear that their consumption will be discovered and that they will be subject to a variety of unpleasant consequences, random drug testing seeks to:

- deter the use of prohibited substances among employees
- prevent and reduce harm or loss to the public, the employer, fellow employees, and employees themselves

The Objective of Drug Testing for Cause

By requiring employees to provide urine samples when they are judged unfit to work on specific occasions and when such unfitness is thought to result from drug use, drug testing for cause seeks to:

- confirm or disconfirm the supervisor's or manager's suspicion that this causal relationship exists
- deter the use of prohibited substances among employees

The Objective of Routine Drug Testing for Employees in Safety-Sensitive Positions

By instilling in users and potential users of certain drugs the knowledge that their consumption of such substances will be monitored and that, if detected, such consumption will lead to their being judged unfit for work, drug testing for employees in safety-sensitive positions seeks to:

- prevent harm or loss to the public, the employer, fellow employees and employees themselves
- deter the use of prohibited substances

In the discussion of objectives above, the emphasis is upon harm reduction and prevention through the imposition of measures about which employees have little choice. Refusal to take a drug test in itself invites discipline up to and including dismissal. Drug testing, as other chapters in this volume make clear, is an intrusive intervention that involves invasion of individual rights of personal privacy, dignity, and security. Thus, it is evident that if the objectives of drug testing are to be achieved at all, they must be achieved at considerable cost to the individual in terms of personal autonomy, even though in some cases the individual can be considered a beneficiary of such intrusive measures; after all, the purpose of testing for cause and testing in safety-sensitive positions is to prevent employees from harming *themselves,* as well as others or the property of others. The problem lies in the extent to which such measures are nonconsensual—that is, imposed against the will of the individual. The trade-off between harm to the individual resulting from the assaults upon autonomy associated with drug testing and benefit to the individual and to others resulting from the same is influenced to some degree by the actual effectiveness of the measures involved. If they are highly effective in achieving their objectives, the harm to the individual is offset by the benefit, at least to some extent. If they are relatively ineffective, however, the harm is for nothing. Other chapters in this book have drawn attention to the fact that drug testing often appears to fall short of achieving its objectives. If this is the case, other alternatives would tend to weigh heavily in the balance against drug testing if they could demonstrate some effectiveness at little or no cost to the individual. It is in this context that one might usefully review the objectives of EAPs and HPPs, together with whatever evidence can be adduced about their effectiveness.

3. THE OBJECTIVES OF EMPLOYEE ASSISTANCE PROGRAMS

By providing opportunities for employees who are experiencing personal problems to seek help through clinical and other counseling programs, EAPs attempt to do the following:

- restore health and well-being
- restore job performance to optimal levels
- prevent further harm or loss to employees, fellow workers, employers, customers, the public, or shareholders
- reduce costs associated with harm and loss resulting from the effect of such problems
- help supervisors manage such employees with minimal disruption and cost to their employers

It is evident from this description of EAP objectives that insofar as this intervention is directed toward identification of drug users, it is as part of a general strategy for providing troubled employees with opportunities to help themselves. The EAP, in other words, attempts to achieve *more* than drug testing, and it does so with the interests of the employee in mind. Rehabilitation is a key part of the EAP; indeed, it is its very essence.

The Effectiveness of EAPs

EAPs have been able to demonstrate clearly that they are of relevance to the control of drug abuse in the workplace (Roman, 1989). EAPs began as interventions aimed at alcohol abusers but expanded to deal first with other drugs and then later with a wide variety of other personal problems to the point where, today, the typical new program is broadbrush (See, e.g., Shain & Groeneveld, 1980; Trice & Schonbrunn, 1981). As noted above, EAPs are conceived as interventions that allow employees to consult helping professionals when they feel that personal problems are becoming too difficult to manage. Traditional programs included a strong formal component whereby supervisors were encouraged to do "constructive confrontation" with employees whose job performance had deteriorated and where "normal" efforts to restore it had failed (Shain & Groeneveld, 1980; Trice & Beyer, 1984; Shain, 1992a). Of late, this formal component appears to have fallen into disrepute, the emphasis shifting toward the voluntary use of programs delivered by third-party providers external to the workplace (for a discussion, see Harley, 1991). This trend appears to have been accompanied by a tendency for new programs to see proportionately fewer alcohol and drug cases, although no clear, comprehensive picture of the situation is currently available. It is certain, however, that the overall number of EAPs has increased dramatically over the last 15 years. More than half of all organizations with 500 or more employees report some form of EAP (U.S. Department of Labor, 1989), and in Ontario more than 32% of organizations with more than 50 employees have them (Macdonald & Wells, 1993).

The relevance of EAPs as alternatives to drug testing depends very much upon the design of the specific program. Surprisingly few data are available on the proportion of drug users actually seen in EAPs, but reports that are available suggest a wide variation in the effectiveness of such programs with regard to the identification and referral of this target group. For example, a comparison of reports between 1985 and 1990 shows that EAPs are capable of identifying as much as 1.35% of the workforce (Foote, 1990) or as little as 0.15% (Martin, Heckel, Goodrick, Schreiber, & Young, 1985). A third study (Ashenberg Straussner, 1988) shows variation in the referral of drug users according to whether the EAP is run from within the organization (0.19% referral rate) or by a third-party provider (0.28% referral rate). If one were to estimate that at least 2% of the work force consisted of employees who abused drugs and needed help, these "penetration" figures would convert into a range between 7.5% and 67.5% of the population at risk of being identified (or identifying itself) through the

EAPs discussed in the above mentioned reports. A number of factors may account for this enormous range.

1. *The actual prevalence and type of drug-related problems varies between workplaces.* It stands to reason that variations of this sort will be found according to the kinds of work being done and the kinds of people doing it. In some workforces there will be more illicit drug use; in others, more abuse or misuse of prescribed and over-the-counter medications. For example, in a series of Canadian health needs/risks surveys conducted in the framework of the "Workplace Health System," a variation between 6.3% and 18.9% was found in relation to the use of drugs "for recreational purposes" when all levels of frequency were taken into account.* Frequent use, however, varied between 0.3% and 3.4% (Addiction Research Foundation and Health and Welfare Canada, 1987–1989). Such drug use excluded alcohol and tobacco, as well as painkillers, tranquilizers, or sleeping pills when utilized for their intended purposes.

2. *Different types of EAPs will attract and deter different types of potential program users.* For example, EAPs can be differentiated according to their focus (alcohol/drug emphasis versus a broad appeal); whether they encourage voluntary and direct self-referral to care providers without the use of in-house intermediaries such as nurses, physicians, and coordinators; whether they incorporate a formal constructive-confrontation component; whether they employ the services of an outside service provider; the quality of such service and the training or qualifications of the providers; and the internal governance of the EAP (run by management only versus a joint management/employee team approach). These and other variations in EAP structure can all be related to what has been described as the "ideal model" of such programs (Shain & Groeneveld, 1980) and as their "core technology" (Roman & Blum, 1985, 1988).

3. *Differences in the availability and quality of treatment for severely dependent drug abusers will occur across the country, influencing the readiness of troubled employees and their potential "motivators" to initiate referrals.* If a high-quality treatment facility exists in one's own community, for example, access may be perceived as relatively easy (problems of confidentiality and anonymity aside) compared with the prospect of a trip to a place, however fine, many hundreds of miles away.

Because of the way in which the factors listed above influence referral rates, it is difficult to pinpoint exactly what will contribute to the maximum effectiveness of EAPs with regard to drug abusers. It is fairly safe, however, to assert the following broad principles.

*The Workplace Health System is a planning and implementation framework through which a comprehensive strategy for the prevention and management of employee health problems can be pursued. See section 4, "Comprehensive Health and Assistance Policies and Programs."

- The EAP should make confidentiality its first priority. This means that a drug user should be able to consult a care provider with minimal risk of being identified by anyone outside the therapeutic relationship as someone seeking help for a drug problem. Many believe that external or third-party providers can deliver better assurances of this kind of confidentiality (Besenhofer & Gerstein, 1992; Roman & Blum, 1985; Shain, 1985).
- EAP providers, be they in-house or run by third parties, must be perceived by drug users and referral agents as having the competence to deal with their problems. There is informal evidence that EAPs are recruiting more professionals *without* such competence, even though they may be well trained in other respects.
- EAP providers must make potential clients aware of their services by actively broadcasting what they can do and how they can help the work force at large. Even very well-run EAPs can falter when it comes to dissemination of information about their services, and the "riskiest" drug users are likely to be a particularly difficult group to reach simply because they are so troubled. For example, in a Canadian Armed Forces study, 58% of those who had used LSD or other hallucinogens in the last 12 months and 45% of those who had used cocaine fell into the highest-scoring category on an inventory of psychiatric symptoms, compared with approximately 23% of nonusers (Shain & Suurvali, 1991).
- EAPs that hope to reach drug users cannot rely exclusively or perhaps even mainly upon voluntary or self-referrals. There is a need to reinforce the formal component of programs so that supervisors and managers know how to use constructive-confrontation techniques (Harley, 1991; Shain, 1992a; Trice & Beyer, 1984). The failure of organizations to promote such techniques successfully has no doubt helped open the door to drug testing as a last resort. But drug testing cannot be a substitute for sound management practices. EAPs have long been the standard-bearers of such practices as they are applied to alcohol- and drug-abusing employees who tend to deny the nature and extent of their dependence unless confronted with unequivocal evidence of its effect upon job performance. This evidence must be gathered through careful documentation of deteriorating job performance over a period of time and must be presented to troubled workers in ways that command their attention and inspire remedial action on their part.

Although the ultimate threat of job loss is present in such a process, this form of progressive discipline is in fact the best protection for drug-dependent employees, because it is in some cases the only way of diverting them from dismissal. At the very least, attention to constructive confrontation requires supervisors to observe the behavior of employees,

> thus raising the odds that problems will be noticed at the earliest possible stage. It should be stressed, however, that constructive confrontation is meant to be aimed at improving job performance exclusively, rather than at diagnosing reasons for its deterioration (Trice & Beyer, 1984).

EAPs, then, clearly have relevance to the control of drug abuse in the workplace, but they could have a much greater impact if they were managed more explicitly for this purpose. Properly designed and applied, EAPs are strong candidates for the role of prime alternative to drug testing. They have the powerful appeal of interventions that concentrate upon job performance and fitness for work rather than upon drug taking, which may or may not affect behavior at work. They have the strong advantage, too, of being offered on a voluntary self-referral basis as well as on a formal basis, thus multiplying the routes through which troubled employees may access help.

Impressive claims have been made for the effectiveness of EAPs in terms of their rehabilitative effect upon alcohol abusers (see discussion in Shain, Suurvali, & Boutilier, 1986, pp. 185ff). Data of this sort concerning drug abusers are less available, although two recent accounts suggest that EAPs aimed at drug abusers are both effective and cost efficient (Browne Miller, 1988; Kertesz, 1989). It seems very likely, though, that success rates will vary enormously, just as penetration rates do, according to the quality controls built into the specific EAP in question (Kertesz, 1989). It is important to note, however, that when comparing drug testing and EAPs, the *rehabilitation* potential of the latter is not the main issue, although undoubtedly evidence of effectiveness in this regard adds to its appeal. Drug testing per se offers no rehabilitative potential, and it is therefore with regard to identification of drug users and their removal from harm's way that the most fruitful comparison with EAPs can be made. If a drug user is identified through an EAP (at least, if a supervisor or manager is involved), the employer is alerted to the fact that the employee in question may be a risk to self and others. It is this knowledge that allows preventive action to be taken in the future. Even if treatment of the user is ineffective, the employer has the information he or she needs to divert employees at risk from jobs where they can do themselves and others harm. Again, however, the effectiveness of this stratagem relies upon the robust functioning of the constructive-confrontation component of the EAP. Self-referrals to EAPs do not activate the same vigilant response of the employer, but it is hoped that the same responsible attitude of the drug user that leads him or her to seek help without obvious pressure from supervisors or managers will also cause him or her to choose to avoid risky work.

EAPs cannot guarantee the identification of drug use that might lead to or be associated with loss and harm in the future. They can identify current job performance problems, though, and they have a good chance of discovering drug involvement through the assessment process that is essential to the effective functioning of these programs. EAPs (at least in their formal application) have the advantage of starting from the perspective of job performance and fitness for work, rather than from the perspective of drug use per se. To a large extent, this approach avoids spurious associations between drug use and job performance deficits that emerge from concentration upon identifying the former rather than the latter.

There remains the question of whether EAPs have any *auxiliary* (as opposed to alternative) role to play with regard to drug testing. In a sense, EAPs take over where drug testing leaves off in that they provide an answer (other than discipline) to the question of "Now what?" after an employee has tested positive for a prohibited drug. That is, they provide a rehabilitative response to identification of people with drug problems. There is some evidence that the two methods can and do coexist (Roman, 1989). Indeed, according to Roman, drug referral activity in EAPs that operate in companies with drug testing tends to be *higher* than in companies without drug testing. Roman himself, however, expresses uncertainty about the process linking the two interventions. It may be that in some cases drug testing (particularly for cause and after accidents) directs more people into EAPs, or perhaps employees with (emerging) drug problems make use of the EAP before they are confronted with a drug test.

Obviously, more needs to be learned about the interaction between the two forms of intervention. An EAP is a way of identifying drug users in its own right, however, so it may be redundant to have both an EAP and drug testing if the former is operating at full potential. It appears that EAP drug referral activity is highest in organizations where the program is integrated into supervisory and management practices (Roman, 1989). Thus, when progressive discipline, using EAP as a branch in the trail, is endorsed, drug referral rates tend to be higher, suggesting (as above) that there is no substitute for good management and that EAP is part of it. Given that EAP is the less drastic means of containing harm, one might favor it for that reason over drug testing.

4. THE OBJECTIVES OF HEALTH PROMOTION POLICIES AND PROGRAMS IN THE WORKPLACE

HPPs are directed primarily toward the enhancement of well-being and secondarily toward the prevention of health-related problems. They might be considered alternatives to drug testing in the sense that, if successful, they would reduce the need for such drastic means, even though they might not be expected to eliminate it. With regard to substance abuse, such policies and programs are intended to be preventive at a much earlier stage than drug testing. Although the objectives of both types of intervention use the language of prevention, they refer to quite different procedures. Indeed, it is important that one distinguish at the outset the objectives of health promotion *policies* from those of health promotion *programs*.

The Objectives of Health Promotion Policies in the Workplace

By being incorporated into the technical, physical, and social organization of work, and by providing services consistent with the principle that the workplace environment has a profound influence on well-being, health promotion policies seek to:

- make the workplace more supportive of employee efforts to protect and improve their own mental and physical health
- make the workplace less likely to produce harm or loss as a result of erosion of or threat to employee mental and physical health.

The Objectives of Health Promotion Programs in the Workplace

By providing information about health-related matters and by teaching participants a variety of skills related to maintaining, regaining, or improving their health and energy levels, health promotion programs seek to:

- prevent and reduce harm or loss to employees and employers resulting from premature morbidity and mortality
- enhance the quality of life of employees
- enhance the quality and quantity of products and services provided by the host organization

The main difference between health promotion policies and programs, as outlined above, is that the former concentrate on the workplace environment, whereas the latter concentrate on the individual employee. Neither is uniquely directed toward the prevention of drug problems, but each is relevant to this end.

Policies may be thought of as providing a context for programs. This context may support the effectiveness of specific initiatives, or it may detract from it; consequently, I will consider policies first.

Health Promotion Policies

These policies may be directed at the technical, physical, or psychosocial dimensions of working environments. Sometimes they will encompass all three under a broad "health and safety" umbrella. Such comprehensive policies tend to acknowledge the interdependence of technical, physical, and psychosocial environments, just as they acknowledge interactions between mental and physical health. For example, on the surface, the provision of safety equipment is a matter pertaining to the physical environment of the workplace; but how decisions are made about what equipment to buy and the ways in which it is to be used are psychosocial matters. It is fair to say, therefore, that the effectiveness of physical solutions to safety problems will depend in no small measure upon the psychosocial processes used to arrive at them.

It should be the primary responsibility of employers to do no harm to the employees they hire. This is a "floor" standard in that it represents a minimum expectation of employers. A higher standard might be reflected in the goal of establishing a health-promoting work environment, but this is not a legal requirement, whereas the "do no harm" imperative is. Consequently, the first obligation of employers—before considering HPPs or EAPs, and certainly before considering drug testing—should be the provision of a working environment that in itself does not predispose employees to abuse drugs or in some way precipitate their use. As a moral and legal prerequisite to more specific, programmatic interventions aimed at preventing substance abuse, this obligation is rarely discharged. Much more common is the tendency for employers to import programmatic solutions aimed at individual employees, who are expected to take preventive or remedial action themselves even though they may be surrounded by working conditions that promote harm.

Obviously, it makes sense for employers to have in place specific policies aimed at reducing the availability and use of psychoactive substances on workplace premises and at preventing employees from reporting for duty in an impaired condition. But such policies are virtually fatuous if implemented in environments that, from every other point of view, promote substance abuse through "psychotoxic" forms of work organization. Psychotoxic organization of work refers to methods of planning, dividing up, and executing labor in ways that defeat employee morale. This adverse effect appears to be achieved most readily through conditions of work characterized by having too much to do in too little time, with very little control or influence over such pressure, and with very little social support to buffer its negative impact (Karasek & Theorell, 1990; Shain, 1990a; Shehadeh & Shain, 1990). These conditions of work are known to contribute to a variety of interconnected mental and physical health problems, including substance abuse (Shehadeh & Shain, 1990).

Of course, other conditions of work can more obviously influence the probability that substances will be abused. Examples cluster around workplace subcultures in which drinking and drug use are normative (see, e.g., Ames & Janes, 1987; Plant, 1979). Interestingly, both the studies that link high pressure and low control to psychotoxicity and those that link "culture" to abuse of substances contain within them certain implications for reforming the organization of work to make it healthier and less conducive to drug dependence. These implications revolve around the idea of increasing the involvement of employees in the process of defining and solving organizational problems.

Many will be familiar with examples of this idea in the context of increasing productivity (see, e.g., Peters & Waterman, 1982). Productivity gains may be expected from serious-minded efforts to increase the participation of employees in the organization and design of work. Participation can also be important in the definition of and search for solutions to problems associated with substance abuse. Examples of specific applications of this approach can be found in the form of peer intervention strategies, often in the context of EAPs (Molloy, 1989; Sonnenstuhl, 1982). A broader application, though, awaits testing in the form of deliberate efforts to involve the work force as a whole in efforts to define and resolve substance abuse problems. Of course, if the counsel of employees is ignored after an apparently genuine consultation, the result can be worse than having never involved them in the first place (Nitkin, 1991).

The authentic participation of employees in identifying and finding solutions to substance abuse problems is a far cry from unilaterally imposed, invasive drug testing. It is far more consistent with the employer's duty to do no harm and certainly meets the "least drastic means" criterion set out at the beginning of this chapter. It is conceivable, nonetheless, that the process of employee participation could result in recommendations to utilize drug testing—perhaps under very limited circumstances; this is, in fact, what happened at one large petrochemical company (Nitkin, 1991). If the process of involving employees is thorough and the intention to be guided by the results of such participation is genuine, however, an emergent drug testing policy would likely meet the least-drastic-means test by virtue of its being declared to do so by the "constituent assembly" of the work force as a whole. After all, if the community most affected by a policy has been involved in determining a need for it and in designing it, one might fairly say that for local purposes, it had by definition balanced the social good resulting from a limited form of drug testing against the curtailment of individual rights that is necessarily involved in its implementation.

The participation of employees requires that they take active ownership of a problem and come up with solutions acceptable both to themselves and to the employer. In other words, participation involves duties and responsibilities to the employer. Although superficially it may be seen as a rollback of management rights to govern the workplace, participation can be implemented in ways that compensate for this effect by tapping the creative resources of employee ingenuity and goodwill (Shain, 1992b). There is a further advantage to participative solutions: The process of being involved in decisions is known to be beneficial to mental health because it improves the individual's sense of "efficacy"—the sense that one can influence one's life course in important ways (see, e.g., Aronsson, 1989; Israel, House, Schurman, Heaney, & Mero, 1989; Jackson, 1983; Johnson, 1989).

So, when employees are involved in seeking solutions to substance abuse problems in the workplace, not only do they find more acceptable alternatives, but in so doing they feel better about themselves, which is a benefit in itself. This philosophy of participation is the foundation for any effective drug strategy in the workplace. Though it needs to be expressed in overall management policies and specifically in seeking solutions to substance abuse problems, it represents also the guiding spirit of the more traditional alternatives to drug testing considered in this chapter. If, for example, HPPs and EAPs are simply "laid on" without consultation, it is likely that they will be ineffective and never have the chance to demonstrate whether or to what extent they are viable alternatives to drug testing.

Health Promotion Programs

HPPs exist in many forms, and their objectives vary from the simple provision of information to basic changes in attitudes, beliefs, and behavior. Their presence in the workplace has increased considerably over the last 10 years (Shain, 1990b). The most common subjects of HPPs are smoking cessation, fitness/exercise, weight loss/nutrition, and stress management. Such programs, when evaluated, have yielded mixed results, probably because they reflect such a variety of technologies and approaches.

A recent review of such evaluations suggests that certain key components need to be incorporated into the design of any HPP if it is to have a chance of being effective (Shain, 1990b; Suurvali & Shain, 1989). These components are (a) attention to the needs of participants to gain or regain a sense of efficacy, competence, or control in relation to their health generally or in relation to a particular health practice such as exercise or eating; and (b) attention to the fact that health practices tend to be highly interdependent. For example, patterns of activity, eating, drinking, smoking, sleeping, and stress management tend to be closely interwoven (Shehadeh & Shain, 1990). A scan of 84 articles over the last 5 years claiming to deal with HPP evaluations, however, showed that only 8 involved a study or consideration of these two components together (Erfurt, Foote, & Heirich, 1992; Health and Welfare Canada, 1990a; Health Insurance Association of America, undated; Heirich, Cameron, Erfurt, Foote, & Gregg, 1989; Klesges & Glasgow, 1986; McDowell, Black, & Collishaw, 1988; Wood, Olmstead, & Craig, 1989). These and other components now form an essential part of the "Workplace Health System," an innovative Canadian intervention combining HPPs, EAPs, and environmental initiatives in one comprehensive approach (Health and Welfare Canada and Addiction Research Foundation, 1991).

Some HPPs offer information about alcohol and other drug use, but few are directed toward these subjects as their sole target (Shain et al., 1986). One might therefore question the relevance of HPPs to drug users; however, their *potential* relevance lies in the fact that drug users (the employed ones, at least) are not unidimensional beings whose lives revolve exclusively around the acquisition and consumption of psychoactive substances. They have other concerns and worries, some of which are related to their health. This begs the question of who drug users are, because clearly one cannot design HPPs that are likely to be effective with this group unless something is known of their characteristics, needs, and wants. Other chapters in this book deal with this subject, but here it is worth offering a few additional observations on the characteristics of drug users from the perspective of HPP design and marketing to this population.

The first thing we must do is define what we mean by drug use. Clearly, the term must embrace the ingestion of illicit drugs—marijuana, cocaine, hallucinogens, and so forth. But even with this pattern of use (the one that probably springs to most people's minds when the term *drug use* is employed), it is important to observe that most consume illicit substances infrequently. Only a few among the employed population use illicit substances (or any other psychoactive agent, for that matter) on a regular basis. For example, in a recent survey of the Canadian Armed Forces, of the 46% who said they had ever used marijuana or hashish, only 6.7% had used it in the last 30 days, and only 15.3% in the last year (Canadian Forces Health and Lifestyle Survey, 1989). Consequently, the "fit" between illicit drug users and HPPs may not be as bizarre as it first appears. Most illicit drug users who are still in the work force have normal needs and wants. Only a relative few are highly disturbed individuals who need the kind of help that EAPs can provide.

It is interesting, however, that of those in the Canadian Armed Forces who had used cannabis products during the year before the survey, more than half said they had experienced job performance problems because of *drinking* or its aftereffects, and almost the same proportion reported trouble with their supervisors in this regard. The important point here is that the alcohol use of cannabis users presents a door for potential HPP intervention. Indeed, 42% of those who had used cannabis in the previous 12 months reported that they consumed more than 14 standard drinks of alcohol per week. Of course, not all of these users are in any way motivated to examine their drug or alcohol consumption; perhaps only a minority will want to do so.

In another workplace study (Health and Welfare Canada, 1990b), it was found that among 98 "recreational" drug users, 10 wanted to quit or cut down on their use. Of the latter group, 60% wanted also to quit smoking and to cut down on their drinking. So even if it seems unrealistic to approach illicit drug users directly on the basis of their actual drug use through HPPs, it may be possible to engage them in efforts to deal with other health practices—such as smoking and drinking—through properly designed campaigns. This indirect approach is based on the principle that health practices tend to reinforce each other and therefore that each is, in a sense, a "door" to the other. We may be able to address drug use by helping users to examine their smoking and drinking patterns, which are very likely woven together with their consumption of illicit and other drugs.

This indirect approach is relevant not only for cannabis users but also for cocaine and hallucinogen users. The Canadian Armed Forces study showed that both of these other drug-using groups were heavy alcohol consumers (64% of cocaine users and 65% of hallucinogen users drank 14 or more standard drinks per week). Both cocaine and hallucinogen consumers, however, reported extremely low levels of efficacy (i.e., sense of influence over their health and their work), thus posing a major challenge to designers of HPPs—who, judging from the reported literature, have a tendency to assume that everyone can become healthy if they have the "will" (Shain & Suurvali, 1991). Half the recreational drug users who said they wanted to quit or cut down in the Health and Welfare Canada (1990b) study indicated that they were *too depressed* to take action.

It may well be that the illicit-drug-using population in the workplace falls along a continuum from those who are easily reachable by HPPs (a minority) to those who would be difficult if not impossible to attract (another minority). In between lies a large group of people who could be reached by better designed HPPs, by EAPs, or even by both. Again, it would be useful and extremely desirable to involve employees (including motivated drug users) in the design of better HP programs. This is far from impossible and ought to be tried, given the imperative of the least-drastic-means test described earlier.

As noted above, though, drug use refers to more than just those who consume illicit substances. We must also consider employees who take such licit substances as painkillers, tranquilizers, and sleeping pills. These substances could easily be the subject of drug screening, leading to some sort of official action if tests were positive. But screening for these substances raises a major question concerning who their users are and the employer's interest in them. In fact, it appears that users of these drugs are not very well understood. There is evidence, for example, that many employees who take painkillers, tranquilizers, and sleeping pills have experienced an illness or injury in the last year that kept them off work for some time, and that their current use of these drugs is a way of coping with the residual pain or discomfort from these episodes (Shehadeh & Shain, 1992). Although, presumably, much of the use of sleeping pills and tranquilizers is a result of prescriptions made out by physicians, many (around 75%) say that their consumption patterns reported for the last month are "typical" or even less than typical, suggesting long-term utilization of substances intended largely for the short-term amelioration of specific conditions (Shehadeh & Shain, 1992). What is striking, too, is that more than 34% of males and 32% of females who used either of these drug types reported the use of *both* at least occasionally.

Some of these employees are clearly troubled, reporting high levels of job stress and financial worries. Among this troubled group, drug usage is higher, increasing even more when combined with low efficacy (the sense that little can be done by the individual to change his or her situation). A recent German study showed similar results in that a higher proportion of workers who experienced "high intensity work-loads" reported the use of medications for dealing with pain (63% of women with high loads versus 36% with low loads; 48% of men with high loads versus 32% with low loads; Ziegler, 1991).

HPPs are a potential source of help for some of these employees; it is likely that stress management programs* could be tailored to their needs and that other interventions aimed at weight reduction, increasing activity, or quitting smoking could also be made relevant. Relevance in this context refers to making the program *look* appealing to users of sleeping pills, tranquilizers, and painkillers who want to cut down on their use. It also refers to engaging and keeping their attention once they are in the program. HPP designers need to be aware that this neglected group of drug users exist and are at risk in the work force. Surprisingly, relatively few such users report that they want to quit or cut down: In the Health and Welfare Canada study referred to earlier, only 8% of this group expressed such a desire. This may suggest a pattern of dependence on the drugs in question, or a belief that their use will be extinguished when life returns to normal. The reported typicality of their drug use, however, suggests further that this belief may be wishful thinking. As with any drug-using group, it is likely that such persons could be reached by either HPPs, EAPs, or both if deliberate efforts were made in this direction. Clearly, much thought will have to be given to making HPPs appealing to risk groups of the sort described above. As noted earlier, employees at large could be usefully involved in this design exercise.

5. COMPREHENSIVE HEALTH AND ASSISTANCE POLICIES AND PROGRAMS

In the last few years a type of workplace intervention has emerged, a generic term for which might be "comprehensive health and assistance policies and programs" (CHAPPs). CHAPPs build upon the technology of EAPs and HPPs in several ways that are expected to make them more than simply the addition of the two founding components (Shain & Boyle, 1985). Essentially, they are planning and implementing frameworks for policies and programs aimed at the prevention, remediation, and management of health-related problems in the workplace. They are intended to bring consistency to policies and programs, locating all of them within a common philosophical and theoretical context. In one application of the CHAPP model, the Workplace Health System,

*In one study of a relaxation training course conducted by Shain and Bay, it was found that in comparison with an untrained group, those who were taught how to relax reduced their use of painkillers, at least in the short run. This reduction in use was seen to be correlated with lowered scores on standard measures of anxiety (Shain et al., 1986).

the first step is to obtain the commitment of senior management and employee representative groups to the principle that the health-related needs and risks of the whole work force will be studied (Health and Welfare Canada and Addiction Research Foundation, 1991). Second, on the basis of understandings gleaned from these surveys, a plan is developed that is intended as a response to the health-related needs and risks of the whole work force. Third, the process of study and planning is regulated by an in-house committee comprising representatives of management, employees, and special staff such as EAP and wellness coordinators. Fourth, the plan is meant to contain strategies for addressing the health needs and risks of employees not only by proposing that programs such as EAPs and HPPs be delivered to individuals and groups, but also by designating initiatives for making the organizational environment a healthier, safer place in which to work. These latter initiatives may span everything from providing more nutritious food in the cafeteria to making communication flow more easily within and between departments.

All such proposals, of course, must be rooted in the results of the health needs/risks surveys, because these are what provide the joint steering committees with their authority to act (Shain, 1990c). Because the surveys contain many interwoven opportunities for employees to demonstrate or comment upon the effect of the workplace environment on their health, however, it becomes almost inevitable that the committee's plan will contain recommendations of some sort for making this environment more health promoting. As noted earlier, the participation of employees in the search for solutions to problems that they themselves have had a hand in defining tends to be health promoting in itself, because this kind of involvement is thought to build efficacy and therefore to be good for mental health. For this reason, CHAPPs (and the Workplace Health System in particular) are likely to be useful vehicles for addressing the health-related needs and risks of drug users. To the extent that drug users respond to the surveys—which many seem to do quite readily—the results can be used to define the nature of the group or groups at need and at risk. If further validation or clarification of survey results is required, special group sessions may be held with and among the target population as long as the committee can establish bonds of trust. This process of direct consultation is likely to be valuable in itself and may be used instead of questionnaire-type surveys, provided that the physical and psychosocial environment of the workplace is examined in as much depth as the individual health practices of employees.

CHAPPs provide opportunities for synergism to develop between EAPs and HPPs. Because a common joint committee oversees both programs and all other health-related interventions, it becomes possible to promote cross-referrals between the more remedial EAPs and the more preventive HPPs. It becomes more likely, too, that no employee group will be neglected in the process of program design, because everyone has a chance to participate in the survey and the results concern everyone. CHAPPs are the most likely of all the workplace health-related interventions to make a difference in the *culture* of the host organization, although this effect remains to be studied. One might, however, anticipate this effect when employees participate to the greatest extent possible in all stages of the formulation and implementation of a comprehensive plan.

6. CONCLUSION

It is evident that EAPs, HPPs, and CHAPPs have considerable potential as alternatives to drug testing. Some of this potential has been realized in practice, but a great deal of it remains to be exploited because little determined effort has been made to bend these programs to the task of preventing or dealing with drug abuse in any serious way. EAPs are the most-used vehicle for reaching drug abusers in the workplace, and even they are of dubious value as stand-alone methods for controlling the problem. It is clear that EAPs can reach a sizable proportion of the drug-using population at risk, however, if the will is present to make the program work in this way.

In the context of the least-drastic-means principle discussed at the beginning of the chapter, it becomes imperative to pursue these alternative avenues to drug testing. Only when such alternatives have been seriously tried and have fallen short should drug testing be considered as a way of closing the gap between policy objectives (reduction of drug abuse consequences to an acceptable or minimal level) and actual outcomes. In the process of implementing these alternatives a cardinal principle should be observed—namely, the requirement that employees themselves be involved as much as possible in helping to define and seek solutions to the problems associated with drug abuse in the workplace.

REFERENCES

Addiction Research Foundation and Health and Welfare Canada, 1987–1989, *Reports on Employee Health Needs and Risks at Selected Worksites*, Addiction Research Foundation, Toronto.

Ames, G. M., and Janes, C. R., 1987, Heavy and problem drinking in an American blue-collar population: Implications for prevention. *Soc. Sci. & Med.* **25**(8):949.

Aronsson, G., 1989, Dimensions of control as related to work organization, stress and health, *Int. J. Health Services* **19**(3):459.

Ashenberg Straussner, S. L., 1988, A comparative analysis of in-house and contractual employee assistance programs, *Employee Assistance Quarterly* **3**(3/4):43.

Bayer, G. A., and Barkin, A. C., 1990, Employee assistance program utilization: A comparison of referral sources and problems, *Employee Assistance Quarterly* **5**(4):63.

Besenhofer, R. K., and Gerstein, L. H., 1992, Referrals to EAPs: Characteristics of hypothetical supervisors, EAPs, and substance abusing workers, *Employee Assistance Quarterly* **7**(2):41.

Browne Miller, A., 1988, New perspectives on chemical dependence treatment evaluation: A case study, *Employee Assistance Quarterly,* **4**(2):45.

Canadian Forces Health and Lifestyle Survey, 1989, "How we stand" and "Alcohol and drugs, 1982–1989," Directorate of Preventive Medicine, Surgeon General Branch, Dept. of National Defense, Ottawa.

Editor, 1989, McDonnell Douglas Corporation's EAP produces hard data, *The ALMACAN* **19**(8): Research Issue.

Erfurt, J., Foote, A., and Heirich, M. A., 1991, Worksite wellness programs: incremental comparison of screening and referral alone, health education, follow-up counselling and plant organization, *J. Employee Assistance Research.*

Foote, A., 1990, EAPs and early intervention for alcohol problems at the workplace, in: *Alcohol problem intervention in the workplace* (P. M. Roman, ed.) pp. 227–236, Quorum Books, New York.

Goodspeed, R. B., and DeLucia, A. G., 1990, Stress reduction at the worksite: An evaluation of two methods, *Am. J. Health Promotion* **4**(5):333.

Harley, D. A., 1991, Impaired job performance and worksite trigger incidents: factors influencing supervisory EAP referrals, *Employee Assistance Quarterly* **6**(3):51.

Health and Welfare Canada, 1990a, *Health promotion in the workplace: A sampling of company programs and initiatives,* Health and Welfare Canada, Supply and Services, Ottawa.

Health and Welfare Canada, 1990b, *Report on the health needs and risks survey at a pulp and paper company.* confidential report, Health Promotion in the Workplace Branch, Health Promotion Directorate, Health and Welfare Canada, Ottawa.

Health and Welfare Canada and Addiction Research Foundation, 1991, The Workplace Health System: Overview. Health Promotion in the Workplace, Supply and Services Canada, Ottawa.

Health Insurance Association of America/American Council of Life Insurance and U.S. Dept. of Agriculture, undated, *Wellness at the Worksite: A Manual,* Washington, D.C., Resource Center, Sun Life of Canada, Toronto.

Heirich, M. A., Cameron, V., Erfurt, J. C., Foote, A., and Gregg, W., 1989, Establishing communication networks for health promotion in industrial settings, *Am. J. Health Promotion* **4**(2):108.

Israel, B. A., House, J. S., Schurman, S. J., Heaney, C. A., and Mero, R. P., 1989, The relation of personal resources, participation, influence, interpersonal relationships and coping strategies to occupational stress, job strains and health: A multivariate analysis, *Work and Stress* **3**(2):163.

Jackson, S. E., 1983, Participation in decision-making as a strategy for reducing job-related strain, *J. Applied Psychol.* **68**(1):3.

Johnson, J. V., 1989, Collective control: Strategies for survival in the workplace, *Int. J. Health Services,* **19**(3):469.

Karasek, R., and Theorell, T., 1990, *Healthy Work: Stress, Productivity and the Reconstruction of Working Life,* Basic Books Inc., New York.

Kertesz, L., 1989, McDonnell Douglas EAP trims health care costs, *Business Insurance,* November 13, 1989:1.

Klesges, R. C., and Glasgow, R. E., 1986, Smoking modification in the worksite, in: *Health and industry: A behavioural medicine perspective* (M. F. Cataldo and T. J. Coates, eds.), pp. 231–254, John Wiley and Sons, Toronto.

Macdonald, S., and Wells, S., 1993, *Employee Assistance, Health Promotion, and Drug Testing Programs at Ontario Work Sites,* Addiction Research Foundation, Toronto.

Martin, D. W., Heckel, V. M., Goodrick, G. K., Schreiber, J. M., and Young, V. L., 1985, The relationship between referral types, work performance, and employee problems, *Employee Assistance Quarterly* **1**(2):25.

McDowell, I., Black, A., and Collishaw, N., 1988, The "Healthstyles" health promotion program: description and behavioural outcomes, *Can. J. Pub. Health* **79**:447.

Molloy, D. J., 1989, Peer intervention—An exploratory study, *J. Drug Issues* **19**(3):319.

Nitkin, D., 1991, Alcohol and drug testing in the Canadian workplace, *The Corporate Ethics Monitor* **3**(6):90.

Peters, T. J., and Waterman, R. H., 1982, *In Search of Excellence,* Warner Books, New York.

Plant, M. A., 1979, Drinking careers: Occupations, drinking habits and drinking problems, Tavistock Publications, London.

Roman, P. M., 1989, The use of EAPs in dealing with drug abuse in the workplace, in: *Drugs in the Workplace: Research and Evaluation Data,* NIDA Research Monograph Series, U.S. Dept. of Health and Human Services, Rockville, MD.

Roman, P., and Blum, T., 1985, The core technology of employee assistance programs. *ALMACAN* **15**:8.

Roman, P. M., and Blum, T. C., 1988, Formal intervention in employee health: Comparisons of the nature and structure of Employee Assistance Programs and Health Promotion Programs, *Soc. Sci. Med.* **26**(5):503.

Shain, M., 1985, An exploration of the ability of broad-based E.A.Ps to generate alcohol-related referrals, in: *The Human Resources Management Handbook: Principles and Practice of EAP* (J. L. Francek et al., eds.), Praeger Press, New York.

Shain, M., 1990a, My work makes me sick: Evidence and health promotion in implications, *Health Promotion* **29**(3):11.

Shain, M., 1990b, Health promotion programs and the prevention of alcohol abuse: Forging a link, in: *Alcohol Problem Intervention in the Workplace* (P. M. Roman, ed.), pp. 163–179, Quorum Books, New York.

Shain, M., 1990c, Worksite community processes and the prevention of alcohol abuse: Theory to action, *Contemporary Drug Problems* 1990:369.

Shain, Martin, 1992a, Constructive confrontation, *Employee Assistance* **5**(5):23.

Shain, M., 1992b, "Labor Law is a Hazard to your Health: Implications for Reform," Issues in Health Promotion Series, #1, Centre for Health Promotion, University of Toronto.

Shain, M., and Boyle, B., 1985, Toward coordination of Employee Health and Assistance Programmes, in: *The Human Resources Management Handbook: Principles and Practices of EAPs,* (J. L. Francek et al., eds.) New York: Praeger Press.

Shain, M., and Groeneveld, J., 1980, *Employee Assistance Programmes: Philosophy, Theory and Practice.* Lexington, Toronto.

Shain, M., and Suurvali, H., 1991, *The Efficacy Factor in CAF's Lifestyle Survey Data: A second look at "How We Stand"* Report prepared for Dept. of National Defense under contract DSS 19 SV.W8477-1-SC13, Preventive Medicine Directorate, Department of National Defense, Ottawa.

Shain, M., Suurvali, H., and Boutilier, M., 1986, *Healthier Workers: Health Promotion and Employee Assistance Programs,"* Lexington Books, D. C. Heath, Toronto.

Shehadeh, V., and Shain, M., 1990, *Influences on Wellness in the Workplace,* Health and Welfare Canada Technical Report, Supply and Services Canada, Ottawa.

Shehadeh, V., and Shain, M., 1992, *Use of painkillers, calming medications and sleeping pills in selected worksites,* Manuscript in preparation, Addiction Research Foundation, Toronto.

Sonnenstuhl, W. J., 1982, Understanding EAP self-referral: toward a social network approach, *Contemporary Drug Problems,* Summer, 1982:269.

Suurvali, H., and Shain, M., 1989, *Components found in workplace health promotion programs: an analysis of the literature,* Addiction Research Foundation, Toronto.

Trice, H. M., and Beyer, J. M., 1984, Work-related outcomes of constructive confrontation strategies in a job-based alcoholism program, *J. Studies on Alcohol* **45**(5):393.

Trice, H. M., and Schonbrunn, M., 1981, A history of job-based alcoholism programs: 1900–1955, *J. Drug Issues,* **11**:171.

U.S. Department of Labor, 1989, *Survey of employer anti-drug programs,* Dept. of Labor Statistics, Report No. 760, Washington, D.C.

Wood, E. A., Olmstead, G. W., and Craig, J. L., 1989, An evaluation of lifestyle risk factors and absenteeism after two years in a worksite health promotion program, *Am. J. Health Promotion* **4**(2):128.

Ziegler, H., 1991, Workplace drug and alcohol programs in Germany, Paper presented at Washington Tripartite Symposium on Drug and Alcohol Abuse Prevention Assistance Programs at the Workplace, U.S. Dept. of Labor, Washington, D.C.

13

The Interrelations of Drug Testing with Other Human Resource Management Practices and Organizational Characteristics

TERRY C. BLUM, DAIL L. FIELDS, STUART H. MILNE, AND CHESTER S. SPELL

This chapter examines drug testing of employees and applicants for employment by work organizations, specifically as it is interrelated with other human resource management practices and organizational characteristics. A model is presented incorporating drug testing into the overall realm of human resource functions, and data from a research project involving a diverse sample of work sites in the state of Georgia are presented to illustrate further the role of drug testing in human resource management. In particular, the beliefs and attitudes of human resource managers toward drug testing as a human resource tool and the prevalence and form of drug testing over the variety of work-site types represented in the sample will be discussed. In addition, rates of positive drug tests are presented for the various types of testing programs present at these work sites.

TERRY C. BLUM, DAIL L. FIELDS, STUART H. MILNE, and CHESTER S. SPELL • School of Management, Georgia Institute of Technology, Atlanta, Georgia 30332. The order of authorship is alphabetical. The authors would like to acknowledge support from Grants R01-AA-07192 from the National Institute on Alcohol Abuse and Alcoholism and R01-DA-07417 from the National Institute of Drug Abuse. The authors also wish to thank James Rawson for his contribution in analysis of data.

Research Advances in Alcohol and Drug Problems, Volume 11: Drug Testing in the Workplace, edited by Scott Macdonald and Paul M. Roman. Plenum Press, New York, 1994.

1. THE HUMAN RESOURCE MANAGEMENT SYSTEM

Figure 1 is drawn from Blum (1989) and illustrates how the components of the human resource system interact with both the external environment and the objectives of an organization to reduce uncertainties about the firm's human resources. Drug testing enters into this diagram primarily in the staffing and performance management areas, but has implications for other human resource management functions as well.

Organizations decide to adopt drug testing programs for a variety of reasons. One may be to prevent entry of current drug users into the organization, leading to preemployment drug screening for all job types. Drug testing of employees involved in work-related accidents or suspected of drug use by their supervisor may be implemented in an attempt to discourage drug use that could increase the chances of personal injuries or property losses. Testing employees at random may also be implemented to achieve safety-related goals, but it is more likely to be mandated for safety-sensitive jobs by the U.S. Department of Transportation, other government agencies, customers, or insurers. In addition, drug testing may be implemented by some organizations to discourage employee drug use in hopes of reducing expensive health care risks, based on the underlying assumption that drug-free individuals are generally healthier than drug users.

Each type of drug testing program, regardless of original intent, potentially affects other parts of the human resource function of the firm. Preemployment screening influences employee selection and staffing and therefore enters into the human resource model (see Figure 1) in that area. Preemployment drug testing may be viewed as a method by which the firm can limit the likelihood that new employees will exhibit problems related to substance abuse that may seriously affect their on-the-job performance. Preemployment drug testing may also be viewed by management as sending a message to existing employees that the company is serious about its drug policies and is concerned with their safety and welfare by assuring that new employees are not using drugs. It may also be used by the organization as a sign to employees that the firm is actively attempting to contain health care costs and to maintain benefits. Drug testing of job applicants may be viewed by both management and workers as emphatic enforcement of stated policies against drug use at the work site and evidence of the firm's commitment to take actions that reduce the impact of employee drug use and abuse.

A significant question raised by preemployment drug screening is how it affects the types of workers available and selected for hire. In other words, does such screening limit a firm's ability to attract candidates with skills critical to its long term success? Because employees using drugs are generally assumed to be performing below acceptable levels, employee drug testing performed on a reasonable-suspicion or random basis is associated primarily with the perfor-

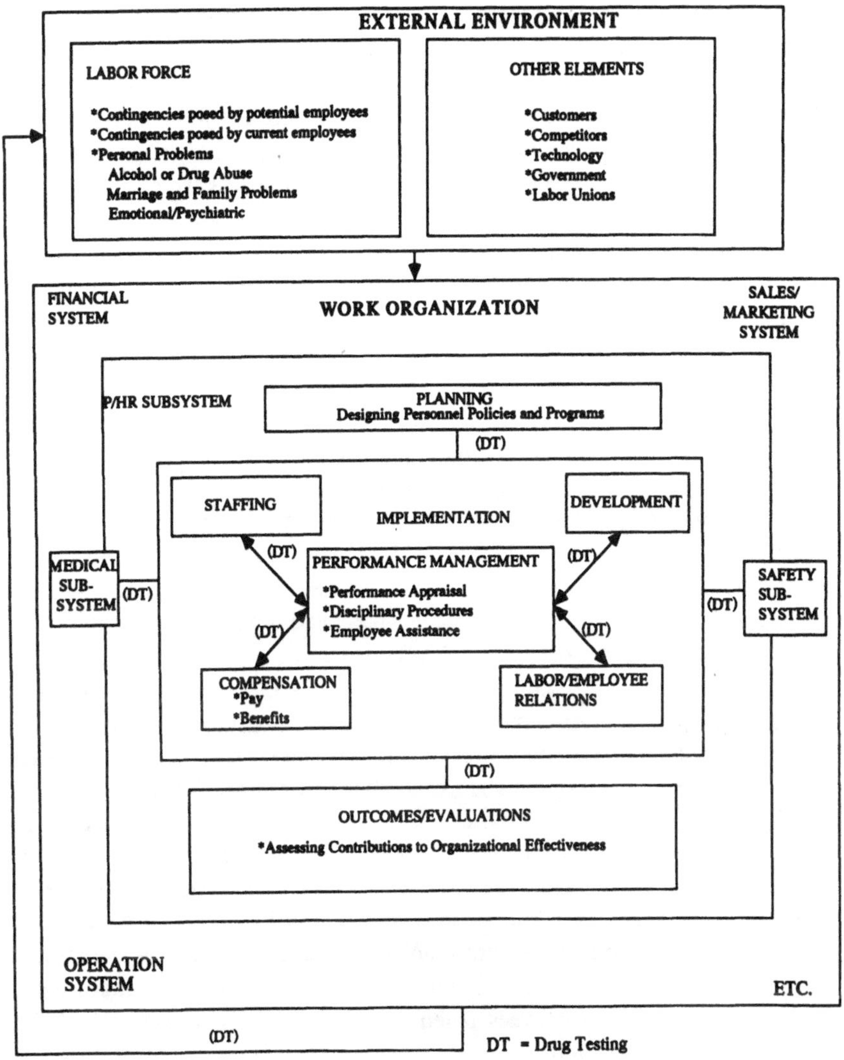

Figure 1. Personnel/Human Resource System.

mance management practices of a firm and thus enters the human resource model (Figure 1) in that area. In addition, drug testing current employees requires the firm to address its handling of employees identified as having used drugs: Does a positive test result in termination, disciplinary actions, or rehabilitation?

A key point in an organization's drug testing program is the position it occupies vis-à-vis other staffing and performance management functions. Is the drug testing a stand-alone function, primarily used to exclude individuals from the work force and/or terminate current employees who test positive, or is it integrated with an employee assistance program (EAP), insurance coverage for rehabilitation, or employee health promotion or prevention programs designed to discourage drug abuse? Employers who implement employee drug testing without provision for rehabilitation may use it as a shortcut for identifying and eliminating undesirable workers. Eliminating applicants who test positive may be a substitute for other procedures firms could use to assess the character of an employee (background checks, police records, references, etc.).

Preemployment drug testing as a stand-alone practice may only affect the supply of available new workers to the company if the firm adopts the practice of never hiring those who fail drug tests. Such testing, when integrated with other forms of suitability testing for applicants including skill tests, background checks, and/or psychological tests, may provide another indicator of prospective employee success in the firm. In addition, whether the firm drug screens applicants for all positions may affect the importance attached to drug policies and practices by employees and by the public in general.

The combination of employee drug testing with a consistently enforced policy covering work-site drug use, an EAP to help those testing positive receive counseling and rehabilitation, and affordable health care benefits that cover alcohol and drug treatment represents an integrated approach that uses related programs to help supervisors and employees deal more effectively with employee drug use problems. These comprehensive programs might also be linked with health promotion programs, substance abuse prevention programs, and testing for alcohol use in critical safety situations to form an even more comprehensive plan. These integrated programs are generally aimed at employee conservation and development, as well as more immediate substance abuse prevention goals.

Testing employees for drug use as a stand-alone practice, however, is essentially a program of employee surveillance and discipline. This approach may have negative effects on employee morale, because it appears to be simply a method for the firm to identify undesirables among present workers and remove them from the organization. Aside from the potential impact on morale, stand-alone drug testing of employees potentially removes experienced and skilled workers from the work force.

In particular, as Figure 1 illustrates, EAPs combined with drug screening programs may be useful vehicles for helping supervisors or managers effectively and efficiently detect employee problems that hamper work performance and obtain services that are helpful in resolving them. In this role, EAPs may limit the supervisory time consumed by such problems, reduce the effect of one employee's problems on other workers, and help protect the firm's investment in employee training and company-specific skill development. EAPs also may be viewed as a symbol that the firm is concerned about the welfare of employees and is willing to provide some measure of help to workers whose personal or family difficulties begin to affect their jobs.

2. RESEARCH RESULTS FROM A SURVEY OF WORK SITES

As part of a study involving human resource managers at a sample of work sites in Georgia, data were collected in 1988 and 1991 concerning work-site demographics, employee benefit programs, and personnel practices, including aspects of any drug testing programs at the work site. Two hundred ninety-seven work sites, each with more than 250 employees, agreed to participate in 1988. Although all the sites were in Georgia, the sample was a diverse one, with all of the major industrial classes found in the Standard Industrial Classification (SIC) codes represented. Of the sites, 150 (53%) were involved in manufacturing; 14 (6%) were involved in wholesale or retail trade; 23 (8%) were involved in the financial, insurance, or real estate industries; and 14 (5%) were hospitals. The remaining sites (28%) were involved in either agriculture, mining, construction, or transportation.

Face-to-face structured interviews were conducted with the highest-ranking human resource manager at each work site in 1988 and again in 1991. At the time of each interview, the respondent was also asked to complete a questionnaire and return it to the researchers by mail. The response rate to the questionnaire was 82% in 1988 and 83% in 1991. The sample size in 1991 was reduced to 279 worksites; 11 sites had closed in the period since the first interview, and 7 sites refused to participate in the second round of data collection.

Human Resource Managers' Beliefs and Attitudes Concerning Drug Testing

Incorporated into the questionnaire in both 1988 and 1991 were 15 items designed to assess the respondents' perceptions of various issues concerning the efficacy, efficiency, and legitimacy of drug testing as a human resource practice. All respondents were asked to respond to these items regardless of whether drug testing was present at their work site at the time of the survey. The items were presented in a 5-point Likert scale format ranging from "strongly disagree" to "strongly agree." Although not identified as such on the survey instrument, the items were generally representative of four major areas of issues related to drug testing: (a) effects of drug testing on the workplace and work processes (4 items), (b) employee relations and the direct effects of drug testing on employees (4 items), (c) the practice of drug testing itself (4 items); and (d) drug testing and broader societal concerns (3 items). For the purposes of this chapter, the responses are presented grouped according to these issues and compared, first, for the overall sample in 1988 and 1991; second, for those work sites doing no drug testing, preemployment testing only, current employee testing only, and tests of both applicants and employees in 1991; and third, for those work sites that had either preemployment or employee drug testing *and* an EAP in 1991, and those who had such testing *without* an EAP in 1991. These comparative results are summarized in Table 1, with responses presented as the percentage of respondents in each category who indicated agreement or strong agreement with each item (4 or 5 on the response scale). The results are also discussed further below.

Drug Testing Beliefs and Attitudes: Overall Sample, 1988 to 1991. A comparison of data collected in 1988 and 1991 shows a definite movement toward more favorable attitudes among human resource managers relative to drug testing. Respondents in both years were very positive about the effectiveness they perceived drug testing to have on workplace safety, and somewhat neutral about its effect on productivity or morale. Relatively strong disagreement was expressed in both years to the suggestion that drug testing may not be necessary. With the exception of the issue of drug testing and productivity, these results show a significant mean shift toward more favorable positions relative to drug testing from 1988 to 1991.

Turning to issues of employee relations and drug testing, one continues to see this positive trend. In both years human resource managers appeared convinced that drug testing presented little threat to individual privacy, but significantly more so in 1991 than 1988. They also were significantly more likely in 1991 to see drug testing as a benefit to employees who do not use drugs and not to see it as a potential demoralizing agent. On the issue of drug testing actually helping drug users, opinion remained relatively neutral between these years.

On issues related to the drug testing process itself, the trend toward more positive attitudes expressed by respondents in the later survey is also evident. Respondents in both years appeared convinced that drug testing was not inaccurate, too costly, or opposed by management, and in 1991 were also significantly less likely to see it as potentially inaccurate. Regarding the presence of employee opposition to drug testing at the work site, the 1991 responses were significantly less in agreement with this statement than were those of 1988. The responses for 1991 did indicate, however, that 29% of the human resource managers still believed that employees were opposed to drug testing at their worksites, possibly indicating less positive sentiments than the trend data alone.

Only in the area of drug testing and general societal issues was the positive trend between these years not evidenced. Between 1988 and 1991, responses on issues regarding drug testing and public safety, as well as drug testing and public trust, did not change significantly, and responses on the issue of such testing aiding national security actually showed a significant negative shift. Overall, the responses on these items in both years appear to indicate that respondents were essentially undecided on these issues.

The implications of these results are several. First, drug testing is apparently becoming perceived as a more acceptable, legitimate, and worthwhile workplace practice, and increasing exposure to and experience with drug testing is not diminishing this. Second, drug testing is increasingly being viewed as not detrimental to employees and indeed often as beneficial, rather than as a "necessary evil" that organizations are forced to adopt. Third, drug testing is increasingly being seen as a workplace rather than a societal issue, which would support the concept of the integration of drug testing into the total human resource structure (as proposed in this chapter).

Beliefs and Attitudes by Drug Testing Type Present: 1991. An interesting pattern is revealed when the responses are examined based on type of drug testing present at the work site. As might be expected, those who do no drug testing have the least favorable attitudes toward such testing. Those who test employees only, however, generally did not differ significantly in their responses from the nontesters, whereas those who tested only applicants or both applicants and employees fell together as significantly more positive toward drug testing than the other two groups. It would seem that those who test applicants find drug testing most palatable and easily embraced, whereas those who test employees only may view the process more as a necessary control procedure or legal requirement. This could indicate that many organizations do indeed view preemployment testing as a panacea for their perceived drug-related problems; considering the difference in responsibility an organization faces when dealing with an applicant as opposed to a current employee, this is a possibility that those concerned with the broader societal impact of these policies might find troubling.

Beliefs and Attitudes by EAP Presence: 1991. Comparisons of those sites that tested for drugs and supported an EAP in 1991 to those sites with testing that did not support an EAP at that time seem to support further the presence of a quick-fix notion of drug testing. Those sites that did not support an EAP were significantly more likely to view drug testing favorably in virtually all of the areas related to the workplace and employee relations, whereas little difference was shown between the site groups in the areas of drug testing processes or societal issues. The non-EAP sites seemed to view drug testing as a far more comprehensive and efficacious practice vis-à-vis human resource management than the EAP sites, further supporting the notion that stand-alone drug testing may be perceived as a technological short cut to solving drug-related problems and as a substitute for a comprehensive approach to substance abuse in the workplace.

Drug Testing Practices: 1988–1991

In 1988, 177 (60%) of the 297 work sites in the sample were involved in drug testing for employees, applicants, or both; by 1991, 214 (78%) of the 279 work sites remaining in the sample were involved. Fifty-two sites either initiated or expanded their drug testing programs between the 1988 and 1991 visits, whereas only 6 discontinued some form of drug testing during this period (4 were preemployment screening programs, and 2 were programs testing employees

Table 1
Comparisons of Human Resource Managers' Attitudes and Beliefs Concerning Drug Testing by Year, Type of Testing Present, and EAP Presence

	Percentage of Respondents Agreeing or Strongly Agreeing							
	1988[a] (n = 233)	1991[a] (n = 226)	No DT[b] (n = 50)	App[b] (n = 29)	Emp[b] (n = 17)	Both[b] (n = 130)	EAP[c] (n = 110)	No EAP[c] (n = 66)
Workplace issues:								
DT is an effective means of dealing with safety.	**70**	**77**	**58**	**79**	**76**	**84**	**79**	**88**
DT is an effective means of dealing with productivity.	47	47	42	52	41	48	**43**	**58**
DT is an effective means of dealing with morale.	**30**	**34**	**20**	**38**	**29**	**40**	**32**	**50**
DT is not necessary.	**16**	**8**	**14**	**14**	**6**	**5**	**10**	**2**
Employee relations issues:								
DT is an invasion of privacy.	**21**	**11**	**18**	**10**	**12**	**8**	10	6
DT is a benefit to employees who do *not* use drugs.	**59**	**66**	**44**	**69**	**47**	**77**	**67**	**82**

DT provides help to employees who *do* use drugs.	59	59	**42**	**76**	**41**	**65**	68	58
DT has a potentially negative impact on morale.	**48**	**34**	**50**	31	**47**	**26**	**34**	**20**
Drug testing process issues:								
DT is inaccurate.	**20**	**12**	**12**	**10**	**18**	**11**	11	12
DT is too costly.	22	17	**24**	**17**	**29**	**13**	16	14
DT is opposed by management.	16	11	**20**	**17**	**23**	**5**	**12**	**4**
DT is opposed by employees.	**44**	**29**	**38**	**34**	**53**	**22**	**34**	**15**
Societal issues:								
DT is an effective means of dealing with public safety.	66	57	52	59	59	59	55	65
DT is an effective means of public trust.	31	38	26	48	29	40	**37**	**49**
DT is an effective means of dealing with national security.	**52**	**36**	28	45	18	39	34	45

[a]Comparison of responses 1988 to 1991.
[b]Comparison of 1991 responses from worksites with no drug testing, testing of applicants only, testing of present employees only, and testing of both applicants and employees.
[c]Comparison of 1991 responses from worksites with drug testing and an EAP, and testing without an EAP.
Note: Figures in boldface type represent response differences that are statistically significant at the 0.05 level.

"for reasonable cause"). When respondents were able to give specific reasons for the discontinuation of these programs, cost and the logistic hassle of administering them were most often cited.

All of the work sites testing employees and applicants in 1991 indicated an intention to continue these programs into the foreseeable future. Of those sites not testing applicants in 1991, 32% indicated a reasonable likelihood of beginning such a program within the next year, whereas 42% of those not testing current employees for reasonable cause indicated this probability. The trends reflected in these data would appear to run counter to a recent Bureau of Labor Statistics report that indicated a general stability, and in some areas a decline, in the number of drug testing programs (Hayghe, 1991).

Random Drug Testing: 1991

Because random drug testing is largely confined to particular segments of the work force at a relatively small proportion of work sites in this sample, it is discussed separately in this section but will be combined with other types of employee testing in the remainder of this chapter. The results of the study seem to indicate that of the possible types of drug testing options available to work sites, the random testing of current employees has enjoyed the least popularity and generated the greatest concern. None of the 214 work sites with testing were involved in random testing alone, and only 48 (17%) included it as part of a larger drug testing effort. Sites with random drug testing were somewhat more likely to be in rural locations (36%) than the sample as a whole (31%), and they were heavily concentrated in manufacturing (47%) and transportation (11%). They were only slightly less likely to have a union presence (23%) than the general sample (26%). Approximately 80% of the random testing programs were initiated after 1988. Fifty-eight percent of the work sites indicated that not all positions were subject to random testing, and 62% of those worksites indicated that only positions under legal mandate were subject to random testing. Where legal constraints were not an issue, clerical, managerial, and non-safety-sensitive positions were most often cited as exempt from random testing.

Although 95% of the respondents at work sites engaged in random drug testing reported there were benefits associated with such testing, 34% also believed there were serious problems with it. Benefits cited were reduction of the drug problem (53%), improved employee morale (97%), improved safety (40%), and a general positive effect on the worksite (32%). Problems cited were ethical issues (100%) and employee opposition (44%).* Overall, however, 98% of the respondents at work sites involved in random testing believed its benefits out-

*Citing more than one benefit or problem was possible, so percentages total to more than 100%.

weighed its problems, and 96% of them indicated a high likelihood of this practice continuing at that site into the foreseeable future.

The consequence to an employee of a positive random drug test result was reported as immediate termination at 35% of the work sites, progressive discipline at 7%, and counseling at 37%; the remainder of the sites indicated each case would be handled in an individual manner. Considering the potential ramifications of random drug testing to both the employee and the organization, it is interesting that only 90% of the random drug testing sites indicated that a positive test result would be confirmed, and of this group only 94% indicated that it would be done by an alternative methodology. The extent of implementation and actual impact of these programs is also of interest: 11 (28%) of these work sites had performed no random tests in the past year, and the median number of tests actually performed was 50. Of the sites doing random testing, 60% tested fewer than 10% of the employees at the site in the year prior to the interview, whereas 23% tested between 10% and 25% of the employees, and 16% tested more than 50% of the employees. Of those sites actually performing tests, 47% had no positive results; the median percentage of positives was 2% of those tested.

Given that 83% of the work sites in this study were not involved in random testing, whereas 77% of the sites were involved in some other form of drug testing, the reasons for not doing random drug testing would seem particularly significant. Reasons given for not engaging in random testing included cost (7%), legal concerns (43%), ethical concerns (19%), perceived employee opposition (11%) lack of perceived need (29%), and inconsistency with corporate culture or general policy (9%).* Of the work sites in the sample with a union presence that did not engage in random drug testing, 33% cited reported union opposition as a reason for not doing so.

Finally, respondents at 83% of the sites not engaging in random testing projected little or no likelihood of this practice being initiated in the near future. Clearly, in this sample at the time of the interview, random drug testing had not achieved the degree of diffusion or general acceptance that other forms of drug testing had attained.

Extent of Drug Testing Programs: 1991

More than three fourths (77%) of the 279 worksites in our sample had some type of drug testing program in place in 1991. These proportions differ substantially from the survey results reported by Guthrie and Olian (1991), who found that only 48% of their respondents had drug testing programs in place. The fact that all of the locations in the present sample are larger employers—and that many are plant or branch locations of very large (Fortune 500) companies—may

*Again more than one response was possible, so percentages total to more than 100%.

partially explain this difference, because larger organizations may be more likely than smaller ones to have resources available to conduct drug testing programs. Larger firms are also more visible than smaller employers and therefore more likely to be subject to institutional pressures to implement such programs as drug testing (Meyer & Rowan, 1991; Pfeffer & Salancik, 1978). Fifty-six percent of the sites in our sample tested both job applicants and employees, 7% tested employees only, and 14% performed preemployment testing only. The 214 work sites with testing in this sample reported performing a total of 29,206 preemployment drug tests, as well as 3,739 random and 2,821 for-cause tests during the year preceding the 1991 interview.

Most (94%) of the sites in the sample that performed preemployment drug tests reported that they tested applicants for all jobs. The most frequently reported reason for excluding positions from preemployment testing was that the job was not safety sensitive. Likewise, 91% of the sites conducting for-cause tests of employees reported that all jobs were covered. The most common reason that jobs were excluded from for-cause programs was that testing was not mandated by law or regulation for the position.

Almost half (42%) of the sites in the sample reported conducting 50 or fewer preemployment tests in the year prior to our interview; 40% reported doing between 50 and 250 tests, and 18% reported 250 or more preemployment tests in that year. Most (94%) of those sites doing for-cause tests of employees tested fewer than 10% of the employees at the work site in the year prior to our interview. Forty-two percent of the sites doing preemployment tests reported that applicants who tested positive were never hired, whereas the others would consider applicants who tested positive but reapplied after a period of time (the median waiting period for reapplication was 6 months). More than a third (35%) of the sites interviewed reported that implementing preemployment drug testing had reduced the number of job applicants; however, 93% of these sites did not believe that preemployment drug testing had hurt their ability to fill vacant positions.

Sixty-one percent of the sites doing preemployment testing reported paying an average of $30 or less per test; 27% reported an average cost per test between $30 and $50, and 12% reported an average cost per test exceeding $50. The cost per test was not, however, associated with differences in preemployment drug testing practices (e.g., testing only applicants for selected jobs).

Reasons Sites Do Not Test

Based on responses from 80 of the 85 sites that did not conduct preemployment drug screening programs, the three most prevalent reasons for not testing applicants were as follows:

- Lack of need (44%)
- Costs (28%)
- Legal concerns (19%)

Information from 101 of the 103 sites that did not do for-cause drug testing of current employees indicated that the following were the major reasons for their policies:

- Lack of need (42%)
- Legal concerns (30%)
- Union opposition (16%)

Of the sites that did not currently perform preemployment tests, 65% indicated that the chances were low or nonexistent that they would begin such testing during the next year. Conversely, 22% stated that the chances of beginning preemployment testing in the next year were high, and the remainder reported some chance of starting such testing. Similarly, 21% of the sites not performing for-cause drug tests of employees indicated that the likelihood was high they would begin in the next year, whereas 38% reported some chance they would start such testing; 41% did not plan to initiate such a program in the next year.

Drug Testing and Other Human Resource Practices

Ninety-six percent of all the work sites in our sample reported having in place a formal policy prohibiting drug use and possession at the work site by employees. Most (69%) of the human resource managers in the sample reported that this drug policy was always enforced, whereas 27% reported that their policy is usually enforced. More than half of the sites interviewed either refer employees who violate the drug policy to counseling or rehabilitation (30%) or report that drug policy violations by employees are handled on a case-by-case basis (27%); however, 29% terminate drug policy violators.

Human resource managers were asked during interviews to rate the impact of employee drug abuse on the work site. Only 4% of the 279 sites reported a major drug problem. These sites were significantly more likely than the overall sample to have a testing program, as well as to test both applications and current employees. Similarly, the work sites that described their drug problem as moderate (26%) were also more likely to test for drugs. The sites that reported that employee drug use had no impact on the worksite (12%) were less likely to test employees; however, they were as likely as the overall sample to utilize preemployment drug testing.

These results seem to suggest that human resource managers view drug testing as an effective tool in discouraging existing drug use among employees, as well as a defense against hiring people who may introduce drug problems into the workplace. Comparison of drug problem ratings collected in 1991 with those provided in 1988 also supports this view. Specifically, 30% of the sites in the sample reported that employee drug abuse was a greater problem in 1991 than in 1988. Thirty-five percent of these sites did no drug testing (compared to 23% in the sample overall), and they were much less likely to test employees than the rest of the sites. Conversely, those sites that reported a diminished employee drug abuse problem in 1991 (32%) were much more likely to have a drug testing program, and they were more likely than the overall sample to use both pre-employment and employee testing.

Respondents were also asked to describe whether alcohol or drug abuse presented a more severe problem for the work site to address. Only 28 sites (10%) reported neither to be a significant problem. Drug testing of applicants or employees was much less likely at these sites. Thirty-one percent of the respondents reported that alcohol was a greater problem for the work site than drugs; these locations were less likely to use preemployment testing but were more likely to have a program for testing employees only. The sites where drugs were reported as a more severe problem than alcohol (43%) were more likely to have a drug testing program in place, and to conduct preemployment tests, than the sample as a whole.

More than half of the respondents in the sample (51%) reported that their work site required employees to be tested if they were suspected of inebriation on the job. Almost all of these sites (92%) also had some type of employee drug testing program in place. In contrast, only 32% of the sites reporting that they did not use for-cause alcohol testing of employees had an employee drug testing program in place.

Twenty-two percent of the respondents interviewed in 1991 reported that some form of surveillance was used at their work site to detect employee drug or alcohol use or possession. In addition, 25% of the respondents reported that employee property had been searched to detect drugs or alcohol. The drug testing practices of those using surveillance were not significantly different from those of the overall sample. The sites where searches were performed were significantly more likely than the other sites to do drug testing of any type, and they were also more likely to test employees.

Almost two thirds (61%) of the sites in our sample reported having an employee assistance program (EAP) in operation at the time of the interview. The sites without an EAP were less likely than the others to have a drug testing program of any type in place, and they were much less likely than the overall sample to perform employee drug tests. This may reflect a recognition that stand-alone drug testing (without integration with other programs for employee well-being) may have negative consequences on the supply of qualified human resources. This perspective is supported by the 66% of our sample that performed employee drug testing and also reported having an EAP. Further, the 98 sites

(33%) that did not support health promotion activities were significantly less likely than the others to have any type of drug testing program in place.

Most of the sites (82%) with EAPs reported that fewer than 10% of the employees had used the EAP for any reason in the year prior to the interview. An additional 15% of the respondents reported that between 10% and 25% of the employees at their work site had used the EAP during the same period. Sites in each category of EAP use did not differ significantly from the overall sample in their drug testing practices.

Virtually all of the work sites in our sample offered at least some health benefits to their employees. As was expected, the quality and coverage of benefits and the cost to the employees varied greatly. Whereas 54% of the sites in the sample reported that employee insurance costs for individual coverage averaged $20 or less per month, 7% of the sites reported employee costs for individual coverage exceeding $50 per month. There were no significant differences in drug testing practices among sites with different levels of employee premiums for individual coverage. The 119 sites (41%) in the sample where family coverage premiums for employees were less than $50 per month, however, were more likely to have both preemployment and employee drug testing programs. Conversely, sites where employee premiums for family insurance coverage exceeded $100 per month were less likely than the overall sample to do drug testing at all and also less likely to use preemployment and employee testing. The willingness of employers with lower insurance cost to employees to use both preemployment and employee drug testing may reflect a belief that drug testing helps avoid excessive health benefit utilization by drug users and therefore helps maintain the relatively favorable premium rates.

Drug Testing and Work Site Characteristics

The extent to which sites with differing organizational characteristics (e.g., industry type, number of employees, location) conducted no drug testing at all, did preemployment screening only, tested employees only, or tested both applicants and employees was examined. The type of drug testing programs used at work sites with differing characteristics is shown in Table 2. This table also reports the average percentage of applicants and employees who had positive results for each type of testing program.*

The average proportion of positives reported for all preemployment test programs was 6%. For random and for-cause drug testing, the average percentage of positives reported should be interpreted cautiously, because the distribu-

*The positive test rates are probably attributable to a combination of drug testing practices, organizational characteristics, and employee drug use. The relative impact of each of these factors is not known; however, these rates of positives should be interpreted cautiously and not be used alone as proxies for the prevalence of drug use among applicants and employees of these firms.

Table 2
Differences in Drug Testing by Work Site Characteristics, 1991

	No test (n = 65)	Appl (n = 38)	Emp (n = 20)	Both (n = 156)	Mean % Positive Applicant Test		Mean % Positive Random		Mean % Positive For Cause	
	%	%	%	%	n	%	n	%	n	%
Manufacturing	**12.0**	**13.2**	**6.0**	**68.9**	125	6.23	17	3.24	92	38.81
Nonmanufacturing	**40.2**	**14.3**	**8.9**	**36.6**	46	4.67	17	1.88	31	27.10
Union	**11.3**	**12.7**	**4.2**	**71.8**	56	**7.45**	5	0.80	36	**50.31**
Nonunion	**27.4**	**13.9**	**8.2**	**50.5**	115	**5.02**	29	2.86	87	**29.89**
0–249 employees	**36.4**	**21.2**	**6.1**	**36.4**	17	**3.47**	1	0.00	9	44.44
250–499 employees	**26.7**	**13.9**	**4.0**	**55.4**	61	**5.46**	18	2.39	42	29.71
500–999 employees	**24.4**	**9.3**	**9.3**	**57.0**	48	**8.13**	7	2.14	41	30.61
1000 or more employees	**8.5**	**15.3**	**10.2**	**66.1**	45	**4.71**	8	3.63	31	48.65
Urban	**27.6**	**12.0**	**9.4**	**51.0**	105	6.28	20	2.95	80	35.40
Rural	**13.8**	**17.2**	**2.3**	**66.7**	66	5.08	14	2.00	43	36.72
Turnover < 10%	17.1	11.7	4.5	66.7	81	**4.86**	13	1.85	52	41.79
Turnover 10–25%	20.9	17.9	9.0	52.2	42	**5.24**	4	0.50	33	32.36
Turnover > 25%	31.7	12.9	8.9	46.5	48	**7.92**	17	3.56	38	30.79
Organizational Skill Shortage	23.5	12.6	4.9	59.0	119	6.35	26	2.77	82	39.52
No Organizational Shortage	22.3	16.0	10.6	51.1	52	4.58	8	1.88	40	29.20
Labor shortage	18.2	12.1	12.1	57.6	18	5.28	3	3.33	18	43.11
Adequate labor supply	21.8	12.0	4.2	62.0	95	5.22	21	3.86	64	39.88
Labor surplus	10.0	13.3	10.0	66.7	21	6.48	7	2.43	15	28.20
Staffing problem great	28.1	6.3	12.5	53.1	17	6.59	2	1.00	17	45.65
Staffing problem moderate	33.3	18.0	7.7	41.0	41	7.00	7	4.43	27	32.74
Staffing problem small	13.8	12.2	5.7	68.3	86	5.35	21	2.52	59	36.36

Nonwhite < 25%	27.7	18.1	1.1	53.2	60	5.22	13	1.77	34	33.56
Nonwhite 25–50%	22.7	11.8	7.6	58.0	75	5.65	14	1.79	57	35.47
Nonwhite > 50%	15.4	7.7	13.5	63.5	31	7.61	5	7.20	29	39.45
Women < 34%	5.3	13.3	1.3	80.0	65	6.23	11	2.45	44	35.68
Women 34–66%	24.4	12.2	4.9	58.5	76	6.01	18	2.89	54	35.61
Women > 66%	40.0	17.1	14.3	28.6	27	4.15	3	0.67	21	36.38
Avg. employee age < 30	37.5	16.7	4.2	41.7	26	7.73	4	0.00	17	22.47
Avg. employee age 30–39	23.3	10.0	8.7	58.0	94	5.53	24	3.24	70	34.51
Avg. employee age > 39	14.3	17.5	3.2	65.1	45	5.49	3	0.67	30	44.63
Avg. education < HS	**16.9**	**16.9**	**10.2**	**55.9**	38	7.74	4	**9.25**	30	30.53
Avg. education = HS/GED	**18.1**	**11.0**	**4.7**	**66.1**	90	5.90	20	**1.90**	67	34.99
Avg. education = some college	**34.4**	**12.5**	**6.3**	**46.9**	33	3.94	8	**1.50**	20	44.85
Avg. education = college	**50.0**	**11.1**	**16.7**	**22.2**	6	3.50	1	**0.00**	3	50.00
Avg. Salary < 15K	**34.9**	**6.3**	**14.3**	**44.4**	30	8.03	7	3.50	32	33.95
Avg. Salary 15–25K	**16.3**	**14.6**	**4.9**	**64.2**	86	5.22	16	3.06	56	44.67
Avg. Salary > 25K	**20.5**	**13.7**	**5.5**	**60.3**	51	5.88	10	1.60	33	41.06
Absenteeism Rate < 3%	**20.1**	**12.2**	**6.1**	**61.6**	109	5.95	20	2.70	84	36.96
Absenteeism Rate = 3–6%	**22.2**	**22.2**	**0.0**	**55.6**	18	5.28	2	3.00	6	29.67
Absenteeism Rate > 6%	**29.5**	**13.6**	**11.4**	**45.5**	44	5.70	12	2.25	33	34.18
Predominant tech = small batch	**33.3**	**18.5**	**7.4**	**40.7**	16	4.50	2	4.00	10	31.00
Predominant tech = mass batch	**9.9**	**11.9**	**5.9**	**72.3**	77	6.66	13	4.15	56	41.07
Predominant tech = continuous	**0.0**	**17.1**	**0.0**	**82.9**	31	6.52	2	0.50	22	40.41
Predominant tech = service	**39.7**	**12.9**	**10.3**	**37.1**	47	4.40	17	1.41	35	26.06
High-tech organization	25.9	12.7	7.8	53.6	100	5.10	14	3.14	66	**44.85**
Not high-tech organization	19.6	15.2	6.3	58.9	71	6.82	20	2.15	56	**25.46**
Employee Assistance Program	20.1	13.6	8.9	57.4	108	**4.79**	15	2.33	75	**41.91**
No Employee Assistance Program	28.2	13.6	4.5	53.6	63	**7.57**	19	2.74	48	**26.42**

Notes: No Test = no drug testing program; Appl = applicant drug testing only; Emp = employee drug testing only; Both = applicant and employee drug testing. Figures in bold type have a statistically significant difference between worksite characteristics at $p \leq .05$. Turnover and work-force data for nonmanagement employees only.

tions of reported positives for these tests were significantly skewed. For example, the distribution of positives reported by 34 sites conducting random tests included 24 sites with mean positive proportions of zero. Consequently, although the mean for random tests for the overall sample was 2.6%, the mean for those who reported a nonzero positive rate was 8.7%. The overall distribution of positive rates for the 123 sites that reported for-cause test results included 49 sites with zero positive rates for this type of drug test. The overall average positive rate for the entire sample was 35.9%, whereas the mean for those reporting a nonzero positive rate was 59.6%. Thirty-eight of the sites with nonzero positive rates had averages of 50% or less; 36 had average rates of 50% or more (including 27 sites that reported all their for-cause tests were positive). The overall rate of positive test results reported for the more than 29,000 preemployment tests conducted by the work locations in the sample in the year prior to the 1991 interview is consistent with the results observed in employment screening tests reported by Anglin and Westland (1989) but is lower than that reported by Hayghe (1991).

Sixty percent of the work sites in the 1991 sample were classified as manufacturing sites. These include locations performing manufacturing of durable and/or nondurable goods, mining, forestry, agriculture, and construction. Sites classified as nonmanufacturing included those providing business or personal services (e.g., insurance, transportation, and communications). The drug testing practices reported by manufacturing sites were substantially different from those of non-manufacturing sites.* Specifically, manufacturing sites were much more likely that nonmanufacturing sites to have some type of drug testing program in place. Only 12% of the manufacturing sites reported doing no drug testing, compared to 40% of the nonmanufacturing sites. Manufacturing sites are also significantly more likely to use both preemployment and employee testing than nonmanufacturing sites. This finding is in conflict with survey results reported by the American Management Association (Greenberg, 1990) which found nonmanufacturing sites to be more likely to test employees.

Unionized work sites in this sample were significantly more likely to have some type of drug testing in place than nonunionized sites. Drug testing at unionized work sites also was more likely to cover both applicants and employees and significantly less likely to cover only employees. This result may reflect union efforts to assure that if drug testing is done, it covers not only current workers (who are union members) but also prospective hires. The average rate of positive results for preemployment tests and of for-cause employee tests reported by unionized work sites are both significantly higher than the comparable rates

*Statistical significance of the differences among firms reported is based on a chi-square test applied to tables cross-referencing firm characteristics with types of drug testing. Differences reported are significant at $p < .05$.

for nonunion sites. The difference in the for-cause positive rate may reflect management's reaction to union pressures that employees be subjected to drug tests only in those cases where there is obvious impairment. If this is the case, however, the 50% positive rate of for-cause drug tests again suggests that supervisory estimations of probable drug use are relatively inaccurate.

Consistent with other reported findings (Greenberg, 1990; Hayghe, 1991), smaller work sites are less likely to have drug testing programs in place than are larger sites. Specifically, of the 33 sites in our sample who had fewer than 250 employees in 1991, 36% reported no drug testing implemented for applicants or employees.* Conversely, only 8.5% of the sites with more than 1,000 employees reported no drug testing program in place. Smaller work sites that had a drug testing program were more likely to undertake preemployment testing only, whereas the larger sites were significantly more likely to test both job applicants and employees. The positive test rates for the smallest (fewer than 250 employees) and largest sites (more than 1,000 employees) were somewhat above the overall mean rate of positives found in for-cause tests of employees; only the rate for the largest sites was statistically different ($t = 1.66$; $p = .05$). This suggests that these sites are more cautious in selecting employees to be subjected to for-cause drug testing. For instance, smaller companies may be motivated to limit such tests as a result of costs and reliance on crucial employees. Larger sites may cautiously implement for-cause tests of employees to minimize threat of legal action and/or negative publicity.

More than two thirds (69%) of the 279 worksites in the sample were located in urban settings. A location was considered urban if it was part of a Standard Metropolitan Statistical Area (SMSA). Approximately 50% of the sample was located in the Atlanta SMSA, whereas the balance of the urban sites were within the other Georgia SMSAs (which include Athens, Albany, Columbus, Macon, Savannah, Augusta, and the Georgia portion of the Chattanooga, Tennessee, SMSA). Sites located in rural areas were significantly more likely than those in urban areas to have some type of drug testing program in place. Work sites in rural areas were also much more likely than urban sites to undertake both preemployment and employee testing. A work site with 250 or more employees in a rural setting is likely to be a dominant employer in the local labor market, offering relatively attractive benefits and pay rates. Consequently, drug testing may be implemented more extensively by these sites because they are less concerned with these practices limiting or reducing their labor supply than are locations in urban areas (where there are more employers competing for labor).

As shown in Table 2, work locations in the sample were also classified according to (a) their turnover rates and whether they reported (b) shortages of

*Although all of the firms initially selected for this study had 250 or more employees in 1988, some had reduced their employment level below 250 at the time of our second interview in 1991.

skilled employees, (c) an overall shortage in labor supply, and (d) problems in satisfying staffing needs. The only labor-related characteristic approaching statistical significance ($p = .06$) in relation to differences in drug testing practices, however, was the level of turnover among nonmanagement personnel. Specifically, 36% of the work sites in the sample reported nonmanagement turnover exceeding 25% per year, 24% reported turnover between 10% and 25%, and 40% reported annual turnover under 10%. Sites that reported annual nonmanagement turnover rates of 25% or more were significantly less likely to have some type of drug testing program in place. Sites in the low turnover group were significantly more likely to test both employees and applicants, and they were less likely to test employees only. The high turnover site were much less likely than others in the sample to use both preemployment and employee testing, whereas the sites with 10% to 25% turnover were somewhat more likely to undertake preemployment drug testing only. Sites with nonmanagement turnover exceeding 25% had significantly higher positive rates for applicant tests than the rate for other sites. As suggested by Zwerling, Ryan, and Orav (1990), the positive association of turnover with positive drug tests may indicate that these sites do not offer very attractive jobs and consequently are dealing with more job applicants who are more likely to have multiple employability problems.

As Table 2 also shows, 66% of the sites indicated that they were having trouble finding qualified workers for some skilled jobs. There are no significant differences in drug testing programs, however, between the sites reporting specific skill shortages and those without such shortages. In addition, only 16% of the sites in the study indicated that they were experiencing an overall labor shortage. Again, there was no statistically significant relationship between drug testing practices and labor supply. There was also no significant relationship between drug testing practices and extent of staffing problems.

The race and gender composition of a site's work force was associated with a significant difference in the drug testing programs present. For example, the 20% of the work sites in our sample that had more than 50% nonwhite employees in nonmanagement positions were more likely to support drug testing of some kind. These work sites were also more likely to test both applicants and employees, whereas those sites with fewer than 25% nonwhite employees (36% of the sample) were more likely to test only job applicants. The rates of positive test results on both employee and preemployment tests, however, were not related to proportions of nonwhite employees.

The greater the proportion of females in a site's nonmanagement work force, the less likely that drug testing was done. Specifically, 26% of the sites in our sample reported that their nonmanagement work force contained more than 66% women; 40% of these sites had no drug testing program in place, compared to 23% for the overall sample. Conversely, of the work sites where females held one third or fewer of nonmanagement jobs, only 5% reported no drug testing program in place. These sites with one third or less female representation (28% of the sample) were also more likely to test both applicants and employees. By comparison, of the sites where females held two thirds or more of nonmanagement jobs, only 28% reported testing both applicants and employees. The positive drug test rates of applicants and employees at sites with differing proportions of women in the work force were not statistically different from the overall sample.

Both average age and education levels of a site's nonmanagement workers were also associated with the extent and type of drug testing. Sites with an average age for nonmanagement workers exceeding 40 (24%) were more likely to have some type of drug testing in place, and they were more likely to test both applicants and employees. Conversely, sites with a nonmanagement work force whose average age was less than 30 (18%) were more likely to do no drug testing, and less likely to do both preemployment and employee testing. Though these trends in drug testing practices are not consistent with Cook's findings (1989) that younger people are more likely to use drugs, it may reflect a tendency among older workers to endorse drug testing as a program that can improve on-the-job safety and help contain increases in employee insurance costs. There were no significant differences in positive test rates for applicants or employees between sites with differing average employee ages.

The greater the average education level of a firm's nonmanagement workers, the less likely that drug testing was done. Those sites with average nonmanagement education levels of some college (24%) and college or graduate degrees (7%) comprised half of the sites in the sample that did no drug testing at all. Those sites with the highest average education levels that did test, however, were more likely than the overall sample to test only employees. Those sites whose nonmanagement work force had an average education level of less than high school (22% of the sample) were more likely to test only applicants, whereas those with an average nonmanagement education level of high school/GED were more likely than the overall sample to test both applicants and employees. The rate of positive results for random tests of employees in sites with average education levels below high school were significantly higher than the comparable rates for sites with higher average education levels. This finding is also contrary to Cook's observation (1990) that marijuana and cocaine use was more prevalent among those employed in the skilled trades, whose average education level would exceed high school/GED.

Drug testing practices also varied among sites according to the average salary levels of nonmanagement positions. The 26% of the sites in our sample that reported average annual nonmanagement salaries of less than $15,000 were more likely to have no drug testing program in place and were less likely than the overall sample to undertake preemployment testing and to test both job applicants and employees. This group of sites, however, was more likely than the overall sample to test employees only. The sites that reported nonmanagement salaries averaging between $15,000 and $25,000 (47%) were more likely to have some type of drug testing program in place and were more likely than the overall sample to test both applicants and employees. The companies reporting average nonmanagement salaries above $25,000 per year showed no significant differences in their drug testing practices from the overall sample. The lack of drug testing programs among sites with lower average salary levels may reflect the difficulty of attracting and retaining employees at lower pay levels. The greater emphasis on drug testing among sites in the midrange group for average pay may simply reflect industry-specific factors: For example, manufacturing sites tend to have higher rates of nonmanagement pay and also tend to drug test more; transportation sites tend to have better-paying nonmanagement jobs, but more positions for which drug testing is mandated by government agencies.

Drug testing practices were also associated with the level of absenteeism among nonmanagement employees. Specifically, 57% of the sites in our sample reported absenteeism rates of 3% or less, 26% reported rates between 3% and 6%, and 17% of the sites reported absenteeism exceeding 6%. The sites with low absenteeism rates were more likely than the overall sample to do some type of drug testing, and they were more likely to use both preemployment and employee testing. The sites with higher absenteeism rates were significantly less likely to do any drug testing, and they were also less likely to test both applicants and employees. The sites with absenteeism rates above 3% were more likely to test only employees than were sites in the overall sample.

The predominant technology that a site uses also influences the extent and type of drug testing. The classification of work-site technology used here is based on Woodward's scheme (1965). Consistent with findings concerning industry type, sites where the predominant technology was providing a service (40%) were much less likely than the overall sample to drug test at all, and less likely to test both applicants and employees. Those sites using primarily continuous-process technology (e.g., mines or chemical refineries; 13% of our sample) all performed drug tests; more than 80% of these sites tested both applicants and employees. The manufacturing sites using primarily small-batch technology (e.g., custom engine repair or aircraft modification) were less likely to do any drug testing. These sites were also less likely than the overall sample to test both applicants and employees, but they were more likely to perform preemployment testing only. Sites using primarily mass-production technology (e.g., assembly lines) were more likely than the overall sample to do drug testing and to test both applicants and employees. There were, however, no significant differences in positive test rates for applicants or employees between groups of sites having different predominant technologies. In addition, there were no significant differences in drug testing practices between the sites in our sample that reported themselves as "high tech" (60%) and those sites that reported themselves as not "high tech."

Work sites with EAPs did not differ significantly from those without EAPs in terms of drug testing practices. Those sites with EAPs had lower positive rates of drug screens among their job applicants, perhaps indicating that these companies attract higher quality (non-drug-using) job applicants. Rates of positives for random testing did not differ between EAP and non-EAP work sites. Positive test rates were higher for for-cause drug testing among EAP work sites, which may indicate that supervisors are more willing to ask for a for-cause test when a referral to an alternative EAP is available, as opposed to only discipline or termination. The positive results for employee drug tests in these sites also suggests that preemployment-only screening will not totally prevent drug use among current employees and may yield a false sense of security for work sites.

3. CONCLUSION

The human resource management model presented in this chapter indicates that drug testing should be conceptualized as a strategy that must be integrated with other human resource management practices to be consistent with an organization's competitive needs and goals.

The data presented from our survey of work sites suggests that drug testing is gaining increasing acceptance by human resource managers. The types of strategies aimed at discouraging employee drug use, though, differ by some organizational characteristics. The data also imply that preemployment testing alone may provide an organization with a false sense of security regarding the elimination of drug users from the work site. In contrast, through practices such as education and well-designed EAPs, more comprehensive, integrated programs seem to offer organizations better ability to limit drug use among current employees, to reduce its effects on other employees, and to assure that the company retains the use of knowledgeable employees.

REFERENCES

Anglin, M. D., and Westland, C. A., 1989, Drug monitoring in the workplace: Results from the California Commercial Laboratory Drug Testing Project, in: *Drugs in the Workplace: Research and Evaluation Data* (S. W. Gust, and J. M. Walsh, eds.), pp. 81–96, NIDA Research Monograph 91, National Institute on Drug Abuse, Rockville, MD.

Blum, T. C., 1989, The presence and integration of drug abuse intervention in human resource management, in: *Drugs in the Workplace: Research and Evaluation Data,* NIDA Research

Monograph No. 91 (S. W. Gust and J. M. Walsh, eds.), pp. 245–270. National Institute on Drug Abuse, Rockville, MD.

Cook, R. F., 1989, Drug use among working adults: Prevalence rates and estimation methods, in: *Drugs in the Workplace: Research and Evaluation Data,* (S. W. Gust and J. M. Walsh, eds.), NIDA Research Monograph No. 91, pp. 17–32, National Institute on Drug Abuse, Rockville, MD.

Greenberg, E. R., 1990, Workplace testing: The 1990 AMA survey, part 2, *Personnel* **67**:26.

Guthrie, J. P., and Olian, J. D., 1991, Drug and alcohol testing programs: do firms consider their operating environment?, *Human Resource Planning* **14**:221.

Hayghe, H. V., 1990, 1988 Bureau of Labor Statistics' survey of employer anti-drug programs, in: *Drugs in the Workplace: Research and Evaluation Data,* Volume II (S. W. Gust, J. M. Walsh, L. B. Thomas, and D. J. Crouch, eds.), pp. 177–208, NIDA Research Monograph 100, National Institute on Drug Abuse, Rockville, MD.

Hayghe, H. V., 1991, Anti-drug programs in the workplace: Are they here to stay?, *Monthly Labor Review* **114**:26.

Kandel, D. B., and Yamaguchi, K., 1987. Job mobility and drug use: An event history analysis, *American Journal of Sociology* **92**(4):836.

Meyer, J. W. and Rowan, B., 1991, Institutionalized organizations: Formal structure as myth and ceremony, in: *The New Institutionalism in Organizational Analyses* (W. Powell and P. Dimaggio, eds.), University of Chicago Press, Chicago, IL.

Normand, J., and Salyards, S., 1989, An empirical evaluation of pre-employment drug testing in the United States Postal Service: Interim report of findings, in: *Drugs in the Workplace: Research and Evaluation Data* (S. W. Gust, and J. M. Walsh, eds.), pp. 111–138, NIDA Research Monograph 91, National Institute on Drug Abuse, Rockville, MD.

Normand, J., Salyards, S., and Mahoney, J. J., 1990, An evaluation of pre-employment drug testing, *Journal of Applied Psychology* **75**:629.

Pfeffer, J., and Sanacik, G., 1978, *The External Control of Organizations,* Harper and Row, New York.

Woodward, J., 1965, *Industrial Organizations: Theory and Practice,* Oxford, London.

Zwerling, C., Ryan, J., and Orav, E. J., 1992, Costs and benefits of pre-employment drug screening, *Journal of the American Medical Association* **267**:91.

II

PERSPECTIVES ON DRUG TESTING

14

Union Perspectives on Workplace Drug Testing

SHAHID ALVI

1. INTRODUCTION

This chapter examines the issue of drug testing from the perspective of organized labor. It aims to provide the reader with a sense of the civil liberties issues attending drug testing and the nature of organized labor's concerns regarding the validity and effectiveness of such testing. Although the chapter focuses mainly on the positions of Canadian unions and their leaders, the views of unions in the United States and other countries are included where possible.

In Canada, unions have not always agreed with management on ways of dealing with alcohol and drug abuse. Alcohol and drug abuse in the workplace was at one time treated as a pathological condition fostering punitive, judgmental, and often repressive ways of treating alcoholic workers. Testing was nonexistent because appropriate technologies did not exist. Today, the Canadian labor movement has largely rejected workplace drug testing in favor of employee education and broadbrush employee assistance programs as ways of counteracting the negative effects of substance abuse. Although some unions and professional associations are not completely uniform in their perspectives on workplace drug testing, the large "umbrella" unions (or labor centrals) that are the focus of

---

SHAHID ALVI • Conference Board of Canada, Ottawa, Ontario K1H 8M7, Canada. The opinions expressed in this paper are those of the author and do not necessarily reflect those of the Conference Board of Canada.

Research Advances in Alcohol and Drug Problems, Volume 11: Drug Testing in the Workplace, edited by Scott Macdonald and Paul M. Roman. Plenum Press, New York, 1994.

this chapter do share basic concerns regarding workplace drug testing.* The largest labor central, the Canadian Labor Congress (CLC), takes a comprehensively negative position on workplace drug testing. Some unions, however, do endorse drug screening under certain circumstances. In particular, in situations where personal and/or environmental safety is an issue, testing is endorsed as one way of guarding against possibly dangerous or life-threatening incidents.

The Canadian union movement is eclectic, and space limitations do not permit a detailed analysis of the subtle differences among various unions on screening for alcohol and drugs in the workplace. Because unions are diverse social organizations, this chapter focuses on the perspectives of some of the larger unions in Canada. The most significant of these—the Canadian Labor Congress (CLC)—is an umbrella union that, as of 1992, represented the views of nearly 60% of unionized Canadian employees. There are more than 2.3 million trade unionists affiliated with the CLC through 92 international and national unions. Another union perspective examined in this chapter is that of the National Automobile, Aerospace and Agricultural Implement Workers Union of Canada (CAW-Canada), a union that represents the interests of 170,000 workers in the automobile, aerospace, telecommunications and electronics, transportation, and food/beverage sectors. Information for this chapter was gathered from interviews with union leaders for another project on corporate responses to substance abuse in the workplace.* In addition, various union position papers on this issue were analyzed, along with several union submissions to the federal government's Standing Committee on Transport.†

2. THE LABOR RELATIONS CONTEXT

Philosophical Differences

Union viewpoints on workplace drug testing must be understood within the general context of labor-management relations and in terms of the pressures

*For instance, some professional societies (e.g., the Canadian Owners and Pilots Association) are against random testing but have accepted drug testing as part of their yearly physical examination process for many years. Similarly, the Canadian Merchant Service Guild is amenable to the idea of screening for drugs periodically or after an accident but is vehemently against random or for-cause testing. Although many professional associations are essentially white-collar unions, in this chapter I deal exclusively with blue-collar unions while noting that the perspective of professional associations is often different from traditional union viewpoints on drug testing and other issues.

*Two hundred organizations were surveyed to determine the nature of corporate responses to substance abuse in the workplace. As part of this research project, 12 union leaders were interviewed in order to understand better labor's perspective on workplace substance abuse. See Conference Board of Canada (1992).

†This committee was constituted to hear various opinions on Transport Canada's proposed program for alcohol and drug use in the transportation industry.

currently affecting unions. There is little question that union perspectives on workplace issues are rooted in significant philosophical differences between labor and management.

Ostensibly, unions serve to express the collective view of workers. This view is premised on the goal of enhancing working conditions and standards, as well as the quality of the social milieu in which working relations are embedded. Within this context, unions see the function of management to be the maximization of productivity through supervision and control of workers. They have traditionally seen management as conceiving of and treating the worker as an "instrument of production . . . as a resource to be exploited and monitored [and] as a cost to be controlled and minimized" (Aktouf, 1992, p. 407). Ultimately, the management function is seen as one of the main engines driving and reproducing a competitive and often "brutally efficient" society, in which the quality of working life is subordinated to the financial success of the firm and labor is viewed as a commodity to be exploited. In effect,

> this allocation of power in the workplace, known as the principle of residual rights, is the legal manifestation of the concept of labor as a commodity and [has] established the priority of property over the principles of democracy. . . . The high conflict/low trust pattern often associated with the handling of distributive or win/lose conflict can spill over into all the issues with which the two parties deal. This can lead to "a cycle whereby conflicts involving some issues drive out the potential for cooperation and problem solving where the parties share common interest." (Ranking, 1990, p. 73)

As pressure to compete on a global scale intensifies, many labor organizations feel that management is now exercising its "right to manage" in a particularly aggressive and antiunion manner. Moreover, as the pendulum of power within working environments swings in the direction of management, organized labor fears the demise or devaluation of its vision of society. As the Ontario Federation of Labor (1988) argues, the notion of "job quality" is very much tied to a vision of society articulated as the difference between a "free market, dog-eat-dog society or a more human and livable community-based nation" (p. 1). Today, many labor leaders feel that they are being asked to subscribe to a largely corporate vision of society that "denies the interests of working people, and the basic tenets of distributive justice" (Kumar & Coates, 1991, p. 30).

Although many unions and their employers are now calling for more cooperative approaches to production, there is no question that the opposing-teams mentality still governs the credos of labor and management. Accordingly, management-labor relations are often confrontational; a winner-take-all attitude prevails, and the parties often assume aggressive, intransigent positions. As might be expected, one consequence of this situation is that labor is often suspicious of management-initiated programs and policies, particularly those (e.g., drug testing) that are perceived to impinge upon the freedom and dignity of the worker.

Economic Pressures

Over the past two decades in North America, unions have assumed an increasingly defensive posture. There have been significant declines in union membership (particularly in the United States), continued strain in the area of labor-management relations, and significant losses at the collective bargaining table. In addition to concerns over wages, pensions, and occupational health and safety issues, many unions are worried about job security, particularly because the continent has just experienced a long wave of organizational restructuring.

Furthermore, these stresses have occurred in the context of a globalizing economy in which many employers are exporting their operations to cheaper locations in the third world, or streamlining domestic operations via downsizing or wage cutbacks (Baer, Grabb, & Johnston, 1991).

In addition, although Canadian unions have been somewhat more successful than their U.S. counterparts in resisting pressures to adjust to "new economic realities," their leaders are still concerned about their ability to motivate and unify the rank and file. A Gallup poll conducted in 1989 showed that half of Canadians believe that the views of labor leadership are not representative of the views of the ordinary labor union member (Coates, Arrowsmith, & Courchere, 1989). Indeed this issue points up one of the central problems of the modern union movement—namely, how to develop and maintain a unified position given the seeming indifference of the rank and file to questions of social and workplace policy and the continued assault on the freedoms and rights of labor to even exist.

In this chapter, the central significance of these economic pressures and the philosophical differences between management and labor are that they provide the lens through which unions interpret many workplace policies. Indeed, these factors contribute importantly to union perspectives on the function and effectiveness of most management policies, including attempts to deal with alcohol and drug abuse in the workplace. In an environment where productivity issues are perceived to dominate management's agenda, unilaterally imposed policies on alcohol and drug abuse are viewed with some skepticism. A senior union executive puts it this way: "Employers see substance abuse as a cost-effectiveness issue, [while] the unions are interested in the overall well-being of their members. . . . That's why we are against drug testing . . . because it is not for the well-being of the employee."

3. UNION PERSPECTIVES ON DRUG TESTING IN THE WORKPLACE

As suggested above, it would be simplistic to suggest that all unions are against workplace drug screening. There are many different circumstances under which drug testing might take place (see Chapter 6), and some unions are supportive (perhaps reluctantly) of carefully designed drug screening policies if testing occurs in specific circumstances and appropriate precautions are taken. Although some may oppose random, periodic, and mandatory testing, they may agree that testing is justified in the investigation of industrial accidents, in monitoring the integrity of some safety-sensitive positions, or for cause. In the majority of cases, however, union leaders argue that drug and alcohol use can and should be reduced by means other than drug testing. Most notable among the suggested alternatives are educational programs wedded to broad-based, jointly designed and administered employee assistance programs (EAPs).

In keeping with the traditional labor concern to link social issues with the experience of work, current union policies on alcohol and drug abuse aim to create a more equitable, less stressful, and safer working environment while recognizing that many social problems (including alcohol and drug abuse) have their roots in conflicts and stresses residing outside the workplace and/or the nature and design of work itself. Union leaders recognize that drug and/or alcohol abuse can have a negative impact on coworkers, the public, and the environment, and they are therefore supportive of the notion that there should be standards in relation to impairment on the job. Screening for substance abuse, however, is viewed as a quick-fix quasi-solution that is intrusive, costly, and ineffectual. In addition, and perhaps most importantly, they are concerned about the civil rights implications of drug testing.

The Factors Motivating Drug Testing: Union Perspectives

Many unions have questioned the motivations behind government and management calls for testing. In Canada, one of the more prevalent perceptions within the labor movement is that national uneasiness over the issue of drugs in the workplace (and within society generally) amounts to gross exaggeration rooted in an ideology imported from the United States. In a series of interviews conducted with Canadian union leaders, most argued that Canada does not have substance abuse problems anywhere close to those of the United States. They contend that the U.S. administration's declaration of a "war on drugs" was merely imitated by the Canadian government, which—in spite of criticism and evidence to the contrary—proclaimed a "drug epidemic" in Canada in 1986, Accordingly, they are concerned that Canadian employers may follow the example of their counterparts in the United States, where, according to data from a 1986 study of the Fortune 500, 30% of firms test job applicants (Stroud, 1987). The CAW-Canada stated that "the issue of mandatory use testing has been placed on the public agenda primarily by corporate interests and conservative politicians in the United States of America, and, to a lesser extent by their 'cousins' in Canada" (Ontario Law Reform Commission, 1990 p. 2).

Underlying this position is the conviction that Canada is tightening political, economic, and ideological links with the United States. It is argued that the United States is Canada's largest trading partner, and that with the implementation of the Free Trade Act (and possibly the North American Free Trade Agreement), the economic links will become stronger. Out of necessity, Canada has become part of the global economy—and, say many union representatives, this economic linkage has included ideological linkage. The case for the ideological nature of the so-called drug and alcohol problem is founded on the premise that media and the state are engaged in a process of creating a moral panic vis-à-vis alcohol and drug use in Canadian society. It is alleged that the mass media, in concert with a corporate elite interested in cementing and homogenizing its links with the corporate environment of the United States has overreacted to the alcohol and drug problem by superimposing U.S. statistics and its corresponding "war on drugs" doctrine on Canada.

Some also argue that drug testing is just a component of the hysteria generated by governments in both the United States and Canada that are unwilling to deal with the root causes of addiction in society as a whole. Advocates of this position believe that governments are reluctant to address the real causes of dysfunctional behavior (including drug and alcohol abuse) because it would force them to reexamine some fundamental aspects of modern society. This perspective is based on the notion that many of today's addictions and dysfunctional behaviors are in fact rooted in stresses occurring within and outside the production process. As such, these advocates locate the causes of alcohol and drug abuse within a paradigm of addictions theory that prioritizes environmental and social factors (e.g., high workloads, long hours, separation from family and friends, stress in relation to job security, and more broadly, stresses deriving from under- and unemployment, relative deprivation vis-à-vis consumer goods, inadequate education, and diminished life chances). Also, as pointed out above, many unions see modern society as founded irrevocably on free-market principles in which maximizing labor productivity is a goal overriding any real attempts to change society in order to regulate the social and environmental correlates of addiction.

It is not surprising, then, that many unions feel that government and some employers have ulterior motives in what is often perceived to be a push toward drug testing. These motives have to do with issues of control over the worker in order to increase productivity, and perhaps even to eliminate unions altogether. As one union executive argued, "What it boils down to is management control [over the worker]. We recognize that management has to have some degree of control in the workplace, but [the question is] where you draw the line and also the quality of the control. Management has the right to manage, they assess job performance, and if you can't do the job or you are drinking on the premises, then fine . . . but we are against draconian tactics."

This quotation also points up the importance of the job performance criteria within the context of substance abuse in the workplace. Unions agree with the position of the Canadian Civil Liberties Association (CCLA) and the Canadian Human Rights Commission that "regardless of a positive test or a refusal to undergo such a test, the employer would have to demonstrate the employee's inability to perform the job at issue. The CCLA also says that by itself, a positive test and an unwillingness to undergo the test cannot support an inference of an inability to perform the job" (Burovoy, 1990). The Privacy Commissioner of Canada (1990) maintains that one of the main shortcomings of the so-called job performance model is that "its focus is limited to productivity and safety in the workplace; it does not deal with the issue of use away from work unless that use affects the job"; however, the model also has some value in that it "allows management to intervene on the basis of legitimate performance expectations and to maintain union support in doing so."

It is also no surprise, then, that many labor organizations see workplace drug testing as having more to do with the productivity of labor than with concerns for the well being of the worker. In the political context, drug testing is seen as "politicians' attempts to appear as if they are doing something about the so-called drug problem . . . that the focus on drug testing diverts attention away from other workplace issues [e.g., health and safety], and that government agencies, such as the police, do not have to be involved with an unpopular and politically dangerous activity" (Energy and Chemical Workers Union, undated).

To summarize, many unions feel that there is no crisis of drug and/or alcohol abuse in society—nor, by extension, is there a crisis in the workplace. Indeed, the notion of "crisis" is interpreted as an artificial construction masking ulterior motives. Some union leaders fear that the underlying reasons for testing in the workplace have more to do with managerial interests in maximizing productivity than with health and safety. They argue that most individuals involved in accidents typically have worked long shifts or under extremely arduous conditions. One union leader stated this perspective clearly:

> The issue is safety in the workplace . . . and safety in the workplace is not going to be enhanced by putting in legislation about testing for substance abuse in the workplace. You tell me how many people you know that can work 16 hours a day and not be at risk of an accident. . . . Legislation is not going to be the factor that deals with the problem. . . . The key is education, making people more aware of the impact of substance abuse, and of alternatives . . . other methods of dealing with the problem.

Moreover, these leaders argue that the drug-free environment is a myth in today's culture and that testing will not necessarily eliminate workplace substance abuse. As one union official puts it, "If somebody is going to do drugs, they're going to do them. . . . If they're an addict, no piece of legislation saying drug testing is mandatory is going to stop them from doing drugs." Another union leader questions the practicality of drug testing:

> I believe . . . that [an] airline pilot should not be under the influence of drugs—but should we test him? If we did, what would we find? We would find that if a pilot wanted to take drugs, and knew that a drug test was a possibility, it would be stupid to report for work with cocaine or marijuana in the body. It's known a line of coke taken within an hour or two before the flight wouldn't show up in the test; but if you tested in midflight, it would. So should we test in midflight? . . . It's nonsense. It doesn't prove anything; it's a simplistic excuse to show that we are really serious about doing something. (Canadian Centre for Occupational Health and Safety, 1988, p. 17).

The emphasis on education, as opposed to draconian drug testing, points up another important issue for unions: the need to educate their membership about the dangers of drug and alcohol abuse and to communicate to them that help is available (e.g., through an EAP). One of the greatest challenges faced by unions, however, has to do with educating the rank and file regarding the perceived shortcomings of drug testing as a method of combatting substance abuse. Some of the union leaders interviewed expressed a concern that many employees are unaware of the shortcomings of drug testing. They argue that educating employees as to the negative aspects of drug testing will pose a challenge for union leadership, especially in light of recent evidence that the general public supports drug testing programs. These leaders maintain that the membership are led to believe that drug testing will alleviate the "problem" of substance abuse and thereby guarantee employee safety. In effect, for these labor leaders, the rank and file is often uninformed, misled, or both.

In addition, in the view of some labor organizations, there is sometimes pressure on employees to "toe the line" in relation to managerial demands, particularly in times of high unemployment. The CLC has argued that "voluntary" drug testing is not voluntary at all: "If a [job] applicant says 'no,' then the applicant does not get the job. If employees say 'no' they come under suspicion, can be harassed, and even fired for insubordination" (Canadian Industrial Relations Personnel Developments, 1987, p. 504). In such circumstances, employees may be likely to trade their beliefs for job security. One interviewee argued that

> people will go along with it because they can't say "Take this job and shove it." If management says in order for you to get from A to B and get this job you have to do this stuff [take a drug test], the person says, "If that what it takes, fine." Given an option, they'd probably tell the company to take their job and shove it. In that sense, drug testing doesn't deal with the problem of alcohol and drug abuse.

Moral and Ethical Problems with Testing

Despite failed attempts to apply principles of civil liberties to the drug testing issue, many trade unionists and human rights activists continue to emphasize the ethical and moral dimensions of drug testing.

Unions argue that some testing procedures could constitute an invasion of the individual's right to the privacy. Under this perspective, blood tests would be viewed as intrusive, whereas direct observation of urination might be viewed as degrading and a violation of personal rights (Macdonald, Wells, & Fry, 1992). Accordingly, many unions point out that drug testing policies should address the potentially demeaning effects of such tests. For example, the International Transport Workers' Federation (1991) calls for a balanced approach to alcohol and drug abuse that safeguards "the individual worker's right not to suffer unwarranted intrusions into his/her private life and violations of their basic human rights either by employers or by national authorities" (p. 2). Other unions have built upon this more conciliatory perspective, suggesting that if drug testing is here to stay, less intrusive measures (e.g., interactive video or hair analysis) might be utilized.

Because procedures such as urinalysis can detect past use but not present impairment, drug testing is seen by some as an objectionable intrusion into the nonworking activities of the worker. According to the Canadian Auto Workers' submission to the Ontario Law Reform Commission (1990) project on drug and alcohol testing,

> The state has no business in a non-criminal, civil context to invade a person's right to his/her privacy and the integrity of his/her person. The State should have no right in a non-criminal, civil context to force a person to give up his/her blood or urine, without his/her consent. . . . Our rights are like threads woven in a tapestry. If we undo one thread [i.e., allow substance use testing in a civil context] we risk unravelling our entire tapestry of rights and freedoms. (p. 1).

Similarly, the International Brotherhood of Electrical Workers (1991) has stated that "no employer should encroach on the privacy and dignity of its employees by subjecting them to random and speculative drug testing."

Some unions feel that drug screening invades privacy but is also a control and surveillance technique used to manipulate worker behavior (CLC Submission to the Standing Committee on Transport). As well, it is argued that such control (via the drug testing program) is often justified in the name of increased safety in the workplace, even though there are as yet no *causal* links between substance abuse and accidents within the workplace.

Finally, there is some concern over the potential for employers to use the information gathered from drug tests to determine a worker's propensity to contract diseases or their pregnancy status. This somewhat Orwellian perspective is constituted by the fear that drug testing may also be used to purge "undesirable" workers from the workplace, or that they could be used to determine the employability and/or future productivity of the worker.

The Costs of Drug Testing

Competitive pressures tend to heighten labor and management awareness of the importance of cost control in all arenas of corporate activity. The concern over the cost-effectiveness of substance abuse programs is reflected in union arguments that drug testing is not cost-effective. With regard to mandatory drug testing, Reg Baskin of the Energy and Chemical Workers Union maintains that "we in the labor movement don't think companies are stupid enough to waste money on a mandatory testing program. It's just not possible to find the profit line with enough money in it to waste $100, $200 or $300 on each test" (Canadian Centre for Occupational Health and Safety, 1988, p. 16). Similarly, the Canadian Labor Congress feels employers need to be convinced of the efficacy of jointly designed and administered employee assistance programs as a partial solution to alcohol and drug abuse in the workplace. They maintain that such programs would cost far less than drug testing programs.

In effect, the use of alcohol and drug screening programs could be very costly and may provide little in the way of return on investment. Within current literature, there is some evidence to support this contention. For instance, Henriksson (1991) has argued that unions are in the position of demanding that employers use the most costly drug screening analysis methods to ensure accuracy. As well, union demands that employer drug testing programs address issues of accuracy, confidentiality, and reliability may exacerbate these costs. In addition, some leaders have argued that the use of drug testing will merely identify an individual who already has an addiction and may have had one for years. In effect, "Testing will do nothing but confirm what has otherwise been observed" (Ontario Law Reform Commission, 1990, p. 9).

Another important cost is less tangible: the cost associated with decreased morale and diminished or negative labor relations that might occur as a result of the implementation of drug screening programs. Many union leaders feel that drug testing policies are anathema to harmonious labor relations, particularly in an era in which labor-management cooperation is being cited as critical to the ability of organizations to compete on a global scale. For this reason, unions once again contend that the key to successful treatment of workplace substance abuse is the joint (i.e., union and management) development of substance abuse programs. As one union leader put it,

> In joint programs the emphasis is on the effect of workplace stresses in causing the problems the employees are having. . . . What we try to do in the labor movement is to address the needs of the worker through education and preventative programs in the short term for that person's immediate needs, and in the long term . . . well, if you see four people coming out of a department with nervous breakdowns, then you know that something is going on . . . and we turn it over to our health and safety department. . . . We take a more community oriented approach.

This perspective has much to do with the union perception that government is following a short-term strategy by jumping on the drug testing bandwagon. One CLC official interviewed for this chapter argues that "in our submissions to government we have said 'why are you testing right off the bat? You've never given good joint EAP's a chance." . . . You have to try that first and failing that, then you might be justified in using drug testing. . . . Not that we're endorsing drug testing . . . it's just that it is not a quick fix, and that's what the government wants."

Shortcomings in Drug Testing Technology and Process

Some unions argue that there are important shortcomings inherent in the drug testing technology and processes now utilized by employers. For instance, one interviewee argued that false positives may result in devastating consequences for an individual because of the stigma of being initially identified as a potential drug addict. This feeling is still prevalent despite the contention of some drug testing experts that proper testing technologies, used in concert with one another, are infallible. For instance, although EMIT (urinalysis) may produce false positives, most experts argue that a confirmatory test using gas chromatography/mass spectrometry (GC/MS) should be made a mandatory component of the drug testing process. Moreover, these experts argue that such techniques must be used in conjunction with rigorous patient interviewing in order to determine whether the patient has used an illegal drug or has consumed poppy seeds that might contain morphine (Stroud, 1987).

The union response to such arguments has often been that confirmatory tests such as GC/MS are very expensive. Because management pays for the testing process, it may be reluctant to pay further for confirmatory tests in order to ensure accuracy. In addition, notwithstanding management's assurances of confidentiality, some labor leaders argue that even if someone tests positive and later tests negative with the confirmatory test, the damage may already be done. In effect, they argue that the stigma associated with negative labeling may be an outcome of the testing process, even if that person later tests clean. As well, unions argue that the chain of custody may well break down on occasion—for instance, a sample may be lost, misplaced, or mixed up with another, resulting in inaccurate conclusions and concomitant negative consequences for the employee. In short, "Drug testing has proven to be very unreliable, with error rates reaching up to 66 per cent. . . . Results from drug-testing can confuse legal and harmless foodstuffs with illegal drugs [such as] cranberry juice, poppy seeds, herbal tea, ephedrine, antihistamines used in asthma and cold prescriptions and propanolamine in appetite suppressants" (Canadian Industrial Relations and Personnel Developments, 1987).*

Another criticism is that current testing technology has distinct limitations of scope. For example, it is well known that urinalysis, the technique preferred

*It should be noted, however, that this 66% figure stems from a report by the U.S.-based Center for Disease Control, which cited this rate on the part of one laboratory.

by the majority of organizations now testing, can detect past use of a drug but not the level of use, the degree to which addiction is prevalent, or the extent to which the individual was impaired. Moreover, urinalysis cannot determine whether an individual is impaired on the job, a problem that is critical from the union perspective because it speaks to the issue of job performance. In short, some labor organizations contend that although drug testing may indicate that a worker has used drugs in the past, it may say nothing about that person's ability to do her or his work. Deficiencies in job performance associated with alcohol and drug abuse may have more to do with adverse working conditions, other health problems, or stress than with use or abuse of alcohol and drugs. Moreover, opponents of drug testing argue that if widespread testing becomes law, many labs will quickly be needed to deal with an exponential increase in demand for drug tests. A consequence of this may be watered-down standards that could entail an increase in false positive tests.

In outlining the limitations of drug testing, unions also argue that the drug-free workplace is unattainable, and that the problem of abuse must be dealt with in the context of cooperative labor relations. Accordingly, their solution emphasizes treatment of substance abuse in the context of a disease model, rather than a punishment model.

Another important issue revolves around the question of the net that is cast by drug testing policies. Drug testing entails a widening of the net in that it has the potential to invade continually the privacy of innocent employees. As well, some unions are concerned that drug testing policies will simply identify (and possibly punish) those individuals who, by definition, already hold jobs and are therefore not the most impaired drug users in society. As one union pamphlet asks, "What will happen to the (probably) light or recreational drug users who are caught and dismissed from legitimate employment? The most likely result will be the creation of more heavy drug users and dealers, with society as a whole picking up the cost" (Energy and Chemical Workers Union, undated).

4. UNION SOLUTIONS: EDUCATION AND JOINT EAPS

It should be obvious by now that most unions would rather not see drug testing installed in the workplace and that they are more amenable to solutions to workplace alcohol and drug abuse which address the root causes of the problem. Among the most popular of these proposed solutions is the jointly designed and administered employee assistance program (EAP). A recent Conference Board of Canada study of 97 private- and public-sector organizations found that in organizations where some part of the working population was represented by a union, one third used a joint management/union committee to design and implement an EAP (Conference Board of Canada, 1992, p. 6). The majority of these programs are broad based, meaning that they focus on a wide variety of problems as they relate to each other. Implicit in this approach is the recognition that alcohol and drug abuse can only be dealt with through education, and that other stressors (both inside and outside the workplace) are strongly associated with alcohol and drug abuse.

This approach is seen by many unions as the only viable alternative to dealing with abuse issues because it falls within a treatment modality in which abuse is viewed as "a health problem requiring treatment [in a cooperative manner]"; conversely, testing is viewed as part of a punitive strategy where "the abuser is [viewed as] a criminal who must be disciplined, fired or jailed. Management seeks to throw away the problem with the problem employee" (Dugan 1987, p. 8). Attending this perspective is the argument that such programs have not been given the time or resources to demonstrate their effectiveness in many organizations.

In addition, many unions would like to see more attention paid to working conditions as they relate to the creation of stresses that employees often "resolve" through the use of alcohol and/or drugs. One union leader reiterated that workplace testing programs are being contemplated today because "the U.S. told us to do it" but added that "today's pressures, long hours the stresses of the workplace, etcetera. . . . All of that contributes to accidents, from injuries to oil spills. . . . Substance abuse could be a factor in that equation . . . but I stress *could* be a factor."

5. CONCLUSION

Clearly, many unions see drug testing in the workplace not only as a short-term, Band-Aid solution but as an assault on the freedoms of workers and, in broader terms, as a method of controlling the labor power, productivity, autonomy, and political will of organized workers. Many of these concerns are entrenched in historically conditioned antagonisms over social and working conditions, as well as the rights and roles of working people.

As they enter the uncertainties of the 1990s, many unions will continue to emphasize their objections to drug testing while promoting employee education, jointly designed programs dealing with worker wellness, and less stressful working conditions. And in light of the perception that there is no "drug crisis" in Canada, they will continue to advocate a made-in-Canada solution to substance abuse in the workplace and society.

REFERENCES

Aktouf, O., 1992, Management and theories of organizations in the 1990's: Toward a critical radical humanism?, *Academy of Management Review* **17**(3).

Alvi, S., 1992, *Corporate Responses to Substance Abuse in the Workplace* (Report No. 87-92). Conference Board of Canada, Ottawa.

Baer, D., Grabb, E., and Johnston, W., 1991, Economic dissatisfaction, potential unionism, and attitudes toward unions in Canada, *Canadian Review of Sociology and Anthropology* **28**(1):68.

Burovoy, A. 1990, Letter to Max Yalden, Chief Commissioner, Canadian Human Rights Commission, General Counsel, Canadian Civil Liberties Association.

Canadian Industrial Relations and Personnel Developments, 1987, CLC opposes mandatory drug testing, *Canadian Industrial Relations and Personnel Developments Newsletter,* January 7, **1**:503.

Canadian Labour Congress, 1990, submission to the Standing Committee on Transport Canada's proposed program for alcohol and drug use in the transportation industry, CLC, Ottawa.

Coates, M. L., Arrowsmith, D., and Courchene, M., 1989, The Current Industrial Relations Scene in Canada: 1989 Labor Movement and Trade Unionism Reference Tables, Industrial Relations Centre, Queens University.

Canadian Centre for Occupational Health and Safety, 1988, *Drug testing in the workplace: A conference,* Canadian Centre for Occupational Health and Safety, Hamilton, Ontario.

Dugan, L., 1987, Drug abuse and testing: A union viewpoint, *Worklife Report* **5**(2):8.

Energy and Chemical Workers Union, undated, *Drug Testing: Just Say No!*

Henriksson, L. E., 1991, The unconvincing case for drug testing, *Canadian Public Policy* **17**(2):183.

International Brotherhood of Electrical Workers (IBEW), 1991, Letter to Manager of Labor Relations, New Brunswick Power from J. E. Cole, Business Manager IBEW, (December 4, 1991).

International Transport Workers' Federation, 1991, October 15–16, Executive Board Meeting: Draft Policy on Drug and Alcohol Abuse.

Kumar, P., and Coates, M. L., 1991, *Canadian Labour Relations: An Information Manual,* Industrial Relations Centre, Queens University, Kingston, Ontario.

Macdonald, S., Wells, S., and Fry, R., 1992, *Issues related to drug screening in the workplace* (paper prepared for the International Labor Organization.) Addiction Research Foundation, London, Ontario.

Ontario Federation of Labor, 1988, *Let Canadians Decide,* Toronto.

Ontario Law Reform Commission, 1990, Submission of the National Automobile Aerospace and Agricultural Implement Workers Union of Canada Project on Drug and Alcohol Testing, C.A.W. Canada, Willowdale, Ontario.

The Privacy Commission of Canada, 1990, *Drug Testing and Privacy,* Minister of Supply and Services, Ottawa.

Rankin, T., 1990, *New Forms of Work Organization: The Challenge for North American Unions,* University of Toronto Press, Toronto.

Stroud, C., 1987, Do what's fair, *Canadian Business* April:68.

15

Drug Testing, the War on Drugs, Workers, and the Workplace

Perspectives from Sociology

JUDITH C. BLACKWELL

1. INTRODUCTION

A sociological perspective on drug testing in the workplace begins with the question of why this new social control measure appeared in the United States in the 1980s. What was the sociohistorical context of this initiative? Can drug screening be seen as a logical outcome of a coherent social policy framework, and is it consistent with the history of labor-management relations in North America? What other social, economic, or political conditions might have made workplace drug testing widely accepted in democratic societies like Canada and the United States?

In sociology, we speak of the "social construction" of social problems. For example, parental abuse of children undoubtedly has existed for millennia. Nevertheless, it was not until the latter half of the twentieth century when child abuse came to be perceived as a social problem that deserved public reaction and was worthy of legislative response (Nelson, 1986; Pfohl, 1977). Similarly, we may ask why workplace impairment was seen as a sufficiently serious social problem in 1980s America to justify drug screening as a policy response.

It is also of sociological interest to determine whether this initiative grew

---

JUDITH C. BLACKWELL • Department of Sociology, Brock University, St. Catharines, Ontario L2S 3A1, Canada.

Research Advances in Alcohol and Drug Problems, Volume 11: Drug Testing in the Workplace, edited by Scott Macdonald and Paul M. Roman. Plenum Press, New York, 1994.

out of concern about workplace impairment at the grass roots level (Jensen, Gerber, & Babcock, 1991) or, alternatively, if it originated in the political realm. Sometimes democratic governments act to legislate morality (Duster, 1970), even though a majority of voters do not wholeheartedly endorse such policies. Other policy initiatives arise from lobbying efforts of interest groups that may or may not have the support of widespread public concern. Was drug testing implemented in response to a well-defined and publicly acknowledged social problem ("from the bottom up") or was it imposed by a powerful group of policymakers ("from the top down")?

In order to understand the acceptance of drug testing programs and the social construction of workplace impairment as a social problem, it is necessary to examine the ideological climate of 1980s North America. To this end, I will explore how the drug problem has been portrayed in successive declarations of "war" on drugs, thereby defining the nature and seriousness of the issue in the public mind. The reader shall see how subtle modifications in the message of the 1980s helped to set the stage for viewing workplace impairment as an urgent social problem. These changes in the drug war discourse also help to explain anomalous aspects of drug screening policies.

2. THE WAR ON DRUGS IN HISTORICAL PERSPECTIVE

There are two fundamental approaches to drug control policy: measures designed to limit the *supply* of specified psychoactive substances, or those intended to reduce *demand* for them. For almost a century, North America has emphasized supply-side or prohibitionist drug policies, characterized by legislative prohibition, criminalization of the user, and strict law enforcement of domestic and international trafficking (Boyd, 1988; Reasons, 1974; Solomon, 1988). Demand-side measures include education for healthy living, treatment of persons with substance-related problems, and amelioration of the social conditions in which unhealthy behaviors flourish. Advocates of drug screening in the workplace claim it is a demand-reduction measure, because working people will be forced to choose between illicit drug use and employment, and therefore should logically opt for the latter.

Over recent decades, the supply-side policy thrust has been promoted by a succession of U.S. presidents, each proclaiming personal commitment to a new "war on drugs" and promising imminent victory. Hosmer (1990) characterizes drug war discourse and prohibitionist policies as a crusade cloaked in "formidable righteousness," where those who refuse to join risk being suspected of irresolution at best and treachery at worst. Furthermore, like every self-respecting military program, the war on drugs is seen to entail a forceful and continuing propaganda campaign (Alexander, 1990; Trebach, 1987).

The goal of destroying the illegal drug trade is widely thought to be an enormous task facing uncertain or even highly unlikely success (Alexander, 1990; Blackwell, 1988a; Boyd, 1991; Trebach, 1987). It could thus be argued that the sheer magnitude of the prohibitionist undertaking justifies military discourse in support of supply-side policy. Certainly, the language seems appropriate to argue for public spending on police, customs, armaments, surveillance technology, and prison construction. The public perception of the "drug problem" in North America, however, is socially constructed through this discourse. To the degree it dominates the public debate, other policy proposals are excluded. Indeed, drug war advocates claim that any criticism of their assertions represents "surrender" (Fratello, 1990).

Drug war discourse has generated strong public support for a supply-side, "tough guy" approach to drug policy (Gardiner & McKinney, 1991). The mainstream media and popular culture have adopted it wholeheartedly. The people of the United States, for example, report that they are very happy to have tax dollars spent on drug enforcement:

> Which should come as no surprise. The horrors of drug abuse are so lavishly documented that in a single day it's possible to hear a report on *Good Morning, America* about a Coast Guard marijuana seizure off Savannah, Georgia; then read in the morning paper about a drive-by shooting in Los Angeles; glance at a drug-free-workplace poster over the water fountain; listen to a call-in radio confessional about addiction; catch up on Richard Dreyfuss's battle against cocaine while waiting in the line at the Safeway; hear from the kids about the D.A.R.E. "drug education" program at school; watch a "kingpin" brought to justice on *Miami Vice;* pop in a video of *New Jack City;* and wind up the day by participating in a crack-house raid on the 10 o'clock news. (Baum, 1992, p. 886)

Most policy analysts would argue that Canada has tended to adopt a less muscular approach to the drug war, although the discourse surrounding the problem has often been borrowed from the United States (Erickson, 1992). In the age of international television and mass distribution of U.S. popular culture, the average Canadian might well have been exposed to almost all of the above on any given day.

With each new drug war, the public comes to believe that drug use is one of the most important problems confronting their country (Jensen, Gerber, & Babcock, 1991) and that supply-side policies are the answer. Politicians, in turn, are sensitive to such strong public sentiment. Thus, the drug war discourse continues, and traditional social policy approaches are perpetuated.

3. CHANGES OF EMPHASIS IN THE 1980S

There were two important changes in drug war rhetoric of 1980s North America. Taken together, they help explain how the stage was set for introducing drug screening in the workplace. First, after decades of division between the dominant supply-side advocates and a minority of demand-side drug policy reformers, the former began to include the control of demand in their prohibitionist agenda. Second, with the support of conservative political administrations, a new phenomenon appeared: citizens' groups that redefined the drug problem to include *all* illicit drug users, not simply those who were demonstrably causing harm to themselves and others. These changes prepared the way for identifying workplace drug impairment as a major cause of North America's economic woes and the loss of U.S. competitiveness on the international market.

Appropriation of Demand-Side Policy by Supply-Side Drug War Advocates

Prohibitionist policy, with its emphasis on eliminating the supply of illicit substances, has been the dominant social control measure of twentieth-century North America. From roughly the 1950s onward, however, new voices began to be heard, suggesting that switching the focus to the control of demand for these substances would be a more humane and effective social policy. Members of the medical profession began to argue that drug addiction was a disease, rather than a crime or evidence of moral failure (Blackwell, 1988b). This led to proposals for medical treatment rather than punishment of users. Social scientists, civil libertarians, legal scholars, and consumer advocates argued for a fundamental rethinking of drug control policy (Brecher, 1972; DiChiara, 1990). A number of U.S. state legislatures passed laws to "decriminalize" the possession of small amounts of marijuana. Many drug policy reformers suggested that attention should be shifted from the drugs per se to the users of these substances. It was argued that the answer to the problem could be found in education, in treatment of problem drug users, and in rectifying the social and economic conditions in which drug use thrives.

For some years, demand-side programs functioned as parallel institutions within the supply-side environment. Agencies concerned with education, health, and welfare conducted social programs and lobbied for funding; law enforcement agencies, meanwhile, continued to receive generous support for their pursuit of supply-side prohibition activities. As Peyrot (1984) characterized the situation, it was "a patchwork accumulation of conflicting approaches" to the perceived social problem of drug abuse.

In the 1980s, however, a new development occurred: Groups traditionally associated with supply-side policies began to claim expertise in demand-reduction. Administrations in the United States and Canada promoted deregulation of capitalist enterprise on the one hand, and withdrew support for social programs on the other (Braun, 1991; Harrison & Bluestone, 1990). Many of the threatened social services were founded on the philosophy of social reformers who argued that lack of economic opportunity led to such social problems as dysfunctional drug use. With the withdrawal of social spending, the drug war propaganda was subtly altered.

It was now argued that the war on drugs could eliminate the demand for drugs, as well as the marketplace for them. Police forces became drug educators, and across the United States, uniformed officers were sent into classrooms in the Drug Abuse Resistance Education (DARE) program. Canada instituted its own version of this initiative, called Police Assisting Community Programs (PACE; Erickson, 1992). The new demand-side drug war would also promote voluntary organizations of concerned citizens. Most notably in the United States, private-ownership drug treatment would be encouraged to take the place of state-funded social programs (Trebach, 1987). Thus, under the rhetoric of getting central government "off the backs of the people"* and reducing national debt, the decade turned its back on social reform and prepared to face a revitalized war on drugs.

The Rise of Citizens' Organizations and Zero Tolerance

In the *1984 National Strategy for Prevention of Drug Abuse and Drug Trafficking,* we find the following words attributed to U.S. President Ronald Reagan:

> No longer do we think of so-called hard drugs as bad and so-called soft drugs as being acceptable. Research tells us there are no such categories; that the phrase "responsible use" does not apply to drug experimentation by America's youth. And so far as the "recreational use" of drugs is concerned, I've never in my life heard a more self-serving euphemism by those who support drug use. (p. 35)

This represents the first official announcement of a new turn in drug war rhetoric. It paved the way for the concept of zero tolerance, as it came to be known—the idea that all forms of illicit drug use were equally unacceptable.

This approach directly contradicts mainstream sociological perspectives of drug users. Sociological research has revealed a diversity of drug-using patterns involving varying degrees of risk.† Just as not all alcohol consumers "hit the skids," many people can use illicit drugs, including heroin and cocaine, without disastrous effects (Blackwell, 1983, 1985; Erickson, Adlaf, Murray, & Smart, 1987; Schasre, 1966; Waldorf, Reinarman, & Murphy, 1990; Zinberg, 1984). Indeed, social or recreational users of illicit substances far outnumber users with drug-related problems (Wisotsky, 1986), just as social drinkers are more common than alcoholics.

*This was a phrase used in Ronald Reagan's campaign against "big government" (Harrison & Bluestone, 1990).

†This research has largely been in the ethnographic tradition of studying the social realities of "deviants" in their own social worlds, rather than theorizing about their motivations and behavior or studying those who have come to the attention of social control agencies as a result of their problems (e.g., Becker, 1953; Plant, 1975; Preble & Casey, 1969; Ramos & Gould, 1978; Waldorf, 1973).

Research has shown that the so-called drug problem is not the homogeneous monolith it was once thought to be, but rather a heterogeneous complex of illicit *and* licit drug usage patterns representing varying degrees of social damage (Mitchell, 1990). This understanding calls for sophistication in framing policy responses that are sensitive to the many different types of drug problems and their social correlates (Commission of Inquiry Into the Non-Medical Use of Drugs, 1973).

The 1980s war on drugs, however, repudiated the research on which this scholarship was based. The ideology of zero tolerance encompassed all forms of illicit drug use, and it remained mute on the issue of problems related to the use of legally available substances. In short, the new definition of the "drug problem" was a return to the uncomplicated conceptions of the past.

In the 1980s, there was an extraordinary growth of private-sector drug treatment programs based on the "tough love" philosophy (Trebach, 1987), and citizens' groups such as the Parent Resources Institute on Drug Education (PRIDE)* in the United States, and Alcohol and Drug Concerns and the Council on Drug Abuse (CODA) in Canada. The zero-tolerance platform can be traced to U.S. government reliance on this "parent peer" movement for demand reduction, as well as the use of profit-oriented treatment to fill gaps in the social assistance network (Trebach, 1987).

All of the elements that were to appear in the U.S. national drug strategy can be found in PRIDE's 1982 national conference proceedings. Carleton Turner, senior drug policy advisor to the Reagan White House, was a keynote speaker. He took the platform to stress an injunction against the use of certain words in discussions of drug use, including *responsible* and *recreational*. Robert DuPont, the founding director of the U.S. National Institute on Drug Abuse (NIDA), also spoke:

> Drug dependence does not require a defective child or defective family. The power of the chemical . . . [is not based] on deficiencies of either the family or the individual, but on the process of drug dependency itself. And that process begins with drug experimentation. Neither the drug user nor his family can control that process once it begins. Until we get that life-saving message across, we are going to have a hard time with our prevention efforts. We are also going to continue to have a hard time with the scientists and many of their studies. (Gleaton, Schuchard, & Moore, 1982, p. 86)

The threat of "a hard time with the scientists" was not an empty one, resulting in pressure that has been characterized as academic censorship (Blackwell, 1987; Morgan, 1991). Indeed, official outcry over research findings continued to the end of the decade.*

*Not to be confused with the Canadian organization PRIDE (People to Reduce Impaired Driving Everywhere), which eventually became a Canadian branch of the U.S. group MADD (Mothers Against Drunk Driving).

*A notable example can be found in a speech by William Bennett, director of the Office of National Drug Control Policy, on "drug policy and the intellectuals." His address to an audience at Harvard University included the following: "But in the great public policy debate over drugs, the academic

Robert DuPont's statement revealed the overall strategy of the new war on drugs (Blackwell, 1987). The U.S. government was relying upon voluntary organizations to reduce demand for illicit drugs. Yet the lifeblood of the membership of these groups flowed in the veins of concerned parents, and for the most part *concerned* could be translated as "being middle class and having offspring who use drugs or who might someday do so." This was before it became popular to blame most personal problems on "dysfunctional families" (Kaminer, 1992; Rieff, 1991). On the contrary, it would be counterproductive to allow concerned parents to waste their energies fretting over how their family relations might be less than perfect.

The new message was that all illicit drugs were equally dangerous, so there was to be no discussion of how certain drugs or patterns of drug use are more dangerous than others. Most certainly, the young people of North America were not to be educated about relative risks or precautions that might be taken to avoid adverse consequences of illicit drug use (Trebach, 1987); in this drug war, the catchphrase was "just say no."

In a discourse that proclaims *all* forms of illicit drug use to be off limits, the occasional marijuana smoker is classified together with the most troubled "crack" addict. In an atmosphere of zero tolerance, policy proposals that otherwise would be considered unacceptable in democratic societies are seriously debated.* This helps to explain the wide net cast by drug screening, which does not identify alcohol-related risks nor distinguish between illicit drug use associated with workplace impairment and cases where this outcome is highly unlikely.

4. DRUG SCREENING IN THE WORKPLACE AND ECONOMIC POLICY

Supply-side *drug* policy dovetailed with the supply-side *economic* policies of the 1980s. Labelled "Reaganomics" by the media and "neoconservative" by social scientists, the U.S. economic agenda was also welcomed in Canada and the United Kingdom. It promised economic recovery through massive cuts in business taxes, and it encouraged corporate restructuring through economic deregulation. Among other things, supply-side economics was designed to allow

and intellectual communities have by and large had little to contribute, and little of that has been genuinely useful or for that matter mentally distinguished" (Bennett, 1990). Needless to say, academics understand this as a reference to research findings that bring the drug war rhetoric into question. Lester Grinspoon, an acknowledged medical authority on cannabis for over two decades, calls the era described in this chapter as one of "psychopharmacological McCarthyism" (Grinspoon, 1990).

*For example, in the 1980s proposals were seriously entertained to confine "casual" drug users, with no evidence of social dysfunction, in boot-camp settings (Fratello, 1990).

businesses more freedom in setting wages and prices and to "reimpose greater managerial discipline over day-to-day activities in the workplace" (Harrison & Bluestone, 1988, p. 95). Another important component of this approach was a "systematic attack upon social welfare programs" (Braun, 1991). Rather than developing policies to directly address heightened competition from foreign markets or to increase the productivity of the next generation of workers, supply-side economics focused on short-term measures. The aim was to increase business profits by creating a "leaner and meaner" economy, a phrase repeated frequently in news reports of plant closures or wage rollbacks.

Throughout this century, employers have instituted programs to raise the level of respectability and morality of workers. One is reminded here of the Ford Motor Company's "sociological department," which sent company agents into workers' homes to see if Ford's vision of middle-class family values was being realized (Meyer, 1981). Hecker and Kaplan (1989) argue that drug screening in the workplace is consistent with a long tradition in labor-management relations: "The current discourse about substance abuse and the decline of American workers' productivity, taking place against a backdrop dominated by discussions of U.S. 'competitiveness,' fits squarely into [a] historical pattern" (p. 694).

The development of industrial medicine and industrial psychology in the 1920s is an early example of employers' interest in the internal environment of workers' bodies "in an age when workers did not have the right to such information themselves or to complementary knowledge about the hazards of the environment in which they toiled" (Hecker & Kaplan, 1989, p. 700). This observation buttresses the argument that worker surveillance programs have been designed, not for the sake of the workers' welfare, but in the service of factory discipline (Hecker & Kaplan, 1989). Workplace urine screening might be seen as a logical extension of this tradition of "scientific" surveillance.

In the 1980s, the discourse in support of drug screening focused on workplace safety and the alleged contribution of worker impairment to loss of international competitiveness. Although there is good reason to point the finger at American management practices, the war on drugs permitted the blame to be individualized and productivity problems to be attributed to the personal habits of the workers themselves. This tendency to "blame the victim" also has a long history, where individual characteristics of workers (e.g., their personal behavior, accident-proneness, or genetic susceptibilities) have been alleged to be the cause of occupational morbidity and mortality (Hecker & Kaplan, 1989). The crusade of "zero tolerance" for drug use made it possible to attribute the nation's economic difficulties to the behavior of workers, on and off the job.

Interestingly, the evidence rallied in support of the extent and costs of worker impairment does not stand up to close scrutiny, nor does the presumed elevated risk of drug users to experience workplace accidents or injuries (see Chapter 6). Nevertheless, in the United States,

> drug testing is now being implemented, in one form or another, by the armed forces, many large companies, local governments, professional sports leagues, criminal justice agencies, insurance companies, and even by parents, using home testing kits. Perhaps as many as ten million Americans per year are subjected to urinalysis to detect the use of illegal drugs. (Zimmer & Jacobs, 1990, p. 220)

All this would not have been possible except for recent advances in the development of sufficiently inexpensive technology that could allow for a profitable urinalysis industry. Zimmer and Jacobs (1990) have analyzed drug testing in America as an economic enterprise conservatively estimated at $300 million in value. This figure refers to the equipment and chemicals necessary for urinalysis but does not include associated businesses (e.g., courier services, plastics manufacturers, and office supplies). It also does not include another growth industry: privately-run drug treatment centers for workers whose bad habits are unveiled by the testing. The estimate also excludes private consultants hired by businesses to design testing programs.* The drug-testing enterprise appears to be a considerable economic force that, in the course of its business promotion, will continue to communicate a definition of the "drug problem" consonant with the drug war discourse of the United States in the 1980s.

5. THE WAR ON DRUGS AND ANOMALOUS ASPECTS OF A SOCIAL POLICY

Bruce Alexander (1990) argues that propaganda "causes stupidity" (p. 70), whether it is designed in support of true military campaigns or in the aid of drug wars. There are four key elements of drug war propaganda that have appeared in various guises over the century in North America and that help to explain certain logically inconsistent aspects of drug screening as a social policy. The four themes of drug propaganda identified here, although frequently reiterated by politicians and in the media, are highly questionable attempts to portray the extent and nature of the drug problem in a manner that will elicit public support. Those who have taken the time to examine these propositions in detail conclude they are little more than myths in the disguise of conventional wisdom.

Drawing Distinctions between Legal and Illegal Substances

If we accept the premise that workplace impairment is a serious social problem, the question immediately arises as to why drug testing tends to concentrate on *illegal* substances. A recent study of Canadian transportation companies

*Robert DuPont is one of a number of well-known consultants in the field who were formerly "federal drug war establishment" officials (Zimmer & Jacobs, 1990).

showed that employers are much more likely to test for illicit drugs than for prescription drugs or alcohol (Macdonald & Dooley, 1991).

Prohibitionist policy urges people to believe that it is reasonable for the law to distinguish between legal drugs (pharmaceutical products, alcohol, nicotine) and illegal substances (cannabis, hallucinogens, heroin, cocaine, etc.). Yet laws were passed with little factual information available about the relative health risks of the substances undergoing criminalization and without regard to scientific evidence of social harm (Reasons, 1977; Solomon & Green, 1988). The scholars who have questioned the rationale for distinguishing between licit and the illicit substances, whether on pharmacological grounds or on the basis of social harm, are too numerous to list. Nevertheless, they share the belief that a more rational approach to drug policy is needed, and they have proposed various ways in which this might be accomplished (Boyd, 1991; Green, 1988; Mitchell, 1990). Thus, the focus on illicit drugs in drug testing programs may be logically inconsistent, but it rests firmly in a long-standing prohibitionist tradition.

Exaggerating the Social Damage of Illicit Drugs

It was briefly noted above that arguments for workplace drug testing were based on highly contentious data concerning the role of illicit drugs in worker productivity or in workplace accidents (Horgan, 1991). This is consistent with the history of drug war discourse.

As each new drug "epidemic" or war is declared, we are told that it involves the most dangerous and addictive substance yet encountered. We are warned that large numbers of people are involved, that the situation is about to mushroom out of control, and that through damaging themselves, drug users are threatening the fabric of society (Fratello, 1990). At regular intervals, the people are asked to be prepared to support a new military campaign against another manifestation of the old evil. By the time journalists, scientists, and epidemiologists have rallied to examine the statistics presented and to question the validity of some of the statements made in support of new prohibitionist initiatives, policies are usually in place, and public funding already has been allocated to them (Erickson, 1992).* Similarly, the necessity for widespread workplace drug screening was accepted without critical scrutiny of its rationale or effectiveness.

Characterizing Illicit Drug Users as "Outsiders"

A theme heard repeatedly over the century has suggested that illicit drug users are morally inferior, untrustworthy, and threatening (Blackwell, 1988b).

*Recent inflated claims about the number of "crack babies" born to "addict" mothers is only one example of exaggeration in the service of maintaining a crisis mentality (Fratello, 1990).

One can also observe a disturbing tendency to locate the problem as largely one of racial minority or immigrant groups (Lusane, 1991; Musto, 1973). Such presumed alien threats motivated legislators to institute the drug laws in the first place (Reasons, 1974; Solomon & Green, 1988), and subsequently they have been reiterated in associating illicit drug problems with inner-city youths and foreign traffickers. Addicts and other disreputable outsiders from the drug world are portrayed as a menace to the respectable classes, and most particularly to the young people of these classes. Alexander (1990), among others, believes this propensity to "blame the victim" represents a deep need to find a scapegoat for society's problems.

Drug users in the workplace—the "outsiders" who have been singled out as the cause for loss of Western predominance in the global economy—are the latest incarnation of this threat. As noted above, it may seem unfair to relieve management of responsibility by focusing blame on the workers, but this tendency can be observed in labor-management relations throughout the century. In an interesting twist, the "alien threat" has become foreign economies, and the drug war rhetoric has been revised to identify drug-using workers as domestic collaborators.

"Cracking Down" on the Illicit Marketplaces

To future observers, the ultimate irony of the 1980s drug war may be its focus on productivity in the workplace and the need to rescue the North American economy. Indeed, it has been argued that the major conceptual weakness of drug war policy has been its unwillingness to acknowledge that the illicit drug market is a prototype of free-market capitalism.

There is a widespread reluctance to understand how "underworld" trade in illicit goods and services is a textbook illustration of free-enterprise entrepreneurship (Lux, 1990). Indeed, commitment to the accumulation of profit is the primary force that makes the illicit drug trade so resistant to supply-side control measures. In some inner-city neighborhoods in the United States, drug dealing has been characterized as the "major employer of black youth" (Lusane, 1991) and as an important conduit for "unfulfilled entrepreneurial talent" (Myers, 1990). The profits of the international drug trade make it hardly surprising that there always seem to be new candidates waiting in the wings when trafficking networks are broken up, supply routes are severed, or local production areas are closed down.

The financial power of the drug trade is such that it can overwhelm the economies of small countries and undermine the fiscal integrity of larger nations (Blackwell, 1988a). The international politics of illegal arms, drugs, and "hot money" weaves a seemingly impermeable web around the globe (Naylor, 1987). When contradictions arise between U.S. foreign policy and attempts to control international drug trafficking (Epstein, 1990; McCoy, 1991; Scott & Marshall, 1991), the likelihood of eradicating the trade appears even more remote.

The drug war rhetoric of the 1980s retained a belief in the ability of warlike measures to stop an international drug trade that has resisted enforcement measures for the better part of a century. Turning a blind eye to the economic and political power of this marketplace, it promoted a new solution: turning domestic demand reduction over to the private sector by promoting employee surveillance, the drug screening industry, and treatment programs run by and on behalf of private entrepreneurs. In so doing, the war on drugs diverted attention from an intractable geopolitical problem to a domestic "war on users" (Siegel, 1989).

6. PERSPECTIVES FROM SOCIOLOGY: SOME CONCLUDING OBSERVATIONS

This chapter began with the question of whether the problem of workplace impairment was a genuine source of widespread public concern or whether it was a social problem constructed in the political realm. Evidence points to the latter explanation. Jensen, Gerber, & Babcock (1991) have monitored public opinion in 1980s America and come to the conclusion that the war on drugs was socially constructed by powerful interests in the absence of a grass roots social movement.

Ronald Reagan produced a "drug strategy" in 1982 and declared a new drug war in August of 1986. Canada's prime minister, Brian Mulroney, announced an "epidemic" of drug use in 1986 and a new "national drug strategy" in 1987 (Erickson, 1992). In a televised address in September 1989, George Bush announced his "national drug control strategy" while holding a plastic bag of cocaine he said had been purchased in the park across the street from the White House.*

Was the crisis mentality of the 1980s justified? In terms of the epidemiology of drug use, a reasonable observer would have to conclude that rates of drug use overall were generally stable, although cocaine use increased and then declined in certain subpopulations (Jensen, Gerber, & Babcock, 1991; Myers, 1990). The question tends to be obscured by commentators whose policy agendas are served by either inflating or deflating the estimates (Lusane, 1991). Be that as it may, considering the epidemiology of illicit drugs in North America over the past three decades, it would be difficult to argue that increased use rates were sufficiently dramatic to justify the publicity the problem received in the 1980s.

Until the Reagan drug war was officially declared in August 1986, public opinion polls indicated that drugs were not generally considered to be a major social problem (Jensen, Gerber, & Babcock, 1991). By the end of that month,

*The teenager who was lured to the park to make the sale was later found not guilty on the grounds of government entrapment (Lusane, 1991).

though, 86% of Americans agreed that fighting the drug problem was "extremely important." By the fall of that year, both Democrats and Republicans were trying to gain political advantage from this issue. Indeed, during the election campaign politicians appeared on television clutching plastic cups of their urine in proof of their freedom from drugs (Hecker & Kaplan, 1989). Thus, urine testing became a symbol of the shifting battlefront to attack users as well as traffickers in illicit substances.

Just as there is no reason to believe that increased illicit drug use rates justified the imposition of widespread drug screening in the workplace, there is no evidence that workplace impairment had become a more acute problem in the 1980s. To understand the introduction of this social policy and to comprehend its apparent incongruities, one must situate it in its sociohistorical context: the history of drug war rhetoric, global shifts in economic power, technological developments that made an economically feasible drug screening industry possible, and the political philosophy of governments in the United States and Canada.

REFERENCES

Alexander, B. K., 1990, *Peaceful Measures: Canada's Way out of the "War on Drugs"*, University of Toronto Press, Toronto.

Baum, D., 1992, June, The drug war on civil liberties, *The Nation* **29:**886–888.

Becker, H. S., 1953, Becoming a marihuana user, *American Journal of Sociology* **59:**234–242.

Bennett, W. J., 1990, Drug policy and the intellectuals, in: *Drug Prohibition and the Conscience of Nations* (A. S. Trebach, and K. B. Zeese, Eds.), pp. 14–20, Drug Policy Foundation, Washington DC.

Blackwell, J. C., 1983, Drifting, controlling and overcoming: Opiate users who avoid becoming chronically dependent, *Journal of Drug Issues* **13:**219–235.

Blackwell, J. C., 1985, Opiate dependence as a psychophysical event: Users' reports of subjective experiences, *Contemporary Drug Problems* **12**(3):331–350.

Blackwell, J. C., 1987, Academic censorship and the "war on drugs": The case of responsible drug use, Presented at Canadian Law and Society Association annual meeting, McMaster University, Hamilton, Ontario.

Blackwell, J. C., 1988a, Canada in a global setting: Notes on the international drug market, in: *Illicit Drugs in Canada: A Risky Business,* (J. Blackwell, and P. Erickson, Eds.), pp. 326–335, Nelson Canada, Scarborough, Ontario.

Blackwell, J. C., 1988b, Sin, sickness, or social problem? The concept of drug dependence, in: *Illicit Drugs in Canada: A Risky Business,* (J. Blackwell, and P. Erickson, Eds.), pp. 174–185, Nelson Canada, Scarborough, Ontario.

Boyd, N., 1988, Canadian punishment of illegal drug use: Theory and practice, in: *Illicit Drugs in Canada: A Risky Business,* (J. Blackwell, and P. Erickson, Eds.), pp. 301–313, Nelson Canada, Scarborough, Ontario.

Boyd, N., 1991, *High Society: Legal and Illegal Drugs in Canada,* Key Porter Books Ltd, Toronto.

Braun, D., 1991, *The Rich Get Richer: The Rise of Income Inequality in the United States and the World,* Nelson-Hall Publishers, Chicago.

Brecher, E. M., 1972, *Licit and Illicit Drugs,* Consumers Union, Mount Vernon, NY.

Commission of Inquiry Into the Non-Medical Use of Drugs, 1973, *Final Report of the Commission of Inquiry into the Non-Medical Use of Drugs,* Information Canada, Ottawa.

DiChiara, A., 1990, Changing media presentations of the drug user: The social deconstruction of moral devils, in: *The Great Issues of Drug Policy,* (A. S. Trebach, and K. B. Zeese, Eds.), pp. 303–310, Drug Policy Foundation, Washington DC.

Drug Abuse Policy Office, 1984, *1984 National Strategy for Prevention of Drug Abuse and Drug Trafficking,* U.S. Government Printing Office, Washington, D.C.

Duster, T., 1970, *The Legislation of Morality: Law, Drugs and Moral Judgement,* The Free Press, New York.

Epstein, E. J., 1990, *Agency of Fear: Opiates and Political Power in America,* revised edition, Verso, London and New York.

Erickson, P. G., 1992, "Recent trends in Canadian drug policy: The decline and resurgence of prohibitionism," *Daedalus: Journal of the American Academy of Arts and Sciences* **121**(3):239–268.

Erickson, P. G., Adlaf, E. M., Murray, G. F., and Smart, R. G., 1987, *The Steel Drug: Cocaine in Perspective,* Lexington Books, Lexington, MA and Toronto.

Fratello, D., 1990, Under the influence of prohibitionism: Drug policy debate and processes still serve a discredited, dangerously extremist philosophy, in: *The Great Issues of Drug Policy,* (A. S. Trebach and K. B. Zeese, Eds), pp. 283–289, Drug Policy Foundation, Washington, DC.

Gardiner, G. S., and McKinney, R. N., 1991, The great American war on drugs: Another failure of tough-guy management, *Journal of Drug Issues* **21**(3):605–616.

Gleaton, T. J., Schuchard, K. M., and Moore, H. W., 1982, *PRIDE National Drug conference highlights, 1982,* Parent Resources Institute on Drug Education, Atlanta, GA.

Green, M., 1988, Towards rational drug scheduling, in: *Illicit Drugs in Canada: A Risky Business,* (J. Blackwell, and P. Erickson, eds.), pp. 186–208, Nelson Canada, Scarborough, Ontario.

Grinspoon, L., 1990, Marijuana enhances the lives of some people, in: *Drug Prohibition and the Conscience of Nations,* (A. S. Trebach, and K. B. Zeese, eds), pp. 157–162, Drug Policy Foundation, Washington DC.

Harrison, B., and Bluestone, B., 1990, *The Great U-Turn: Corporate Restructuring and the Polarizing of America,* Basic Books, New York.

Hecker, S., and Kaplan, M. S., 1989, Workplace drug testing as social control, *International Journal of Health Services* **19**(4):693–707.

Horgan, J., 1990, Your analysis is faulty, *The New Republic* April 2:33–35.

Horgan, J., 1991, Postal mortem: Drug test results may point to racial discrimination, *Scientific American* February:22–23.

Hosmer, C., 1990, Does calling illegal drugs evil become a trap?, in: *The Great Issues of Drug Policy* (A. B. Trebach and K. B. Zeese, eds.), pp. 28–30, Drug Policy Foundation, Washington, DC.

Jensen, E. L., Gerber, J., and Babcock, G. M., 1991, "The new war on drugs: Grass roots movement or political construction?" *Journal of Drug Issues* **21**(3):651–667.

Kaminer, W., 1992, *I'm Dysfunctional, You're Dysfunctional: The Recovery Movement and Other Self-help Fashions,* Addison-Wesley, Reading, Mass.

Lusane, C., 1991, *Pipe Dream Blues: Racism and the War on Drugs,* South End Press, Boston.

Lux, K., 1990, *Adam Smith's Mistake: How a Moral Philosopher Invented Economics and Ended Morality,* Shambhala Publications Inc., Boston.

Macdonald, S., and Dooley, S., 1991, The nature and extent of EAPs and drug screening programs in Canadian transportation companies, *Employee Assistance Quarterly* **6**(4):23–40.

McCoy, A. W., 1991, *The Politics of Heroin: CIA Complicity in the Global Drug Trade,* Lawrence Hill Books, Brooklyn NY.

Meyer, S., 1981, *The Five Dollar Day: Labor Management and Social Control in the Ford Motor Company* 1908–1921, State University of New York Press, Albany NY.

Mitchell, C. N., 1990, *The Drug Solution: Regulating Drugs According to Principles of Efficiency, Justice and Democracy,* Carleton University Press, Ottawa.

Morgan, J. P., 1991, Medical text survives political assault, *The Drug Policy Letter* **3**(3):3–7.

Musto, D. F., 1973, *The American Disease: Origins of Narcotic Control,* Yale University Press, New Haven.

Myers, S. L., 1990, Drugs and market structure: Is there really a drug crisis in the black community? in: *The Great Issues of Drug Policy,* (A. S. Trebach, S. Arnold and K. B. Zeese Eds.), pp. 98–105, Drug Policy Foundation, Washington, DC.

Naylor, R. T., 1987, *Hot Money and the Politics of Debt,* McClelland and Stewart, Toronto.

Nelson, B. J., 1986, *Making an Issue of Child Abuse: Political Agenda Setting for Social Problems,* University of Chicago Press, Chicago.

Peyrot, M., 1984, Cycles of social problem development: The case of drug abuse, *The Sociological Quarterly* **25**(Winter):83–96.

Pfohl, S. J., 1977, The "discovery" of child abuse, *Social Problems* **24**(February):310–323.

Plant, M. A., 1975, *Drugtakers in an English Town,* Tavistock Publications, London.

Preble, E., and Casey, J. J. Jr., 1969, Taking care of business: The heroin user's life on the street, *International Journal of the Addictions* **4**:1–24.

Ramos, M., and Gould, L., 1978, Where have all the flower children gone?: A five-year follow-up of a natural group of drug users, *Journal of Drug Issues* **8**:75–84.

Reasons, C., 1974, The politics of drugs: An inquiry in the sociology of social problems, *The Sociological Quarterly* **15**(Summer):381–404.

Rieff, D., 1991, Victims all? Recovery, co-dependency, and the art of blaming somebody else, *Harper's* October:49–56.

Schasre, R., 1966, Cessation patterns among neophyte heroin users, *Journal of the Addictions* **1**(2):23–32.

Scott, P. D., and Marshall, J., 1991, *Cocaine Politics: Drugs, Armies, and the CIA in Central America,* University of California Press, Berkeley, CA.

Siegel, R. K., 1989, *Intoxication: Life in Pursuit of Artificial Paradise,* E. P. Dutton, New York.

Solomon, R. R., 1988, Canada's federal drug legislation in: *Illicit Drugs in Canada: A Risky Business,* (Blackwell, J. and Erickson, P. Eds.), pp. 117–129, Nelson Canada, Scarborough, Ontario.

Solomon, R. R., and Green, M., 1988, The first century: The history of non-medical opiate use and control policies in Canada, 1870–1970, in: *Illicit Drugs in Canada: A Risky Business,* (J. Blackwell, and P. Erickson, Eds.), pp. 88–116, Nelson Canada, Scarborough, Ontario.

Trebach, A. S., 1987, *The Great Drug War,* MacMillan Publishing Company, New York.

Waldorf, D., 1973, *Careers in Dope,* Prentice-Hall, Englewood Cliffs, NJ.

Waldorf, D. R., Reinarman, C., and Murphy, S., 1991, *Cocaine Changes: The Experience of Using and Quitting,* Temple University Press, Philadelphia.

Wisotsky, S., 1986, *Breaking the Impasse in the War on Drugs,* Greenwood Press, New York.

Zimmer, L., and Jacobs, J. B., 1990, Mapping the drug testing industry and its implications, in *The Great Issues of Drug Policy,* (A. S. Trebach, and K. B. Zeese, Eds), pp. 219–226, Drug Policy Foundation, Washington, DC.

Zinberg, N. E., 1984, *Drug, Set, and Setting: The Basis for Controlled Intoxicant Use,* Yale University Press, New Haven, CT.

Index

FSC
www.fsc.org
MIX
Papier | Fördert
gute Waldnutzung
FSC® C083411

Kolibri 360 GmbH
Ferdinand-Jühlke-Straße 7
99095 Erfurt, Deutschland
produktsicherheit@kolibri360.de